weather
elements

PRENTICE-HALL INTERNATIONAL, INC., *London*
PRENTICE-HALL OF AUSTRALIA, PTY., LTD., *Sydney*
PRENTICE-HALL OF CANADA, LTD., *Toronto*
PRENTICE-HALL OF INDIA (PRIVATE) LTD., *New Delhi*
PRENTICE-HALL OF JAPAN, INC., *Tokyo*

fifth edition

weather
elements

a text in
elementary
meteorology

THOMAS A. BLAIR

ROBERT C. FITE
Oklahoma State University

prentice-hall, inc. englewood cliffs, n.j.

Library of Congress Catalog Card No.: 65-13636

Printed in the United States of America   94772-C

preface to
the fifth edition

This book is an account of the science of modern meteorology. Its style is designed to interest and inform the layman as well as to challenge and encourage the beginning student of meteorology. A strong mathematical background is not requisite to reader comprehension, yet numerous discussions and problems emphasize the importance of mathematics and physics to the professional meteorologist. It is hoped that this book will challenge many young and capable students to study further and to select meteorology as their profession.

The science of meteorology has grown rapidly in recent years, and it seems certain to remain youthful and vigorous for a long, long time. It is a great challenge to those who "seek to know," for many problems about the atmosphere remain unanswered. Probably no other science discipline offers greater opportunities and rewards for research efforts, both theoretical and applied.

The demand for meteorological forecasters is increasing more rapidly than they can be trained. In addition to the continuing manpower requirements of the U.S. Weather Bureau, the Armed Forces, and the commercial airlines, a great new requirement for meteorologists has developed among private enterprises of all kinds. Television stations, various industries, and even municipal governments are finding meteorologists not only desirable but almost essential to the successful operation of these enterprises.

I am indebted to the U.S. Navy for much basic training, practical experiences, and repeated refresher courses in meteorology. It was my privilege, while on active military duty, to study under some of the leading meteorologists of the world and to make many aircraft reconnaissance flights into typhoons of the tropical Pacific Ocean. This firsthand experience with "weather in action" provided vivid demonstrations of what otherwise might have appeared to be routine theoretical concepts of the thermodynamics of the atmosphere.

I am also indebted to the U.S. Weather Bureau, the National Aeronautics and Space Administration, the U.S. Navy, and many others for materials and illustrations for this edition. Credit is given individually after the figures as appropriate.

R.C.F.

preface to
the first edition

This book aims to present, concisely and systematically, an introduction to the science of meteorology in its present stage of development. My primary purpose is to set forth the facts and principles concerning the behavior and responses of the atmosphere in such a way as to enable the reader to acquire an elementary understanding of the physical processes underlying observed weather phenomena. An important secondary object is to present that general body of information about the weather and the present state of our knowledge concerning it which, it is believed, every intelligent person should possess in relation to this most important element of his environment.

Attention is given to the instruments and methods used in observing and measuring atmospheric conditions, to the complex effects of solar radiation, and to the interrelations of the various weather elements. Other subjects treated are the general circulation of the atmosphere and its modifications, the basis of weather forecasting, the general geographic distribution of the weather elements, and some of the relations of weather and climate to man and his varied life. A brief account is given of the electrical and optical phenomena of the atmosphere, and of the organization and activities of the United States Weather Bureau. Some knowledge of such matters is a necessary foundation for the study of geography, agriculture, and ecology, and of aeronautics, hydrology, and other branches of engineering. In addition, such knowledge is useful in a great variety of professions and occupations, notably in medicine, law, and business. It is hoped, therefore, that the book will prove of value to persons of widely varying interests.

The discussions are necessarily brief and incomplete, and much interesting and valuable material has been omitted, but it is hoped that the most important phases of the subject have been treated in such a way as to arouse an abiding interest and lead to further reading. Meteorology is a growing science and at the present time is undergoing a rather rapid development and transition. An effort is made to present the modern aspects of the subject and to indicate the lines along which research is being conducted and progress being made.

The author of a book on elementary meteorology is inevitably indebted to the pioneers and leaders in the science of the weather in past generations, and also to a great number of contemporary students and investigators. No one can write such a book without becoming aware of meteorology's debt to Sir Napier Shaw and Dr. W. J. Humphreys, among present-day scientists. Dr. H. C. Willett and Mr. Jerome Namias have recently contributed notably to a knowledge of air masses and air-mass analysis. Nearly all the writers listed in the bibliography have provided facts or ideas which have been drawn upon in the preparation of this text. I regret that it has not been possible to identify and acknowledge the original source in each case. For general scope and for the general method of treatment of some of the fundamentals the author is conscious of the influence of the older textbooks, especially those by W. M. Davis and W. I. Milham.

To Dr. Nels A. Bengtson I am deeply grateful, not only for his critical reading of the entire manuscript, but also for his sympathetic interest in the book and his help in many of the details of its preparation. I am indebted to the Chief of the United States Weather Bureau for permission to publish this work, and to the scientific staff at the Central Office of the Weather Bureau for valuable criticisms and suggestions. My thanks are extended to Mr. D. Keith Kinsey, who prepared nearly all the drawings, to Mr. H. Floreen for his cloud photographs, and to Professor J. C. Jensen, Mr. Otto Wiederanders, the United States Weather Bureau, and Julien P. Friez and Sons, for other photographic illustrations. The Taylor Instrument Companies have kindly given permission for the use of some material originally published in Tycos-Rochester (now Taylor-Rochester), and the Denoyer-Geppert Company has permitted the use of its base maps. My wife has given valued assistance and encouragement and has helped in reading the proofs.

T.A.B.

table of contents

1
THE ATMOSPHERE   1

2
OBSERVING THE WEATHER   13

3
SOLAR RADIATION   61

4
ADIABATIC PROCESSES AND STABILITY   79

5
EVAPORATION AND CONDENSATION   100

6
INTERRELATIONSHIPS OF TEMPERATURE, PRESSURE, AND WIND   122

7
THE GENERAL CIRCULATION   135

8
THE SECONDARY CIRCULATION   152

9
AIR MASSES AND FRONTS   169

ix

10
SPECIAL STORMS
AND LESSER ATMOSPHERIC DISTURBANCES   186

11
WEATHER ANALYSIS AND FORECASTING   215

12
AVIATION AND THE WEATHER   245

13
THE UPPER ATMOSPHERE   258

14
CLIMATE   274

15
WORLD WEATHER RELATIONSHIPS
AND CLIMATIC INFLUENCES   307

appendix I
BIBLIOGRAPHY   331

appendix II
CONVERSION FACTORS AND TABLES   338

appendix III
MEAN MONTHLY AND ANNUAL TEMPERATURES
AND PRECIPITATION   343

INDEX   351

list
of illustrations

1.1	Nimbus Meteorological Satellite..............................	3
1.2	Composition of Dry Air by Volume	6
1.3	Relation of Volume to Pressure on a Mass of Gas at Constant Tempera-ture	9
2.1	Thermometer Scales Compared	15
2.2	Maximum and Minimum Thermometers with Townsend Support	16
2.3	Thermograph	16
2.4	Instrument Shelter with Door Open and Instruments in Place	18
2.5	Thermograph Record for a Week in January at Lincoln, Nebraska	19
2.6	Typical Curves Showing Annual March and Annual Range of Tempera-ture	20
2.7	A Simple Mercurial Barometer	21
2.8	Mercurial Barometers Mounted in Case	22
2.9	Barometer Scales Compared	23
2.10	Schematic Drawing of an Aneroid Barometer	24
2.11	Navy-type Aneroid Barometer Calibrated in Inches and Millibars	24
2.12	Barograph	25
2.13	Wind Instruments	28
2.14	Wind Directions	29
2.15	Robinson Three-cup Anemometer	31
2.16	Aerovane	31
2.17	"Smoke Run" at Brookhaven National Laboratory	33
2.18	Wind Rose for New York City	34
2.19	Automatic Atomic-powered Weather Station	35
2.20	Sling Psychrometer	40
2.21	A Generalized Vertical Arrangement of Cloud Types	49
2.22	Cirrus Invading the Sky (C_H1)	50
2.23	Cirrocumulus (C_H9)	50
2.24	Cirrostratus (C_H7)	50
2.25	Cirrostratus (C_H6)	51
2.26	Semi-transparent Altocumulus (C_M3)	51

2.27 Altocumulus ($C_M 7$) 51

2.28 Altocumulus Increasing and Thickening ($C_M 5$) 52

2.29 Thin Altostratus Covering Entire Sky ($C_M 1$) 52

2.30 Thick Altostratus ($C_M 2$) 52

2.31 Stratocumulus ($C_L 5$) 53

2.32 Stratocumulus from the Spreading Out of Cumulus ($C_L 4$) 53

2.33 Stratus ($C_L 6$) 53

2.34 Stratus fractus of Bad Weather ($C_L 7$) 54

2.35 Cumulus humilis ($C_L 1$) 54

2.36 Cumulonimbus calvus ($C_L 3$) 54

2.37 Cumulonimbus capillatus ($C_L 9$) 55

2.38 A Standard 8-inch Rain Gauge with Measuring Stick 56

2.39 The Fergusson Weighing Rain Gauge 57

3.1 Electromagnetic Spectrum Showing Wave Frequencies and Wave
Lengths 62

3.2 Pyrheliometer 65

3.3 Electrical Sunshine Recorder 66

3.4 Earth's Orbit About the Sun 68

3.5 Effect of Angle of Incidence on Insolation 69

3.6 Diagrammatic Representation of the Distribution of Solar Radiation ... 71

3.7 Transfer of Heat by Convection 76

3.8 Convectional Circulation in a Liquid 77

4.1 Radiosonde in Flight 81

4.2 Hurricane Becky 83

4.3 Adiabatic Changes of Temperature 85

4.4 The Mechanics of Equivalent Potential Temperature 86

4.5 The Adiabatic Chart 88

4.6 Lapse Rate Showing a Stable Atmosphere 91

4.7 Lapse Rate of an Unstable Atmospheric Condition Below the 880-mb Level   92

4.8 Conditional Instability 93

4.9 Instability of Lifting 95

5.1 Class A Evaporation Station 102

5.2 Orchard Heaters in a California Citrus Grove 105

5.3 Wind Machine for Fighting Freezes 105

5.4 Penetrative Convection Producing Summer Cumuli 112

5.5 Snow Crystals 114

5.6 Typical Large Hailstones Showing Layer Structure 116

5.7 Glaze Ice Storm Near Atlanta, Georgia, March 1961 117

5.8 Cloud-seeding Generator 119

6.1 Isobars and Pressure Gradient 123

6.2 Vertical Cross Section of Isobaric Surfaces and Resulting Air Movement   124

6.3 Effect of the Coriolis Force 125

6.4 Three Forces Affecting the Wind 126

6.5 Surface Winds in Relation to the Isobars 127

6.6	Sea Breeze	128
6.7	Land Breeze	129
7.1	Mean Annual Sea-level Pressure in Inches and Millibars for the World	137
7.2	Pressure and Wind Belts of the World	138
7.3	Schematic Representation of the Cells of Atmospheric Circulation	139
7.4	Mean January Sea-level Pressures and Wind Directions of the World	141
7.5	Mean July Sea-level Pressures and Wind Directions of the World	142
7.6	East-West Transport of Air in the General Circulation	146
8.1	Station Model for Plotting Synoptic Weather Data	153
8.2	Synoptic Weather Map of the United States, September 22, 1953	154
8.3	Synoptic Weather Map of the United States, September 23, 1953	156
8.4	Synoptic Weather Map of the United States, September 24, 1953	157
8.5	Barometric Depression Showing Cyclonic Circulation in the Northern Hemisphere	158
8.6	Typical Paths of Cyclones Appearing in Various Regions of the United States	160
8.7	Anticyclone and Clockwise Circulation in the Northern Hemisphere	161
8.8	Typical Paths of Anticyclones Appearing in Various Regions of the United States	162
8.9	Wedge of Cold Air Invading a Warm Current	164
8.10	Pressure Profile of the Tropics	165
8.11	Streamline Chart of the Caribbean Area	166
9.1	Three-dimensional Representation of a Cold Front	178
9.2	(a) Surface and (b) Vertical Sections of a Warm Front	179
9.3	(a) Surface and (b) Vertical Sections of a Cold Front	180
9.4	(a) Cold Front and (b) Warm Front Types of Occlusion	182
9.5	Stages in the Life Cycle of a Wave Cyclone	183
10.1	Panorama Inside the Eye of a Typhoon	187
10.2	Regions and Generalized Paths of Tropical Cyclones	190
10.3	Five Hurricanes Photographed by Tiros III	192
10.4	Tropical Hurricane	194
10.5	A Mature Thunderstorm	196
10.6	Average Annual Number of Days with Thunderstorms in the United States	199
10.7	Direct Lightning Discharge	202
10.8	Ball Lightning	203
10.9	Tornado at Wichita Falls, Texas, April 3, 1964	206
10.10	Small Waterspout	209
10.11	Diagram of Foehn Wind and Resulting Changes in Air Condition	210
10.12	Dust Storm, Johnson, Kansas, April 14, 1935	212
11.1	Atmospheric Cross Section from Denver to Atlantic City	221
11.2	Pressure-contour (Constant-pressure) Chart, 500 Mb, February 21, 1945	222
11.3	Isentropic Chart	225
11.4	Pressure-contour Chart, 700 Mb, February 5, 1946	227

11.5	Facsimile	229
11.6	Synoptic Weather Map of the United States, September 25, 1953	231
11.7	Synoptic Weather Map of the United States, September 26, 1953	232
11.8	Synoptic Weather Map of the United States, September 27, 1953	233
11.9	Radar PPI Scope	236
12.1	Flight Forecast Cross Section	247
12.2	Rime and Glaze on Wing of Aircraft	250
12.3	Icing in Frontal Conditions	251
12.4	Carburetor Icing	252
12.5	GCA Radarscope	253
12.6	Eddy Turbulence in Mountains	254
13.1	Radiowave Receiving Apparatus at Stanford University	260
13.2	Effects of Solar Activity	262
13.3	Variations of Temperature with Altitude	264
13.4	Atmospheric Stratification	267
13.5	Van Allen Radiation Belts	268
13.6	Auroral Displays at Fairbanks, Alaska	270
14.1	Mean Annual Sea-level Temperatures, World, °F	280
14.2	Mean January Sea-level Temperatures, World, °F	281
14.3	Mean July Sea-level Temperatures, World, °F	282
14.4	Mean Annual Range of Temperature, World, °F	284
14.5	January Mean Daily Range of Temperature in the United States	285
14.6	Mean Annual Precipitation, World, Inches	287
14.7	Types of Rainfall Distribution by Months	288
14.8	Average Annual Number of Days with .01 Inch or More of Precipitation in the United States	289
14.9	Climates of North America	298
14.10	Iowa Precipitation, 1873–1955	301
14.11	Geologic Evidences of Climatic Changes	302
15.1	Frequency Polygon of January Precipitation at Cleveland, Ohio, During a Sixty-four-year Period	309
15.2	Frequency Polygon for Length of Growing Season at Indianapolis, Indiana, for a Sixty-year Period and Curve Showing the Probable Distribution of Frequencies in a Very Long Record	310
15.3	Departures of Mean Monthly Temperatures from Normal, St. Paul, Minnesota, January 1929, to December 1955	312

weather
elements

1

the atmosphere

The weather has always been a subject of universal interest. Man has been concerned about its fickle ways and geographical variations since the earliest days of recorded history. He has observed the fury of mighty storms, the freshness of gently falling raindrops, the burning sun over a drought-stricken land, and the refreshing breezes of a spring afternoon. He has observed the lands of perpetual ice and snow, the middle latitudes with rhythmic yet somewhat erratic annual cycles, and the tropics with perpetual warmth. These things have caused him to wonder about the powers that control the elements. What can cause a pleasant summer afternoon to be changed into a frightful display of wind, fire, hail, or flood? Only recently have we begun to understand these secrets well enough to permit advanced planning and intelligent action, based on what the weather is going to be.

The earth, as it turns on its axis and follows its elliptical orbit about the sun, is forever encompassed by a gaseous shell or envelope called the *atmosphere*. This encircling air is an integral and essential part of the earth. We frequently remain unaware of its presence because of its invisibility; but, we feel its force when it moves rapidly past us, and we know that "when the trees bow down their heads, the wind is passing by." It is an ever-moving air, not fixed like land, nor confined in basins and channels like water, but ever present and all prevailing about the face of the earth.

Air is the medium in which we live and move, the breath of life to men, animals, and plants. Without it, this would be a dead and barren world. We can live for many days without food, for a few days without water, but for only a few minutes without air. The food that we eat and the clothing that we wear are composed in large part of elements obtained from the air. The water that falls on our fields is carried to them by the air. Air supports combustion and transmits sound. In addition to these primary and indispensable functions, air is made to serve us in many practical ways. It is a source of power to sailing ships and windmills. When compressed, it actuates the brakes of moving vehicles and the trip hammers of pneumatic tools; it serves us in many other ways, and finally it furnishes a support and a highway for vast machines, "as the heavens fill with commerce." It is with the behavior of this intangible, colorless, and odorless but all-important atmosphere that this book deals.

EXTENT OF THE ATMOSPHERE

The atmosphere extends to a height of several hundred miles above the earth's surface. The effective upper limit of the atmosphere is reached at a much lower altitude when the air becomes extremely rarefied. Although it seems light, there are approximately 11,850,000,000,000,000,000 pounds of air weighing down upon the earth at all times. Being compressible, the air is more dense near the surface of the earth than at higher altitudes because of pressure from the upper layers on those below. It becomes so rare at only 15,000 feet (5 km) elevation that supplementary oxygen must be provided for air travelers; and at 18,000 feet (6 km), half of the mass of the atmosphere lies below.

Knowledge of the upper atmosphere has been growing rapidly since the development of sounding rockets. Previously, observations had been restricted to those made by instrumented balloons and observations of the auroras, meteors, and noctilucent clouds. During the early 1950's, some four hundred sounding rockets were fired by the United States, primarily devoted to learning more about the ionosphere, the region above 100 km. During the International Geophysical Year (IGY) of 1957–1958, at least two hundred additional launches were made from sites in both hemispheres More recently, several weather satellites have proved highly successful in making weather observations from outer space (Fig. 1.1).

It is possible that the air at extremely high altitudes affects surface weather conditions, either directly or indirectly. Whether or not this is so, there is little doubt that more high altitude observations from rockets and satellites will permit greater accuracy in forecasting the weather of the

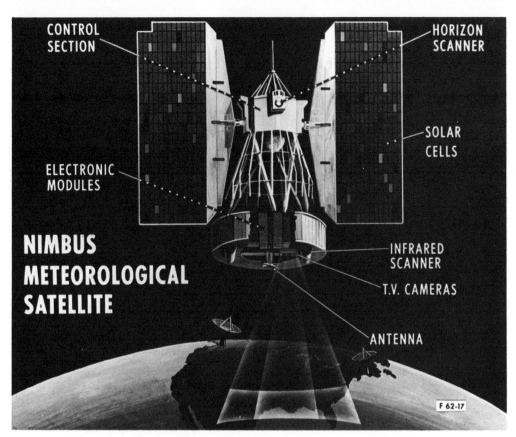

CONTROL SECTION

HORIZON SCANNER

SOLAR CELLS

ELECTRONIC MODULES

NIMBUS METEOROLOGICAL SATELLITE

INFRARED SCANNER

T.V. CAMERAS

ANTENNA

F 62-17

Nimbus Meteorological Satellite. This satellite was designed especially for **FIG. 1.1** weather reconnaissance. It contains TV cameras which are always oriented toward the earth. When launched in a polar orbit and aided by the earth's rotation, the Nimbus satellite can provide complete surveillance of the clouds and weather of the atmosphere once every twenty-four hours. *Courtesy, National Aeronautics and Space Administration.*

future. In general, however, weather is a low-level phenomenon. Clouds frequently are found at elevations of 30,000 feet (9.1 km), but rarely reach 40,000 feet (12.2 km) except in thunderstorms where they may reach more than 80,000 feet (25 km). The study of meteorology is therefore restricted mainly to a study of a thin boundary layer of the atmosphere about 15 miles (24 km) in thickness.

METEOROLOGY DEFINED

Meteorology is the science of the atmosphere and its phenomena—those phenomena which we call the weather. Because of their infinite variety and their intimate relation to all of our activities, the phenomena of the weather are subjects of never-ending interest. They are not only of interest, but are also of great importance, since weather is one of the chief elements in man's environment, far reaching in its influence and affecting all phases of his life. One of the reasons for the daily interest in the weather in regions outside of the tropics is that it is new every morning. It is never stable for long but always in a state of becoming something different. In this it is typical of all nature; but, since weather changes are more rapid and noticeable than most other natural changes, "changeable as the weather" has become a time-worn simile.

Meteorology combines physics and geography. It not only applies the principles of physics to the behavior of the air treated as a mixture of gases, but it considers the whole atmosphere and its movements as they are affected by such geographic factors as latitude, topography, altitude, and distribution of land, water, and mountains. The geography of the earth has a pronounced effect on its weather. Insofar as meteorology deals with the physics of the air, it is a branch of physics; insofar as it is descriptive and explanatory of the environment of man, as affecting his modes of life and his ways of earning a living, it is a branch of geography. In combining the two to account for actual weather and climate, it is something different from either; it is a separate branch of science. Moreover, the data accumulated in the study of meteorology and climate are capable of infinite applications to the life of man. They are of importance in the study of history, geology, and biology. They are used directly and daily by the farmer and the engineer, by the physician, the lawyer, and the businessman.

The science of meteorology has advanced by the following steps:

1. The development of a desire to understand the nature of weather changes and weather variations.

2. The invention of instruments for measuring various elements of the atmosphere.

3. The accumulation of observational data.

4. The classification and organization of these data for the purpose of analyzing various characteristics of the atmosphere.

5. The development of theories to interpret observed interrelationships between the atmospheric elements and flow patterns.

6. The repeated testing and modification of these theories to improve forecasting accuracy.

7. The application of the knowledge thus acquired for useful purposes.

Some of the Greek philosophers, notably Hippocrates, Aristotle, and Theophrastus, approached the study of weather and climate in a scientific spirit and made progress in interpreting the phenomena of the atmosphere —rather remarkable progress, in view of the limited knowledge of physics and chemistry existing in their day. We derive the name "meteorology" from Aristotle's treatise, *Meteorologica*. This treatise included a discussion of much that we now call astronomy, physical geography, and geology, but about one-third of it was devoted to atmospheric phenomena.

During the Middle Ages, weather events were given many irrational and mystical interpretations. The weather was a matter of signs and portents, often assumed to be related to human conduct as warning, punishment, or reward. Some of the mystery remains in many minds, and superstition still survives when men discuss the weather. And yet, the elementary facts about atmospheric phenomena and their causes are simple and easily acquired, and they are necessary to an intelligent appreciation of our daily life. It is true, on the other hand, that much is yet unknown about the behavior of the air. The atmosphere is so vast as to preclude, perhaps forever, the possibility of a complete analysis of its forces and activities. Therein lies an opportunity and a challenge for additional accumulation of facts and for further investigation and research.

Upon examination, the atmosphere is found to be a complex system, not a simple chemical element nor even a compound, but a relatively stable mixture of a number of gases. First, there are several chemical elements which remain permanently in gaseous form under all natural conditions. Second, gaseous water, known as *water vapor*, is a variable part of this mixture. Under certain conditions, liquid and solid forms of water also occur in the air, but these are not included in the definition of air. Finally, the air always contains, but not as essential ingredients, a great number of solid particles of various natures, known collectively as *dust*.

Composition of the Atmosphere

PERMANENT GASES

The two permanent gases that make up 99 per cent of the volume of the air, after the water vapor and the dust particles have been removed, are the chemical elements nitrogen and oxygen. These two elements, in combination with others, also make up a large portion of all living matter and the earth's crust. Nitrogen forms about 78 per cent of the total volume of dry air, and oxygen about 21 per cent (Fig. 1.2). Of the remaining 1 per cent, the greater part is argon, and only about 0.04 per cent remains, of which approximately 0.03 per cent is carbon dioxide and the remainder is neon, helium, krypton, hydrogen, xenon, ozone, radon, and other gases.

The relative percentages of the principal permanent gases remain remarkably constant throughout the world from the surface of the earth to heights of several miles. We breathe the same air everywhere.

The active energizing element of the air is oxygen, which combines readily with other chemical elements and is necessary to life. The carbon dioxide which is exhaled by animals is absorbed by plants, and its oxygen constituent later released to the air. This reciprocal use by plants and animals plays a part in maintaining a relatively constant ratio of these two gases. The waters of the ocean also exercise a control over the concentration of carbon dioxide in the air: when the amount of carbon dioxide increases, more is absorbed by the water; when it decreases, some of the gas returns to the atmosphere. The other permanent gases appear to have no special natural functions except to increase the density of the atmosphere and to dilute its oxygen. But some soil bacteria take nitrogen from the air and make it available to plants, and man has also learned how to utilize atmospheric nitrogen. The rare gases neon, krypton, and xenon are also obtained by extraction from the air.

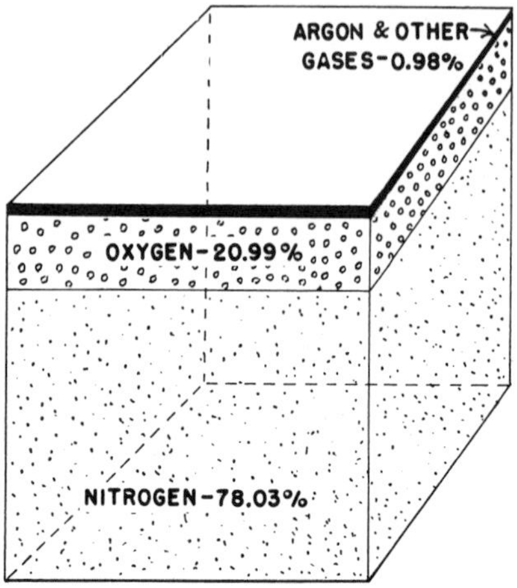

FIG. 1.2

Composition of Dry Air by Volume. Water vapor is also present in the air, but varies from near zero to 4 per cent.

WATER VAPOR

Water vapor is contributed to the air by evaporation from water surfaces, soil, and living tissues and by combustion. It is an all-important constituent of the atmosphere, but, unlike the other gases, is quite variable in amount, ranging from a minute proportion in the air of deserts and polar regions to a maximum of approximately 4 per cent by volume in the warm and humid tropics. Some water remains in the air as a gas at all temperatures; but the amount that may be mixed with the other gases of the air at low temperatures is small compared with the possible amount when the temperature is high. The importance of atmospheric moisture to all forms of life is so universally recognized that no additional emphasis need be given here. However, less well known is the very important role which it plays in the physical processes of the atmosphere. Water vapor in the air affects its temperature, density, and humidity and its heating and cooling characteristics; these will be explained later.

DUST

The gases of the atmosphere maintain in suspension an immense number of nongaseous substances of various kinds which are collectively called dust. In addition to the visible dust which sometimes fills the air and darkens the sun in dry regions, the air always, or nearly always, carries small particles of organic matter, such as seeds, spores, and bacteria. Much more numerous, however, are the microscopic, inorganic particles which contribute to the formation of haze, clouds, and precipitation. Some of these are fine particles of soil or of smoke, or salts from ocean spray, which are lifted and diffused by the winds and rising air currents. The dust particles are naturally more numerous in the lower atmosphere, but some of them are carried to heights of several miles. Large amounts of even finer particles are thrown into the air by volcanic explosions, and many more result from the burning of meteors in the upper air, thus furnishing a supply of dust to the air at great heights.

Many of these particles are very minute, but they have two important effects on the weather. First, many of them are water absorbent and are the nuclei on which condensation of water vapor begins. Second, they intercept some of the heat coming from the sun. When there is an unusual amount of such dust, as in a time of great volcanic activity, the result may be to reduce the average temperature of the globe. Dust plays a part in the creation of the varied colors of sunrise and sunset. For three years after the violent explosion of the volcano Krakatoa in the East Indies, in 1883, brilliant twilight colors were seen around the world, as the dust gradually spread from its source until it encircled the globe. In mid-ocean, the air has been found to contain from 500 to 2,000 of these microscopic and submicroscopic dust particles per cubic centimeter, and in dusty cities more than 100,000 per cubic centimeter. In the aggregate, large quantities of atmospheric dust are continually exchanged between the earth and the atmosphere. Many rain-making and weather-control theories now being tested are based on the importance of these hygroscopic dust particles to the weather processes.

Properties of the Atmosphere

By the "properties" of the atmosphere we mean the qualities or attributes of the air and its various constituents that contribute to the weather elements and atmospheric phenomena. Since the atmosphere is essentially a mixture of gases, it behaves as other gases do—according to the natural laws of gas behavior.

GENERAL CHARACTERISTICS

The principal characteristics of gases are their extreme mobility, compressibility, and capacity for expansion. The atmosphere is sometimes called the *ocean of air*, and winds are compared to streams of water; but when these analogies are used, the greater freedom with which air moves in all directions, its greater fluidity and mobility, should be kept in mind. A gas has neither definite shape nor size. We cannot have a vessel half full of air; a small amount of air will fill a large vessel completely and uniformly. (Strictly speaking, exact uniformity is not attained, because the air at any point in the vessel is compressed by the weight of the air above it. This effect is negligible for most purposes in dealing with small volumes of air, but is of great importance in considering the atmosphere as a whole.) This property of indeterminate expansion is due to the fact that gases themselves exert a pressure which tends to change their volume to fit any container. This pressure is proportional to the density and the temperature of the gases and is exerted in all directions. According to the molecular theory, gases are made up of large numbers of minute molecules which are in a constant state of irregular motion. The effect of frequent collisions by these molecules may be observed in pressure and temperature characteristics. With this goes the property of great compressibility. The air is readily compressed; that is, its volume is decreased and its density increased when pressure is applied to it, and it readily expands when the pressure is diminished. Under the same pressure, it expands with an increase of temperature, but it occupies less volume and becomes denser with a decrease of temperature. In general, solids and liquids also change volume and density with change of temperature, but gases change to a much greater degree and with more uniformity.

LAWS OF THE GASES

The characteristics just described are more definitely expressed in the following gas laws. These laws apply with close approximation to all the permanent gases of the air, but not so closely to water vapor. They refer to a fixed quantity (mass) of gas.

Boyle's Law. Robert Boyle (1627–1691), a British physicist and chemist, discovered that, for a given mass of a gas at constant temperature, the product of the pressure times the volume is a constant (Fig. 1.3). Stated otherwise, the volume of a given mass of gas is inversely proportional to the pressure, provided the temperature is unchanged. Algebraically, this may be written:

$$PV = K,$$

where P is the pressure, V is the volume, and K is a constant. A comparison of pressure and volume under different sets of conditions may be expressed as: $P_1 V_1 = P_2 V_2 = P_3 V_3$, and so on. Since density means the ratio of the mass to the volume, density varies inversely to the volume, and therefore the density of a gas at constant temperature is directly proportional to its pressure, or $P/D = K'$, where D is the density and K' is a constant.

Law of Charles and Gay-Lussac. Two French physicists, Jacques Charles (1746–1823) and Joseph Gay-Lussac (1778–1850), discovered an additional gas law near the beginning of the nineteenth century. The law states that when the volume remains constant the pressure of a gas increases at a rate of 1/273 of the initial value at 0°C for each centigrade-degree increase in temperature. Algebraically, this law may be expressed as follows:

$$P_t = P_o \left[1 + (1/273)T\right] \text{ at constant volume,}$$

where P_t is the pressure at any given time and P_o is the pressure at 0°C.

It can also be shown that at constant pressure, the volume of a gas increases at the rate of 1/273 of its initial value at 0°C for each centigrade-degree increase in temperature. This relationship may be expressed as:

$$V_t = V_o \left[1 + (1/273)T\right] \text{ at constant pressure,}$$

where V_t is the volume at any given time and V_o is the volume at 0°C.

One consequence of the first equation is that at a temperature of −273°C a gas should cease to exert any pressure, that is, its molecules should cease to move. This temperature is called the *absolute zero* because, according to this law, no lower temperature can possibly exist, since neither pressure nor movement can be less than zero. It has been found that gases do not follow this law exactly at very low temperatures. Absolute temperatures are temperatures measured in centigrade degrees and calibrated to absolute zero.

Combining the laws of Boyle, Charles, and Gay-Lussac, we may obtain a single simple equation expressing the relations among pressure, volume, and temperature for a given mass of any one gas:

$$PV = RT,$$

where T is the absolute temperature and R is constant for any one gas, but variable with different gases.

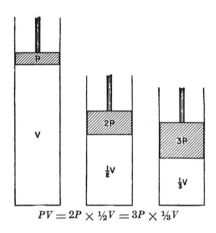

$$PV = 2P \times \tfrac{1}{2}V = 3P \times \tfrac{1}{3}V$$

FIG. 1.3

Relation of Volume to Pressure on a Mass of Gas at Constant Temperature.

PRESSURE

The air is held to the earth by the force of gravity. It therefore has weight, which is indicated by atmospheric pressure. At sea level, this pressure amounts to about 14.7 pounds per square inch, on the average, or about one ton per square foot. It decreases from this amount with increasing elevation and it also fluctuates slightly at sea level with changes in atmospheric conditions.

The weight of air per unit volume can be expressed as its *density*, dense air being a large quantity occupying a small volume. The weight of a cubic foot of air at sea level is about 1.2 ounces, or 0.08 pound. The density of the air is, therefore, 0.08 pound per cubic foot. Except for rare and temporary circumstances, the density and pressure of the air decrease with increasing height, rather rapidly at first and then more and more slowly.

The first step in the development of a physical science **Elements** is to observe, measure, and record phenomena as they **of Weather** occur. From his early beginning, man has doubtless given attention to weather phenomena, but for thousands of years his observations were haphazard and were mere personal impressions, soon forgotten or distorted. Although some rainfall measurements were made at a very early date, it was only about three hundred years ago that man first began to measure the condition of the air and to record his observations for historical and comparative purposes. Such measurements necessarily awaited the invention of the thermometer and the barometer. The former is credited to Galileo (1564–1642) in about the year 1590; Torricelli (1608–1647) invented the mercurial barometer in 1643.

Shortly after the invention of these instruments, some systematic observations of the temperature and pressure of the air were begun, but such observations did not become widespread, continuous, and comparable with one another until early in the nineteenth century. Today, when a meteorologist speaks of "making an observation" of the weather, he implies the careful use of instruments of precision for the purposes of determining and recording various physical facts about the condition of the atmosphere by methods so standardized that his observations are comparable with those of others throughout the world. His observations, however, are unlike those of the physicist in the laboratory; they are comparable rather to those of a physician in observing and measuring the condition of a patient. The constant and uncontrollable variations in the atmosphere are analogous to the changes in a living, moving organism.

THE METEOROLOGICAL ELEMENTS

There are a number of physical properties and conditions of the atmosphere that may be measured quite accurately. Others must be observed or measured with less exactness because of the lack of mechanical measuring devices. All of these changeable properties must be measured accurately if we wish to determine what happens in the air and how it changes, or if we wish to describe the weather as it is at a given time and place. The most important of these are: (a) the temperature of the air, (b) the pressure that the air exerts, (c) the direction and speed of the air's motion, (d) the humidity of the air, (e) the amount and type of cloudiness, and (f) the amount of precipitation. These are the six fundamental weather elements. Other items are included in a complete weather observation, as will be noted later. It is evident that instruments giving results which can be set down in figures are necessary for obtaining an accurate knowledge of conditions and permitting a comparison of weather at different times and places. In Chapter 2, the instruments and methods used in making the primary and essential observations are described briefly. Instruments and observational details have been largely standardized in this country by the United States Weather Bureau.

WEATHER AND CLIMATE

Weather comprises the condition and characteristics of the atmosphere at a given time; *climate* implies the totality of weather conditions over a period of years. Climate is not merely the average weather; it includes also the extremes and variability of the weather elements, for example, the greatest and least rainfall, the highest and lowest temperatures, and the maximum wind velocity for a given period. Since the weather is constantly changing, we need a long series of observations in order to have reasonably accurate information concerning the average and most frequent conditions and the probable variations.

Many of the data dealing with weather and climate are expressed in *normal* values. In meteorology, the word *normal* is used for the average, or mean, value of a weather element for a considerable period of time. Ordinarily a mean value is not considered a normal value unless there are at least ten years of record, and much longer records are required in most cases to establish an approximately stable normal value. No such thing as an absolutely unchanging normal is known in climatic records. The normal, or average, value of a weather element is not necessarily its most probable value at any given time.

PROBLEMS

1.

A rigid container with a volume of 1 cu yd is filled with air. If the temperature of the air is 0°C and the pressure is 15 lbs per sq in., what will be the resulting pressure if the temperature is increased to 10°C.?

2.

From problem 1, what volume would be required to contain the original air at 10°C and 15 lbs per sq in. of pressure?

3.

Again from problem 1, what would be the pressure per square inch if the original air is compressed into a container of 1 cu ft capacity while the temperature is held constant at 0°C?

4.

If the pressure on a given mass of gas is reduced, what will happen to the volume? Temperature?

5.

Assuming the pressure of the air to be 14.7 lbs per sq in. and its density to be 0.08 lb per cu ft, if air is removed from a 12-inch cubical vessel until the density is one-third that of the outside air, how much pressure on the vessel will tend to crush it?

6.

What is the weight of the air remaining in the vessel of problem 5?

7.

At constant temperature, what would be the pressure inside the vessel of problem 5 if enough air is pumped into it so that it weighs 1 pound?

8.

What is the density of the air in problem 7?

9.

If one doubles the pressure in a fixed volume, what will happen to the temperature?

10.

Explain the difference between weight and pressure.

2

observing
the weather

A weather element of primary concern is the temperature of the air. Temperature in many parts of the world is subject to wide extremes and sudden changes; it is a weather element to which human life, and also plant and animal life, are sensitive; it is an important factor in determining the conditions of life and the productiveness of the soil in the different regions of the world; the varying temperature of the air is responsible for many other weather changes. These are some of the reasons for the importance of temperature measurements.

In the molecular expansion of the constitution of mat- **Temperature** ter, all substances are made up of molecules in more or **Observations** less rapid motion among themselves. As the velocity of its intermolecular motion increases, the temperature of a body rises. Matter in motion possesses energy; it is capable of exerting a force and of doing work; and the energy due to molecular motion is called *heat*. Heat is, therefore, a form of energy, and a measurable quantity, although not a substance. It may be transformed into other forms of energy. Although the human body is responsive to atmospheric temperatures, it is not an accurate instrument for the measurement of the temperature of the air. For this purpose we need thermometers.

THERMOMETERS

Thermometers are instruments designed to respond accurately to changes of temperature. There are various types and forms of temperature-measuring instruments. They may be classified on the basis of construction into four major groups:

1. *Liquid-in-glass thermometers* which contain either mercury or some organic spirit such as ethyl alcohol or pentane. This is the most common type of thermometer for making surface weather observations.

2. *Deformation thermometers* include the Bourdon thermometer (a curved, flattened, liquid-filled tube) and the bimetallic thermometer which is actuated by the unequal expansion of two dissimilar metals.

3. *Liquid-in-metal thermometers* are variations of the Bourdon thermometer and are especially used by industry. The expansion of the liquid takes place in a separate, sealed container, and the change of pressure is transmitted through a small bore to the Bourdon tube, which may be located at considerable distance from the temperature being measured.

4. *Electrical thermometers* are based on the change of the resistance to current as the temperature of the conductor is changed, or on the thermo-electric principle that when an electric circuit is made of two dissimilar metals and the junctions are not at the same temperature, a current will flow. Electric thermometers are not widely used for surface observations but are commonly used for upper-air measurements.

On the *Fahrenheit* thermometer, invented in 1710 by Daniel Fahrenheit (1686–1736), a German physicist, the temperature of melting ice is 32° and that of boiling water, 212°. Although invented by a German scientist, the Fahrenheit thermometer is now in common use only in English-speaking countries. On the *centigrade* scale, the freezing and boiling points of water are called 0° and 100°, respectively. The centigrade thermometer is also sometimes called the *Celsius thermometer*, after the Swedish astronomer, Anders Celsius (1701–1744), who invented it in 1742. Temperatures below the zero of either scale are written with a minus sign. A change in temperature from 32° to 212°, being a change of 180° on the Fahrenheit scale, corresponds to a change of 100° on the centigrade scale, making each Fahrenheit degree equal 5/9 of a centigrade degree (Fig. 2.1). For some scientific purposes, it is preferable to use a scale which has its zero at −273°C. and ascends in centigrade units. This is called the *absolute scale* and is indicated by the symbol °K (Kelvin) following the number. The following formulas may be used to convert from one scale to another:

$$°C = 5/9 (°F - 32) = °K - 273,$$
$$°F = 9/5°C + 32,$$
$$°K = °C + 273.$$

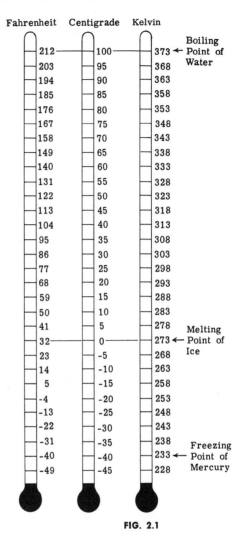

An accurate thermometer meets the following requirements: the bore is uniform, the fixed points are accurately determined, and the gradations are correctly spaced and etched on the stem. It contains a suitable fluid, one that does not freeze at the temperatures to be measured and does not readily vaporize or decompose. To meet the requirement of a nonfreezing liquid, alcohol is used instead of mercury under very cold conditions, for mercury freezes at $-38.7°F$ ($-39.3°C$). The size and shape of the bulb and the size of the bore determine the instrument's sensitiveness and quickness of response.

Maximum thermometers. Special thermometers are used for obtaining the highest and lowest temperatures occurring during any time interval. The maximum thermometer has a constriction of the bore just above the bulb, through which the mercury is forced out of the bulb as the temperature rises, but which prevents the return flow as the temperature falls (Fig. 2.2). The top of the column therefore remains at the highest point reached since the last setting of the thermometer. The maximum thermometer is set by whirling it around a mounting near its upper end. The centrifugal force thus generated forces the mercury back into the bulb. After setting, the thermometer indicates the correct temperature at the time, called the *current temperature*. The maximum thermometer should be mounted nearly horizontal with the bulb slightly *higher* than the other end to lessen the tendency for the mercury to retreat into the bulb.

Minimum thermometers. The liquid used in a minimum thermometer is alcohol. A small, dumbbell-shaped glass index is placed within the bore

FIG. 2.1

Thermometer Scales Compared.

Maximum and Minimum Thermometers with Townsend Support. Courtesy, **FIG. 2.2** Bendix Corporation, Friez Instrument Division.

of the instrument. The thermometer is mounted horizontally, with the index within the liquid and in contact with its surface at the end of the column. As the temperature falls and the column shortens, the index is carried toward the bulb by the surface tension of the liquid. When the temperature rises, the liquid flows past the index and leaves it at the lowest temperature reached. After the minimum temperature is read, the index is returned to the top of the liquid, which is the current temperature, by simply turning the thermometer bulb-end up. By making readings of a maximum and a minimum thermometer once a day, the highest and lowest temperatures reached during the twenty-four hours are obtained. A reasonably regular reading hour should be established that is not likely to coincide with either of the extreme temperatures.

Thermographs. Various types of recording thermometers, or thermo-

Thermograph. A clock mechanism rotates the cylinder beneath the record- **FIG. 2.3** ing pen. Temperature changes cause changes in the curvature of the Bourdon tube, A, resulting in vertical movements of the arm, B. Courtesy, Bendix Corporation, Friez Instrument Division.

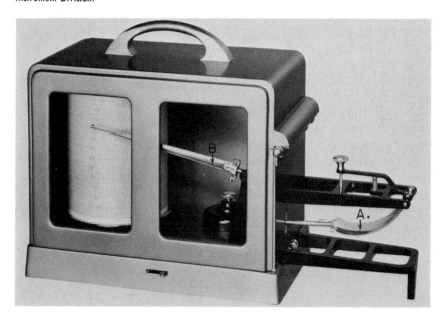

graphs, are used to obtain a continuous record of the temperature. One common type uses a Bourdon tube, which has a flattened, curved metal tube filled with liquid, sealed and fastened rigidly at one end. With change of temperature, there is unequal expansion or contraction of the liquid and the metal, producing a change of curvature in the tube, thus moving the free end. This movement is communicated to a pen, which is caused to move up or down on a drum that is being slowly rotated by a clock within it. In this manner, a continuous record of the temperature is traced on a ruled sheet surrounding the rotating drum (Fig. 2.3). Such a record is less accurate than one obtained by readings of a mercury thermometer, but if the thermograph trace is checked and corrected occasionally by comparing it with an accurate and similarly exposed thermometer, the results are sufficiently accurate for general meteorological purposes.

OBTAINING THE TEMPERATURE OF THE AIR

To determine the air's temperature, more is required than an accurate thermometer. It is equally important to make sure that the thermometer assumes the temperature of the air. A thermometer indicates its own temperature, but sometimes that is not the same as the temperature of the air surrounding it. If the thermometer is exposed to direct sunshine or to reflected heat from ground or buildings, it becomes hotter than the air around it. If it is close to a good radiating surface at night, it becomes colder than the air. If it is exposed where the air does not move freely, it may indicate the temperature of the air immediately around it but not of the general mass of air. These are some of the reasons why even good thermometers disagree. Most privately owned thermometers are not properly exposed, yet this is just as important as having a good thermometer. There often are actual differences in air temperature within short distances, and thermometers in the same city should not necessarily agree; but in many cases the disagreement is due to a failure to secure the temperature of the free mass of air.

To obtain the correct temperature reading, thermometers are exposed to the freely moving air in such a way that they are screened or sheltered from other influences. The *instrument shelter* in standard use in the United States is a white box with a base about 2 by 2 1/2 feet, and about 33 inches high (Fig. 2.4). It has a sloping double roof with open air space between. All four sides are louvered to permit free movement of air through it while protecting the instruments from sunshine, rain, and snow. The bottom is nearly closed but permits some movement of air through it. It is preferably mounted over sod, about four feet above the ground, to get above the influence of the surface temperature and into a layer of air that is moving freely. Shelters embodying the same principles are used in meteorological services throughout the world.

FIG. 2.4

Instrument Shelter with Door Open and Instruments in Place. Courtesy, U.S. Department of Commerce, Weather Bureau.

USES OF TEMPERATURE OBSERVATIONS

Standardized observations of temperature have been made in some places in Europe for more than 100 years, and in the United States for more than seventy-five years. Many stations in each state have records longer than fifty years. For stations having sufficient length of record, normal annual, monthly, and daily values may be obtained; also, the mean maximum and minimum temperatures and the actual extremes of highest and lowest temperatures are determined. Monthly and annual temperature normals based on ten years of record are frequently used, but thirty to forty years give more trustworthy normals. Hourly values may be observed and recorded by an observer or, more frequently, read from the thermograph sheets in stations equipped with this instrument (Fig. 2.5). The mean temperature for a given day may be obtained by taking the mean of the twenty-four hourly readings, but the sum of the maximum and minimum divided by 2 is generally used instead. The average temperature of a given month is the average of the maximum and minimum temperatures for that month. The average annual temperature is the average of the twelve monthly averages.

From the hourly values, or the thermograph record, the *daily march of temperature* may be observed. On the average, the highest temperature for the day occurs in mid-afternoon, between 2 and 5 p.m. Most heat is received from the sun at noon, but during a portion of the afternoon, the earth and the air near it continue to receive more heat than they lose, and hence the temperature continues to rise until a balance between incoming and outgoing heat is reached. This delay in the occurrence of the maxi-

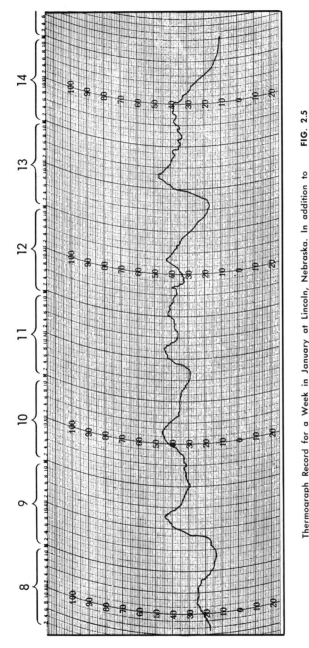

Thermograph Record for a Week in January at Lincoln, Nebraska. In addition to the diurnal changes, some irregular changes may be noted.   **FIG. 2.5**

mum until a few hours after noon is known as the *retardation,* or *lag,* of the maximum. From the time of the maximum, the temperature usually falls rather rapidly until about 8 to 10 P.M., and then more slowly until additional heat is again received from the sun. The minimum therefore occurs about sunrise. These are average conditions; on any one day there may be irregular fluctuations which upset this daily march of temperature. The difference between the highest and lowest temperatures for any day is called the *daily range* of temperature. Different daily ranges indicate important climactic differences. For example, the average daily range at Key West, Florida, is about 10°F, and at Winnemucca, Nevada, about 30° F, indicating that Key West, Florida, has little change in temperature from day to night, and Winnemucca, a large change.

The *annual march* of temperature in most parts of the Northern Hemisphere makes January the coldest month and July the warmest. The reverse is true in the Southern Hemisphere. In the interior of the United States, daily normals of temperature reach a maximum about July 15–25 and a minimum about January 15–25, but the most heat is received on June 21–22 and the least on December 21–22. There is thus a retardation of both maxima and minima of about one month (Fig. 2.6). Where temperatures are influenced by large bodies of water, the retardation is often greater than one month. In middle latitudes, individual years are marked by great irregularity in the march of temperature; that is, by irregularly alternating spells of warm and cool weather of unequal length, so that in a given year June or August may be warmer than July, and December or February colder than January. The *annual range* of temperature means the difference between the average temperature of the warmest and the coldest month.

Typical Curves Showing Annual March and Annual Range of Temperature.   **FIG. 2.6**

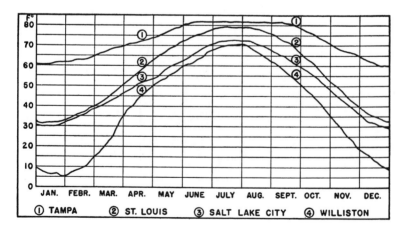

The pressure of the air at a given place is a force exerted in all directions in consequence of the weight of all the air above it. As a result of the air's constant and complex movements and the changes in its temperature and its water-vapor content, the weight of air above a fixed point is continually changing. The pressure, therefore, like the temperature, is never constant for long; but, unlike temperature changes, variations in pressure are not ordinarily perceptible to human senses. They are, nevertheless, an important feature of the weather by reason of their relations to other weather changes.

Pressure Observations

MERCURIAL BAROMETERS

The instrument used to measure the atmospheric pressure accurately is the mercurial barometer. When a glass tube about three feet long is filled with mercury and then inverted and the open end immersed in a cup of mercury, the mercury will flow out of the tube into the cup until the weight of the column in the tube (above the surface of the mercury in the cup) is balanced by the pressure of the air upon an equal cross section of the liquid surface (Fig. 2.7). The length of the column of mercury thus becomes a measure of the pressure of the air. This is the instrument invented by Torricelli in 1643. The instruments in use today are only mechanical refinements of the original barometer. It becomes obvious that fixed gradations on the tube for measurement of the column height would not be satisfactory unless a method were devised to keep the height of the mercury in the cup, or cistern, at a constant level. In the Fortin type of mercury barometer, the cistern has a flexible bottom to which is attached an adjusting screw by which the level of the mercury in the cistern is set at a fixed point before each reading (Fig. 2.8). A thermometer is attached to the frame of the barometer for reasons to be explained later.

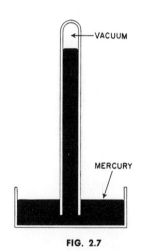

FIG. 2.7

A Simple Mercurial Barometer.

Units of pressure measurement. In this country, the barometer scale is usually graduated in inches. In countries where the metric system is in use, the scale is marked in millimeters. When we say that the barometer reads 29.92 inches or 760 millimeters, we mean that the pressure of the air supports a column of mercury of that length. This value, 29.92 inches or 760 millimeters, is taken as the normal

Mercurial Barometers Mounted in Case. From left to right, Fortin type with   **FIG. 2.8**
screw to adjust level of mercury in cistern, fixed-cistern type, and a barometer combining principles of the other two. *Courtesy, U.S. Department of Commerce, Weather
Bureau.*

value of the pressure at sea level at latitude 45°, and is called the *normal atmosphere,* or simply *one atmosphere.* There has now come into general use another unit of atmospheric pressure, called the *bar,* which is not a measure of length but a direct statement of force per unit area, that is, of pressure. Barometer scales are frequently marked in *millibars* (mb)—thousandths of a bar. The bar is equal to 1 megadyne (1,000,000 dynes) per square centimeter. Under standard conditions of temperature and gravity, a pressure of 29.53 inches = 1 bar = 1,000 millibars. The millibar, as a unit of measure of atmospheric pressure, is in widespread use among the weather services today, and pressures are seldom converted to inches of mercury except for public uses. A comparison of the three scales for measuring atmospheric pressure is made in Fig. 2.9. Note that 1013.2 mb = 29.92 in. = 760 mm.

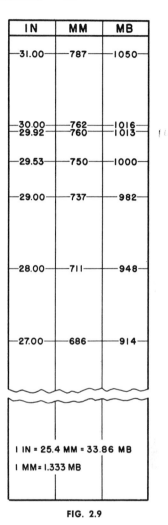

IN	MM	MB
31.00	787	1050
30.00	762	1016
29.92	760	1013
29.53	750	1000
29.00	737	982
28.00	711	948
27.00	686	914

1 IN = 25.4 MM = 33.86 MB
1 MM = 1.333 MB

FIG. 2.9

Barometer Scales Compared.

BAROMETER CORRECTIONS

Four corrections are necessary to render a barometer reading comparable to other readings at other places, and only by comparing pressures at many places is it possible to know what the pressure pattern is like.

1. A *temperature* correction is necessary because the density of mercury changes with changes in temperature. For this purpose a thermometer is attached to the barometer, and all readings are corrected to a standard temperature.

2. The force of gravity varies over the earth's surface making a *gravity* correction necessary. This is so because the earth is not a perfect sphere. Its equatorial diameter is about 27 miles (43 km) greater than its polar diameter. Hence, the same actual pressure would give a higher barometer reading at the equator than at the poles. This correction therefore depends on the latitude of the instrument's location.

3. Most barometers are found to have certain divergencies due to scale

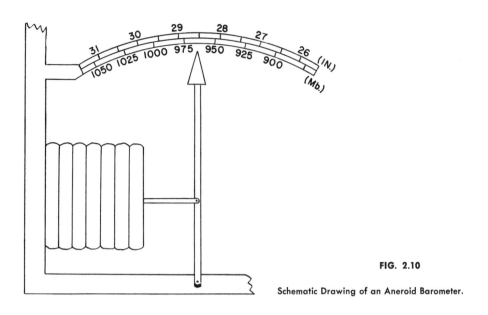

FIG. 2.10

Schematic Drawing of an Aneroid Barometer.

Navy-type Aneroid Barometer Calibrated in Inches and Millibars. Courtesy, *Bendix Corporation, Friez Instrument Division.*   **FIG. 2.11**

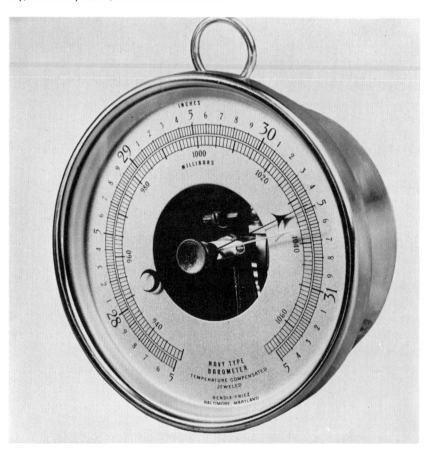

inaccuracies and capillarity which are grouped together as "instrumental error" and may be considered an *instrument* correction. When these three corrections are applied to the barometer reading, the result is the station pressure.

4. Finally, an *altitude* correction must be made if any two or more barometer readings from locations with different elevations are to be compared. Generally, all barometer readings are reduced to sea level for the purpose of comparison.

ANEROID BAROMETERS

Another instrument in general use for the measurement of pressure is the aneroid barometer. It consists essentially of a flexible metal box, or chamber, which is hermetically sealed after being nearly exhausted of air, and is kept from collapsing by a spring within it. The flexible chamber then responds sensitively to pressure changes, and the resulting movements are communicated to an index hand moving over a dial (Fig. 2.10). Aneroid barometers are compensated for temperature and require no gravity correction; the station pressure is read directly from the dial. Instrumental errors, however, are considerable and variable, and these instruments are less reliable than are mercury barometers and should be checked frequently with them. Aneroids are light and easily carried without injury, if not subjected to severe jarring, and are therefore useful for travelers and explorers and on vessels at sea (Fig. 2.11).

A *barograph* is an aneroid barometer that makes a continuous record of the pressure. It consists of several metallic chambers, one on top of the other. The combined motion of these is communicated to a lever, terminating in a pen. The pen writes a record of the pressure upon a ruled sheet of paper wound around a drum while the drum is being rotated slowly by a clock within it (Fig. 2.12). The continuous records of pressure thus ob-

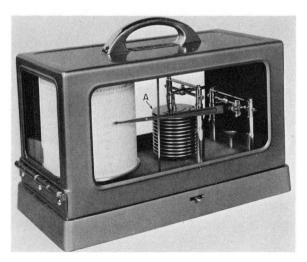

FIG. 2.12

Barograph. The flexible, metallic chambers, A, are partially exhausted of air, and a system of internal springs are balanced against the outside air pressure. Changing air pressure results in compression or expansion which causes a vertical movement of the pen. *Courtesy, Bendix Corporation, Friez Instrument Division.*

tained are valuable in showing the march of pressure, the extremes, and how the pressure is varying at any time. The *barometric tendency*, meaning the change in pressure during a given period of time (usually, the three hours preceding an observation) is of importance in forecasting the weather.

VARIATION OF PRESSURE WITH HEIGHT

As we rise above sea level, we get above some of the weight of the air, and the pressure falls rather rapidly at first in the dense lower air, and then more slowly as the air becomes thinner. As a first approximation, we may say that the pressure decreases one-thirtieth of its value at any given moderate altitude with an increase of 900 feet in height (275 m). Starting with a pressure of 30 inches at sea level, at 900 feet above sea level it will have fallen to 29 inches; during the next 900-foot rise to 1,800 feet elevation, it will have fallen one-thirtieth of 29 inches to 28.03 inches; continuing at this geometric ratio for each successive change of 900 feet. But the density and weight of the air depend upon its temperature and, to a lesser extent, upon the proportion of water vapor in it and the force of gravity. Hence, no accurate correction for altitude can be made without a consideration of these factors, especially the temperature.

Reduction to sea level. In studying the distribution of pressure over the earth, it is necessary, then, to take account of the differing altitudes of the places at which the pressure was measured. In doing this, all readings are customarily "reduced to sea level." For places above sea level, this means adding to the station pressure an amount assumed to represent the weight of the air in a vertical column extending from the point of observation to sea level. Since no such column exists beneath a land station, assumptions as to its temperature, density, and moisture content are fictitious, and the results are only approximations. When the altitudes are considerable, as in the Rocky Mountain region, the reductions thus made are subject to considerable error.

The various corrections to be applied in reducing pressures to sea level, or conversely, in determining heights by the barometer, are published in detail in the *Smithsonian Meteorological Tables.* By applying these corrections, the difference in altitude between two nearby places may be determined with considerable accuracy if simultaneous observations of pressure, temperature, and humidity are obtained at the two stations.

Altimeter. The relation of pressure to height above sea level has long been used by travelers, explorers, and surveyors in making estimates of altitudes and differences in altitude, and now has a wide application in connection with aviation. The *pressure altimeter,* carried by all airplanes, is an aneroid barometer graduated to read directly in heights instead of pressures. The rate of decrease of pressure with height varies with the temperature of the air column and to a lesser degree with the pressure distribution and the humidity of the air. The elevations indicated by such an altimeter are correct only under the assumed standard conditions. If the air is colder than the standard atmosphere, the instrument indicates too high an altitude; if the air is warmer than the standard, the reading is too low. Another source of error lies in the fact that the pressure differs widely from time to time at the same place, and also differs from place to place at the same height above sea level.

Before taking off on a flight, the aviator adjusts his altimeter to an *altimeter setting*, which is the pressure at the airport reduced to sea level by assuming standard atmospheric conditions, not by using current temperatures. His instrument will then read the correct altitude of the airplane at that moment. As the time since the altimeter was set increases, and as the plane gets farther from the place where it was set, the probability of serious error in the indicated altitude increases. The error may amount to several hundred feet. Obviously, it is wise to check the altimeter setting frequently with points along the flight route, and especially to adjust the instrument to the correct altimeter setting at the destination before landing. An instrument developed during World War II, using the radar principle, is called the *radio altimeter*. It is installed on all larger aircraft today and enables the aviator to make a direct determination of his true elevation above the ground and is therefore an *absolute altimeter*.

RESULTS OF PRESSURE OBSERVATIONS

Pressure observations began in Italy about the middle of the seventeenth century and have been carried on more or less continuously in various parts of the world from that time to the present. Especially during the past hundred years, observations have been numerous and widely distributed. Yearly, monthly, daily, and hourly normals have thus been established, more or less definitely, throughout the world. The normal annual pressure is found to differ in different parts of the world, and the monthly normals at any one place change with the seasons. Outside the tropics, there are also comparatively large irregular variations from day to day, independent of seasonal changes but more marked in winter than in summer.

Diurnal variations. Finally, there are regular daily variations of small amounts, resulting in two maxima and two minima each day. The maxima occur about 10 A.M. and 10 P.M. local time, and the minima about 4 A.M. and 4 P.M., varying somewhat with the season of the year. These diurnal variations are greatest in equatorial regions, where they amount to about 0.1 inch (3 mb), and decrease steadily toward the poles. In higher latitudes, they are practically masked by the larger irregular variations and may not be apparent except in the averages of a long period. A complete physical explanation of these daily changes is difficult, but they seem to be long atmospheric waves similar to the ocean tides, which move around the earth about two hours in advance of the sun and are in a complex way associated with the gravitational attraction of the sun and the daily changes in temperature.

Wind is air in horizontal motion. Vertical movements in the air are commonly called *currents*. Winds are of fundamental importance in making our weather what it is. In the first place, the motion itself is a weather factor of importance— a quiet winter's day may be pleasant and a windy day may be disagreeable. In the second place, the physical condition of the air is largely a function of its source and horizontal movement. Winds become moist when moving over large water areas, and they carry this moisture to the land. Air becomes cold over frozen or snow-covered regions and moves, as wind, to warmer regions. Similarly, warm air is transported to normally cold regions. To describe the movement itself without reference to the condition of the moving air, two facts about the wind must be observed, namely, its direction and its speed.

Wind Observations

WIND DIRECTION

Wind vanes have been in use since ancient times as indicators of the direction of the wind. A wind is named for the direction from which it comes, that is, the direction toward which the arrow of the wind vane points (Fig. 2.13). Winds are said to *veer* when they change in a clockwise direction, such as east to south or west to north, and are said to *back* when they change in the opposite order.

An automatic record of the wind direction may be obtained by connecting a vane by electrical circuits to a recording device actuated by clockwork. A recording instrument in common use is the *meteorograph* or

FIG. 2.13

Wind Instruments. These instruments are mounted on the tower support on top of the observatory of the central office of the U.S. Weather Bureau, Washington, D.C. From left to right, Dines (pressure tube) anemometer, thunderstorm indicator (generating voltmeters), 4-foot wind vane, and three-cup anemometer. The anemometer is whirling quite rapidly so that the cups are not discernible. Courtesy, U.S. Department of Commerce, Weather Bureau.

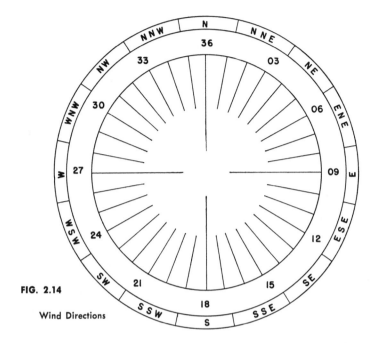

FIG. 2.14

Wind Directions

triple register. It records not only wind direction, but also wind speed, sunshine, and rainfall, as will be noted later. Hence the name "triple register," because it records three weather elements.

Other devices are in use, called *anemoscopes,* which give a continuous record of wind direction. There are also wind-direction indicators showing exact directions at any instant by a pointer on a dial. Both surface winds and winds aloft are observed according to 36 points of the compass, or to the nearest 10 degrees (Fig. 2.14). Wind direction is plotted on a weather map by means of a *wind shaft* drawn toward the station from the direction of the wind. A surface wind is plotted as W, WNW, NW, NNW, and so forth, and speed is shown by *feathers* on the shaft. Winds aloft are represented in the same manner with accuracy to 36 points of the compass.

WIND SPEED

Moving air exerts a force or pressure against objects in its path, and that force is proportional to the square of its velocity.[1] This may be expressed by the equation: $P = KV^2$, where P is the pressure exerted by the wind, V is its velocity, and the value of K depends upon the units used. If pres-

---

[1] In strict usage, velocity is a vector quantity and equals speed in a particular direction. In common usage and as ordinarily tabulated, wind velocity refers to speed of motion without reference to direction.

sure is expressed in pounds per square foot and velocity in *knots*,[2] then $P = 0.0053V^2$, approximately, for a flat surface normal to the wind, where pressure includes also the suction on the rear of the surface. (When velocity is expressed in miles per hour, the formula becomes $P = 0.004V^2$.) By reason of this force exerted by the wind, its velocity can be estimated without instruments by its effect on surrounding objects. For this purpose a scale was developed, known as the *Beaufort scale*. Originally used by Admiral Beaufort of the British Navy in 1805, this scale was at first expressed in terms of the effect of the wind on the sails of a ship but was later adapted for both land and sea use. It involved a scheme of wind arrows with "feathers" to graphically represent both wind direction and speed. More recently, a simplified scheme of this system has been more or less universally adopted where the "feathers" indicate wind speeds to the nearest 5 knots. A lined feather is made into a pennant to indicate 50 knots. The two symbols $\digamma$ and $\not\digamma$ represent 15 knots and 65 knots, respectively.

For a mechanical measurement of wind velocity, several types of *anemometers* have been developed. A simple *deflection anemometer* consists of a board, hinged at the top and swinging in the wind, having an attached arc to indicate the angular amount of its deflection from the vertical. From this deflection the velocity may be calculated. A *pressure tube anemometer* consists of a U-shaped tube containing a liquid and having one of the open ends directed toward the wind. The difference in level of the liquid in the parts of the tube is a measure of the pressure of the wind and hence of its velocity.

Robinson cup anemometer. For meteorological purposes, the Robinson cup anemometer has long been in general use in this country. In this type of instrument, a set of hemispherical cups is mounted on a vertical axis attached to a spindle which actuates a dial (Fig. 2.15). As the cups revolve in the wind, distances are indicated on the dial in knots or miles per hour.

By fitting the dial with posts that press against a spring and thus close an electric circuit for each mile, an automatic record of the wind movement is obtained on the meteorograph on the same sheet with the record of the direction. Both the anemometer and the wind vane may also be connected electrically with an indicator located in an office at some distance in such a manner as to enable the observer to determine the direction and speed of the wind at any time without visiting the instrument.

Aerovane. A recent development is the Bendix-Friez aerovane wind transmitter, a combined anemometer and wind vane. It uses a three-bladed propeller for measuring the speed of the wind, and a streamlined vane for direction (Fig. 2.16). The propeller rotates at a rate proportional

---

[2] The knot, one nautical mile (6,080.20 feet) per hour, has become the standard unit of wind velocity in the United States. The term originated at sea from divisions in the log line arranged to measure a ship's speed through the water.

FIG. 2.15

Robinson Three-cup Anemometer. Totalizing dials indicate the total miles of wind, and electrical contacts operate a speed indicator and recorder. Courtesy, Bendix Corporation, Friez Instrument Division.

FIG. 2.16

Aerovane. Instantaneous direction and speed of the wind may be read remotely from the dials connected to this instrument. Courtesy, Bendix Corporation, Friez Instrument Division.

to the wind speed. The vane performs two functions: it indicates the wind direction, and it keeps the propeller axis pointed into the wind. Both are connected with indicating or recording instruments.

GUSTINESS OF WINDS

The record made by a cup anemometer gives the time between successive miles of wind, but a pressure tube anemometer may be arranged to give a continuous graph of the fluctuations of the wind. Other types of instruments to indicate the gustiness and instantaneous speed of the wind have been devised. A recording mechanism may be attached for making a continuous, permanent graphic record. The records obtained by such instruments show that the flow of air near the surface of the earth is never steady. It is not a streamline flow, but a movement in successive gusts and lulls of a few seconds' duration. This *turbulence* is greater the higher the wind velocity; it is greater over land than over ocean surfaces, and greater over forests and cities than over bare, level ground. Evidently, the turbulent motion is caused, in part at least, by surface irregularities and friction.

Friction at the earth's surface induces gustiness by checking the flow of the lowest layer, letting the layers above it break over it like the waves along a sloping seacoast. Surface obstacles turn the air out of its course and into numerous cross currents. Eddies around buildings and through city streets are familiar examples of turbulent motion, but all the trees and shrubs and all the little irregularities of the land cause similar eddies in relation to their size, changing both the speed and the direction of the wind in their vicinity. The effect of such obstructions extends to five or six times their altitudes. These effects are, therefore, local and confined to the air near the earth's surface, unless other forces aid in causing unsteady motion.

EFFECT OF ALTITUDE

The average velocity of the wind increases with height above the ground. There is a marked increase in the first 100 feet (30 m). In general, the velocity at the height of 33 feet is about twice that at 1 1/2 feet, and the velocity at 100 feet is 1.2 times that at 33 feet. This reduced velocity near the surface is evidence of the "frictional drag" of the earth. Notwithstanding the increased velocity, there is less turbulence as we rise into the free air, but some effects of surface eddies are felt at heights of 6,000 to 9,000 feet (1,800–2,700 m). Turbulence also sometimes originates in the upper air through the contact and resulting friction of winds of different directions or velocities and different densities.

EXPOSURE OF WIND VANE AND ANEMOMETER

Considering the effects of surface turbulence and surface drag, it is evident that, in order to get records truly representative of the general condi-

"Smoke Run" at Brookhaven National Laboratory. Periodically, smoke is   **FIG. 2.17**
released from three different levels of this 410-foot tower to supplement
weather data obtained from instruments, including those attached to the steel arms projecting from
the lefthand side of the tower. It is common to find considerable sheer in the wind direction through
small changes in elevation. *Brookhaven National Laboratory Photo.*

tions in a region, the place of exposure of the wind instruments must be
carefully selected. They should be placed where they are as free as possible of interference from local irregularities, that is, as far as possible from
adjacent high objects and as much as possible above them. Often they are
placed on the roofs of buildings at varying distances from other buildings
of comparable height. Conflicting results might be obtained from instruments exposed at different heights (Fig. 2.17). Observations from the roofs
of buildings and at varying elevations are unsatisfactory for comparative
purposes. It would be better if all instruments could be exposed in the open
and at standard heights above the ground.

RESULTS OF WIND OBSERVATIONS

The records obtained by continued observations of the wind afford
valuable information which may be summarized in various ways. Official
records in the United States give the prevailing direction and the average
velocity for each day, month, and year, and the monthly and annual
normals; also, the maximum velocities by months, and the number of days

when velocities of 32 miles per hour (16 mps) or more occurred. Also calculated are the percentages of the time that the wind blew from each of the principal directions and the percentages of the total movement from each direction. Wind data may be graphically presented by means of a *wind rose,* in which the relative lengths of the radiating lines indicate the relative frequency of the winds from the different directions (Fig. 2.18).

Wind variations. The accumulated observations show that there is an annual change in both direction and the speed of the wind in most parts of the world. The velocity is greater, on the average, in winter and spring than in summer and autumn. The reason for this is the greater contrast in temperature between high and low latitudes in winter and spring seasons, as will be noted later. Usually March is the month of highest average velocity and August the month of the lowest; but in a large part of the Mississippi and Missouri valleys, April is windier than March. In Rocky Mountain and Pacific Coast regions and in the vicinity of the Great Lakes, there is con-

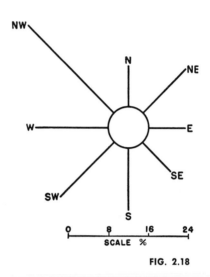

FIG. 2.18

Wind Rose for New York City. Average annual percentage of winds from eight directions.

siderable local variation in the months of highest and lowest average velocity. The prevailing direction of the wind also frequently changes with the seasons, owing to changing temperature contrasts between land and ocean areas.

The velocity of the wind is generally greater by day than by night over land surfaces, especially in summer and on clear days. The highest average occurs from 1 to 3 P.M., and the lowest about sunrise. These diurnal variations are caused by the heating and rising of the surface air by day and the descent of cooler air from aloft. This explanation is confirmed by the fact that at sea, where the surface does not become diurnally heated, there is little difference between day and night velocities. The conditions under which vertical interchanges of air take place are discussed in Chapter 4. In most coastal regions, there is a daily change in wind direction, which will be considered in more detail in Chapter 6.

Although the annual and daily variations of the wind movement recur with more or less regularity, they are subject to continual interruption by irregular changes due to special causes. Sometimes these erratic variations occur as *squalls*—sudden marked increases in velocity, like gusts but lasting much longer. At other times, the wind may shift radically in both direction and speed and may continue from the new direction for several hours or even days. An explanation of these irregular wind variations must be delayed for later discussion.

REMOTE WIND OBSERVATIONS

One of the real problems in meteorological analysis is to obtain observations at critical locations even though it is not convenient to have an observer located there. One recognizes the scope of this problem when it is realized that nearly three-fourths of the earth's surface is covered by the oceans. The Navy has recently developed an atomic-powered NOMAD weather station which is designed to operate unattended for periods up to ten years (Fig. 2.19).

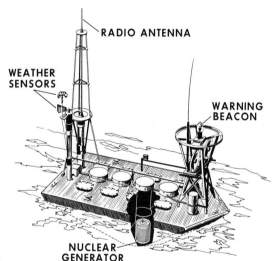

FIG. 2.19

Automatic Atomic-powered Weather Station. This station is powered by a generator developed by the Martin Company of Baltimore, Maryland. Heat from the decay of radioactive materials is converted to electricity which operates the instruments. Courtesy, Office of Naval Research.

In addition to wind speed and direction, the NOMAD (Navy Oceanographic Meteorological Automatic Device) radios air temperature, sea temperature, and barometric pressure every three hours. When the weather becomes severe, a storm sensor causes the transmission frequency to increase to once each hour. The first of these stations is moored at 20°N Latitude and 90°W Longitude in the middle of the Gulf of Mexico.

Similar, but land-based, unmanned weather stations have been operating successfully for more than two years at opposite ends of the earth. The first nuclear-powered station was installed in the Canadian Arctic at Sherwood Head, Axel Heiberg Island, on August 17, 1961. A short time later another station was placed at Minna Bluff, Antarctica. It is now anticipated that a worldwide network of automatic weather observation stations will be developed.

Humidity Observations

Water vapor is the most variable of the gases of the atmosphere, ranging from almost zero to a maximum of about 4 per cent by volume. It is extremely important to man's existence on the earth and constitutes one of the primary elements of weather. It not only contributes to the heating and cooling of the earth's surface but is directly related to the distribution and extent of precipitation over the earth.

Some of the molecules at the surface of a liquid are continually escaping and entering the air as gaseous molecules, thereby reducing the volume of the liquid. For any surface of a given liquid, such as water, the number of molecules that escape in a period of time depends solely upon the speed at which they are moving, that is, upon the temperature of the surface of the liquid. Raising the temperature increases the velocity of the molecules and the rate at which they break free from the liquid surface. In this way, water vapor enters the air from water surfaces, moist soil, and growing plants. The process is called *evaporation*, and it occurs in all liquids. Ice and snow sometimes change directly from the solid to the gaseous state. This process is called *sublimation*. In breaking away from the attraction of the other molecules, the escaping molecules use heat energy at the expense of the immediate environment. The heat energy so lost does not warm the gas but is used solely in effecting the change of state, and is called *latent heat of vaporization*, or *latent heat of sublimation*, as the case may be. This latent heat is again returned to the environment upon condensation of the water vapor. The wide use of evaporative cooling units throughout the western half of the United States is evidence that cooling by evaporation contributes much to the temperature characteristics of the atmosphere.

MIXING RATIO

The mass of water vapor per unit mass of dry air is a convenient parameter by which to express the relative composition of the mixture. The parameter is called the *mixing ratio* of the moist air and is denoted by the symbol r. The mixing ratio r of moist air can therefore be defined as the ratio of the mass m_v of water vapor to the mass m_a of dry air with which the water vapor is associated:

$$r = \frac{m_v}{m_a}.$$

SATURATION MIXING RATIO

The symbol r_w is used to denote saturation mixing ratio of moist air with respect to a plane surface of pure water. The symbol r_i denotes saturation mixing ratio of moist air with respect to a plane surface of pure ice. Moist air at temperature T and at total pressure p is said to be saturated if its moisture content is such that it can coexist in neutral equilibrium with a plane surface of pure water (or ice) at the same temperature and pressure.

VAPOR PRESSURE AND SATURATED VAPOR

When water vapor escapes into space and mixes with the other gases of the air, it exerts a pressure in all directions as do the other gases. This partial pressure is known as the *vapor pressure* of the air. John Dalton, founder of the atomic theory, first stated in 1802 that the total pressure p of a mixture of gases is equal to the sum of the pressures of the individual gases if each occupied the same volume alone at the same temperature. This is known as *Dalton's law of partial pressures*. The vapor pressure e' of water vapor in moist air at total pressure p and with mixing ratio r is defined by:

$$e' = \frac{r}{0.62197 + r} p.$$

It is expressed in the same units as the total air pressure.

Considering an open water surface, we find not only an escape of molecules from the liquid to the air, but also some return of the gaseous molecules to the liquid. At first the number of molecules escaping will be greater than those returning to the liquid, and we say that evaporation is occurring. But as the number of molecules of vapor in the air increases, there is an increase in the vapor pressure and in the number of molecules returning to the liquid. Finally, an equilibrium point is reached when the number of molecules returning is just equal to those escaping. The net evaporation is then zero and the air is said to be saturated, that is, the space can hold no more water vapor under the existing conditions. If the temperature of the air is now increased, the tendency of the water molecules to return to the liquid would be decreased and more water vapor would have to be added to keep the space saturated. At constant pressure and a given temperature, the saturation vapor pressure has a fixed value, but it changes rapidly with changes in temperature (Table 2.1 on page 42). For example: at 0°F and 30.0 inches of barometric pressure, saturation vapor pressure is 0.038 inch; at 50°F, 0.360 inch; and at 100°F, 1.916 inches.

ABSOLUTE HUMIDITY

In dealing with the moisture in the atmosphere, one quantity that may be measured is the actual mass of water vapor in a given volume of air. It may be expressed, for example, as the number of grams of water vapor in a cubic meter of moist air. We thus obtain the *absolute humidity*, which is defined as the mass of water vapor per unit volume of air.

SPECIFIC HUMIDITY

Another parameter of water vapor in the atmosphere is *specific humidity,* defined as the mass concentration or moisture content q of moist air as determined by the ratio of the mass m_v of water vapor to the mass $(m_v + m_a)$ of moist air in which the mass of water vapor is contained:

$$q = \frac{m_v}{m_v + m_a}.$$

Notice that absolute humidity is the relation of the mass of vapor to the volume occupied, and specific humidity is the relation of mass of vapor to mass of air. Again, since pressures exerted by gases are proportional to the masses, specific humidity may be obtained by dividing the partial pressure due to the water vapor by the total pressure of the air. Specific humidity is usually expressed in grams of water vapor per kilogram of air, and the equation becomes: $q = 621.97e'/p$. When a quantity of air expands or is compressed, the total pressure and the vapor pressure change in the same ratio, so that the value of e'/p remains the same. Hence, the specific humidity is constant under these conditions; it does not change unless water is added or removed.

DEW POINT AND CONDENSATION

The *dew point* of a given mass of air is the temperature at which saturation occurs when the air is cooled at constant pressure without the addition or removal of water vapor. It is determined by the amount of water vapor in the air and is entirely independent of the free-air temperature. The dew-point temperature is compared with the temperature of the free air to determine humidity conditions. The dew-point temperature is often used in empirical formulas to determine the height of convective clouds and to predict the occurrence of fog, dew, frost, or precipitation.

If the air is cooled below its dew point, some of the water vapor becomes liquid. This process of changing from a gas to a liquid is called *condensation.* Just as heat is transformed in the process of evaporation to cool the environment, condensation releases an equal amount of energy in the form of heat (called *latent heat of condensation*), which results in adding heat to the environment. Ordinarily condensation begins as soon as the temperature of the air falls below the dew point, but under certain conditions the change of state is delayed until the temperature of the air is considerably below the dew point. When this happens the air is said to be supersaturated.

RELATIVE HUMIDITY

Relative humidity is a common parameter for expressing water-vapor content of the air. It is the percentage of water vapor present in the air in comparison with saturated conditions. Relative humidity U (in per cent) of moist air is defined by:

$$U = 100 \, \frac{r}{r_w},$$

where r is the mixing ratio of moist air at pressure p and temperature T and r_w the saturation mixing ratio at the same temperature and pressure.

Vapor pressure, absolute humidity, specific humidity, and mixing ratio are different ways of expressing essentially the same thing; thus, any of these parameters may be used to obtain relative humidity if the existing condition and the saturated condition are known. Relative humidity or dew point is commonly used to express the moisture content of the air at a given time and place, while vapor pressure, mixing ratio, absolute humidity, and specific humidity are more useful expressions when dealing with the thermodynamics of the atmosphere.

MEASUREMENT OF HUMIDITY

The dew point may be determined directly by a simple laboratory experiment. When water is placed in a thin-walled, brightly polished silver cup and kept well stirred, the temperature of the liquid and the cup will be the same. When sufficient ice is added to cool the water and the cup below the dew point of the surrounding air, the outer polished surface of the cup will be visibly clouded by beads of water. The temperature of the water (thoroughly stirred) at the time this clouding begins is the dew point of the surrounding air to a close approximation. An instrument of this kind is called a *dew-point hygrometer*.

The absolute humidity may be measured by passing a known volume of air through a chemical which absorbs the moisture, and noting the resulting increase in weight of the absorbing substance. By more elaborate instrumental means, the saturation vapor pressures at different temperatures have been experimentally determined with great care. From such laboratory determinations and from the known physical relations between the various humidity factors, tables of humidity values have been prepared and published. The authoritative publication in this country is *Smithsonian Meteorological Tables,* Sixth Revised Edition, published by the Smithsonian Institution, in 1951.

Psychrometers. In meteorological practice, a psychrometer is commonly used for humidity measurements. The *whirled psychrometer* consists of two mercury thermometers with cylindrical bulbs, mounted vertically within the instrument shelter upon a frame that can be turned rapidly. The two thermometers are alike, but one has a thin piece of clean muslin tied around the bulb. This bulb is dipped in water, and the two are whirled. After a minute or two of whirling, the two thermometers are read. The reading of the thermometer with the dry bulb is the current temperature of the air; the wet-bulb thermometer will ordinarily be found to have a lower reading. The whirling is repeated until no further reduction in the reading of the wet-bulb thermometer can be obtained. This reading is called the *wet-bulb temperature.* It will remain constant as long as the covering remains wet and the whirling is continued, provided the air retains the same temperature and the same moisture content. The cooling of the mercury is due to the evaporation of the moisture around it and is directly proportional to the dryness of the air. The difference in temperature between the dry-bulb and the wet-bulb thermometers, therefore, gives a measure of the moisture of the air. Given this difference, which is called the *depression of the wet bulb,* it is possible to read the dew point, vapor pressure, and relative humidity from the *Smithsonian Meteorological Tables.* A *sling psychrometer* is a similar instrument except that the two thermometers are mounted together on a metal back and are whirled by hand by means of an attached cord or chain (Fig. 2.20). The *aspiration psychrometer* has the two thermometers enclosed in a tube through which air is drawn by a fan.

Another humidity-measuring device is called the *telepsychrometer.* As the name implies, it shows the wet-bulb and dry-bulb readings on an

Sling Psychrometer. Courtesy, Bendix Corporation, Friez Instrument Division.   **FIG. 2.20**

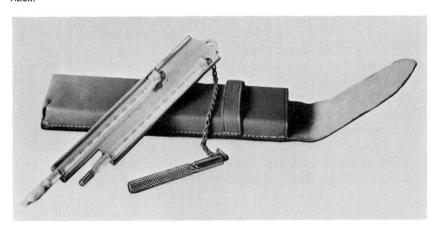

indicator dial mounted in the weather office while the measuring instrument is favorably exposed to the free atmosphere some distance away. The telepsychrometer permits the observer, by means of electric controls, to perform the necessary operations for a reading without leaving the office. A heater element is incorporated to permit the telepsychrometer to function at temperatures below freezing.

In Table 2.1, condensed from the *Smithsonian Meteorological Tables*, will be found the saturation vapor pressures for various temperatures, and also a table for obtaining dew points from psychrometric observations. Differences between the readings of the wet-bulb and dry-bulb thermometers are given at the head of the columns 1 to 30. The dew point corresponding to a given air temperature and a given depression of the wet-bulb thermometer is found in the body of the table. For example, when the temperature is 50° and the depression is 6°, the dew point is 37°; also, when the temperature is 65° and the depression 14°, the dew point is 37°. Similarly, Table 2.2 gives the relative humidity in terms of the air temperature and the cooling of the wet-bulb thermometer. It will be seen, for example, that the relative humidity is 55 per cent when the temperature is 20° and the depression is 3°, and also when the temperature is 70° and the depression is 10°.

Hygrometers. The *hair hygrometer* is an instrument which gives a direct reading of the relative humidity. The oils are removed from a strand of human hair, which is then so attached that its changes in length (in response to humidity changes) actuate a pen moving over a scale which is calibrated between 0 and 100 per cent. In the *hair hygrograph*, the pen moves over a cylinder and makes a continuous record of the relative humidity. The hairs change their length in proportion to the changes in relative humidity, getting longer as the humidity increases. In using psychrometers or hygrometers, it must be remembered that maintaining an active movement of air past the instrument is essential to obtaining a correct reading.

The psychrometer is rather inaccurate at temperatures below freezing, because ice forms on the bulb. The hair hygrometer needs frequent calibration and is slow in responding to humidity changes. The time lag increases as the temperature decreases, and is so great as to make the instrument practically useless at temperatures a little below 0°F. These shortcomings make the hair hygrometer unsatisfactory for use on airplanes or for other upper-air measurements because of the low temperatures and rapid changes in humidity encountered. An *electric hygrometer* has been developed to replace the hair hygrometer, especially on airplanes and radiosondes. It makes use of the fact that the resistance through an electrical conductor coated with a moisture-absorbing material varies as the relative humidity varies.

TABLE 2.1   Saturation Vapor Pressure in Inches of Mercury and Temperature of Dew Point in Degrees Fahrenheit

(Barometric pressure, 30.00 inches)

AIR TEMP. (°F)	SATURATION VAPOR PRESSURE (IN.)	DEPRESSION OF WET-BULB THERMOMETER													
		1	2	3	4	6	8	10	12	14	16	18	20	25	30
0	.038	-7	-20												
5	.049	-1	-9	-24											
10	.063	5	-2	-10	-27										
15	.081	11	6	0	-9										
20	.103	16	12	8	2	-21									
25	.130	22	19	15	10	-3	-15								
30	.164	27	25	21	18	8	-7								
35	.203	33	30	28	25	17	7	-11							
40	.247	38	35	33	30	25	18	7	-14						
45	.298	43	41	38	36	31	25	18	7	-14					
50	.360	48	46	44	42	37	32	26	18	8	-13				
55	.432	53	51	50	48	43	38	33	27	20	9	-12			
60	.517	58	57	55	53	49	45	40	35	29	21	11	-8		
65	.616	63	62	60	59	55	51	47	42	37	31	24	14		
70	.732	69	67	65	64	61	57	53	49	44	39	33	26	-11	
75	.866	74	72	71	69	66	63	59	55	51	47	42	36	15	
80	1.022	79	77	76	74	72	68	65	62	58	54	50	44	28	-7
85	1.201	84	82	81	80	77	74	71	68	64	61	57	52	39	19
90	1.408	89	87	86	85	82	79	76	73	70	67	63	59	48	32
95	1.645	94	93	91	90	87	85	82	79	76	73	70	66	56	43
100	1.916	99	98	96	95	93	90	87	85	82	79	76	72	63	52

TABLE 2.2   Relative Humidity, Per Cent

(Barometric pressure, 30.00 inches)

AIR TEMP. (°F)	DEPRESSION OF WET-BULB THERMOMETER													
	1	2	3	4	6	8	10	12	14	16	18	20	25	30
0	67	33	1											
5	73	46	20											
10	78	56	34	13										
15	82	64	46	29	12									
20	85	70	55	40	25	1								
25	87	74	62	49	36	16								
30	89	78	67	56	45	27								
35	91	81	72	63	52	37	10							
40	92	83	75	68	57	44	22	7						
45	93	86	78	71	61	49	31	18	6					
50	93	87	80	74	65	54	38	27	16	5				
55	94	88	82	76	68	58	43	33	23	14	5			
60	94	89	83	78	70	61	48	39	30	21	13	5		
65	95	90	85	80	72	64	52	44	35	27	20	12		
70	95	90	86	81	74	66	55	48	40	33	25	19	3	
75	96	91	86	82	75	68	58	51	44	37	30	24	9	
80	96	91	87	83	76	70	61	54	47	41	35	29	15	3
85	96	92	88	84	78	71	63	56	50	44	38	32	20	8
90	96	92	89	85	79	72	65	58	52	47	41	36	24	13
95	96	93	89	86	79	72	66	60	54	49	44	38	27	17
100	96	93	89	86	80	73	68	62	56	51	46	41	30	21

HUMIDITY RECORDS

From readings of the psychrometer, one obtains the dew point, relative humidity, and vapor pressure. Many stations also obtain a continuous record of the relative humidity by means of the hygrograph. In addition to fluctuations due to local weather changes, the relative humidity shows both diurnal and annual variations; it is, on the average, greatest during the coolest part of the day and of the year and least during the warmest portions.

A cloud is a visible aggregate of minute particles (less than 100 microns) of water or ice, or both, in the free air. It may contain larger particles of water or ice as **Cloud Observations** well as nonaqueous materials. Clouds are easily sustained and transported by air movements as slow as one-tenth of a mile per hour.

IDENTIFICATION AND GROUPING OF CLOUDS

Clouds are prominent and often spectacular features of the sky in nearly all parts of the world. Much can be determined about the state of the weather by carefully observing them. Luke Howard, an Englishman, devised a basic cloud-classification system in 1803 which has become the foundation of later cloud nomenclature. He recognized three principal cloud forms: (a) *Cirrus*, (b) *Stratus*, and (c) *Cumulus*. Cirrus appears to have a delicate and fibrous texture, generally white in color, often of a silky appearance and occurring in varied forms as tufts, featherlike plumes, or thin uniform veils. Stratus is found in more or less uniform layers at various heights. The stratified character of the cloud is the predominant feature. Cumulus is characterized by its vertical development. The upper surface is usually dome-shaped but may exhibit various protuberances or turrets.

The elevation of clouds provide another useful tool for identification and classification; even though the height varies on different occasions and in different latitudes, they have been divided vertically into three *etages*. High clouds (C_H) are always composed of ice crystals of the Cirrus type and are observed at elevations of 4 to 8 miles (5–13 km). Middle clouds (C_M) may have either a Cumulus or Stratus character and are generally observed at heights of 1 to 4 miles (2–7 km). The prefix *alto* is utilized to help denote these clouds. Low clouds (C_L) are also composed of various gradations and combinations of Cumulus or Stratus, or both, and are found at elevations up to about 6,500 feet (2 km). A unique situation occurs when Cumulus of the C_L group develops vertically through the height ranges of C_M and C_H clouds. These seem to indicate the need for a fourth category which might be called *clouds with vertical development;* but, since these originate in the C_L range, it is convenient to continue to classify them as C_L clouds.

CLOUD GENERA

Every student of meteorology should become familiar with the following ten cloud genera and make a practice of studying their appearance in the sky.[3]

C_H Cirrus (Ci) has a delicate and fibrous appearance, often with hooks or filaments called *mares' tails.* Because of their great altitude, Cirrus sometimes reflect beautiful hues of red or yellow before sunrise and after sunset.

C_H Cirrocumulus (Cc) is relatively rare. It appears as small white flakes or small globular masses, without shadows, and associated with Cirrus or Cirrostratus. The globular masses of Cirrocumulus are often arranged in rows.

C_H Cirrostratus (Cs) is a thin, whitish veil which does not obscure the outline of the sun or moon but gives rise to halos. Sometimes Cirrostratus merely gives the sky a milky look. Sometimes it shows a fibrous structure with disordered filaments.

C_M Altocumulus (Ac) is observed in layers or patches of flattened globular masses, with or without shadows. The globules frequently have definite dark shading. Sometimes they occur in a regular pattern of lines or waves, producing what is called a *mackerel sky.*

C_M Altostratus (As) is a stratified veil of clouds ranging in color from grey to dark blue with a ground-glass appearance. The sun or the moon is visible through thin Altostratus, but without the halo phenomenon which is characteristic of Cirrostratus.

C_M Nimbostratus (Ns) is an amorphous, rainy layer of clouds of dark-grey color. The height of the base of Nimbostratus is usually much lower than that of Altostratus. When Nimbostratus produces precipitation, continuous rain or snow results; but, the characteristic cloud formation is called Nimbostratus even when no precipitation occurs.

C_L Stratocumulus (Sc) occurs in layers or patches of flakes or globular masses. The smallest of the regularly arranged elements appear fairly large; they are soft and grey with darker parts arranged in groups, lines, or rolls. Often the edges of the rolls join together to make a continuous cloud cover with a wavy appearance.

C_L Stratus (St) is a uniform layer of cloud resembling fog, but not resting on the ground. When this low layer is broken up into shreds, it may be designated as *Stratus fractus* of bad weather.

C_L Cumulus (Cu) is a thick cloud with significant vertical development in comparison with its horizontal extent. The base is nearly horizontal while the upper surface is dome-shaped with various protuberances. When the light comes from the side, Cumulus clouds exhibit strong contrasts of light and shade;

---

[3] The names and abbreviations of cloud genera should always be written with an initial capital letter.

against the sun, they look dark with bright edges. During bad weather, Cumulus clouds may be shredded by the winds until they have a very ragged appearance and are called *Cumulus fractus.*

C_L Cumulonimbus (Cb) is a heavy mass of cloud with great vertical development whose summits rise in the form of mountains or towers, develop a fibrous quality, and often spread out in the shape of an anvil. Lightning and thunder are associated with Cumulonimbus as well as rain, snow, or hail. The base of a Cumulonimbus often has a layer of low, ragged Stratus fractus below it.

Cirrus, Cirrocumulus, Altocumulus, and Cumulus occur in detached masses, usually covering only part of the sky. Precipitation normally does not fall from them. Cirrostratus, Altostratus, Nimbostratus, Stratocumulus, and Cumulonimbus form almost continuous layers and often cover the entire sky. Precipitation may occur from any of these except Cirrostratus. *Cumulus congestus* (a species of the Cumulus genus) and Cumulonimbus develop to great heights, their tops often extending 2 to 5 miles (3–8 km) above their bases.

CLOUD SPECIES

Peculiarities in the shape of clouds and differences in their structure have led to the subdivision of most cloud genera into *species*. A cloud belonging to a certain genus may bear the name of only one species. The species are mutually exclusive but may be common to more than one genus. On the other hand, a genus may be used without a species if none of the species seem appropriate. The *International Cloud Atlas* defines the following fourteen species:

Fibratus. Detached clouds or a thin cloud veil, consisting of nearly straight or more or less irregularly curved filaments which do not terminate in hooks or tufts. The term applies mainly to Cirrus and Cirrostratus.

Uncinus. Cirrus often shaped like a comma, terminating at the top in a hook, or in a tuft the upper part of which is not in the form of a rounded protuberance.

Spissatus. Cirrus of sufficient optical thickness to appear greyish when viewed toward the sun.

Castellanus. Clouds which present, in at least some portion of their upper part, cumuliform protuberances in the form of turrets which generally give the clouds a crenelated appearance. The turrets, some of which are taller than they are wide, are connected by a common base and seem to be arranged in lines. The castellanus character is especially evident when the clouds are seen from the side. This term applies to Cirrus, Cirrocumulus, Altocumulus, and Stratocumulus.

Floccus. A species in which each cloud unit is a small tuft with a cumuliform appearance, the lower part of which is more or less ragged and often accompanied by virga. This term applies to Cirrus, Cirrocumulus, and Altocumulus.

Stratiformis. Clouds spread out in an extensive horizontal sheet or layer.

This term applies to Altocumulus, to Stratocumulus, and, occasionally, to Cirrocumulus.

Nebulosus. A cloud like a nebulous veil or layer, showing no distinct details. This term applies mainly to Cirrostratus and Stratus.

Lenticularis. Clouds having the shape of lenses or almonds, often very elongated and usually with well-defined outlines. Such clouds appear most often in cloud formations of orographic origin, but may also occur in regions without marked orography. This term applies mainly to Cirrostratus, Altocumulus, and Stratocumulus.

Fractus. Clouds in the form of irregular shreds, which have a clearly ragged appearance. This term applies only to Stratus and Cumulus.

Humilis. Cumulus of only a slight vertical extent; they generally appear flattened.

Mediocris. Cumulus of moderate vertical extent, the tops of which show fairly small protuberances.

Congestus. Cumulus which are markedly sprouting and are often of great vertical extent; their bulging upper part frequently resembles a cauliflower.

Calvus. Cumulonimbus in which at least some protuberances of the upper part are beginning to lose their cumuliform outlines but in which no cirriform parts can be distinguished. Protuberances and sproutings tend to form a whitish mass, with more or less vertical striations.

Capillatus. Cumulonimbus characterized by the presence, mostly in the upper portion, of distinct cirriform parts of clearly fibrous or striated structure, frequently having the form of an anvil or a plume. Cumulonimbus capillatus is usually accompanied by a shower or by a thunderstorm, often with squalls and sometimes with hail; it frequently produces very well-defined virga.

CODE FOR CLOUD OBSERVATIONS

Since the World Meteorological Organization published *The International Cloud Atlas* in 1956, it has received widespread acceptance as the official guide for observers in coding cloud observations for purposes of communication. It is very important for all observers, even in different countries of the world, to classify clouds alike. Twenty-seven different cloud codes are used to report the possible variations in the "state of the sky." The following code numbers and descriptions are listed in the order of preference (if there is doubt about which code number is most appropriate in a given situation) for each of the three etages, C_H, C_M, and C_L.

C_H9 Cirrocumulus (Cc). Coded as C_H9 when Cirrocumulus is alone at the high-cloud level or if it exceeds the total Cirrus and Cirrostratus that are present.

C_H8 Cirrostratus (Cs). Coded as C_H8 if the Cirrostratus does not cover the whole sky and is not invading the celestial dome.

C_H7 Cirrostratus (Cs). Coded as C_H7 if Cirrostratus covers the entire sky.

C_H6 Cirrostratus (Cs). Coded as C_H6 if the Cirrostratus is invading the sky more than $45°$ above the horizon but does not cover the whole sky.

C_H5 Cirrostratus (Cs). Coded as C_H5 if the Cirrostratus is invading the sky but the continuous veil has not reached 45° above the horizon.

C_H4 Cirrus (Ci). Coded as C_H4 if Cirrus is invading the sky.

C_H3 Cirrus (Ci). Coded as C_H3 if C_H4 is not applicable and if dense Cirrus originating from Cumulonimbus is present.

C_H2 Cirrus (Ci). Coded as C_H2 if there is dense Cirrus with sproutings in the form of turrets or battlements and tufts which exceed the combined sky cover of Cirrus in filaments, strands, and hooks.

C_H1 Cirrus (Ci). Coded as C_H1 if the combined sky cover of Cirrus in the form of filaments, strands, and hooks is greater than the total of other forms of Cirrus.

C_M9 Chaotic Sky. Coded as C_M9 if the sky is chaotic and Altocumulus is present.

C_M8 Altocumulus (Ac). Coded as C_M8 if C_M9 is not applicable and Altocumulus is present with sproutings in the form of turrets or battlements or with the appearance of small cumuliform tufts.

C_M7 Altocumulus (Ac). Coded as C_M7 if C_M9 and C_M8 are not applicable and Altostratus or Nimbostratus is also present or if the Altocumulus occurs at two or more levels, or if it is quite opaque.

C_M6 Altocumulus (Ac). Coded as C_M6 if the Altocumulus if formed by the spreading out of Cumulus or Cumulonimbus.

C_M5 Altocumulus (Ac). Coded as C_M5 if 9, 8, 7, and 6 are not applicable and Altocumulus is invading the sky.

C_M4 Altocumulus (Ac). Coded as C_M4 if 9, 8, 7, 6, and 5 are not applicable and the Altocumulus is continually changing in appearance.

C_M3 Altocumulus (Ac). Coded as C_M3 if a higher code is not applicable and the greater part of the Altocumulus is semitransparent.

C_M2 Altostratus (As) or Nimbostratus (Ns). Coded as C_M2 if the Altostratus is opaque or if Nimbostratus is present.

C_M1 Altostratus (As). Coded as C_M1 if the Altostratus is semitransparent and no Nimbostratus is present.

C_L9 Cumulonimbus (Cb). Coded as C_L9 if the upper part of at least one of the Cumulonimbus is fibrous or striated.

C_L3 Cumulonimbus (Cb). Coded as C_L3 if none of the tops of the Cumulonimbus present is clearly fibrous or striated.

C_L4 Stratocumulus (Sc). Coded as C_L4 if the Stratocumulus is formed by the spreading out of Cumulus.

C_L8 Cumulus (Cu) and Stratocumulus (Sc). Coded as C_L8 if C_L4 is not applicable and Cumulus and Stratocumulus with bases at different levels are present.

C_L2 Cumulus (Cu). Coded as C_L2 if C_L4 and C_L8 are not applicable and the Cumulus have moderate to great vertical extent.

C_L7 Stratus (St) or Cumulus (Cu). Coded as C_L7 if above classifications are not applicable and the low clouds are predominately Stratus fractus or Cumulus fractus, or both.

C_L6 Stratus (St). Coded as C_L6 if the low clouds are predominately Stratus in a more or less continuous sheet or in ragged shreds (other than Stratus fractus of bad weather), or both.

C_L5 Stratocumulus (Sc). Coded as C_L5 if the predominant low clouds are Stratocumulus other than those formed by the spreading out of Cumulus.

C_L1 Cumulus (Cu). Coded as C_L1 if the low clouds are predominantly Cumulus with little vertical extent and are not clouds of bad weather.

These code characteristics should help to identify the various cloud forms, but it should be remembered that there are many gradations between them, and in some cases one form merges into another. Frequently, it is impossible to identify clouds with certainty unless one can interpret the physical processes that are producing them.

A Generalized Vertical Arrangement of Cloud Types. *From* Atmosphere   **FIG. 2.21**
and Weather Charts. *Courtesy, A. J. Nystrom and Company.*

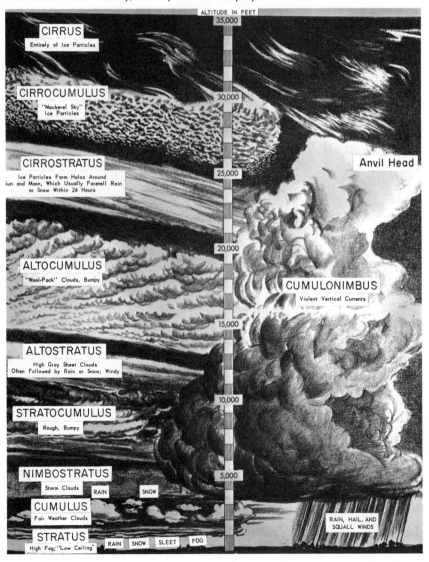

FIG. 2.22

Cirrus Invading the Sky (C_H1). Delicate Cirrus composed of irregularly arranged filaments oriented in various directions and showing a tendency at lower left to fuse together into Cirrostratus. *Courtesy, U.S. Department of Commerce, Weather Bureau.*

FIG. 2.23

Cirrocumulus (C_H9). Closely packed, small, globular masses are arranged in lines or ripples, associated with Cirrostratus at lower right. *U.S. Army Photo.*

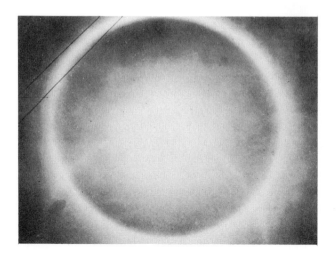

FIG. 2.24

Cirrostratus (C_H7). A well-defined halo of 22° around the sun is visible as well as a parhelic circle through the sun.

FIG. 2.25

Cirrostratus ($C_{II}6$). A thin veil extends above $45°$ at upper left, a fibrous structure with parallel bands shows at left center, and patches of Altocumulus lentricularis and Altostratus below. *Courtesy, U.S. Department of Commerce, Weather Bureau.*

FIG. 2.26

Semi-transparent Altocumulus ($C_{M}3$). A layer of Altocumulus at one level composed of soft, flat, rounded masses, thick enough to be rather heavily shaded in places, but with interstices where the blue appears. *Courtesy, U.S. Department of Commerce, Weather Bureau.*

FIG. 2.27

Altocumulus ($C_{M}7$). Patches of Altocumulus with Stratocumulus below and Altostratus at upper right. *Courtesy, U.S. Department of Commerce, Weather Bureau.*

FIG. 2.28

Altocumulus Increasing and Thickening ($C_M 5$). Bands of Altocumulus are advancing from left to right across the sky. *Courtesy, U.S. Department of Commerce, Weather Bureau.*

FIG. 2.29

Thin Altostratus Covering Entire Sky ($C_M 1$). Two well-defined masses of Stratocumulus lenticularis are at the center. *Courtesy, U.S. Department of Commerce, Weather Bureau.*

FIG. 2.30

Thick Altostratus ($C_M 2$). Below the Altostratus layer is band of Stratocumulus, and fog can be seen in the valley below. *Courtesy, U.S. Department of Commerce, Weather Bureau.*

FIG. 2.31

Stratocumulus ($C_L 5$). Light and shade contrasts are apparent near the zenith, and parallel rows can be seen near the horizon. *Courtesy, U.S. Department of Commerce, Weather Bureau.*

FIG. 2.32

Stratocumulus from the Spreading Out of Cumulus ($C_L 4$). The dark shadows indicate considerable thickness of the clouds. *Courtesy, U.S. Department of Commerce, Weather Bureau.*

FIG. 2.33

Stratus ($C_L 6$). Low Strati are moving over a small, rocky island. These clouds move in at very low altitudes over the West Coast to form fog. *Courtesy, U.S. Department of Commerce, Weather Bureau.*

FIG. 2.34

Stratus fractus of Bad Weather (C_L7). Dark grey, more or less homogeneous clouds cover the sky. Light snow was falling, but because of the use of infrared film, it is not shown and the visibility appears greater than it was. *Courtesy, U.S. Department of Commerce, Weather Bureau.*

FIG. 2.35

Cumulus humilis (C_L1). The scattered masses have a flat and deflated appearance, the horizontal extension being greater than the vertical. *Courtesy, U.S. Department of Commerce, Weather Bureau.*

FIG. 2.36

Cumulonimbus calvus (C_L3). The characteristic anvil of fibrous cloud has not yet developed. Showers can be seen falling from the base of the cloud. *Courtesy, U.S. Department of Commerce, Weather Bureau.*

FIG. 2.37

Cumulonimbus capillatus $(C_L 9)$. An aerial view of the Cumulonimbus anvil shows the striated structure which is very different from the rounded Cumulus form below. Courtesy, U.S. Department of Commerce, Weather Bureau.

RECORDS OF CLOUDS AND CLOUDINESS

When a weather observation is being made, the kind of clouds visible should be recorded, the amount of each kind, and the direction from which each is moving. The amount is estimated in tenths of the sky covered. Such observations give information with regard to the direction, velocity, and turbulence of the wind at different elevations, and are often of direct aid in foreseeing weather changes. The weather bureau records each day as clear, partly cloudy, or cloudy, according to the average cloudiness during the time between sunrise and sunset; clear, if the average cloudiness is three-tenths or less; partly cloudy, if between four- and seven-tenths; and cloudy, if eight-tenths or more.

Precipitation Observations

Precipitation, in meteorology, means either the falling of moisture to the earth in any form, or the quantity of water so deposited, expressed in depth of water. Precipitation takes various forms, such as rain, snow, hail, and other special formations, which are discussed in more detail in the chapter on condensation (dew, frost, and fog are not regarded as precipitation). Amount of precipitation always means the liquid content. The word *rainfall* is often used as synonymous with precipitation, meaning the amount of water in whatever form it may have fallen.

RAIN GAUGES

The object of a rainfall measurement is to obtain the thickness of the layer of water that has fallen, assuming it to be evenly distributed over the surface in the vicinity of the measurement. Any open vessel of the same cross section throughout and exposed vertically will serve as a rain gauge. A cylindrical vessel is preferable. The accuracy of measurement can be increased by measuring the catch in a vessel smaller than that in which it is received, if the ratio of the cross sections of the 2 vessels is accurately known.

The 8-inch rain gauge. The 8-inch rain gauge is a cylindrical receiver exactly 8 inches in diameter, provided with a funnel-shaped bottom (Fig. 2.38). This funnel conducts the rain caught by the receiver into a cylindrical measuring tube 20 inches long and one-tenth of the cross-sectional area of the receiver. The depth of the rainfall is, accordingly, magnified just ten times. For 1 inch of rain, the water is 10 inches deep in the measuring tube. Thus, the amounts can easily be measured with great precision. The depth is measured by a small rule or measuring stick, graduated in inches and tenths. The receiving funnel fits over an outer tube, 8 inches in diameter, which serves to support the receiving funnel and also to hold excess water when more than 2 inches of rain falls, as the inner measuring tube, which is 20 inches long, consequently overflows. The funnel and the outer tube protect the water caught in the inner tube from appreciable evaporation.

Recording gauges. The tipping-bucket recording rain gauge has a 10-inch receiving funnel. At the mouth of the funnel is a bucket of two compartments, so mounted that one or the other receives the water coming from the funnel. As one compartment fills, it tips, thereby emptying its water and presenting the other compartment to the mouth of the funnel. The compartments are of such size with reference to the receiving funnel that each tip represents 0.01 inch. As the bucket tips, it closes an electric circuit connected with the meteorograph. A permanent record is thus obtained of the time of occurrence of each 0.01 inch of rain, and consequently the amount of the fall in any given period.

The *Fergusson weighing rain and snow gauge* is also in common use (Fig. 2.39). In this instrument the accumulating weight of the water or snow caught in an 8-inch cylinder moves a platform supported by a spring balance. This movement is

FIG. 2.38

A Standard 8-inch Rain Gauge with Measuring Stick. Courtesy, Bendix Corporation, Friez Instrument Division.

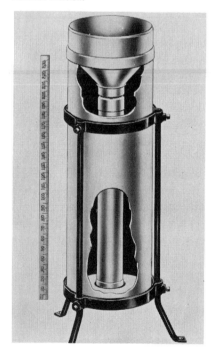

communicated to a pen, which then writes a continuous record on a drum driven by a clock. The record reads directly in inches of precipitation rather than in units of weight. It indicates the rate of fall for any desired interval in addition to total fall since the previous reading. There are other devices for obtaining continuous records of rainfall, one of which is a method of recording the movement of a float that rises as water accumulates in the gauge.

Exposure of rain gauge. To obtain a correct catch of rain with any gauge, the gauge should be exposed on the ground in an open, level space at least as far from trees, buildings, or other high objects as they are high, in order that rain falling obliquely may not be intercepted. Windbreaks at a distance greater than their height are desirable as a means of checking the velocity of the wind. If the gauge is placed much above the ground, the higher wind velocities carry more of the water around and over it. An exposure on the edge of a roof is especially bad because of eddies of wind around the gauge in that location.

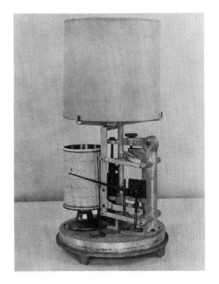

FIG. 2.39

The Fergusson Weighing Rain Gauge. This instrument makes a permanent continuous record of the rate and amount of rainfall. The Outside cover has been removed. *Courtesy, U.S. Department of Commerce, Weather Bureau.*

MEASUREMENT OF SNOW

Two quantities are desired in the measurement of snowfall, namely, the actual depth of the snow and its water equivalent. Both measurements present some difficulty in practice. Snow does not ordinarily lie at a uniform depth over the ground, but drifts, even in moderate winds. Hence, measurements of the depth should be made at several places and the average of these measurements considered the depth of the snow, recorded in inches and tenths.

To obtain the amount of precipitation from snow, that is, its water equivalent, the snow may be melted and measured as rain, or it may be weighed. Since snow readily blows around the top of a gauge instead of falling into it, the amount caught by the gauge is ordinarily considerably less than the actual fall. Gauges with windshields around the cylinder, intended to break up the eddies and insure a more nearly correct catch, have been devised and are widely used, especially in mountain regions. To obtain a representative sample for melting, the outer, overflow tube of the

8-inch gauge may be forced downward through a representative layer of snow, and the section thus cut out may be lifted by sliding a thin board or sheet of metal beneath it. This sample should be melted and poured into the measuring tube and the depth determined as in the case of rain. The best way to melt snow without loss is to add a measured quantity of warm water to it. The Fergusson weighing gauge may be used for snow as for rain, but the amount caught is subject to error.

The amount of water in a given volume of snow varies greatly, according to the texture of the snow and the closeness with which it is packed. The texture of snow changes with its temperature from dry and feathery to moist. The closeness of packing depends not only on the texture as it falls, but also on the depth of fall, the length of time it has lain on the ground, and the temperatures to which it has been subjected since falling. In moist, newly fallen snow, 6 inches of snow may make 1 inch of water, while in small amounts of dry, fluffy snow, the ratio may be as high as 30 to 1. In the absence of definite information, the ratio of 10 inches of snow to 1 inch of water is frequently used as an average. In large drifts which have accumulated all winter and are melting in the spring, 2 inches of snow may be equivalent to 1 inch of water.

PRECIPITATION RECORDS

A daily precipitation record should include the kind and amount of precipitation, and the time of beginning and ending. A record is made of the depth of snowfall since the last observation and also of the total depth on the ground. From the recording rain gauge, the amounts of rain during selected intervals of time can be tabulated. When *excessive rainfall* occurs, the accumulated amounts in successive five- or ten-minute periods should be recorded. Rainfall is considered excessive when it falls at the rate of 0.25 inch in five minutes, 1 inch in one hour, or 2.50 inches in twenty-four hours.

From a long series of such records at a fixed point, normal daily, monthly, and yearly values may be determined; also, the greatest and least yearly and monthly amounts, and the greatest amounts in short periods of from five minutes to forty-eight hours. The record should also show the number of rainy days by months and by years, and their averages over the period of record. A rainy day is a day on which 0.01 inch or more of precipitation occurs, that is, a day on which only traces of rain occur is not counted as a rainy day in this country. Unusually long periods without rain, known as *droughts*, should also be noted because of their great economic significance.

IMPORTANCE OF WEATHER OBSERVATIONS AND RECORDS

The importance of accurate weather records can not be overemphasized. What appears to be relatively insignificant at the time it is observed may prove to be a key to more accurate weather forecasting in the future. This is especially true as we increase the use of electronic computers to process weather data for meteorological and climatological forecasts. Only if accurate data are fed into the machine can reliable analyses be expected.

In addition to the weather observations described in this chapter, we shall soon find that there are many other important techniques used to measure and evaluate the intricate forces acting on our atmosphere. Some of these include observations of evaporation rates, visibility, height and thickness of clouds, vertical distribution of temperature and humidity with respect to pressure, duration and intensity of sunshine, and even the influences from outer space.

PROBLEMS

1.

Express the following Fahrenheit temperatures in the centigrade scale:
86°; 44°; 23°; —13°.

2.

Change the following centigrade temperatures to Fahrenheit: 35°; 23°;
10°; —10°; —20°.

3.

The following barometer readings are given in inches: 28.75; 29.54; 30.15; 30.36. Express them in millimeters and in millibars.

4.

What is the approximate barometric pressure in inches and in millibars at an elevation of 1,800 feet? 2,700 feet? 1 mile?

5.

Since a column of mercury 29.92 inches high is balanced by an atmospheric pressure of 14.7 pounds per square inch, what is the weight of a cubic inch of mercury?

6.

What is the pressure in pounds per square inch at the elevations in problem 4?

7.

Calculate in round numbers the total weight (pressure at the surface) of the earth's atmosphere.

8.

From data given in Table 5, Appendix 3, on page 343, draw graphs of the annual march of temperature at Honolulu, London, Moscow, Freetown, Melbourne, and note variations in annual range and in retardation of maximum and minimum. Compare with Fig. 2.6 on page 20.

9.

What pressure does the wind exert against a wall, 60 by 140 feet, if it is blowing at the rate of 12 knots? 24 knots? 50 knots?

10.

Find dew point, relative humidity, and vapor pressure when the dry-bulb thermometer reads 60°F and the wet-bulb thermometer reads 52°F.

11.

Find dew point and vapor pressure when the temperature is 73°F and the relative humidity is 28 per cent.

12.

Find relative humidity and vapor pressure when the temperature is 35°F and the dew point is 21°F.

13.

Outside air at a temperature of 25°F and a relative humidity of 62 per cent is taken into a room and warmed to a temperature of 75°F without the addition or loss of moisture. What is its new relative humidity?

14.

Air having a temperature of 50°F and a relative humidity of 49 per cent cools during the night to a temperature of 32°F. What does its relative humidity become?

15.

If the total pressure of the air at a given time and place is 29.620 inches, and the partial pressure due to the water vapor is 0.250 inch, what is the specific humidity of the air in grams per kilogram?

16.

A fall of 1 inch of rain amounts to how many tons of water per acre? Per square mile? (A cubic foot of water weighs 62.4 pounds.)

17.

The area of North Carolina is 54,426 square miles, and its average July rainfall is 5.78 inches. What is the weight of the water that falls?

18.

What is the diameter of the cylindrical measuring tube used with the 8-inch rain gauge?

3

solar
radiation

In observing and measuring the weather and its changes, we have noted how extraordinarily variable is the temperature of the air. It is now necessary to examine more closely the way the air is heated and cooled, and some of the physical effects of its variations in temperature, for most of the phenomena of the weather have their origin in temperature changes.

If you stand before a fireplace, the heat that reaches **Radiant Energy** you from the burning coals is said to travel through the intervening space as radiant energy. It would reach you in the same way if there were no air in the space. The fuel loses the energy which is thus sent out through space in a form having many of the characteristics of transverse waves. These are known as *electromagnetic waves*, and the energy thus transferred is called *radiant energy* or *radiation*.

RADIATION

Radiation refers both to the radial emission of energy from an object and to the energy so transferred. The movement of energy through "empty space" in a manner suggesting waves, but without the agency of any material medium, seems mysterious. But there is much evidence that waves of energy do travel in this way and that every object in the universe, whether hot or cold, has the faculty of thus emitting some of its energy. For example, the earth loses some of its heat to space continuously day and night, and is said to "cool by radiation." Of course, when the sun is shining clearly, the illuminated side of the earth is gaining more energy from the sun than it is losing to space. The rate of radiation increases as the fourth power of the temperature expressed in the absolute scale; doubling the absolute temperature of a body results in its sending out radiant energy sixteen times as fast.

CHARACTERISTICS OF RADIANT ENERGY

All electromagnetic waves travel through space at the approximate speed of 186,000 miles per second. This is generally called the *speed of light*. The length of a wave is the distance between two adjacent crests or pulses. The frequency is the number of crests that pass a given point per second. It follows that the product of the wave length and the wave frequency is constant, or that the two quantities are inversely proportional.

The properties of the various electromagnetic waves are related to their lengths and frequencies. When arranged according to their lengths, they form a continuous arrangement known as the *electromagnetic spectrum* (Fig. 3.1). At the left end are the extremely short waves known as *cosmic rays, gamma rays,* and *X rays;* next in order with increasing wave length come the *ultraviolet rays,* the visible *light rays,* and the infrared or so-called *heat rays;* and finally come the *Hertzian electric waves,* including those used in radio transmission. The visible rays of light have a length extending from about 3.8 to 7.6 ten-millionths of a meter; the waves used in radiobroadcasting may vary from less than 10 to more than 30,000 meters.

Electromagnetic Spectrum Showing Wave Frequencies and Wave Lengths. **FIG. 3.1**
The advantage of the metric system is obvious in this figure. Conversion from one unit of measurement to another is much easier than when dealing with English units.

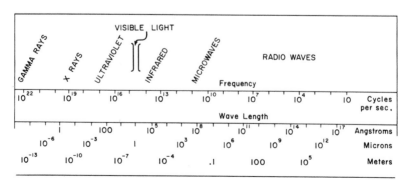

The waves received from the sun and those sent out by the earth are those with which we are particularly concerned in meteorology. The sun's rays include not only the visible light rays but extend throughout the spectrum. Radiation from the earth is always in long heat waves. The use of the expression *heat waves*, as applied to the long-wave radiation emitted by warm or hot bodies, is misleading, since all electromagnetic waves produce heating effects when absorbed.

TRANSMISSION, ABSORPTION, AND REFLECTION

Not only does radiant energy travel through space without the presence of any material substance, but portions of it also pass through certain kinds of matter. Light rays, for example, travel through air, water, and glass, and X rays and other short waves through denser substances opaque to visible light. In these cases the radiation is said to be *transmitted;* it is not itself affected and has no visible effect on the matter through which it passes. Most substances show a selective transmission; that is, some of the wave lengths get through but others do not. For example, window glass admits the light from the sun, but it does not readily transmit outward the long heat waves originating in the room. Different substances select different wave lengths for transmission.

That portion of the radiant energy which enters a substance but is not transmitted through it is said to be *absorbed.* It thereby ceases to be radiant energy and is changed into some other form of energy, often into heat, but sometimes into the energy used in evaporation or in chemical changes. Only the radiation that is absorbed has any effect on the object with which it comes in contact. Selective transmission implies selective absorption; those wave lengths not selected for transmission are absorbed. A radio receiving set illustrates the selective transmission and absorption of electromagnetic waves. It has a device by which certain wave lengths are selected for amplification and others are "tuned out." Some of the waves reaching a material surface may be *reflected,* that is to say, turned back without entering the substance. The only result is to change the direction of motion of the waves. The reflection may be *regular,* as from a mirror or other smooth surface, or *diffuse,* like that from the surface of the ground. Objects are made visible by reflection; those that reflect no light cannot be seen, unless they themselves are emitting light waves.

The heat of the atmosphere and of the surface of the earth is derived almost wholly from the sun. The amounts received from the moon, planets, stars, and the earth's interior are negligible in comparison, as is evident when we remember how the temperature ordinarily rises by day under the influence of sunshine and falls by night, when these other factors are equally

Incoming Solar Radiation

as effective as by day. That part of the incoming solar radiation that reaches the earth's surface is given the special name of *insolation*.[1]

SOLAR CONSTANT

Although the earth receives but a minute portion of the total radiation emitted by the sun (approximately $1/2 \times 10^9$), owing to the small angle subtended by the earth as seen from the sun, the amount received is great. A quantity of heat is measured in calories, a *calorie* being the heat required to raise 1 gram of water from 14.5°C to 15.5°C. The average intensity of the solar radiation is found to be about 1.94 calories per square centimeter per minute, at the average distance of the earth from the sun when measured on a surface perpendicular to the solar beam at the outer limits of the atmosphere. This is called the *solar constant*, so named when the intensity was assumed to be invariable within the errors of measurement. Later investigations indicate that there are slight variations in short periods of a few days. There is more conclusive evidence that there are variations, amounting to about 3 per cent, in periods of a few years. The variations are associated with changes in sunspot activity. If we assume that in the course of a year, half of the energy expressed in the solar constant reaches the earth at latitude 40°, the energy received amounts to more than 5 million kilowatthours per acre.

The observations fixing the average value of the solar constant and its variations have mostly been made and are being continued by the Smithsonian Institute. They are made on mountains in arid regions in the southwestern United States and in Chile and Sinai. These sites were chosen in order to avoid as much of the dust and moisture of the lower atmosphere as possible. Furthermore, methods have been devised by which the remaining errors introduced by variable losses in the atmosphere can be largely eliminated. These observations have been made since 1918 and disclose a probable range in the solar constant of not more than 5 per cent. The variation is found to be in the blue, violet, and especially the ultraviolet portion of the spectrum, rather than in the greater wave lengths.

SOLAR RADIATION MEASUREMENTS

Continuous records of two values in connection with solar radiation are now obtained at a number of places in various parts of the United States and in other countries. One quantity measured is the intensity of direct solar radiation at normal incidence, that is, on a surface kept at right angles to the sun's rays; the other is the total radiation received on a horizontal surface, including radiation reflected from sky and clouds as

---

[1] The word *insolation* is sometimes used more technically to mean the rate at which direct solar energy is received at the earth on a horizontal surface.

Pyrheliometer. Two circular rings of equal area, one black and the other   **FIG. 3.2**
white, are connected by thermocouple to produce an electromotive force
proportional to the intensity of solar radiation. Courtesy, *Eppley Laboratory, Inc., Newport, R.I.*

well as that coming in a direct line from the sun. An instrument used to
measure solar radiation is called a *pyrheliometer*, and is based on the
thermoelectric effect—differential heating produces an electromotive force
that is closely proportional to the amount of radiation received (Fig. 3.2).
The resulting current is recorded by a potentiometer. The data obtained
by the use of these instruments are converted into units of solar radiation

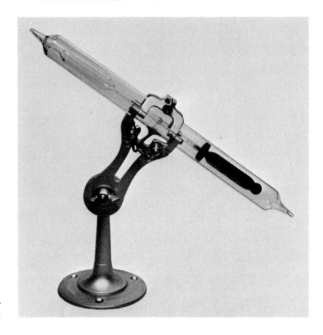

FIG. 3.3

Electrical Sunshine Recorder. Courtesy, Bendix Corporation, Friez Instrument Division.

for use by meteorologists and botanists. They are also of importance to architects, illumination engineers, and other specialists.

Another instrument which measures the duration of sunshine is the *Marvin transmitter* (Fig. 3.3). The transmitter consists of two glass tubes with a vacuum between the inner and outer tubes. The inner tube has a long blackened bulb at the lower end. When sun shines on the instrument, the black bulb absorbs radiant energy and causes a mercury switch to close, permitting a current to flow through a recorder. The amount of *actual* sunshine in comparison with *possible* sunshine becomes valuable data, especially for climatologists.

It is evident that the energy received from the sun at the surface of the earth differs from the solar constant and averages considerably less. The actual amount received at any point depends on several factors.

Insolation at a Fixed Location

ABSORPTION AND REFLECTION

The amount of insolation received changes as the solar constant varies, that is, as the actual energy emitted by the sun changes, but the percentage change in the solar constant is small at most. Of much greater importance in determining the amount of radiation received by the earth is the fact that this varies as the amount absorbed and reflected by the atmosphere varies. Changing conditions of cloudiness, dustiness, and humidity of the atmosphere are continually altering the amount of radiant energy transmitted to the earth. A large and variable amount is reflected back to space by clouds. The most important absorbing constituent of the atmosphere is water vapor.

DISTANCE OF EARTH FROM SUN

Since radiation spreads out spherically from its source, the amount intercepted by a given area varies inversely as the square of its distance from the source. The distance of the earth from the sun averages about 93,000,000 miles (150,000,000 km) but varies somewhat during the year because the earth moves in a slightly elliptical orbit. The earth is about 3,000,000 miles nearer the sun on January 1 than on July 1. In consequence, the total solar energy reaching the entire earth's atmosphere is about 7 per cent greater in January than in July, although it is evident that we of the Northern Hemisphere receive more heat in July than in January. The distance factor would lead one to believe that the Southern Hemisphere should experience hotter summers and colder winters than the Northern Hemisphere. This is not true. Examination of a globe will reveal that a much larger portion of the land area of the earth is north of the equator. Land heats and cools more rapidly than the oceans and thus renders the seasonal variation in distance from the earth to the sun of little consequence. Of much greater importance in determining the amount of insolation received at a fixed location are two other influences next to be considered.

LENGTH OF DAY AND ANGLE OF INCIDENCE

During the course of the earth's journey about the sun, the earth's axis maintains a nearly constant direction in space, making an angle of 66 1/2° with the plane of its orbit. In consequence, the angle at which the sun's rays strike a point on the earth changes with the changing orientation of the earth's axis relative to the sun. On June 21, the sun is vertically overhead at noon at the *Tropic of Cancer* and has its greatest noon elevation at all latitudes north of the tropic and its least elevation at all points in the Southern Hemisphere. Six months later, on December 21, the relative positions of the hemispheres are reversed and the noon sun is directly overhead at the *Tropic of Capricorn* (Fig. 3.4). These dates are the *summer solstice* and the *winter solstice,* respectively, in the Northern Hemisphere. The time of winter and summer are reversed for the Southern Hemisphere.

As time progresses from December 21, the vertical rays of the noonday sun move northward, and are directly overhead at the equator on March 21. They continue northward to the Tropic of Cancer, arriving there on

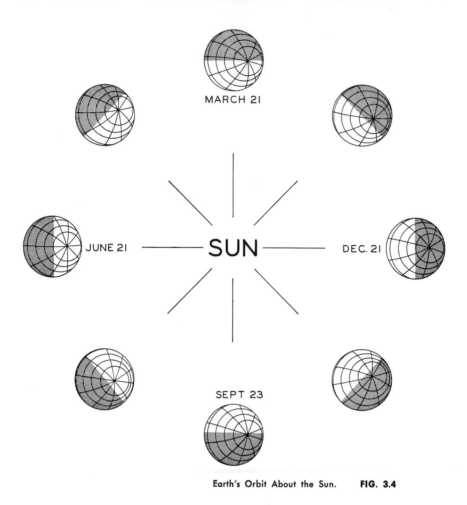

MARCH 21

JUNE 21 ——————— SUN ——————— DEC. 21

SEPT 23

Earth's Orbit About the Sun.   **FIG. 3.4**

June 21, and return to the equator about September 23. These dates are called the *vernal equinox, summer solstice,* and *autumnal equinox,* respectively. At equinox, days and nights are of equal length throughout the world. At other times of the year, days and nights are not of equal length except on the equator. The dates of equinoxes and solstices vary at times by one day or so because our calendar year is not an exact representation of a solar year.

The variations in the angular elevation of the sun produce changes in the amount of insolation received. A given surface receives most rays when they fall perpendicularly upon it. The same amount of incoming radiation is represented by the two lines A in Fig. 3.5. When the rays are perpendicular, they cover an area one of whose sides is A, but when the elevation of the sun is represented by the angle x, they cover the greater area whose side is $A + B$. The same amount of insolation is thus spread over a greater surface, and the energy received per unit area is less in the ratio of A to $A + B$. The *angle of incidence* is defined as the angle which the sun's rays make with the perpendicular. In the case of vertical rays, the angle is zero; in the case of the slanting rays in Fig. 3.5, the angle of incidence is $90 - x$. The angle of incidence at solar noon for any place on the earth can be determined by the following rule: *The number of degrees in the angle of incidence is equal to the number of degrees of latitude between the observer and the latitude where the sun's rays are vertical.* As the angle of incidence increases, the amount of insolation decreases if other variables do not interfere.

There is also a secondary effect of the angle of incidence on the amount of radiation received at the earth's surface. As the inclination of the rays from the vertical increases, the length of their path through the air increases, in the ratio of C to D, which is the same ratio as A to $A + B$. The longer the path through the air, the greater is the absorption and scattering by the air, especially the lower air. Hence, when the sun is near the horizon, its effect is weakened not only by the spreading out of the rays, but also by the loss of heat in passing through much moist and dusty air. Whether the losses due to absorption are more important than those due to inclination depends upon the condition of the atmosphere. It has been found that at Montpelier, France, 71 per cent of the incoming solar radiation reaches the earth in December, and only 48 per cent in the summer months. There the increased amount of moisture (specific humidity) in the summer air reduces the seasonal temperature several degrees.

Not only is the angular elevation of the sun greater in summer than in winter, but the duration of sunshine is greater, the days are longer, and the nights are shorter. It is evident that, other factors being equal, the amount of insolation received is directly proportional to the length of time during which it is being received. This fact has a very important effect in

Effect of Angle of Incidence on Insolation. Disregarding atmospheric ab-   **FIG. 3.5**
sorption, the intensity of insolation when the sun has an angular eleva-
of x, compared with the intensity when the sun is vertical, is the ratio A to A + B, which is *sin x*.
The length of path when the sun is vertical, compared with the length when the sun's elevation is
x, is the ratio C to D, which is also *sin x*.

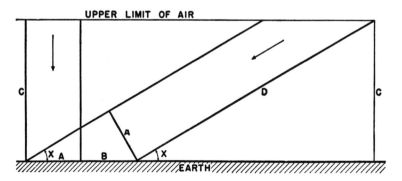

UPPER LIMIT OF AIR

increasing summer insolation in the middle and higher latitudes. The effect increases toward the poles, where the sun is continually above the horizon in the summer, and decreases toward the equator, where the days and nights are always of the same length. See Table 3.1. At latitude 40° there are about fifteen hours of possible sunshine in midsummer as compared with about nine in midwinter. On June 21, the North Pole receives more energy from the sun than does a point on the equator on the same date, but the total amount received during a year at either pole is only about 41 per cent of that at an equatorial location. This statement considers only the effect of position on the earth with respect to the axis of rotation. Actually, lines of equal insolation do not follow the circles of latitude exactly because of many local influences, such as prevailing cloudiness, to be discussed later. An important practical result of the long summer days in high latitudes, however, is that wheat and other crops can be grown far poleward in spite of a very short summer because of the great amount of sunshine during the brief growing season.

TABLE 3.1   Length of Day at Each 10 Degrees of Latitude

Read down for the Northern Hemisphere

LATITUDE	MARCH 21	JUNE 21	SEPT. 23	DEC. 21
0°	12 hrs.	12 hrs. 0 min.	12 hrs.	12 hrs. 0 min.
10°	12 hrs.	12 hrs. 35 min.	12 hrs.	11 hrs. 25 min.
20°	12 hrs.	13 hrs. 12 min.	12 hrs.	10 hrs. 48 min.
30°	12 hrs.	13 hrs. 56 min.	12 hrs.	10 hrs. 4 min.
40°	12 hrs.	14 hrs. 52 min.	12 hrs.	9 hrs. 8 min.
50°	12 hrs.	16 hrs. 18 min.	12 hrs.	7 hrs. 42 min.
60°	12 hrs.	18 hrs. 27 min.	12 hrs.	5 hrs. 33 min.
70°	12 hrs.	2 months	12 hrs.	0 hrs. 0 min.
80°	12 hrs.	4 months	12 hrs.	0 hrs. 0 min.
90°	12 hrs.	6 months	12 hrs.	0 hrs. 0 min.
LATITUDE	SEPT. 23	DEC. 21	MARCH 21	JUNE 21

Read up for Southern Hemisphere

Direct Effects of Solar Radiation

The energy coming to the earth from the sun in the form of solar radiation is either absorbed, reflected, or scattered. Varying conditions over the face of the earth and in the atmosphere cause the distribution of energy received to vary with time and with geographical location.

The ratio at which light rays are reflected from a surface in comparison to the total rays striking the surface is called the *albedo* of that body. The

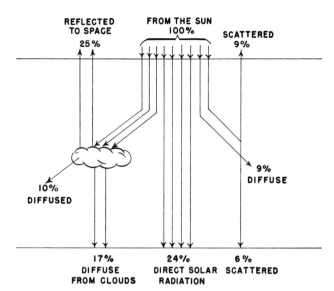

REFLECTED
TO SPACE
25%

FROM THE SUN
100%

SCATTERED
9%

9%
DIFFUSE

10%
DIFFUSED

17%
DIFFUSE
FROM CLOUDS

24%
DIRECT SOLAR
RADIATION

6%
SCATTERED

FIG. 3.6

Diagrammatic Representation of the Distribution of Solar Radiation. Of the incoming radiation, some is absorbed by the atmosphere, some is reflected back to space, and the remainder is absorbed by the earth. The heat balance is maintained by the earth losing its heat back to space through long-wave radiation, latent heat, and sensible heat. *After H. G. Houghton.*

reflectivity of the earth's surface, assuming average cloud cover and other atmospheric conditions, increases from the equator to the poles and averages approximately 34 per cent.[2] The earth is then said to have an albedo of 0.34. Clouds have greater albedo than land surfaces, averaging about 0.55 and 0.10, respectively. In addition to those solar rays which are reflected, some are scattered by dust particles and other impurities in the atmosphere, some are absorbed by the atmosphere, and the remainder are absorbed by the earth's surface. About 19 per cent of solar radiation is absorbed in the atmosphere and about 47 per cent is absorbed at the earth's surface (Fig. 3.6). Assuming that the earth and the surrounding atmosphere become neither warmer nor colder over a long period of time, all of the heat absorbed must eventually be reradiated back to space.

EFFECT ON AIR

Most of the reflection from the atmosphere is from the upper surface of clouds. Clouds have a high reflective power which varies with their thickness and the amount of liquid water they contain. Clouds of ordinary thickness and density probably reflect from 75 to 80 per cent of the incident radiation. The greater part of this reflection is directed outward and so is lost to us, but a part of the reflection is from the upper surface of one cloud to the lower surface of a higher cloud, and thence to the earth. Some of the heat and light we receive on partly cloudy days consists of this reflected radiation. The earth and lower air cool less rapidly on a cloudy night than on a clear night, not because radiation from the earth is less rapid, but because much radiation is reradiated from the clouds to the earth. If the air were free of dust and moisture, only a small

---

[2] Henry G. Houghton, "On the Annual Heat Balance of the Northern Hemisphere," *Journal of Meteorology,* XI (1954), 1-9.

fraction of solar radiation would be absorbed; nearly all would be transmitted to the earth without alteration. Such air would be heated very little by sunshine, for it is only absorbed radiation that increases temperature.

Oxygen and nitrogen are practically transparent to the sun's radiation, and such absorption as occurs in air, except by dust and moisture, is accounted for largely by water vapor and carbon dioxide in the long-wave "heat rays" of the infrared, and by ozone in both the ultraviolet and the infrared waves. The greater part of the absorption by the gases of the air is by water vapor, which absorbs most of the long-wave radiation. Since the radiation emitted by the earth is all longwave, the water vapor absorbs a much greater proportion of earth radiation than of solar radiation, and thus acts as a trap to conserve the energy received from the sun. Coincident with these absorption processes, reradiation from the atmosphere is active and continuous.

Solid particles of dust and smoke in the air, and liquid or solid particles of water in the air, absorb and reflect considerable, but extremely variable, amounts of solar radiation. The dry air of deserts, if it is not filled with dust, absorbs little radiation, and hence the sun has an intense heating effect on solid objects. High plateaus and mountains are above much of the dust and moisture of the air, and consequently there is little absorption by the air above them. Hence the air remains cold, and the sun's rays have much energy left to be absorbed by objects at the surface. That is why one is often warm on winter days in the mountain sunshine, but cold in the shade, the difference between sunshine and shade being much greater than in the lowlands.

EFFECT ON LAND SURFACES

Of the radiation that gets through the atmosphere and reaches the surface of the earth, a part is reflected back into the atmosphere and the remainder is absorbed at the surface. The proportion that is reflected by land surfaces varies greatly with the condition and color of the surface. If the land is covered with grass or trees, or is black, cultivated soil, the reflection may be in the neighborhood of 10 per cent. A bare, hard, sandy soil may reflect 20 per cent, and freshly fallen snow 70 to 80 per cent of the incident radiation.

The remaining percentage of the radiation that reaches the earth is absorbed and changed into other forms of energy. It is thus that the soil is warmed. Land surfaces are good absorbers and therefore heat rapidly when the sun is shining on them. Moreover, heat does not penetrate deeply into the soil but remains in a thin surface layer. For this reason also the surface heats rapidly. The daily variation is small below 4 inches, but a slight daily change may occur to a depth of about 3 feet.

A good absorber is a good radiator, and the land surface that warms rapidly by day cools rapidly by night. Thus a large part of the heat received is soon returned to space. A sandy desert soil exemplifies the maximum of rapid changes in a thin layer. Under such conditions, a change of 49°F from day to night has been observed in the surface layer of soil, whereas the change was only 1°F at a depth of 16 inches. Moist soil does not heat so rapidly as dry soil since some of the energy received is used in evaporating moisture and it takes more energy to heat water than soil.

Snow reflects much solar radiation. It absorbs the remainder and also absorbs or reflects downward the radiation from the soil. A good snow cover protects the land from large daily changes and often prevents its freezing through severe weather. In the spring when the snow disappears, after having persisted for a considerable period, it is often found that the ground beneath is unfrozen, even where near-by bare ground is still frozen hard. In such cases the snow acts as a blanket; heat is conducted from lower ground levels to the surface, but it cannot escape to the air and therefore keeps the surface layer of soil warm.

With the increased insolation of summer, outside the tropics, not all the heat stored by day is lost in the short nights, and the soil becomes progressively warmer. In winter more heat may be lost by radiation through the long nights than is received by day. A land surface therefore becomes hot by day and in summer, and cold by night and in winter. It does not store a large amount of heat.

EFFECT ON WATER SURFACES

Reflection of insolation from a water surface depends upon the smoothness or roughness of the water, and especially upon the angle of incidence of the sun's rays. When the sun is not more than 5° above the horizon, 40 per cent of the insolation may be reflected. As the sun's elevation increases, the percentage reflected steadily decreases until not more than 3 or 4 per cent is reflected when the sun is 50° or more above the horizon. On the average it is probable that the reflection from water surfaces is about the same as from land. Hence, the absorption is about the same. But water surfaces and land surfaces respond quite differently to the absorbed insolation.

There are four important ways in which the effects differ: (a) Radiation penetrates to much greater depths in water than in land. More than one-third of it reaches a depth of 3 feet, and about one-tenth is transmitted to 30 feet. Small amounts of light have been observed at depths of 1,700 to 1,900 feet (520–580 m) beneath the surface of the sea. (b) Of even greater importance in distributing the heat through a considerable depth are the wave movements and general turbulence of the sea surface. Because of this mixing of the waters, and because 90 per cent of the absorption is in the first 30 feet, it may be assumed that the heating effect is uniformly distributed through a 30-foot layer. Thus, there is a great volume of water to be heated as compared with a 4-inch layer of land. In addition, the heat absorbed is often transported great distances by currents, tides, and other movements of the water. The cooling of the water surface by night also contributes to the mixing effect. As the water becomes cooler, it becomes denser; it sinks and is replaced by warmer water from below.

Two other reasons why insolation has comparatively little effect on the temperature of water surfaces are: (c) A large part of the energy absorbed by the water, probably about 30 per cent of it, is used in evaporating the water and is therefore not available for raising its temperature. Furthermore, evaporation increases the salinity, and hence the density, of sea water at the surface and thereby contributes to vertical mixing of the water to considerable depths. Evaporation is greatest when the water is warmer than the overlying air, because then the vapor pressure at the surface is greater than in the air. (d) The specific heat of water is greater than that of other natural substances. Raising the temperature of 1 pound of water 1°F requires three times as much heat energy as heating 1 pound of soil 1°F.

For all these reasons, water areas heat slowly, store much energy, and cool slowly. They are great storehouses of heat energy. Large land areas have great and rapid temperature changes and little storage capacity. The oceans are conservative; the continents, radical. This difference is of fundamental importance in meteorology and climatology, as we shall find. It should be noted, however, that an ice-covered body of water acts much as a snow-covered land surface. It reflects a high percentage of the incident radiation; it warms little by day and cools rapidly by night.

One primary cause of temperature changes in the   **Conduction**
lower air is conduction of heat to or from the earth's
surface. *Conduction* is the process by which heat is transferred through matter, without transfer of the matter itself. When one end of a silver spoon is heated, the other end soon becomes hot by conduction; but when one end of a piece of wood is heated, the other end remains cool. Silver is a good conductor of heat; wood, a poor conductor. Conduction is always from the warmer to the colder point. On a sunny day, the earth's surface is warmed by absorbing insolation, and then, after the earth's temperature has increased above that of the air, the air in contact with it is warmed by conduction as well as by radiation. Similarly, at night, the first process is the cooling of the ground, and then the cooling of the air as it conducts and radiates some of its heat to the ground. Thus, air tends to have the same temperature as the surface with which it is in contact.

Air is a poor conductor, however, and the actual conduction during the course of a day or night affects only 2 or 3 feet of air. Wind and turbulence, however, bring fresh air in contact with the surfaces and distribute the warmed or cooled air to a considerable height. The exchange of heat by conduction is less than that by radiation.

AIR TEMPERATURES

The temperature of the air lags behind that of the earth and changes less; the air is not so warm as the land, in the sunshine, nor so cool during outgoing radiation at night. This fact applies to air locally heated or cooled—not to warm or cold air that may be brought in from other regions. The poor conductivity of the air and its slow loss of heat by radiation explain why frosts sometimes occur when the general air temperature is considerably above freezing. The grass, the paving, and other surfaces where frost forms are colder than the mass of air a few feet above them. It is clear also why a thermometer must be sheltered from radiation, direct or reflected, if it is to assume by conduction the temperature of the surrounding air.

The question "What is the temperature in the sun?" (meaning in sunshine) has no answer. Each different object exposed to the sun's rays absorbs radiation differently and takes on a different temperature. Black objects become warmer than light-colored ones, and dry ones warmer than moist ones. When a black-bulb thermometer, that is, a thermometer with a large bulb coated with lampblack, is exposed to solar radiation, it often has a temperature 60°F or 70°F higher than that of the surrounding air. A piece of black fur exposed to the sun's rays in winter in the Alps reached a temperature of 140°F when the air temperature was 41°F. On the other hand, such an object gets much colder than the air at night. It is the temperature of the air, and not of absorbing and radiating solid bodies, that is of primary concern in discussions of the weather.

EARTH TEMPERATURES

As previously stated, the heating of a land surface by insolation is confined to a thin surface layer. This is so because land is a poor conductor. Heat is conducted downward so slowly that the diurnal change of temperature ordinarily penetrates but 2 or 3 feet into the soil. Before it has reached that depth, night has arrived, and the surface is cooling. Even the annual variation in temperature disappears in all latitudes at a depth of only a few feet. The amplitude of the change in this surface layer diminishes rapidly with depth and depends largely upon the seasonal differences in air temperature. The temperatures at 100 feet below the surface vary with the latitude, being comparable to the mean annual temperature of the air at the surface. At greater depths, the temperature of the earth increases slowly but not uniformly.

Conduction, absorption, and emission of radiation are   **Convection**
processes which originate temperature changes in a
substance, whether solid, liquid, or gaseous. Another method of transferring heat is of great importance to the behavior of the air, although it
is not an original source of gain or loss of heat energy. This is *convection*,
the transfer of heat by internal mass movements of the substance con-

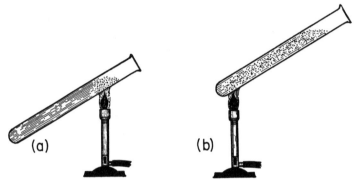

Transfer of Heat by Convection. (a) Water heated at the top while lower   **FIG. 3.7**
portion remains cool. (b) Water heated at the bottom; all becomes nearly
equally heated.

taining the heat. Such movements result from temperature differences
within the substance, and can occur only in liquids and gases, not in
solids. As used in meteorology, convection refers to vertical movements
of the air while *advection* is the term used with reference to the horizontal
transport of winds and slow drifting movements of the air.

CONVECTION IN A LIQUID

If a test tube is filled with water, and a flame is applied near the top,
the water at the top may be brought to the boiling point while that at the
bottom is relatively cool (Fig. 3.7a). In this case, the lower water is heated
only by conduction. If the flame is applied near the bottom of the tube,
the heated water expands and is displaced by the cooler, denser liquid
above it, setting up a *convectional circulation,* in which heat is transferred
by the movement of the water (Fig. 3.7b). Thus, the entire mass becomes
heated to the boiling point at nearly the same time. Figure 3.8 illustrates
a convectional circulation set up in a vessel of water which is being heated
at the bottom over a small part of its area.

CONVECTION IN THE AIR

Gases move even more freely than do liquids and likewise expand when
heated, thereby becoming lighter than before, volume for volume. Fa-

miliar examples of convection in the air on a small scale are the draft up a chimney and the rising of air over a heated radiator. In these cases air is warmed at the bottom, and colder, heavier air pushes it upward out of the lowest place. The effectiveness of a warm-air furnace in heating a house depends upon this method of transferring heat. We have noted that, while the earth's surface is heated by absorption of insolation, it is for many reasons very unequally heated, and that the lower air is heated by radiation and

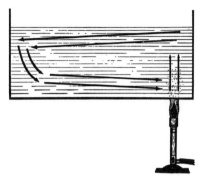

FIG. 3.8

Convectional Circulation in a Liquid.

conduction and likewise unequally heated. We should therefore expect to find convectional currents, involving downward and upward movements of the air, between areas of contrasting temperatures, as, for example, between the oceans and the continents, and on a large scale between equatorial and polar regions. It will be seen, as we proceed, that such movements are of primary importance in the study of meteorology.

PROBLEMS

1.

Tie a string around a globe to represent the boundary between the light hemisphere and the dark hemisphere on June 21. Measure several latitude circles, including the equator, to determine the relative lengths of day and night on that date.

2.

Repeat the above exercise for September 23, December 21, and March 21.

3.

Why are days and nights always of equal length at the equator?

4.

What is the maximum difference in the noon elevation of the sun (expressed in degrees) during a year at any point outside the tropics?

5.

Explain how a navigator can use the sun to determine his latitude if he knows the date and the angle of incidence of the noon sun.

6.

Find the exact latitude of your school, and on the day this problem is assigned, measure the angle of incidence of the sun at noon with a protractor. At what latitude are the sun's rays vertically overhead?

7.

Assuming there are no clouds to intercept the sun's rays, what will be the duration of sunshine in one year at a point on a circle of latitude of 0°? 30°? 60°? 90°?

8.

Explain why the product of the wave length times the wave frequency of radiant energy is always constant.

9.

The wave length of a cosmic ray might be only 10^{-10} centimeters long. This value is what fraction of an inch?

10.

The wave length of a radio wave might be 10^{10} centimeters long. Express this value in feet.

4

adiabatic processes and stability

We have seen that the sun is practically the only source of heat for the atmosphere. It is now necessary to consider how the atmosphere reacts to heat energy. All air does not have the same properties, nor does the same air necessarily maintain its properties for any given period of time. The atmosphere may be compared to a very temperamental person whose response to a stimulus is quite unpredictable unless one is thoroughly acquainted with the characteristics of that individual.

You have learned many of the atmosphere's characteristics. The gas laws of Boyle, Charles, and Gay-Lussac were discussed in Chapter 1. Combined, these laws express a universal characteristic of the atmosphere: *Pressure times the volume equals a constant times the temperature* $(PV = RT)$. In the last chapter, it was shown how heat is transferred to and by the atmosphere through radiation, conduction, and convection. Convection unlocks other potential forces of the atmosphere, and we shall proceed to study these in more detail, but first let us see how we are able to observe these forces and processes in the free air above the earth's surface.

The conditions existing in the free air above the earth's surface are important to theoretical studies of the atmosphere and form one of the most basic tools for weather forecasting.

Upper-air Observations

OBTAINING UPPER-AIR DATA

In Europe and America, mountain observations have been made regularly since 1870. These observations have given valuable information, but the conditions on mountaintops are not representative of free-air conditions at the same altitudes. At various times during the nineteenth and twentieth centuries, free or captive balloons manned by one or more passengers and equipped with meteorological instruments were released to explore the upper air. These flights produced interesting and valuable data, but it became evident that a more complete and regular coverage of upper-air conditions was desirable. Free balloons bearing recording instruments and an offer of reward to the finder for their return also proved less than satisfactory.

From 1898 to 1933, the United States Weather Bureau maintained kite-flying stations at which systematic upper-air records were obtained. Box kites carrying light recording instruments sometimes reached a height of four miles, but no flight could be made when the surface wind was not strong enough to launch the kite. This operation was replaced in 1933 by regular airplane flights from several points over the United States. These flights were synchronized and ascended over their respective stations as nearly vertically as practical to an elevation of about 17,000 feet (5.2 km). Such flights were expensive and required about one and one-half hours for completion, and the records were not available until the flights were completed. Since 1938, airplanes have been replaced by radiosondes in the regular network of upper-air observations in the United States. In addition to the radiosonde, other types of upper-air data are currently obtained by pilot balloons, rawins, aircraft reconnaissance, and research involving rockets and satellites. These methods will be discussed in greater detail.

PILOT BALLOONS

When fully inflated with helium or hydrogen, the *pilot balloon* is about 30 inches in diameter. It floats freely in the air but carries no instruments. The course of the balloon is watched and plotted from the ground by the use of a telescopic theodolite. If two theodolites at a known distance apart are used, the height and position of the balloon at the end of each minute can be computed accurately. If only one theodolite is used, it is necessary to assume a certain rate of ascent, and for this an empirical formula is used. From such observations, the direction and speed of the wind at various levels and the height of the clouds can be quickly determined. Regular flights of pilot balloons every six hours are made at a large number of weather stations throughout the United States, particularly along and near the main air routes. The soundings thus obtained are called *pibals*.

RADIOSONDES

Since 1938, the use of *radiosondes* throughout the world has been increasing rapidly. The device consists of a small box containing temperature, humidity, and pressure instruments and a miniature radio-sending station. It is carried aloft by a large gas-filled balloon which is also equipped with a parachute to lower the instruments harmlessly to the ground after the balloon bursts (Fig. 4.1). The balloons are of good quality and frequently rise to a height of 15 or 20 miles (24–32 km) before bursting. In a systematic fashion, the three weather elements are measured and transmitted by

FIG. 4.1

Radiosonde in Flight. Courtesy, Bendix Corporation, Friez Instrument Division.

radio to a receiving station on the ground. The records become available for immediate use while the radiosonde is still in flight. Elevations corresponding to the reported pressure levels can be computed very accurately when the temperature and humidity characteristics of the air column are known. Records from the radiosonde are known as *raobs*. They provide some of the most extensive and reliable data available on upper-air conditions. Severe thunderstorms and heavy rains may cause instrument failure or interfere with radio reception, but otherwise the radiosonde may be used in all kinds of weather.

RAWINSONDES

Although the pilot balloon is an inexpensive and fairly accurate source of upper-air wind data, it disappears from sight when there are clouds, or with strong winds, it soon drifts beyond the range of the theodolite. The development of radar and radio-directional receiving techniques during World War II made the *rawinsonde* (rawin) possible. This instrument consists of a tracking device at the station which measures the direction and angular elevation of an ascending balloon. It is included with the radiosonde and no extra balloon is necessary. By combining this observation with the radiosonde record, wind direction and speed at various elevations or pressure levels can be easily determined. About two hundred radiosonde and rawin stations are operated in the United States by the Weather Bureau, the Air Force, and the Navy.

AIRCRAFT WEATHER RECONNAISSANCE

With the development and expansion of aviation and the increased need for complete weather information in the military operation of aircraft, the use of airplanes in the collection of upper-air data has been resumed and expanded under the name of *weather reconnaissance*. Airplanes are dispatched to learn the sky conditions over a selected target and along the route to the target, or to keep watch on the weather over a considerable area and make radio reports of existing conditions. As a part of the peacetime activities of the United States Air Force and the Navy, flights by aircraft-carrying meteorologists and specially designed meteorological instruments are scheduled at regular intervals along chosen patterns for the purpose of obtaining complete records of atmospheric conditions in areas where raobs and other upper-air reports are missing. In other words, the airplane becomes a flying weather station that can cover not only a large area, but a changing area, which may be chosen on each flight to provide important information. Radiosondes are sometimes dropped from these planes, transmitting reports of weather conditions as they descend by parachute. Such instruments are called *dropsondes*.

One of the most important and exciting aspects of aircraft weather reconnaissance is locating and tracking hurricanes and typhoons. These severe tropical cyclones originate over the oceans, in low latitudes where little weather data are available. They have caused great property damage and loss of life upon arriving unannounced at populated coastlines. Aircraft reconaissance has become the principal source of weather data useful in reducing the death and destruction caused by these storms. Planes fly around and into the storm centers to determine their exact location, size, intensity, speed, and direction of movement. Although some progress has been made toward forecasting tropical cyclones, reconnaissance still remains our most important defense against their fury.

ROCKET AND SATELLITE OBSERVATIONS

The newest mode of upper-air research is through instrumented rockets and satellites. The total value of these observational instruments has not yet been determined. Even so, we already have learned much about the atmosphere, or lack of it, from the lower reaches of the stratosphere to the limitless space beyond, and there is hope that these research tools will provide a long-awaited breakthrough in improving weather forecasting.

Figure 4.2 shows an Atlantic hurricane which was discovered by the

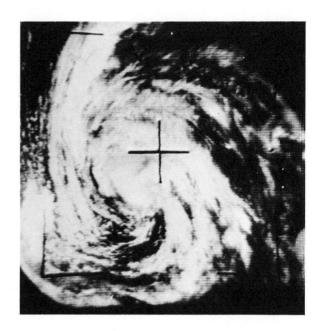

FIG. 4.2

Hurricane Becky. This photograph was taken by the Tiros V weather satellite about 500 miles off the coast of West Africa in the summer of 1962. It was relayed from the satellite to the ground station at Wallops Island, Virginia, and showed the storm to be about 750 miles in diameter. *Courtesy, National Aeronautics and Space Administration.*

"eyes" of a television camera in a weather satellite. These kinds of data are proving so valuable that weather satellites have already become standard observation instruments.

Adiabatic Temperature Changes

When air ascends, the pressure on it decreases, and the gases expand according to the gas laws. Expansion constitutes work in the physical sense and uses energy. The energy expended is heat energy, and the effect is to cool the air. Almost everyone has observed this temperature phenomenon at one time or another. The tube of a bicycle- or automobile-tire pump will become heated as air is forced by the piston into the tire, or frost may occur on a warm summer day about the escape valve of a pressure tank when compressed air is being released.

Ascending air cools as it expands under decreasing pressure and descending air is warmed by compression as it comes into regions of greater pressure. Note that these tempertaure changes are not related to any transfer of heat to or from the air. The air becomes cooler or warmer without any conduction or radiation. The change in temperature is an internal change as a result of the change of pressure upon it. Such changes in temperature are called *adiabatic* changes, the word implying "without transfer of heat." It may be shown by a mathematical discussion of the properties of gases that when dry air rises, the dynamic cooling due to expansion is at the nearly uniform rate of 5.5°F per 1,000 feet, or 1°C per 100 meters. The rate of warming with descent is the same. This is the *adiabatic rate* for unsaturated air.

When considerable moisture is present in rising air, the cooling caused by rising and expansion may result in saturation and then in condensation of some of the water vapor. The level at which condensation begins is known as the *lifting condensation level* (LCL). Beyond this point, two factors influence the air temperature. The dynamic factor continues to cool the air adiabatically, but the release of latent heat by condensation tends to warm the air. (See page 36.) The net result is a retarded rate of cooling. Thereafter, while condensation continues, rising air cools at a retarded adiabatic rate. This retarded rate of cooling is called the *saturation adiabatic rate* or *wet adiabatic rate*. It is not so nearly constant as the dry adiabatic rate, but depends on the temperature and pressure, and on how much of the condensed moisture is carried along with the rising air or precipitated out of it. Under changing conditions, the wet adiabatic rate varies from about 0.4°C to nearly 1°C per 100 meters. The average value for warm temperatures is about 0.5°C per 100 meters or 3°F per 1,000 feet.

Descending air is dynamically warmed by compression. The capacity of the air to hold water vapor is thereby increased. It follows that there will be no more condensation, but, on the contrary, there will be evaporation if liquid water is present in such air. This evaporation will retard the warming of the descending air. If evaporation is sufficient to maintain saturation as the air descends, its rate of warming is a wet adiabatic rate. If there is no condensed moisture present, descending air warms at the dry adiabatic rate. Usually, when condensation has occurred, some condensed moisture is present when the air begins its descent, but this disappears as the temperature rises, and for the remainder of its descent the air is unsaturated (Fig. 4.3). If condensation has occurred during the adiabatic processes, the air returns to its point of origin somewhat warmer than the original temperature.

Note that adiabatic changes occur only when air is expanding or being compressed, and that they occur without any heat being added to or taken from the air. Let us consider whether such a condition ever occurs in nature. Let us take, for example, a large mass of rising air, such as that which precedes the formation of Cumulus. A small part near the outer surface of the rising mass may have its temperature affected by mixing with the surrounding air; also, near the outer surface there is some interchange of heat by radiation and absorption. But air is a poor conductor and a poor absorber, and these modifications do not reach any great distance into the interior of the rising column. The greater portion of the ascending air is subject to no appreciable loss of heat to, or gain from, the outside. Hence, its changes in temperature are essentially adiabatic, the result of expansion under decreasing pressure, and are treated as such for practical purposes in interpreting the behavior of the cloud.

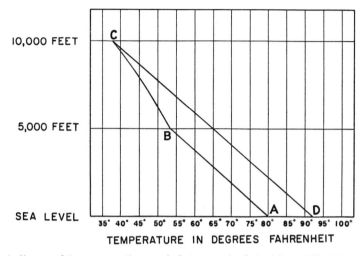

Adiabatic Changes of Temperature. If a parcel of air at sea level, A, with   **FIG. 4.3**
a temperature of 80°F, be lifted 5,000 feet before becoming saturated, it
would have a temperature at that level of 52 1/2°F. On being lifted to 10,000 feet, the same parcel would have a temperature of approximately 37 1/2°F. On returning to sea level, D, this parcel
of air would have a temperature of 92 1/2°F.

POTENTIAL TEMPERATURE

We have seen that the actual temperature of a sample of air varies greatly as it responds to changes of pressure. Sometimes it is desirable to recognize and make use of a more conservative temperature value.

Suppose that a quantity of unsaturated air at or near the surface of the earth and subject to a pressure of 1,000 millibars has a temperature of 70°F. If it is now forced to rise 1,000 feet and remains unsaturated, it cools at the dry adiabatic rate and its temperature will be reduced to 64.5°F (70° − 5.5°). If it then descends to its original level where the pressure is 1,000 millibars and warms adiabatically, it will return to its original temperature of 70°F. No matter how far this quantity of dry air rises or descends, or what pressure changes it undergoes, it will always return to a temperature of 70°F when it returns to a pressure of 1,000 millibars, provided that it remains unsaturated and is subject only to adiabatic influences. In general terms, *potential temperature* is defined as the temperature that a quantity of air would have if brought by the dry adiabatic process to a pressure of 1,000 millibars. Potential temperature is the actual temperature reduced adiabatically to a standard pressure. Changes of elevation result in changes in the existing temperature but make no difference in the potential temperature of unsaturated air.

Suppose, now, that the air, having been lifted 1,000 feet and having reached a temperature of 64.5°F, becomes saturated at that point, but continues to rise another 1,000 feet, with condensation occurring. During the second thousand feet of rise, it will have cooled only 3°, and at the top will have reached a temperature of 61.5°F. If it now descends to its original level, warming all the way at the dry adiabatic rate, when it reaches the standard pressure its temperature will be 61.5° + 11.0° = 72.5°F instead of the 70°F at which it started. We see that the potential temperature may be increased by adiabatic processes, when these involve condensation.

EQUIVALENT POTENTIAL TEMPERATURE

An even more conservative property of a parcel of air is its *equivalent potential temperature*. Again let a quantity of air, starting at the standard pressure of 1,000 millibars, rise until it has lost all its moisture, cooling first at the dry adiabatic rate and later at the wet adiabatic rate. This is a *pseudoadiabatic process* equivalent to adding to the air the heat of condensation latent in all of its vapor. Let this completely dry air then descend to the standard pressure. The temperature it then assumes is called its *equivalent potential temperature*. The equivalent potential temperature can be calculated when the original temperature and humidity are known.

The potential temperature of a given mass of air is unchanged by dry adiabatic processes. The equivalent potential temperature remains the same even though the vertical movements involve condensation and precipitation. It can be changed only by the addition of water vapor through evaporation, or by the loss or gain of heat to or from outside sources.

In Fig. 4.4, if air at 1,000 millibars pressure and 18°C (64.4°F) rises

The Mechanics of Equivalent Potential Temperature.   **FIG. 4.4**

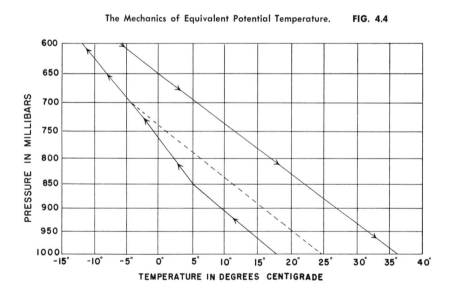

and cools at the dry adiabatic rate to the 857-mb level (4,500 feet) where it becomes saturated, its potential temperature is still 18°C. If it then cools at the retarded rate to the 700-mb level (10,000 feet), its potential temperature becomes 25°C. If it continues to rise until all its moisture is condensed and the latent heat absorbed, and then returns adiabatically to 1,000 mb pressure, its temperature will be 36°C. This is the equivalent potential temperature of the air.

THE ADIABATIC CHART

One of the very important tools of the meteorologist is the *adiabatic chart*. It is simply a graphical means of solving many complicated mathematical relationships existing among the properties of the atmosphere. There are many variations in the manner in which a chart may be constructed, but always the ordinate is some function of pressure (decreasing upward) and the abscissa is temperature increasing toward the right (Fig. 4.5). The primary horizontal lines then become lines of equal pressure and the vertical lines are lines of equal temperature.

Three additional sets of lines complete the chart. They are drawn at chosen intervals for convenience, but not so numerous as to impair legibility. Each set of lines represents a function which is dependent on temperature and pressure. If a given function is to be traced from a point not lying on a printed isoline of that function, the constant value is simply parallel to the function line.

1. Dry adiabats, or lines of equal potential temperature. They are the straight dashed lines sloping from upper left to lower right and graphing the dry adiabatic lapse rate of 5.5°F per 1,000 feet (1°C per 100 m).

2. Saturation adiabats, or lines of equal equivalent potential temperature. They are the curving dash-dot lines varying slightly to the right of the dry adiabats and numbered in °A according to the equivalent potential temperature of a saturated parcel of air situated on the line.

3. Lines of constant saturation mixing ratio, or lines of equal specific humidity (in parts per thousand) of saturated air. (See page 37.) The almost vertical orientation of these dotted lines shows that temperature is a more important factor than pressure in determining the capacity of the atmosphere to hold water vapor.

Sometimes lines of equal height are also drawn because they do not coincide exactly with lines of equal pressure. For practical approximations, however, the 1,000-mb level is at or near the surface, 850 mb is about 5,000 feet high (1.5 km), 700 mb is near 10,000 feet (3 km), and the 500-mb level is almost 20,000 feet (6 km) above sea level. Soundings from radiosondes and other sources are plotted on the adiabatic chart to aid in the analysis of the characteristics and potentialities of the upper atmosphere.

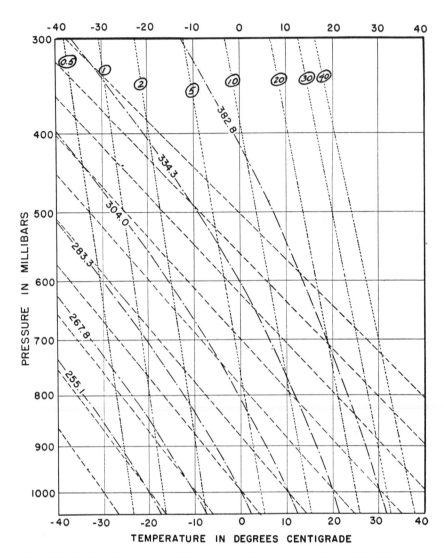

The Adiabatic Chart. Since pseudo adiabats (saturated) are shown on the chart, it may be more appropriately referred to as a pseudoadiabic chart.   **FIG. 4.5**

We have seen that ascending or descending air changes   **Lapse Rates**
temperature at a definite rate as a result of the changing pressure upon it. This does not mean that the overlying air always
grows colder at these rates. There are many reasons why the rate of
change of temperature of the air above a given point at a given time
should only rarely coincide with the adiabatic rate of change. In the first
place, air is not always rising or falling, and therefore not always changing

adiabatically. Second, air is constantly gaining and losing heat by radiation, absorption, and conduction, and often also by evaporation and condensation. Third, horizontal movements bring warm or cold air from other sources. For these reasons, the real vertical distribution of temperature is frequently quite different from the adiabatic rates.

The actual change of temperature with elevation, whatever it may be, is called the *lapse rate* of the air. *Vertical temperature gradient* expresses the same idea, but "lapse rate" is a shorter and more convenient term. The word *lapse* means in this connection the gradual passing from a higher to a lower temperature. In case the air grows warmer with increasing height, the lapse rate is negative. *Lapse rate* is the general term; *adiabatic* and *saturation adiabatic changes* are particular lapse rates occurring under special conditions.

VARIABILITY OF LAPSE RATES

During the past fifty years, a great many records of the temperature of the air within a few miles of the surface of the earth have been obtained by means of balloons, kites, airplanes, and radiosondes. The lapse rates found in different individual ascents have great variability from day to day and at different levels in the atmosphere on the same day, especially in the first 2 miles (3 km). Beyond 2 or 3 miles (3–5 km), the rates are likely to be more nearly uniform. That is to say, the temperature of the air below 2 or 3 miles changes very irregularly, being influenced by irregular wind movements from various sources. These movements sometimes cause a temporary lapse rate that is greater than the dry adiabatic rate, and, on the other hand, the lapse rate is often less than the wet adiabatic rate.

In some cases, instead of decreasing with altitude, the temperature increases, as shown in the curves just mentioned. Such a condition is called an *inversion of temperature*, or simply an *inversion*. On calm, clear nights, as the soil cools rapidly by radiation, the air near the surface is cooled both by radiation and by contact with the cold earth. Thus it often becomes colder than the air higher up. Inversions, or negative lapse rates, frequently occur in this way, but they also occur at higher levels, by reason of winds of different temperatures blowing from different directions.

Observations of air temperatures aloft have now been made in many parts of the world and are sufficiently numerous to establish a fairly definite normal or average value. This *average lapse rate* is found to be about 3.3°F per 1,000 feet (0.6°C per 100 m) in the lower levels of the atmosphere. It increases slightly with higher elevations until the outer limit of the troposphere is reached. It is easy to confuse the ordinary decrease in temperature with altitude and the adiabatic temperature changes resulting from vertical air movements. The lapse rate of the air is ordinarily less than the dry adiabatic rate and about equal to the saturation adiabatic rate. Normally the lapse rate is less when the pressure is high than when it is low, and less in winter than in summer.

The word *stability* is used in studying the weather to indicate a condition of equilibrium. For example, a ruler lying flat on the table is in stable equilibrium; if **Stability and Instability** one end is raised and then released, it returns to its original position. A ruler standing on one end is in unstable equilibrium; if the upper end is moved slightly, the ruler does not return to its former position, but takes a more stable position. Let us examine the effect of various lapse rates upon the stability of the air, that is, upon its tendency to move up or down or remain in the original position.

STABILITY

It is evident that when a certain mass of air is heavier than the surrounding air, it will tend to fall or settle downward; if lighter than the surrounding air, it will be displaced upward by the heavier air. If the temperature of the air is exactly the same throughout the first 1,000 feet above the ground, for instance, the air at the bottom is a little denser because of the added pressure upon it, and hence a little heavier, volume for volume, than that at the top. Because it is heavier, it tends to stay at the bottom; but suppose by some means we force a certain portion of it to rise through the surrounding air. This rising portion cools at the adiabatic rate. Therefore, at any level to which the rising portion ascends within this assumed layer of equal temperature, it is colder and heavier than the air around it. When the outside force which caused it to rise is no longer effective, it sinks back to the surface. The air tends to return to its original position under such conditions, and is therefore said to be *stable,* or in *stable equilibrium.* In the case of an inversion, in which warm air overlies a surface layer of cold air, the atmosphere at that time and place would be very stable.

Let us assume that the temperature falls with elevation, but that the rate of fall is less than the adiabatic rate, as shown in Fig. 4.6. Any portion of the air having a vertical movement will change its temperature at the adiabatic rate. If started upward, it will become colder and heavier than the surrounding air and will settle back to its original position. If pushed downward, it will warm adiabatically and become lighter than the surrounding air. This will cause the displaced air to return to its initial position. This air is stable, and any air is stable if its lapse rate is less than the adiabatic rate. The general rule may be stated thus: *Unsaturated air is stable when its lapse rate is less than the dry adiabatic rate, and saturated*

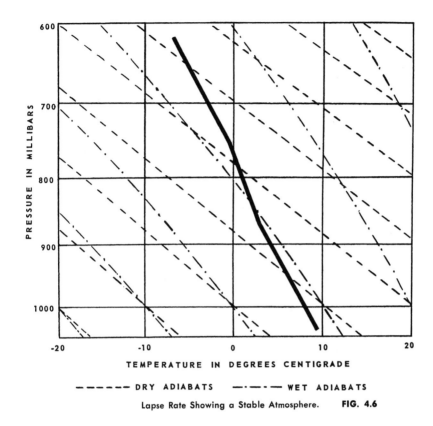

DRY ADIABATS   WET ADIABATS

Lapse Rate Showing a Stable Atmosphere.   **FIG. 4.6**

air is stable when its lapse rate is less than the saturation adiabatic rate. Such air stays in position or returns to its position if forced out of it. Thermal convection is not possible so long as the air remains in this condition.

INSTABILITY

If the lapse rate, as indicated by the heavy line in Fig. 4.7, is greater than the adiabatic rate, air starting at any point and moving upward becomes progressively warmer than its surroundings and therefore continues to rise indefinitely, as long as the given lapse rate of the surrounding air continues. Likewise, air starting downward becomes progressively denser than the surrounding air and continues downward to the earth's surface. This is a case of instability; a little push in either direction sets the air moving in that direction. If air is heated near the surface and starts to rise, it will continue to rise as long as it is surrounded by air that is colder than itself. *Air is unstable when its lapse rate is greater than the dry adiabatic rate.* This condition is favorable to convection. If the lapse rate just equals the dry adiabatic rate, the air is in *neutral equilibrium*. For any lapse rate greater than the dry adiabatic rate, the air is unstable but generally requires an impetus to start vertical movement. It does not start moving up or down automatically.

The maximum possible lapse rate, except momentarily, is one in which the air gets cold so rapidly with height as to offset the tendency of expansion with decreasing pressure, and thus to give the air a constant density in the vertical. This effect requires a fall of temperature of 19°F per 1,000 feet (3.5°C per 100 m) of elevation, and is an extremely unstable condition. Such a lapse rate would result in automatic and almost explosive overturning of the air. It would require no impetus to start the movement; it would be *autoconvective*. This condition may occur momentarily in tornadoes and in a thin layer of air in contact with an intensely heated ground surface.

If the lapse rate changes in Fig. 4.7, as indicated by the heavy dashed line, the layer of air above the point of change is stable. Air from the unstable layer will descend until it meets the surface or it will rise until it reaches a point in the stable layer having a temperature identical with its own, and it will go no farther. Such a change in lapse rate may be oc-

Lapse Rate of an Unstable Atmospheric Condition Below the 880-mb Level.   **FIG. 4.7**

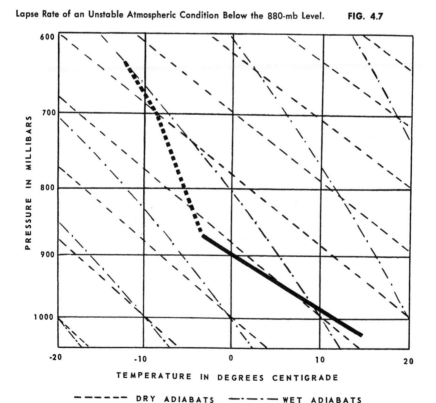

TEMPERATURE IN DEGREES CENTIGRADE

------ DRY ADIABATS   —·—·— WET ADIABATS

casioned by a warm current in the upper air, and such a current limits convection. Convection will stop at, or somewhat above, the bottom of the warm current, and if the air has not already been cooled to its dew point, there will be no condensation, no clouds, and no rain. Conversely, if there is a cold current in the upper air, convection will continue through it and the rising air will probably cool below its dew point, resulting in cloudiness and rain. A stable condition of the atmosphere, therefore, favors fair weather; an unstable condition is conducive to cloudiness and rain.

CONDITIONAL INSTABILITY

The foregoing illustrations of stability and instability assumed that the rising air did not become saturated. When condensation occurs, rising air cools at the saturation adiabatic rate, and it is that rate rather than the dry adiabatic rate which then determines stability or instability. The condition of the atmosphere is at times such that the lapse rate may be represented by a line lying between the dry and wet adiabatic curves (Fig. 4.8). The lapse rate is less than the dry adiabatic rate and greater than the wet adiabatic rate. Such air is therefore stable when unsaturated,

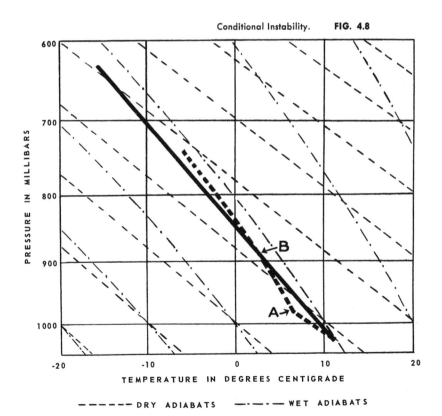

Conditional Instability.   **FIG. 4.8**

but unstable when condensation is occurring in it. It is said to be in a state of *conditional instability*. Whether it is stable or unstable depends on whether or not it has been cooled to saturation.

In many cases, the cooling is adiabatic cooling due to lifting. Assume that a body of air has a considerable moisture content and a lapse rate intermediate between dry and wet adiabatic. If a portion of this conditionally unstable air is forced upward through the mass, it becomes definitely unstable, as illustrated in Fig. 4.8. As it is lifted and is cooled adiabatically, condensation begins at the height A, depending on the moisture content of the air. If the air is forced farther upward, it cools at the saturation adiabatic rate, and becomes warmer than the air around it, and therefore unstable. The height at which instability begins is the *level of free convection, B*.

The instability of the rising air was latent in this case and was realized only when an outside force caused a lifting of the air to the level of free convection. Condensation in air which is forced to rise, therefore, often makes thermal convection possible when it would not otherwise be so, and permits it to extend to greater heights than it otherwise would. When the air is definitely unstable, that is, when the lapse rate is greater than the dry adiabatic rate, condensation makes convection more active by increasing the difference between the temperature of the rising air and that of the surrounding air. Conditional instability is of frequent occurrence in the atmosphere, often in connection with widespread rain.

CONVECTIVE INSTABILITY

Similarly, an entire layer of stable air may become unstable by lifting. The distribution of temperature and moisture must be such that the layer becomes saturated as it rises and that the bottom portion becomes saturated before the upper portion (Fig. 4.9). The latter condition is frequently met, since the relative humidity often decreases rather rapidly from the surface upward. As such a layer rises, it expands under decreasing pressure, causing the upper portion to rise more than the lower. The upper portion therefore cools more than the lower, both because it cools longer at the dry adiabatic rate and because it cools through a greater distance. The lapse rate within the layer is thereby increased and becomes greater than the saturation adiabatic rate. Layers of this character, which, though originally stable, are *convectively unstable* or in a condition of *convective instability* (also called *potential instability*). A layer of air is convectively unstable if the equivalent potential temperature decreases with height through the layer.

SUBSIDENCE

In contrast, a subsiding layer of air has a decreasing lapse rate and its stability increases. As the base of the layer approaches the earth, the

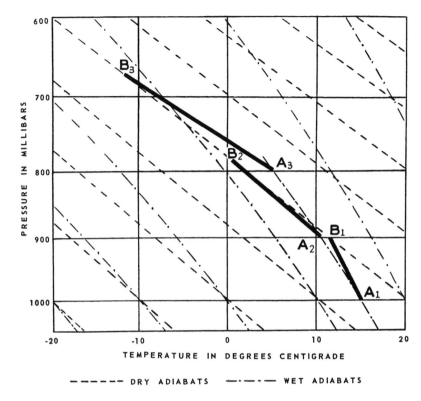

------ DRY ADIABATS   —·—·— WET ADIABATS

Instability of Lifting. The lifting condensation level is at A_1, and the level   **FIG. 4.9**
of free convection is at A_2 for air at the surface.

layer is compressed by the increasing pressure upon it. Hence, the top descends farther than the bottom and is warmed, adiabatically, more than the bottom. This results in a smaller difference in temperature between top and bottom, and in a decreased lapse rate. *Subsidence* therefore increases atmospheric stability and may even cause a temperature inversion.

TURBULENCE IN RELATION TO LAPSE RATES

The atmosphere, especially within a few hundred feet of the earth's surface, but to some extent at all elevations, is turbulent. The many small irregular movements and eddies have vertical as well as horizontal components of motion. This is mechanical turbulence, produced by the action of the winds over the earth's surface. If the air is unstable, such turbulence starts convective currents which will then continue upward. The pilot recognizes these rising currents as "bumps." If the lapse rate is less than adiabatic, the vertical movements started by turbulence are checked and damped. Hence turbulence is more pronounced in unstable air than in stable air. This is illustrated by the usual increase in the gustiness of wind during the day over that at night. By day there is instability and convection, favoring gustiness and increased vertical movement; by night, the cooling of the surface layers favors stability and decreased vertical movement.

The daytime turbulence slows down the heating process by bringing down cooler air. Whatever night turbulence there may be, owing to winds of more than 5 or 6 miles per hour, retards the night cooling by bringing down warmer air, and thereby tends to prevent frosts and to prevent or dissolve ground fogs. The so-called *thermals,* often used by glider pilots, are rising currents of unstable air. Varying stages of instability are also responsible for much cloudiness and rainfall. For these reasons, the degree of stability of the air is of practical significance.

Atmospheric Layers

Until recently it was supposed that the air above the first few miles grew thinner and colder by continuous gradation until it gradually merged into outer space. No change in characteristics, except for the proportions of its constituent gases, was suspected. It was assumed that this high air had little influence on terrestrial affairs and presented few problems of scientific interest or practical concern. Among the most important advances in meteorology since the beginning of the twentieth century has been the discovery that the upper air has a complicated physical structure, with many theoretical and practical bearings. In particular, upper-air exploration has shown that the atmosphere has some structural resemblance to a house of several stories; it is divided into layers, or strata, and each layer has its own peculiar features and behavior.

STRATOSPHERE AND TROPOSPHERE

The first evidence of stratification in the upper air came at the beginning of this century. It has been noted that the normal lapse rate is about the same in all parts of the world and beyond an elevation of about 2 miles becomes quite regular. It was natural to assume that this condition continued upward indefinitely, but the accumulation of data from sounding balloons enabled Teisserenc de Bort and Assmann to demonstrate, between 1899 and 1902, that the air ceases to become colder with elevation at a certain fairly sharp limit in the upper air, at an average elevation of about 7 miles (11 km). From this surface upward for a distance of a few miles, as has been confirmed by many subsequent observations, the temperature remains practically the same, or increases slightly; the lapse rate of the air at these elevations is zero or negative. The region is therefore nearly isothermal in a vertical plane, and was first known as the *isothermal region.* It is now called the *stratosphere.* It is evident that the air in this layer of the atmosphere is in stable equilibrium; there can be no convection through it.

The region between the earth and the stratosphere, where there are frequent unstable and convective currents, is known as the *troposphere.* The prefix *tropo* carries the meaning of a turning or overturning of the air, such as occurs in convectional movements. The boundary surface between the two spheres is known as the *tropopause.*

HEIGHT OF TROPOPAUSE, AND TEMPERATURES IN THE LOWER STRATOSPHERE

In the temperate latitudes of Europe, where records were first obtained and studied, the stratosphere was found to begin at a height of about 7 miles (11 km). With the accumulation of records from other parts of the world, it is now known that the height of the tropopause varies with latitude. The height is about 10.6 miles (17 km) in equatorial regions, from which it gradually decreases toward the poles, both north and south, descending in polar regions to an elevation of only 4 or 5 miles (6–8 km), and possibly less. In addition to this marked change in height with latitude, there are smaller changes related to the seasons and to barometric pressure at the surface. The tropopause is higher in summer than in winter and higher when the surface pressure is high than when it is low.

Although vertical surfaces in the lower portion of the stratosphere are nearly isothermal, it is by no means true that the stratosphere is everywhere of the same temperature. The temperatures at the same elevation in different parts of the world vary widely. In equatorial regions, the normal lapse rate continues to a height of about 10 miles (16 km), until the temperature has fallen to −80° or −100°F (−62° or −73°C). A temperature of −134°F was once registered at a height of 10 miles, above Batavia, Java. In polar regions, the temperature decreases to a height of only 4 or 5 miles (6–8 km) above the earth and falls to −40°F or −50°F (−40° or −45°C). In middle latitudes, the temperature at the tropopause, about 7 miles (11 km) above the surface, is about −60°F. The higher the tropopause, the longer the lapse of temperature continues, and the lower is the temperature of the stratosphere. Hence, at heights of 5 miles (8 km) or more, it is colder over the equator than over the poles. This is true in all seasons. There are movements of air in the stratosphere, perhaps the result of the temperature differences just mentioned; but in passing from the troposphere to the stratosphere, is has usually been found that the winds decrease in velocity fairly rapidly without changing their direction. For a more detailed discussion of the upper atmosphere, see Chapter 13.

PROBLEMS

1.

Assuming the air to have the average lapse rate and a surface temperature of 60°F, if a certain mass of dry air at the surface is heated to 72°F,
how high will it rise and what will be its temperature at that height?

2.

Assume that the maximum temperature on a quiet summer afternoon will
be the temperature at which the air becomes unstable, as indicated by the
temperatures at the surface and at 3,600 feet. What will be the maximum
temperature if the air at 3,600 feet has a temperature of 70°F? 45°F?

3.

Let air having a temperature of 15°C at the surface of the earth rise 3
miles, with condensation occurring during the last mile of the rise. What is
its potential temperature at the surface and after it has risen to 3 miles
when the pressure is 1,000 millibars at the surface? at 528 feet elevation?

4.

On a certain day, air has the following temperatures at the elevations
given: 50°F at the surface; 42°F at 1,000 feet; 45°F at 2,000 feet;
41°F at 3,000 feet; 38°F at 4,000 feet. Make a chart of height against
temperature and plot the lapse rate. What part of the air is stable? What
part is unstable? When the surface air is heated 10°F, how high will it
rise if no condensation occurs?

5.

On a September day at Drexel, Nebraska, the following upper-air data
were obtained. (Altitudes are expressed in meters and temperatures in
degrees centigrade. The ground has an elevation of 396 meters.)

Altitude	Temperature
396	8.7
627	13.9
1,187	11.1
2,443	−0.3
3,094	−5.0
3,292	−7.0

Plot the lapse rate. What part of the air is stable? What part is conditionally unstable?

6.

Why is it more difficult for the surface temperature to fall below the
freezing level after it has been raining than when it is dry?

7.

Think of the conditions under which an icicle forms. Is there a relationship between the formation of an icicle and the latent heat of water vapor?

8.

Did you ever see a dust devil? Would you say it was probably the result of an autoconvective atmosphere? Why?

9.

How are thermals used by glider pilots?

10.

What makes long-range radio broadcasting possible? Why can not television programs be transmitted in the same manner?

5

evaporation
and condensation

Water is an essential constituent of living organisms' environment. The earth is habitable only because of the large amount of moisture at its surface and in its atmosphere. The evaporation of water into a vapor which mixes with the other gases of the atmosphere, and its condensation again at or above the earth's surface constitute necessary steps in the all-important *hydrologic cycle*. The hydrologic cycle, involving evaporation, transportation, condensation, precipitation, percolation, and/or runoff, holds the key to moisture distribution over the face of the earth and is intricately related to all the phenomena of meteorology.

It is generally conceded that most of the water vapor of the atmosphere comes from the oceans. It is from the oceans, particularly from the tropical oceans, that great streams of air become laden with water vapor which is later distributed over the face of the earth through some form of precipitation. Evaporation observations, however, are generally restricted to land stations. Although evaporation is of primary importance in meteorology as

**Evaporation
Observations**

a source of water vapor, it is also important as it affects soil conditions, plant growth, and water storage.

AMOUNT OF EVAPORATION

The amount of water evaporated from a given water surface in a given time depends in the main upon the following factors:

1. *Temperature of the water surface.* For any free water surface with a temperature T, there is a corresponding saturation vapor pressure as shown in Table 2.1 on page 42.

2. *Vapor pressure of the air.* The pressure exerted by the water vapor in the air is known as *vapor pressure,* and it varies directly with the humidity. Evaporation from a water surface is rapid when there is a great difference between the vapor pressure of the air and the saturation vapor pressure.

3. *Wind movement.* Wind removes the moist air in direct contact with the water and replaces it with drier air. Hence, evaporation increases with wind velocity.

4. *Salinity.* The presence of dissolved minerals or salts in the water retards evaporation. Evaporation from sea water is about 5 per cent less than from fresh water, other conditions being the same.

MEASUREMENT OF EVAPORATION

The evaporation from a water surface is often measured by use of a shallow circular pan, 4 to 6 feet in diameter and 10 to 12 inches deep. This pan is filled with water nearly to the top and the decrease in depth is measured carefully every twenty-four hours by a hook gage (Fig. 5.1). The loss of water from such a pan will depend not only on the general factors mentioned in the preceding paragraph, but also on the size of the pan and its methods of exposure—whether it is buried in the ground, resting on the surface of the ground, or raised above ground with air circulating beneath. All of these factors affect the temperature of the water. The evaporation from such a pan is not the same as from a lake under similar weather conditions, partly because the lake water takes on a different temperature, and partly because the moisture content of the air is increased in moving across a considerable body of water.

Evaporation from plant and soil surfaces is great, and the rate is affected by other factors in addition to those applying to a water surface. In the case of the soil, evaporation is influenced by the texture and tilth of the soil and by its water content. In the case of plants, it varies for each species and, in the same species, with the leaf surface and the growing condition of the individual plant. No satisfactory formulas have been developed to connect the measured evaporation from a pan with the loss from larger bodies of water or from plants and soil, as the relations are

Class A Evaporation Station. From left to right the instruments and equipment are an instrument shelter, a weighing rain gauge, an evaporation pan with stillwell and anemometer, and a standard 8-inch rain gauge. Courtesy, U.S. Department of Commerce, Weather Bureau.   **FIG. 5.1**

complex in all cases. However, records made in different localities with the same kind of pan, similarly exposed, give valuable comparative results, showing the relative amounts of evaporation in different climates.

Another method of measuring evaporation has been developed by Thornthwaite and Holzman. They mounted two small instrument shelters on a tower, one near the surface and one several feet directly above the other. Recording instruments within these shelters give a continuous record of pressure, temperature, and relative humidity. From these data the specific humidities of the air at the two shelters, and the density of the air, are calculated. Continuous records of the wind velocity at the two points are also obtained. The differences between the specific humidities and between the wind speeds at the upper and lower points, taken together with the density of the air, give a measure of the vertical flow of water vapor. That is, they determine the mass of water moving upward in a given time, and hence the loss by evaporation from the surface, including the transpiration from plants. The method can be used over either land or water surfaces.

In the greater part of the western half of the United States, where precipitation is light, the annual evaporation from a water surface is greater than the annual rainfall. In parts of Arizona it has been found to be more than nine times the rainfall. In spite of difficulties in the application of evaporation data to specific problems, such data are of much practical value; for example, to hydraulic engineers, in the planning of storage reservoirs and irrigation systems; and to plant scientists, in the study of the relations of plants to their environment.

In the long run, the amount of water vapor in the air **Condensation** becomes neither greater nor smaller. It follows that **on Solid Surfaces** evaporation into the air is balanced by condensation from the air. Over the earth as a whole, precipitation plus deposits of dew, frost, and fog must equal evaporation.

It has already been shown that water vapor is caused to condense when it is cooled. Cooling is the only significant cause of condensation from the free atmosphere. Near the earth's surface, condensation begins on solid surfaces because these get colder than the general mass of air. The earth and all solid objects are better radiators of heat than is the air; at night they cool more rapidly than the air, this being especially true when the sky is clear. The air then loses some of its heat by radiation and conduction to the colder surfaces.

DEW

Air that comes in contact with cold surfaces may thus be cooled below its dew point, in which case some of its moisture is condensed and deposited as dew on the cold objects. If the air is quite calm, the lower 3 or 4 feet may be appreciably cooled by conduction during a single night. Usually, only the air that comes in direct contact with the cold surfaces is cooled to its dew point. It is hardly correct, then, to say that dew falls; rather, it condenses where it is deposited. If the air is quiet, the cooling of the lower air produces an inversion of temperature, which decreases turbulence and so contributes to further stability and calmness. The air at the ground is thus left long in contact with the cold surfaces and is given a good opportunity to reach its dew point. By this process the air within a few inches of the ground may become considerably colder than that immediately above it. On the other hand, movement and turbulence in the lower air cause a mixing to a height of several feet. The cooling extends to a greater elevation than in quiet air, but, since more air is affected by the cooling process, it may be that none of it reaches its dew point. Hence, wind tends to prevent the formation of dew.

FROST

When the dew point of the air is below 32°F, moisture passes directly from the gaseous to the solid state. This process is called *sublimation,* and results in the formation of ice crystals called *frost* or *hoarfrost.* Note that frost is not frozen dew. Frosts are classified as light, heavy, or killing. A *killing frost* is defined as a frost that is destructive of the staple crops of the locality. Only the last killing frost in the spring and the first one in the fall are of special significance. The words *frost, black frost,* and *dry freeze* are sometimes used in a broader sense to denote freezing weather unaccompanied by hoarfrost. Light and heavy frosts are distinguished largely by the amount of the deposit and are without exact definition.

Frosts occur most readily in low places, especially if there is no outlet. The cold, heavy air drains along the sloping surfaces into such low places and accumulates there, becoming still and stable and considerably colder than the general mass of air, thus creating a temperature inversion. In many parts of the world, fruit is grown successfully on slopes and in foothill regions, but not on adjacent valley floors for this reason. Even on level ground, frosts may form when the general air temperature is well above freezing, especially if there is not sufficient wind to move and mix the air. On a cold winter day, frost often occurs on the inside of a window in a general air temperature of 70°F within the room for the same reason that frost occurs outside, that is, by the loss of heat to a cold surface. An electric fan directed toward the window will clear it of frost by replacing the cold air.

The conditions necessary for the formation of dew or frost in nature are: (a) clear sky (except that in cloudy winter weather a damp wind moving over cold ground may produce frost), (b) still, cool air in stable equilibrium, and (c) sufficient moisture to reach the dew point with a moderate amount of cooling. The prediction of frost takes account of these factors and of one further consideration in respect to the dew point. If the dew point is above 32°F, condensation will begin as dew, and the latent heat thus set free will retard the further cooling. Freezing temperatures are thus less likely to occur when the dew point is above freezing than when it is below 32°F. The same process that causes dew and frost causes the sweating of cool objects on a hot summer day and the sublimation of ice on cold pavements in winter. If the temperature falls below freezing but does not fall to the dew point, there will be a freeze but no deposit of frost.

PROTECTION AGAINST FROST

In western and southwestern fruitgrowing regions, most injurious spring frosts or freezes occur on "radiation nights"—that is, under clear and quiet conditions, with cold air at the surface and an inversion layer not over 30 or 40 feet above the surface. Many citrus orchards in those regions, particularly in California, are protected from injury under such conditions by the use of small diesel-oil-burning heaters, giving much heat and little smoke. These are placed among the trees, sometimes as many as sixty to the acre (Fig. 5.2). By this means it is possible to raise the temperature of the greater part of the grove by as much as 12°F.

In the use of these heaters, three factors are effective in preventing injury: (a) The lower air is warmed by the heat produced; (b) the fires create small convection currents which mix the air to about the heights of the tree tops; (c) such smoke as is formed acts as a blanket to retard cooling by radiation. But smoke is avoided as much as possible because it is

FIG. 5.2

Orchard Heaters in a California Citrus Grove. Note the return stack on each heater, a feature developed to reduce air pollution. *Sunkist Photo.*

FIG. 5.3

Wind Machine for Fighting Freezes. This type of device is being extensively used in the California citrus groves. Most freezes are associated with sharp temperature inversions and may be averted by thoroughly stirring the lower air. *Sunkist Photo.*

a public nuisance and because, when it remains in the air by day, it retards surface warming. Larger fires would be less effective, because they carry the heat above the trees, and could be dangerous to the trees as well. It is evident that such protection is not feasible where freezing temperatures occur with cold winds and not as a result of radiation.

Following World War II, the availability of war-surplus airplane equipment led to the development of wind machines like the one in Fig. 5.3. Such machines do not heat the air, but they do stir the low inverted layer, forcing it to mix with warmer and lighter air from above. When properly operated, wind machines will usually prevent frost with no smoke and with less inconvenience than is associated with orchard heaters.

No considerable part of continental United States is entirely immune from frost, but in the southern half of Florida, certain limited areas in California and Arizona, and a small area in southern Texas, frosts are sufficiently rare to permit the growth of citrus fruits and winter vegetables, but not without occasional losses. The state of Hawaii is entirely free of frost at elevations below 2,500 feet, as is Puerto Rico.

Any visible atmospheric phenomenon, except clouds, that depends on the presence of water in the air is called a *hydrometeor.*[1] Hydrometeors are mainly the result of the condensation or sublimation of the water **Condensation Above the Earth's Surface** vapor in the air. Condensation in the free air, as at the surface, is the result of cooling. Condensed moisture takes many forms, because of variations in the moisture content of the air, in its movements and turbulence, and especially in its temperature and its rate of cooling. These forms have been described in detail and given specific names and symbols by an international meteorological committee. The same symbols are in use on weather maps in all the principal countries of the world. The more important condensation forms are discussed in this chapter.

NUCLEI OF CONDENSATION

If air is perfectly free from dust, it may be cooled below its dew point without any condensation; the air is then supersaturated. Moreover, ordinary mineral dust, as from a land surface, may be added to such supersaturated air without starting condensation. But if smoke or salt spray from the ocean is added, rapid condensation occurs. In fact, with such substances in the air, moisture will begin to condense before 100 per cent humidity is reached. Some of the ocean salts and some of the products of combustion have the quality of absorbing moisture from the air and for this reason are said to be *hygroscopic.* Apparently the presence of hygroscopic particles is essential to the condensation of moisture in the air in important amounts. Such particles are called *nuclei of condensation.* This term refers to particles of microscopic size, not to the visible dust or

---

[1] This description agrees with the United States Weather Bureau definition but does not agree, with regard to fog and haze, with the definition of the International Meteorological Organization. See Weather Bureau Publication No. 1445, *Weather Glossary* (Washington, D.C.: Superintendent of Documents, 1946), p. 155; and Sverre Petterssen, *Weather Analysis and Forecasting* (New York: McGraw-Hill Book Company, 1940), p. 37.

smoke particles in the air. Fires, ocean spray, explosive volcanoes, and burning meteors furnish large numbers of hygroscopic nuclei. Tests that have been made show that condensation nuclei are usually present in the free atmosphere in large numbers.

FOG, HAZE, AND DRIZZLE

Fog may be defined as almost microscopically small drops of water condensed from and suspended in the air near the surface of the earth in sufficient numbers to reduce the horizontal visibility to 0.6 mile or less. Fog may also be defined briefly as Stratus cloud near the earth's surface and enveloping the observer. Fog particles vary in diameter from about one-tenth to one-hundredth of a millimeter. Droplets of all these sizes often occur in the same fog. They frequently occur in a supercooled liquid state at temperatures much below freezing, even as low as −20°F. Such supercooled fogs produce a rapid icing of aircraft moving through them.

Accumulations of dust or smoke in the air are sometimes called *dust fogs* or *smoke fogs*, but they should be distinguished from true fogs. Smoke furnishes numerous hygroscopic nuclei and probably facilitates the formation of fog. Certainly smoke darkens fog and reduces the visibility. For this reason, thick fogs are more frequent in smoky cities than in adjoining country districts, but smoke abatement, though very desirable in itself, would not put a stop to fogs. The blend of smoke and fog is called *smog*.

Fogs are now classified in four densities in terms of their effect on visibility: light fog—visibility 5/8 mile or more; moderate fog—visibility between 5/16 and 5/8 mile; thick fog—visibility between 1/5 and 5/16 mile; and dense fog—visibility less than 1/5 mile. Fogs merge gradually into *drizzle* as the droplets become larger. Drizzle implies light rain, which is falling, or at least can be felt on the face. On the other hand, when the fog droplets become smaller and less numerous, fogs grade into *moist haze*. In haze there is no apparent obscuration of objects within about half a mile, but distant objects become blurred and the sky has a gray appearance. Nearly the same effect may be produced by *dry haze*, resulting from dust or smoke or from optical irregularities of the air. Four important processes by which the saturation necessary to produce fogs is obtained are discussed in the following sections.

RADIATION FOGS

The loss of heat by radiation often results in the saturation of the lower air and the development of a fog. Such fogs are named *radiation fogs*. They are of two types: *ground fogs* and *high-inversion fogs*. Ground fogs are a result of the cooling of the earth's surface and the lower air at night, producing an inversion of temperature, which prevents convection and reduces turbulence. They occur principally in the early morning hours. Sometimes only dew or frost follows such cooling, but at other times the entire mass of air to a height of a few feet or a few hundred feet is cooled below its dew point, and then there is fog.

A light wind of 4 or 5 miles per hour is sufficient to produce turbulence when moving over uneven ground or around trees and buildings, and such a wind is conducive to fog; but higher winds carry away the cooled air, destroy the inversion, and prevent fog. Fogs of this character do not extend to any considerable height, frequently not over 100 feet; hence, their name, *ground fogs*. Because clear weather permits rapid cooling, ground fogs are fair-weather fogs; that is, the air is bright and clear above and also at the surface when the sun breaks through the "vapors that did seem to strangle him." But they are most likely to occur when a clear night follows a cloudy day, because then the surface and the lower air start the night cool.

HIGH-INVERSION FOGS

During the winter season, it often happens in certain regions that cool, quiet, moist air overlies the earth and is itself overlain by warmer, drier air at elevations from 300 to 2,000 feet. This occurrence prevents upward movement by convection or turbulence and facilitates cooling by radiation. When this situation persists, the continual cooling of the lower air, night after night, results in a sharp inversion at the boundary of the two layers and the formation at that boundary of a *high-inversion fog*, also called *inversion fog*. This is really a low Stratus cloud. The further cooling of the already cool air by radiation at night often causes the condensation to build downward from the cloud to the earth, causing a dense surface fog at night. When air from polar regions moves over the North Atlantic and becomes stagnant over Europe, such fogs frequently form and persist day and night for several days or even weeks. In this country, in valleys near the seacoast, especially in southern and central California, there are frequent inversion fogs during the winter months. They are especially prevalent and dense in the San Joaquin Valley of California.

ADVECTION FOGS

A second important process by which fogs are formed is the movement of warm, moist air over a cold surface. These are called *advection fogs*. The first essential in the formation of such a fog is the importation of warm, moist air. The second is the cooling of the air to saturation by its movement over the cold surface. Third, turbulent mixing extends this saturated layer to considerable heights. Such fogs may occur with moderately strong winds, and the higher the wind, the deeper the fog layer will be, if formed at all. They often occur, also, with cloudy weather either by day or at night. They are often dense, reducing ceiling and visibility to zero, and they dissipate slowly.

Over continental interiors advection fogs are more frequent in winter, when the ground is cold or snow-covered. On western seacoasts in temperate latitudes, warm, moist, sea air, drifting inland over radiation-cooled land, is often the occasion for such fogs. At sea they occur where there are adjacent bodies of water of contrasting temperatures. The dense and persistent fogs in the vicinity of Newfoundland are of this character and result from the movement of air from the warm water of the Gulf Stream to the cold water of the Labrador Current. Fogs of this type are also frequent from Greenland eastward to Iceland and Spitzbergen, owing to the meeting of relatively warm and cold ocean waters in this region.

EVAPORATION FOGS

When cold air moves over warm water, it often happens that the moisture evaporated from the water and added to the cold air is sufficient to produce saturation and start condensation. This results in a fog, beginning at the water's surface and building upward. It has the appearance of steam rising from the water. Hence such fogs are sometimes called *steam fogs*. The same process is observed when a pan of warm water is placed in cold water. It will be noted that this process involves the advection of cold air, and for that reason these are often classified as *advection fogs*. They may become dense at the surface to a depth of 50 to 100 feet, but they do not extend to any great height. They occur over rivers, lakes,, and oceans, especially in Arctic regions where there is open water overlain by air many degrees below freezing.

Another type of evaporation fog often occurs when rain falls from a warm layer of air through an underlying layer of cold air. Evaporation from the falling warm rain may saturate the cold air, if the temperature of the raindrops is higher than the dew point of the air. If this air is unstable, or if the wind is moderate or stronger, the moisture is carried upward to form a low Stratus or Stratocumulus cloud deck. If the air is stable and the wind light, the condensed moisture remains near the surface, forming a fog. Fogs of this type occur near the boundary between two masses of air of different temperatures. Such a boundary is called a *front*, and the fogs are known as *frontal fogs*. A distinction is sometimes made between *prefrontal* and *postfrontal fogs*.

UPSLOPE FOGS

When air moves upslope against a mountain side or even up a gradually sloping plain, the adiabatic cooling due to ascent may result in saturation and the development of an *upslope fog*. The air must have a rather high relative humidity to begin with and must be stable. If there is convective instability, clouds will form but no fog. Radiation cooling of the air at the surface is often a contributing factor in the development of these fogs.

FOG COST AND DISPERSAL

Dense fogs are very expensive affairs. They are the cause of many accidents; they delay traffic by land and sea, and cause many shipwrecks; they increase cleaning bills and the use of gas and electricity, and are a special menace to aviation. London "pea soup" fogs are perhaps the densest and blackest in the world. There, when the fog is dense, physicians cannot answer calls, mail is not collected, and the fire apparatus goes to a fire at a snail's pace. Methods developed for dissipating fog over airplane landing fields, or other small areas, are based on warming the air above its dew point. This is analogous to the use of orchard heaters to prevent freezing. It is easier under quiet atmospheric conditions, as in radiation fogs, and more difficult in connection with advection fogs. Even in a gentle breeze the cleared air is soon replaced by foggy air, and it becomes necessary to warm a considerable volume of air quickly, if the field is to be kept cleared.

Clouds and Precipitation

In contrast to fogs, which result from cooling by conduction or radiation, clouds are chiefly the result of the dynamic cooling produced by expansion under reduced pressure. By far the most important cause of clouds is the adiabatic cooling resulting from upward movement of the air. Some clouds are probably formed by the mixing of warm and cool air.

The exact process or processes by which the minute cloud droplets grow to sufficient size to fall to the earth as precipitation are still not fully known. One theory that has been widely publicized is the Bergeron ice-crystal theory. This theory assumes that at least the tops of all clouds from which appreciable rain falls are at temperatures below freezing and consist of both ice crystals and supercooled water droplets. The latter are drops of water that were condensed to the liquid form at temperatures above freezing and have remained liquid after being cooled to temperatures below freezing, sometimes much below. There is no complete physical explanation of this phenomenon, but it is of frequent occurrence in the atmosphere. The fact on which the Bergeron theory is based is that the saturation vapor pressure over supercooled water drops is greater than that over ice. When the two exist together in a cloud, there will be evaporation from the droplet and condensation on the ice crystal. It is thus that the crystals grow to sufficient size to fall. As they fall through the cloud, they may grow in size by further condensation and by coalescence with other drops after they melt.

Observations have tended to support this theory in the main, but rain does sometimes fall from clouds in which the temperatures are all above freezing, especially in the tropics. To explain these cases, other processes are suggested as probably effective in the growth of small raindrops. Some of these are: (a) the presence of unusual hygroscopic nuclei; (b) a vapor-pressure gradient due to the presence of drops of differing temperature; and (c) the coalescence of drops of differing size as they collide in the turbulent air.

Rain falls beneath the air in which it is formed, or it is carried short distances by the wind. Even if the space above a given area to the top of the atmosphere were saturated, it would not as a rule contain enough water to make more than an inch of rain. Such a condition of complete saturation never occurs, and moreover, only a small part of the moisture in the air is ever removed by natural processes of condensation.

It is evident, therefore, that a large amount of water cannot fall from a given mass of air, but can come only from a continual renewal of the moisture supply. Hence, one necessary condition for a heavy rain is a continuous supply of moist, rising, inflowing air. Rain may be held aloft by rapidly rising air for a time, and then suddenly be released when the updraft ceases; this results in an extremely heavy rain of short duration and over a small area. Such a downpour may be called a *cloudburst*. The word should be confined to rain of this character but is sometimes erroneously applied to any heavy rain in mountain regions, where the run-off from a large area is collected into narrow valleys, giving the appearance of rain heavier than has actually fallen.

The magnitude of the operations involved in the production of rain is seldom appreciated. One inch of rain weighs 113 tons per acre or 72,300 tons per square mile. A general rain of 1 inch over the state of North Dakota means the precipitation of 5 billion tons of water. All this water has first been lifted high into the air. The tremendous energy of the natural forces involved and the difficulty of trying to control them or to produce important amounts of rainfall artificially are evident. Nature produces the necessary sustained upward movement in one of the ways mentioned in the next three sections.

PENETRATIVE CONVECTION

The uplift may be by means of local convection currents, when certain portions of the lower air become so much heated that they are able to penetrate the overlying air. In such cases, descending columns of air are to be expected between the rising columns (Fig. 5.4). This penetrative convection is to be distinguished from the general expansion and upward movement of an entire, extensive layer of air. In cases of penetrative convection, clouds are likely to occur in relatively small masses, such as detached, flat-base Cumuli. After condensation begins, the retarded cool-

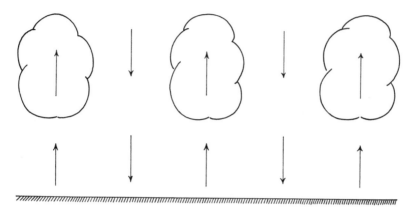

Penetrative Convection Producing Summer Cumuli.   **FIG. 5.4**

ing favors rising of the air and increased thickness of the cloud layer, and thus Cumulonimbus and thundershowers frequently come about. Convective rainfall is therefore usually in the form of heavy showers of short duration—instability showers.

On quiet summer afternoons when such Cumuli are forming by thermal convection, we may reasonably assume that the air is of the same character from the ground level to the cloud bases. With that assumption, the condensation level, that is, the height of the clouds, can be calculated roughly, given the temperature and dew point at the surface. It is to be noted not only that the temperature of the rising air falls at the adiabatic rate (5.5°F per 1,000 feet), but also that its dew point falls. The rate of fall of the dew point varies with different humidities of the air. An approximation often used is 1.1°F per 1,000 feet. The rising vapor expands because of reduced pressure, and this increase in volume decreases the concentration of the vapor and, hence, lowers the dew point. Calling the height of the cloud bases in feet, H; the temperature at the surface, T_o; the dew point at the surface, D_o; the temperature at the bases of the clouds, T_h; and the dew point there, D_h, we have

$$T_h = T_o - (5.5/1,000)H,$$

and

$$D_h = D_o - (1.1/1,000)H.$$

Because H is the height at which condensation is beginning, T_h and D_h represent the same temperature. Hence,

$$T_o - (5.5/1,000)H = D_o - (1.1/1,000)H,$$

from which

$$4.4 \quad H = 1,000(T_o - D_o), \text{ or } H = 227(T_o - D_o).$$

The values of T_o and D_o may be obtained by observation, and then the height of the cloud bases is easily calculated from this equation. This height is the *convective condensation level*.

OROGRAPHIC UPLIFT

Air may be forced upward by the movement of winds over rising ground. When winds move across a mountain range, large masses of air are made to rise. Continuous sheets of cloud of the Stratus type with flat bases, as well as continuous rain, often result. As the air moves downward on the other side of the mountains, it is dynamically warmed and becomes dry and clear. Where winds are prevailingly from one direction across a mountain system, the windward side is wet and the leeward side dry. The Sierra Nevada and the Rocky Mountains are wet on the western slopes and dry on their eastern. Hawaii, with an elevated central backbone, has a very wet side facing the persistent northeast trade winds, and an opposite very dry side. The uplift due directly to the slope of the terrain may not be sufficient of itself to cause rain, but if the air is conditionally or convectively unstable, even a moderate upslope movement may be sufficient to start convection and result in heavy precipitation. This accounts for much of the heavy rainfall in some mountainous regions.

CONVERGENCE AND EDDY MOTION

When winds from different directions converge toward a center, as is the case in some of the storms to be studied later, some of the air is forced up, often resulting in clouds and precipitation. Also, when currents of air of differing temperatures meet at an angle, the heavier air will remain in the lower position, and the lighter air will be forced to rise. In both of these cases the air is said to "converge," and such convergence is a chief cause of cloudiness and precipitation. In stable air, convergence is often attended by continuous cloud sheets and steady, prolonged rain, because the warm air moves slowly up an inclined plane rather than vertically upward, as in convective currents. In other circumstances, convergence furnishes the impetus to the ascent of convectively unstable air, as in the case of orographic uplift, and causes Cumulonimbus clouds and showers.

The upper layer of the atmosphere may have a turbulent wave motion because of a difference in density of air masses moving from different sources. The air at the tops of these waves may be cooled below its dew point, while the lower portions of the waves remain unsaturated. Under these conditions, clouds form in long lines or rows, such as are frequently seen in Cirrocumulus, Altocumulus, and Stratocumulus types. Rain from this wavelike movement is not to be expected.

As the drops of water or particles of ice in clouds in- **Forms**
crease in size, (they begin to fall and eventually reach **of Precipitation**
the ground as precipitation, unless held up by ascend-
ing air currents or evaporated on the way down. Precipitation takes various forms, depending upon the temperature at which condensation takes
place and the conditions encountered as the particles pass through the air.

RAIN

The words *rain* and *rainfall* are often used to include all forms of precipitation, but in this paragraph *rain* refers specifically to moisture which

Snow Crystals. Courtesy, U.S. Department of Commerce, Weather Bureau.   **FIG. 5.5**

falls to the earth in a liquid state. Raindrops vary in diameter from 0.004 inch in mist to 0.2 inch in thunderstorm rain. There is a natural limit to the size of raindrops. Large drops falling through quiet air break up into smaller ones when they attain a velocity of 18 miles per hour. Conversely, no rain can fall through an ascending current of this velocity.

SNOW

Snow is formed by the crystallization (sublimation) of water vapor at temperatures below freezing. Snowflakes are crystals of many beautiful, lacy patterns (Fig. 5.5). The fundamental form is hexagonal, but this is subject to much intricate elaboration, apparently influenced by the temperature, and perhaps also by the rapidity of condensation. Large snowflakes are formed by the combination of many small crystals, usually at temperatures not much below freezing and never at very low temperatures. At very low temperatures there can be but little moisture in the air. Under such conditions, precipitation is likely to be light, but it is never "too cold to snow." Snow has been recorded in Alaska at a temperature of −52°F. As previously noted, a snow cover, being a poor conductor, keeps the soil temperature higher than it would otherwise be under winter conditions, but it keeps the air temperature lower because it is not warmed much by sunshine yet cools rapidly during the night. A snow cover is of much agricultural value in regions where the winters are severe. It prevents the soil's freezing as deeply as it otherwise would, and thus protects the roots of plants. Snow that accumulates in mountain regions during the winter and gradually melts in spring and summer is of great economic value in affording water supplies and maintaining the flow of rivers. On the other hand, the removal of snow from streets, roads, and railroads involves a large annual expense in regions where the snowfall is heavy.

HAIL

Hail consists of hard, rounded pellets of ice, or of ice and compact snow. When a hailstone is cut in half, it is seen to be composed of concentric layers of differing densities and opacities (Fig 5.6). Hailstones as large as marbles are common, and sometimes stones of much greater size occur. At Potter, Nebraska, on July 6, 1928, a few very large stones fell, one of which was 5 inches in diameter and weighed 1½ pounds. Large flattened disks of ice are sometimes found; these are composed of several stones, formed independently, and frozen together while falling. The destructive effects of heavy hail, especially in the beating down of growing crops and the breaking of glass, are great. The area of destruction in any one storm is usually small, although occasionally quite extensive. Hailstorms are frequent in the central valleys of the United States during spring and summer, and losses in that region aggregate many million dollars per year.

Hail falls only from Cumulonimbus. In such clouds there is present an active convectional updraft of warm, moist air. In this rising air, condensation frequently begins as rain, but the drops are carried upward by the rapidly ascending currents. Thus they are lifted into cloud regions where the temperature is below freezing. Here they congeal and also acquire a coating of ice by sublimation. Eventually, they enter a weaker updraft and descend to lower portions of the cloud. Here they gather a coating of water, a part of which freezes around the cold center, and may then encounter another strong updraft and be carried upward again into the ice region. In these journeys they probably grow most rapidly by the freezing upon them of the supercooled water drops with which they collide. This is the older theory of the formation of hailstones.

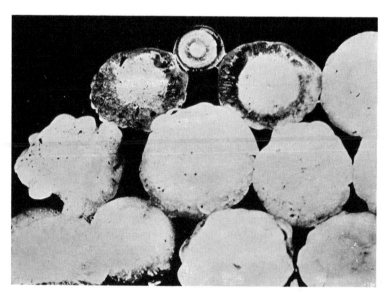

Typical Large Hailstones Showing Layer Structure. Courtesy, U.S. Department of Commerce, Weather Bureau.   **FIG. 5.6**

Another theory—now gaining wide acceptance among some meteorologists—states that hailstones are not necessarily formed by several such rising and falling movements; instead, they are formed simply by falling through subfreezing layers of air and capturing the supercooled water drops with which they collide. Hailstones sometimes acquire several alternate layers of clear and opaque ice and reach a large size before falling to the ground. The ultimate size of a hailstone appears to depend mainly upon the upward velocity of the air, the concentration of supercooled water in the air, and the length of its path through such air.

SNOW GRAINS, SLEET, AND GLAZE

Small grains of snowlike structures, forming opaque white pellets, are known as *snow grains*. Sometimes there is a fall of even smaller and flattened grains, consisting mostly of ice needles. This is called *granular snow*. At other times the grains are larger, rounded, more crisp, and rebound when striking hard ground, and are then called *soft hail*.

Sleet is precipitation in the form of small particles or pellets of ice which originally began to fall as raindrops but were frozen before reaching the ground. It may be safely assumed that most precipitation in the form of sleet occurs when there is a strong temperature inversion above the surface. The precipitation occurs in warm air above a significant layer of subfreezing air.

Precipitation sometimes occurs in the form of rain composed of supercooled drops which freeze rapidly upon striking solid surfaces. This results in the formation of a coating of ice on trees, wires, paving, and other objects. Such a deposit is called *glaze*. Its occurrence is often popularly called an *ice storm*. The damage to trees and wires, resulting from breakage by overweighting, is often large, especially when the storm is followed by high winds (Fig. 5.7). Deposits more than 2 inches in diameter have

Glaze Ice Storm Near Atlanta, Georgia, March 1961. Although ice storms   **FIG. 5.7**
are still prevalent, scenes like this one are becoming rare because most
trunk communication lines are in cable and usually underground, which renders them stormproof.
Courtesy, Southwestern Bell Telephone Company.

often been observed on wires and twigs. The slippery condition produced on paved walks and roads creates a serious hazard to pedestrians and motorists. There will be rapid and heavy icing of aircraft in flight in such a storm.

From the foregoing discussion, it is obvious that much remains to be learned about the physical processes involved in condensation and precipitation. An intriguing discovery by Vincent Schaefer in 1946 has stimulated **Cloud Seeding and Weather Modification** a great amount of research in this direction, especially in the United States and the Soviet Union. Scientists all over the world have become intensely interested in cloud physics and the secrets of the raindrop.

Schaefer first discovered that condensation and precipitation could be artificially induced in the laboratory from supercooled air. Shortly thereafter, Langmuir and Schaefer were able to induce snow to fall by dropping dry ice (frozen CO_2) into clouds from an airplane. It was soon demonstrated that various other nuclei, especially silver iodide, would trigger condensation when the general conditions were favorable. This set off a rash of attempted commercial rain-stimulation activities in various countries of the world.

RAIN STIMULATION

It has now been generally conceded that rain can be artificially induced or increased in amount under certain ideal conditions. Operating on the theory that clouds sometimes fail to release their moisture because of lack of adequate condensation nuclei (see page 106), several commercial companies have contracted to seed large areas with silver iodide crystals. These crystals are known to be good hygroscopic nuclei. They are seeded into the clouds from airplanes or by generators located at strategic places on the ground (Fig. 5.8). The seeding operation cannot create a rain situation at will, but may be able to stimulate more rain from a favorable situation than would fall normally.

Recognizing that far-reaching implications and involvements could ensue from any large-scale form of artificial control of the weather, Congress created the Advisory Committee on Weather Control in 1953. Careful checks of planned field experiments failed to reveal significant increases in precipitation resulting from stimulation techniques. The Committee's efforts did make clear, however, a great need for more basic knowledge of the precipitation processes. Until these fundamentals are understood, any large-scale attempt to control precipitation might result in serious harmful effects by upsetting the balance of nature. A National Center for Atmospheric Research has recently been established on Table Mountain, near Boulder, Colorado, to conduct intensive research on these problems.

Cloud-seeding Generator. Foundry coke is impregnated with a carefully   **FIG. 5.8**
controlled solution of silver iodide and placed in a hopper. A screw-type
feed releases fuel into the furnace at lower right. Silver iodide is vaporized in the intense heat of
the burning coke and is emitted into the air stream at the rate of about 1,000,000,000,000,000
(10^{15}) crystals per minute, each crystal being the potential center of a raindrop. (Note vents at top
of generator.) *Courtesy, Water Resources Development Corp., Denver, Colorado.*

MODIFICATION OF CLOUDS AND FOG

Ordinarily the desire to modify clouds and fog has been restricted to small-scale areas such as airports and harbors, and nearly always to dissipate or to dispel obstructions to vision. In a few cases, such as protecting an orchard from frost, it becomes desirable to be able to induce fog.

Numerous research efforts are underway to discover the most effective chemicals and methods of application to obtain desired results. It should be pointed out that, quite unintentionally, we are artificially modifying clouds and fog in many areas today through ejection into the air of industrial smokes and fumes and the exhausts of millions of cars and trucks.

Weather modification on any large scale presents huge problems and grave responsibilities. This idea was summed up by Dr. Alan T. Waterman, formerly director of the National Science Foundation, in an address to the New York Academy of Sciences in January, 1961:

> We must realize that if in the course of this global study we should acquire the ability to alter the processes of nature on a macroscopic scale, we should do well to enter upon such a course with caution. We are here dealing with forces almost beyond our imagination and we must not forget that we could unwittingly touch off a catastrophic reaction.

PROBLEMS

1.

On a calm, clear spring evening, the temperature begins to fall after 5 P.M. at the rate of 2°F per hour until the dew point is reached, and thereafter at 1°F per hour until 5 A.M. Assuming these basic conditions, answer the following questions, using the 5 P.M. data listed below. When will condensation begin? Will it be dew or frost? What will be the minimum temperature?

Temperature, 50°F; Relative Humidity, 61 per cent
Temperature, 50°F; Relative Humidity, 38 per cent
Temperature, 50°F; Relative Humidity, 80 per cent
Temperature, 45°F; Relative Humidity, 57 per cent

2.

At a noon observation on a quiet summer day, the temperature of the air is 90°, the wet-bulb thermometer reads 67°, and detached Cumulus clouds are observed. How high are the bases of the clouds? What is the temperature at the bases? If the clouds are 1,200 feet thick, what is the temperature at the top?

3.

If air on a plain 3,000 feet above sea level, having a temperature of 42° and a dew point of 36°, is forced over a mountain at an elevation of 12,000 feet above sea level and then descends on the other side. At what height will condensation begin? What will be the temperature at the mountaintop? What will be the temperature when the air has descended on the other side to its original altitude of 3,000 feet? *Note:* At this elevation and temperature, consider the wet adiabatic rate to be 3°F per 1,000 feet.

4.

Make a sketch drawing which shows all of the essential steps in the hydrologic cycle.

5.

If a sample of air has a temperature of 60°F, what is the vapor pressure if the relative humidity is 100 per cent? 50 per cent?

6.

Explain how evaporation can exceed precipitation in a given area. What kind of vegetation would you expect there?

7.

Why are the last killing frost in the spring and the first one in the fall more important than any other frosts?

8.

Write a brief story on the international implications of weather control.

6

interrelationships
of temperature,
pressure,
and wind

In the discussion of convection, we have noted some of the relationships between the pressure, temperature, and movement of the air, with particular attention to vertical movements. Additional relationships between these elements of the weather are now to be noted, especially with reference to horizontal, or approximately horizontal, movements of the air.

Large numbers of pressure records have been accumu-   **Pressure**
lated during the past hundred years from all parts of   **Gradients**
the world, and they show that the pressure of the air
is variable in a number of different ways. First, there is continuous variability of pressure at the same place from hour to hour. Second, pressures differ in adjacent places at the same time. Third, average pressures in different parts of the world are not the same. And finally, average pressures at a given place change with the change of season; they are not the same in winter as in summer. Pressure differences result from vertical and horizontal movements of the air brought about by differences in density, and these, in turn, are due chiefly to temperature differences.

ISOBARS AND PRESSURE GRADIENTS

To represent the various pressures over an area, lines known as *isobars* are drawn on a map through points of equal pressure at a chosen level. They may represent the distribution of pressure at a definite time, or the average distribution for a given period. On surface weather charts, isobars are usually drawn for each 3-mb variation in pressure (Fig. 6.1). Isobars may also be drawn on vertical cross sections through the atmosphere showing the distribution of pressure with height (Fig. 6.2). In the three-dimensional atmosphere, isobars become isobaric surfaces. If one could connect all the points over California having exactly a pressure of 800 mbs, they would form a surface rather than a line; but where the 800-mb surface was penetrated by mountains, there would be an 800-mb isobar along the mountain slope.

The curved lines in Fig. 6.1 represent isobars on a map, showing the pressure decreasing from 1,020 mb at the left to 1,011 mb at the right. Air pressure, as measured by the barometer and represented by isobars, is a force proportional to the weight of the air above the point of measurement. Simultaneous differences of pressure over an area, therefore, cause movements of air tending to equalize the pressure. A force pushes the air from the region of higher barometric pressure toward the region of lower pressure.

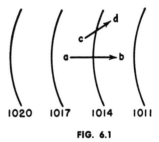

FIG. 6.1

Isobars and Pressure Gradient.

The difference between the pressure at the points *a* and *b* is the force that is pushing the air at *a* toward *b*. In every case, the magnitude of the force depends on the difference of pressure, that is, on the rate of change of pressure with distance. The rate of change of pressure per unit horizontal distance is called the *pressure gradient*. It usually means the change in a direction perpendicular to the isobars, since that is the direction in which the change is most rapid; but note that there are components of this gradient in other directions, also, such as *cd*. The gradient is expressed in millibars per hundred miles, per hundred kilometers, or per degree of latitude. Since the force increases as the gradient gets larger, the rate of movement of the air also increases. Both the direction and the speed of the wind are, therefore, the result of the pressure gradient, but the actual movement of the air is modified by the earth's rotation, by centrifugal force, and by friction.

ISOBARIC SURFACES

The vertical distribution of pressure in the air above a given area may be represented by lines drawn to indicate the heights at which pressures are equal. Such lines then represent isobaric surfaces in the atmosphere. Just as the ground-level pressures are not equal over the earth, the isobaric surfaces above the earth are not, in general, parallel with the ground but are warped in various ways. Although isobaric surfaces are not necessarily parallel to each other, they can never intersect

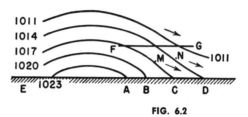

FIG. 6.2

Vertical Cross Section of Isobaric Surfaces and Resulting Air Movement.

because one point cannot have two pressures at the same time. If the points A, B, C, and D in Fig. 6.2 have pressures ranging from 1,023 millibars at A to 1,014 millibars at D, then the isobaric surfaces above ED may be as represented in the figure. The intersections of these surfaces with the ground are isobars. Consider the horizontal line FG at some distance above the earth, and note that the pressure is greater at F than at such points as M and N, although the latter are nearer the ground. There is, therefore, a pressure gradient outward and downward from F, and the air flows out from the region of higher pressure as indicated by the arrows.

A horizontal pressure gradient, if acting alone, would lead to a flow of air along the direction of the gradient, or perpendicular to the isobars. Motion in the atmosphere under a pressure gradient, however, is profoundly modified by an effect due to the rotation of the earth. The result is a flow perpendicular to the gradient instead of along the gradient, except for a greater or less deviation produced by friction in the lower levels.

Gradient Winds and Surface Winds

EFFECT OF THE EARTH'S ROTATION

An object moving in any direction over the surface of the earth tends continually to turn toward the right in the Northern Hemisphere and toward the left in the Southern Hemisphere. This deflection is the effect of the rotational motion of the earth and the movement of the body relative to the surface of the earth. The effect is the same as if the earth were at rest and a force were acting on the moving body. This influence is known as the *deflecting force* of the earth's rotation, or the *Coriolis force*.

Assume that a long-range cannon is located just north of the equator and is aimed due north at a target located on the 60th parallel. When the cannon is fired, the projectile will not travel due north, but will follow a trajectory to the right of north as indicated in Fig. 6.3. This occurrence is due to the relative difference in eastward velocity of points on the respec-

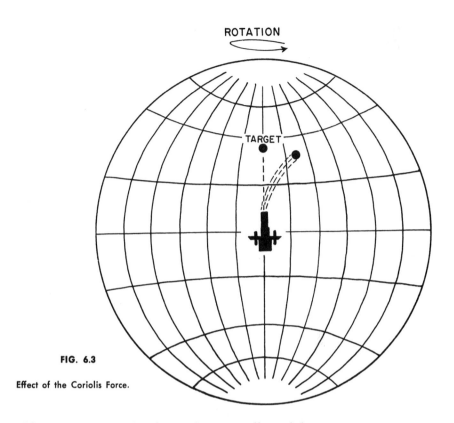

FIG. 6.3

Effect of the Coriolis Force.

tive parallels. In like manner it may be shown that, regardless of direction of movement, the deflection is always to the right in the Northern Hemisphere and to the left in the Southern Hemisphere.

The Coriolis force is not a real force, but only an apparent one, because we determine direction of motion relative to the earth's surface which is also moving in space. The effect of the earth's rotation on wind direction has the dimensions of acceleration. It is usually expressed as $(2V\Omega\sin\phi)$. From a basic law of physics, we recall that a force equals mass times acceleration $(F = ma)$. The Coriolis acceleration becomes a force when applied to a mass of air. It was first expressed mathematically by a French scientist, G. G. Coriolis, in 1844. It can be shown that:

$$C = 2V\Omega\sin\phi,$$

where C is the Coriolis acceleration, V is the speed of the wind, Ω is a constant (angular velocity of the earth's rotation), and ϕ is the latitude where the motion occurs. It can be recognized that the magnitude of C depends on the speed of the wind and the latitudinal location. For a given wind speed, C is zero at the equator and increases toward the poles, because the value of $\sin \phi$ varies from 0 to 1 from the equator to the poles.

The Coriolis force acts at right angles to the horizontal direction of the wind. It does not, however, have any effect on the speed of the wind.

125

The same effect is present in all motions relative to the surface of the earth, but it is inappreciable in most phenomena encountered in everyday experience because they are on a comparatively small scale. It does have to be allowed for, however, in calculating the motions of long-range projectiles. It is of major importance in considering the larger movements of the atmosphere. (See Chapters 7 and 8.) Hence, the fact that *moving air always tends to deviate to the right in the Northern Hemisphere and to the left in the Southern Hemisphere* should be definitely fixed in mind. It should also be remembered that the speed of the wind is not affected by the deflecting influence.

THREE FORCES AFFECTING MOVING AIR

Under a constant difference of pressure, the pressure gradient tends to move air in a straight line, but as soon as motion begins, the effect of the earth's rotation is to cause it to move in a curved path. When the curving motion begins, a centrifugal force is developed, tending to pull the air outward from its center of curvature. Like the Coriolis force, the centrifugal force is not a true force in the physical sense. It is more properly called centrifugal action or reaction. Hence, the movement of the air is the resultant of three influences acting simultaneously, namely, the pressure gradient force, the earth's deflection, and the centrifugal force due to the curvature of the path with reference to the earth. These forces are illustrated in Fig. 6.4. The force *p*, representing the pressure gradient, is always directed toward low pressure. You will note that it is outward from a high-pressure center and inward toward a low-pressure center. The Coriolis force, represented by *d*, is opposite *p* and to the right of the direction of the wind, *w*. The centrifugal force, *c*, is always outward from the center of curvature.

FIG. 6.4

Three Forces Affecting the Wind. Pressure gradient, *p*, starts the wind in motion and is balanced by the centrifugal force, *c*, and the Coriolis force, *d*, to create a gradient wind.

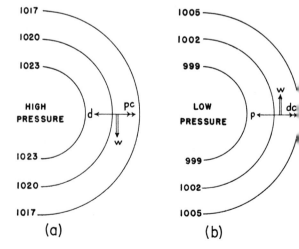

(a)   (b)

GRADIENT WINDS

It can be shown, mathematically, that the resultant direction of motion, under these three forces, is along the isobars instead of across them. The resultant speed and direction, when a steady state is reached, is such that the centrifugal, Coriolis, and gradient forces are in balance. A wind moving along the isobars at such a velocity that these three forces are in balance is called a *gradient wind*. Its instantaneous direction at the point of the forces is represented by the line *w*, parallel to the isobars. The speed of the gradient wind results directly from the pressure gradient, since the other forces exist only after the gradient has initiated the air movement. A special case exists when the isobars are straight and parallel and the gradient does not change over large areas. The centrifugal force in negligible and the gradient force is balanced by the Coriolis force alone. The wind is then called a *geostrophic wind*.

The gradient wind can be calculated when the pressure gradient is known. At heights of 1,500 feet and more above the surface, the actual wind closely approximates the calculated gradient wind, both in direction and in speed. These winds flow perpendicularly to the pressure gradient (parallel to the isobars), directed toward the right of the pressure force in the Northern Hemisphere and toward the left in the Southern Hemisphere.

SURFACE WINDS

Turbulence and friction near the earth's surface reduce the speed produced by a given pressure gradient. Friction has the effect of a new force acting in a direction opposite to the direction of the wind. With reduced wind speed, the deflective and centrifugal forces are less, whereas the pressure force remains the same. The resulting winds are, therefore, pulled around slightly in the direction of the pressure force, as indicated by Fig. 6.5. Wherever there is friction, the wind will tend to move across the isobars in the direction of the pressure gradient.

As a result of all these influences, we have the following general rule for

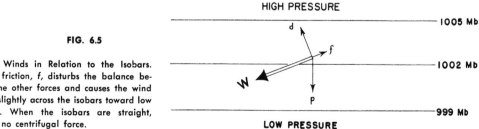

FIG. 6.5

Surface Winds in Relation to the Isobars. Surface friction, *f*, disturbs the balance between the other forces and causes the wind to flow slightly across the isobars toward low pressure. When the isobars are straight, there is no centrifugal force.

HIGH PRESSURE

1005 Mb

1002 Mb

999 Mb

LOW PRESSURE

the movement of the lower air: In a region of low pressure, the air has an inward-curving motion in a counterclockwise direction in the Northern Hemisphere, and clockwise in the Southern Hemisphere. This is called a *cyclonic circulation*. From a region of high pressure, the air moves spirally outward in a clockwise direction in the Northern Hemisphere, and in the opposite direction in the Southern Hemisphere. This is an *anticyclonic circulation*. In 1857, Buys-Ballot gave the following practical rule for determining the distribution of pressure from the wind direction: If you stand with your back to the wind, pressure is lower on your left than on your right in the Northern Hemisphere. The opposite is true in the Southern Hemisphere. This is sometimes referred to as *Buys-Ballot's Law*.

The following well-known winds develop under special circumstances and on a small scale as compared with the general circulation of the atmosphere. They serve to illustrate the direct relationships among tempera-

Winds Due to Local Temperature Differences

ture, pressure, and air movement. Some of them are due to unequal heating of the air and others are due to unequal cooling.

SEA BREEZE

Along the seacoasts, in the summer, the land warms more than the adjacent water by day. The warmed air over the land expands, bending the isobaric surfaces upward, and air flows out over the ocean from the upper surface of the expanded air (Fig. 6.6). This effect decreases the pressure over the land surface and increases it over the water. Air near the ocean surface begins to drift toward land, and thus a partial convectional circulation is set up which is called a *sea breeze*. The circulation is incomplete

Sea Breeze. The first result of diurnal heating of the land is the upward **FIG. 6.6** bending of the isobars over the land, producing an upper-level high; the second is the seaward flow of the upper air, reducing the surface pressure over the land and increasing it over the water; the third is the beginning of the flow of air in from the sea.

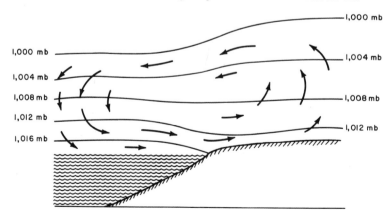

because the air that flows out over the ocean from the top of the expanded layer spreads out broadly, and the downward movement is slow and distributed over a large area. As a result, little of the original air returns to the land, but the lower air along the surface of the ocean flows inland.

Only a shallow layer of the air is affected by these changes; the sea breeze is usually not more than 800 to 1,200 feet (240–370 m) deep. It begins, usually about 10 A.M., some distance off shore and gradually extends inland to a distance of from 10 to 30 miles (16–48 km), and seaward about the same distance. Toward evening it begins to subside. At places around the Great Lakes, notably on the western shore of Lake Michigan, there is a similar lake breeze in summer which extends inland 2 or 3 miles (3–5 km).

Sea breezes have an important moderating effect on the temperature of coastal regions. Where the sea breeze is of daily occurrence, as in parts of California in summer, the afternoon temperatures average materially lower than they otherwise would, and the least agreeable part of the day is often in the forenoon before the breeze arrives. The cities of Chicago and Milwaukee have two summer climates, one within a mile or two of the lake shore, and a considerably warmer one a few miles back from the lake where the lake breeze does not reach.

LAND BREEZE

At night the land cools more than the water, the air over the land becomes denser than that over the water, and the isobaric surfaces aloft slope downward toward the land (Fig. 6.7). When this occurs, air from the ocean begins to flow inland at the top of the cooled mass, thus increasing the pressure over the land and starting a movement out to sea at the surface. This is the *land breeze*, a wind due to local cooling. Again the cir-

Land Breeze. The first result of nocturnal cooling of the land is the settling   **FIG. 6.7**
of the isobaric surfaces over the land, producing an upper-level low; the
second is the landward flow of the upper air, increasing the surface pressure over land; the third is
the beginning of the surface breeze toward the sea.

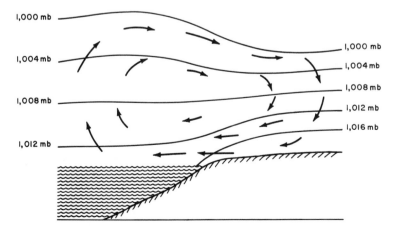

culation is incomplete; the vertical movements are so diffuse and gentle as not to constitute perceptible currents. The land breeze is usually less developed than the sea breeze; it is shallower, has less speed, and extends only 5 or 6 miles (8–10 km) over the sea. The principal reason for this effect is that temperature differences between land and water surfaces are less by night than by day. The effect of the land breeze is to remove the cooled air and to prevent the temperatures from falling so low as they would if the air remained in place. In temperate latitudes, sea and land breezes are most frequent in summer and when skies are clear. In tropical regions, they are frequent throughout the year.

VALLEY BREEZE

The heating of a valley floor and its slopes by day sometimes results in a slow movement of warmed air up the valley or up the sides of mountains. The isobaric surfaces bend upward over the valley, and the air flows toward the sides. With specially favorable topography to concentrate the movement, a strong up-valley breeze may develop by day. In some coastal valleys, sea and valley breezes combine to produce strong winds.

MOUNTAIN BREEZE

Air on mountainsides and sloping plateaus cools by night more rapidly than the free air some distance from the slopes or the air in the valleys below. The draining of cooler, denser air down the slopes into the valleys, under the action of gravity, is somewhat analogous to the flowing of water down hill, but the air spreads out from the mountainsides, as water does not, and mixes with other air. The downward movement results in dynamic warming which, by lessening the density of the air, retards its flow. Hence, the movement is usually slow, but the warming effect of descent is more than offset by radiation cooling. The cold air may collect in pockets in the valleys and produce inversions of temperature, so that in the end (by morning) the valley bottoms are colder than the hillsides from which the cold air has been displaced.

The air may converge in narrow canyons and then gain considerable velocity and extend outward a few miles from the mouth of the valley. In these cases, radiation cooling, which proceeds slowly, may be largely counteracted by adiabatic warming. In Utah the effects of this warming and of the turbulent mixing of the air by reasons of rapid motion are sufficient to prevent early frosts in autumn and thus to prolong the growing season on the bench lands at the mouths of canyons. In some mountain regions, the upslope valley breezes result in the formation of Cumulus clouds and daily afternoon showers during the summer. The rain ceases and the skies clear toward evening, as the valley breeze weakens and the mountain breeze begins to develop.

KATABATIC WINDS

Along the northern coast of the Adriatic Sea, a plateau region rises at the rear of a narrow coastal plain. In the winter, the air over this plateau sometimes becomes quiet and cold by radiation cooling. It then flows down the slopes as a cold, northeast wind, known as the *bora*. The bora occurs either day or night, but is most frequent and strongest when it occurs in the latter part of the night. A similar cold wind, coming from the higher and often snow-covered land to the north, occurs during the winter on the Mediterranean coast of France, where it is called the *mistral*. The bora and mistral are fully developed only when the pressure gradient has a southward component. Such winds as the mountain or canyon breezes and the bora and mistral are given the general name of *katabatic winds, gravity winds, or fallwinds*, due to the flowing of cold, dense air downslope under the pull of gravity. Fallwinds are common along the Norwegian coast, and violent katabatic winds often descend from the glacier-covered interiors of Greenland and Antarctica.

Sea breezes and valley breezes result from daytime heating; land and mountain breezes, from nighttime cooling; katabatic winds in general, from radiation cooling, whether diurnal or of longer period. Hence all are clear-weather phenomena, and all are rather shallow.

Monsoons

Just as along the coastlines the relationship between land and water temperatures changes daily under the influence of insolation by day and earth radiation at night, so in the longer period of a year there are seasonal temperature differences between entire continents and oceans. Continents are warmer than oceans in summer and colder in winter. The resulting tendency is to develop over continents relatively low pressure in summer and high pressure in winter.

Seasonal temperature differences set up convectional circulations analogous to sea and land breezes but having an annual, instead of a daily period. The wind tends to blow toward warm continental interiors in summer and from cold land areas in winter. These winds are called *monsoons*. Monsoons are winds that reverse their direction with the seasons under the influence of seasonal temperature differences between continents and oceans. They are best developed in eastern and southern Asia, where larger phases of the movement of the air are also involved, as will be noted later. They occur to some extent in Australia, the Spanish peninsula, and other places. In a large portion of the interior and eastern United States, the prevailing winds change from southerly in summer to northerly in winter. This reversal of the winds is a monsoon effect, and it is an important factor in the climate of the central and eastern states. It results in the presence of much warm and humid air from the tropical Atlantic and from the Gulf of Mexico in summer, and of much cold, dry air from the interior of Canada in winter.

Because of the great and permanent temperature con- **Polar-Equatorial** trast between tropical and polar regions, we might ex- **Air Movements** pect to find a convectional circulation, analogous to a sea breeze or a monsoon, between equator and poles. On a uniform, non-rotating globe there probably would be a continuous circulation of this kind, with surface winds blowing toward the equator and upper winds toward the poles. On the rotating earth there is, indeed, an interchange of equatorial and polar air, but not a simple continuous exchange in a closed path. The existing temperature differences on the earth do compel movements of air between high and low latitudes, but a number of factors serve to make these movements complex and intermittent.

MODIFYING INFLUENCES

The deflection due to the earth's rotation prevents a simple north-south interchange of air. Winds that start as south winds in equatorial regions become west winds in northern latitudes, and north winds from Arctic regions become east winds. The lack of uniformity in the change of temperature from equator to poles is another factor that prevents a simple interzonal transfer of air. Diversities of the earth's surface, such as the irregular distribution of land and water, the variations in elevation of the land, and differences of surface covering, all result in local or widespread temperature differences which prevent the development of a continuous temperature gradient between equator and poles. These temperature divergences create local pressure gradients not related to latitude, as is illustrated by the monsoons, sea and land breezes, and other local winds. In the third place, these temperature relationships change with the seasons, as the sun's rays shift north and south, thus interfering with a continuous circulation. Finally, there are irregular, moving disturbances of the atmosphere, to be discussed later, which render the actual zonal interchange of air still more complex.

All the winds discussed in this chapter are examples of the propensity of surface air to blow toward a warm area or away from a cold area. They also serve to exemplify Humphreys' concisely stated general principle: "Atmospheric circulation is a gravitational phenomenon, induced and maintained by temperature differences."

PROBLEMS

1.

Given the following sea-level pressure readings in millibars: Omaha, 1,029; Des Moines, 1,023; Davenport, 1,015; Chicago, 1,004; and the following distances between cities: Omaha to Des Moines, 120 miles; Des Moines to Davenport, 140 miles; Davenport to Chicago, 130 miles. What is the pressure gradient per 100 miles between each of the adjacent cities? If the wind velocity between Omaha and Des Moines is 15 miles per hour, what is the velocity between the other cities, assuming it to be proportional to the gradient? From what general direction is the wind blowing?

2.

Draw diagrams illustrating the pressure changes and air movements occurring in sea, mountain, and valley breezes.

3.

Small Cumulus often occur with a sea breeze but not with a land breeze. Why?

4.

Look up the meaning of the *sine* of an angle and explain why the Coriolis force is zero at the equator.

5.

Draw two sets of two concentric circles. Label one set "high pressure" and the other "low pressure." Now draw arrows to or from the four points of the compass to indicate the direction of the pressure gradient in each case. Dash in a deflection to the right of each arrow. This should show the direction of wind flow around high- and low-pressure areas in the Northern Hemisphere. Repeat this operation for the Southern Hemisphere.

6.

Considering the effect of the Coriolis force on wind direction, at what latitude should the wind blow perpendicular to the isobars? Why?

7.

Since the wind in the Northern Hemisphere is always deflected to the right by the Coriolis force, explain how wind can curve to the left around a low-pressure center.

8.

Why is a gradient wind not likely to be found near the surface of the earth?

9.

Are monsoons more pronounced in middle latitudes than in polar or equatorial regions? Why?

10.

Imagine a nonrotating earth with latitudinal heat differences between the poles and the equator like those we actually experience. Make a sketch diagram showing the hemispherical circulation of the atmosphere that could be expected.

7

the general
circulation

Pressure and winds are related phenomena of the same large problem that deals with the distribution of the air over the earth, the changes in distribution, and the processes by which the transportation of great masses of air is achieved. This constitutes the central problem of meteorology, about which many details remain unknown because of the great extent of the atmosphere and the variety and complexity of the influences affecting its movements.

Observations show that there are large areas of the earth where the winds are predominantly from one direction throughout the year, other areas where the prevailing direction changes with the season, and still others where the winds are so variable from day to day that no systematic movement is evident to the ordinary observer. Related to the variability of the wind direction is the fact, previously noted, that pressures are also changeable. Hence, it might be inferred that no simple, permanent plan of distribution of pressure and wind exists. Nevertheless, if, over the globe, we take the average annual pressure and the prevailing winds, we find not only that pressure and winds are closely related, but also that their distribution may be generalized into a simple system, dividing the earth into a few large zones or belts. The average distribution of wind movement is known as the *general circulation.*

The mean annual pressures over the globe are represented in Fig. 7.1. One can see that there is something of an orderly sequence of high and low pressure belts **Yearly Averages of Pressure** girdling the earth. In addition to latitude, the relative positions and size of the land masses contribute significantly to the characteristics of the various pressure belts. Observations made during the International Geophysical Year (IGY) indicate that the average pressure pattern is high over Antarctica but more variable than previously supposed. A study of the chart will disclose the following alternating zones of high and low pressure.

EQUATORIAL BELT OF LOW PRESSURE

In equatorial regions there is a belt where the pressure is less than 29.9 inches (1,013 mb) throughout, and less than 29.8 inches (1,009 mb) in parts of the Eastern Hemisphere. The belt varies in width, but completely encircles the earth. On the average, its center is somewhat north of the equator. Within the equatorial belt, the winds are generally light and variable, with frequent calms, but with an average slow drift from east to west. The entire belt is called the *doldrums,* but this word applied originally only to the ocean areas near the equator, where sailing ships were frequently becalmed.

SUBTROPICAL HIGH-PRESSURE BELTS

Centered at about 35° north and 30° south latitude, there are irregular belts where the average pressure is above 30 inches (1,016 mb) and within which are certain areas averaging more than 30.1 inches (1,019 mb). These are the *subtropical high-pressure belts* or the *horse latitudes.*[1]

The name *subtropical high* is applied especially to the centers of higher pressure within the belts. The northern belt, where large land and water surfaces alternate, is more irregular than the southern belt, which is largely over water and therefore under a more nearly uniform influence. These belts are regions of variable winds, averaging light and changing with the seasons. They are sometimes invaded by traveling disturbances attended by stormy winds.

---

[1] The name *horse latitudes* is said to have arisen in the days of sailing ships, when several Spanish vessels were becalmed at the center of the subtropical high-pressure circulation. The cargoes, consisting mostly of horses destined for the New World, were dumped overboard to lighten the ships and increase their mobility.

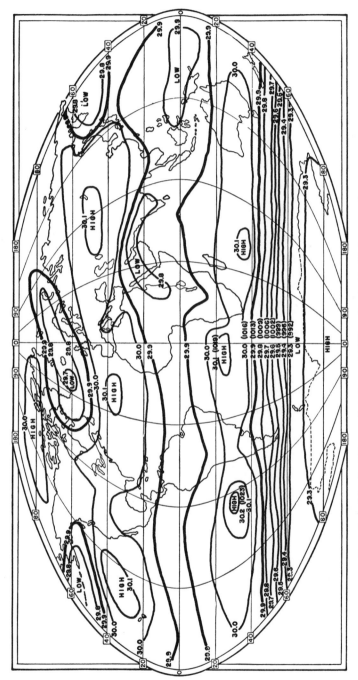

Mean Annual Sea-level Pressure in Inches and Millibars for the World. *Base map by permission of Denoyer-Geppert Co.* **FIG. 7.1**

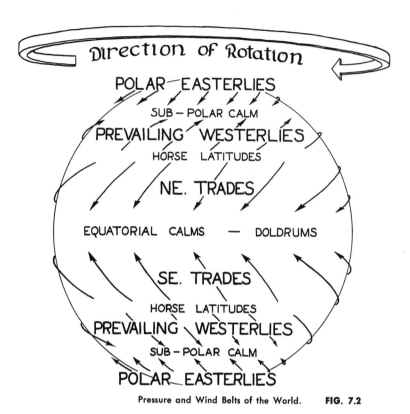

Pressure and Wind Belts of the World.   **FIG. 7.2**

The equatorial belt of low pressure and subtropical belts of high pressure may be explained as the expression of a convectional circulation, air rising in the heated doldrums, moving poleward aloft in both hemispheres, being deflected eastward by the earth's rotation, and finally accumulating and settling in the belts of higher pressure, out of which winds blow toward the equator (Fig. 7.2). The movements are probably not so simple and direct as this explanation implies, but undoubtedly convectional movements like this do occur. These belts are a prominent and permanent feature of the general circulation.

POLAR LOW PRESSURE

There is a continuous belt of low pressure in the Southern Hemisphere between latitudes 60° and 70°. This belt overlies a water surface. In corresponding latitudes in the Northern Hemisphere there are large, cold land masses, and their effect is to increase the pressure; but over the northern oceans there are well-defined areas of low pressure. These are centered in the vicinity of the Aleutian Islands in the Pacific and between Greenland and Iceland in the Atlantic. Winds from the west or southwest blow into these regions of low pressure from the equatorward side in accordance with the pressure gradient as modified by the deflecting influences.

POLAR CAPS OF HIGH PRESSURE

In the Arctic and Antarctic regions there exist more or less permanent caps of high pressure with prevailing easterly winds. In the Northern Hemisphere, the cap is not centered at the pole, but extends from northern Greenland westward across the northern islands of Canada. Even in polar regions where everything remains covered with ice and snow much of the time the different effects of land masses and water bodies are observable.

In Antarctica, the high-pressure cell is probably altered by the extreme height of the continent which averages about 10,000 feet in elevation. This means that the surface circulation is roughly comparable to the 700-mb level. During 1957, the sea-level pressure at Little America (78°S, 162°W) varied between 30.4 inches (1,029 mb) and 27.5 inches (930 mb). It has become apparent from the IGY observations that Antarctica is frequented by storms of great intensity. Winds are typically strong, averaging 15 to 17 miles per hour (7–8 mps) and often vary from the prevailing easterly direction.

CIRCULATION ZONES AND CELLS

In conformity with this general distribution of the pressure in alternating belts of high and low pressure, the general circulation is divided into three *zones* in each hemisphere. One of these is the zone between the subtropical high-pressure belt and the equator, in which winds move equatorward with a large component from the east. The second zone lies between the subtropical high-pressure and the polar-circle low-pressure belts, that is, between latitudes 30° and 60°, approximately, in each hemisphere. In this zone, the air moves poleward but by deflection becomes largely westerly. Finally, in the third zone, the air moves out of the polar cap of high pressure toward the lower pressures at about latitude 60°, becoming easterly by deflection. Thus, instead of a continuous circulation between equator and poles, such as would occur on a uniform, nonrotating earth, we find each hemisphere divided into three more or less independent *circulation zones* (Fig. 7.3).

Schematic Representation of the Cells of Atmospheric Circulation.   **FIG. 7.3**

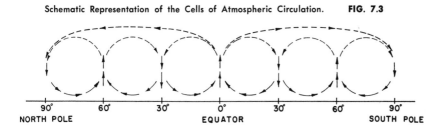

90° 60° 30° 0° 30° 60° 90°
NORTH POLE   EQUATOR   SOUTH POLE

A closer examination of the pressure belts shows that they are not of uniform pressure throughout, but that they are divided into a number of centers, or *cells*. There are centers of low pressure near the equator and near latitude 60°, and centers of high pressure in the subtropical belts of both hemispheres and near the poles. These centers of high and low pressure control or at least influence the air movement around them, resulting in the formation of several *cellular circulations*, some cyclonic, others anticyclonic. These are superimposed upon the zonal circulations, and the result is a meridional (north-and-south) movement of the air on the east and west sides of these cells. But on the whole, as a result of all the complex influences, the latitudinal (east-and-west) circulation is much greater.

The cells just mentioned are known as *centers of action* because it is along their boundaries that most storms originate and travel. They are also called *semipermanent centers* of high and low pressure because they tend to persist in the same general regions, but their exact position and intensity change with time. The entire zones shift northward in the northern summer and southward when it is summer in the Southern Hemisphere. They follow the sun and the seasonal changes, but they lag a month or two behind the sun. The seasonal change in the position and intensity of the cells is a monsoonal effect. The cells of low pressure tend to migrate in summer to the heated continental interiors from the cooler oceans, and the pressure is relatively higher over the oceans. In winter, the cells of high pressure are centered over the cold continental areas and low pressure is intensified over the relatively warm ocean waters.

January and July Averages of Pressure and Winds

The major differences in pressure distribution and wind direction between winter and summer are shown in Figs. 7.4 and 7.5. Let us now examine these charts and note in some detail the outstanding features of the general circulation and its component parts, the zonal and cellular circulations, as these are modified by the distribution of land and water and by the seasonal variations in insolation.

DOLDRUMS

In January, the continuous equatorial belt of low pressure has its centers of lowest pressure over the land areas in the Southern Hemisphere, where it is midsummer. Note the centers in equatorial South America, equatorial Africa, and northern Australia (Fig. 7.4). In July, the belt is almost entirely north of the equator, and low pressure extends far northward over North America and Asia, with minima in northwestern India and southwestern United States (Fig. 7.5). Within the doldrums, the air movement in the lower atmosphere is mostly from an easterly direction, but note that there

Mean January Sea-level Pressures and Wind Directions of the World. Base map by permission of Denoyer-Geppert Co.

FIG. 7.4

141

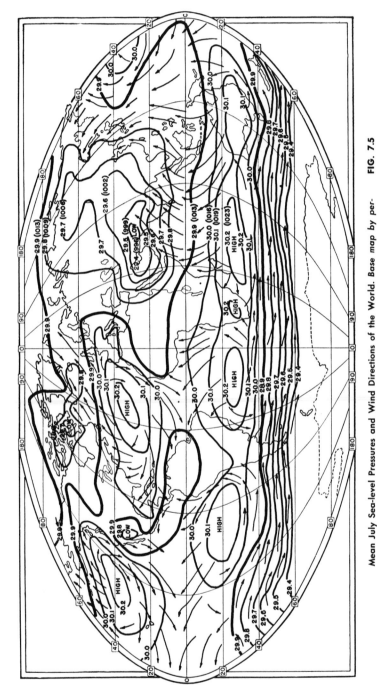

Mean July Sea-level Pressures and Wind Directions of the World. Base map by permission of Denoyer-Geppert Co.   FIG. 7.5

is a shifting between northeast and southeast with the seasons, as the center of the low pressure moves south and north. In January, northeast winds of the Northern Hemisphere extend to, and in some cases south of, the equator. In July, winds from the Southern Hemisphere cross the equator and reach 10° to 20° north latitude. The convergence of these winds in the doldrum region and the resulting vertical movements cause frequent and heavy rains throughout the year.

HIGH-PRESSURE BELTS

In January, the subtropical high-pressure belt is practically continuous in the Northern Hemisphere near latitude 30°, with somewhat higher pressure in the eastern parts of the Atlantic and Pacific than in the western parts of these oceans. In the Southern Hemisphere, where the land is warm in January, there are three maxima over the relatively cool oceans, in each case where the ocean water is abnormally cold for the latitude because of cold ocean currents moving northward.

In July, in the Northern Hemisphere, the high-pressure belt is broken by the development of low pressure over the hot interior regions of southwestern United States and southwestern Asia, but there are well-developed and extensive cells of high pressure over the cool ocean areas. The cell in the eastern Pacific is known as the *Pacific high,* or *Pacific anticyclone,* and that in the eastern Atlantic as the *Azores high,* or *Azores anticyclone.* These two cells are of great importance in their influence on the weather of all temperate regions of the Northern Hemisphere. South of the equator, although pressure has risen over the land areas, the centers of highest pressure remain over the oceans, as in January. The small proportion of land in these latitudes is not sufficient to reverse the pressure distribution as in the Northern Hemisphere.

TRADE WINDS

Between the doldrums and the belts of higher pressure, there are steady, moderate winds, known as *trade winds,* blowing out of the high-pressure areas toward the equator. As they move equatorward, they are deflected to the west and become *northeast trades* in the Northern Hemisphere and *southeast trades* in the Southern Hemisphere. They are best developed on the eastern sides of the oceans, in air flowing out of the oceanic peaks of high pressure. In these situations, they are remarkably constant in direction and speed, blowing almost uninterruptedly, day and night, winter and summer, with a velocity of from 10 to 15 miles per hour (5–8 meters per second). Such steady winds do not occur over large land areas, and even in the western portions of the oceans, the trades are less constant. They are confined to the belt between 30° north and 30° south latitude.

ALEUTIAN AND ICELAND LOWS

In contrast to the continuous belt of low pressure near the Antarctic circle, there are two distinct cells of low pressure near the Arctic circle. That in the north Pacific is known as the *Aleutian low,* and that in the north Atlantic, the *Iceland low.* Both of these are strongly developed in winter, for each is in a region where the temperature of the water is raised by warm ocean currents, and each is near large land masses that become very cold. In summer, Alaska and Siberia become decidedly warmer than the adjacent waters, thus reversing the temperature gradient. This is followed by a reversal of the pressure gradient; the center of low pressure moves to the continents, and the Aleutian low practically disappears. In the Atlantic area, Greenland, Iceland, and northwestern Europe remain comparatively cool during the summer; they do not warm sufficiently to destroy the Iceland low. The Aleutian and Iceland lows exercise an important influence on the weather of North America and of Europe, respectively, as will be noted later.

CONTINENTAL HIGHS OF WINTER

As indicated in the preceding paragraph and as shown in Fig. 7.4, the Aleutian and Iceland lows are separated in winter by areas of high pressure over the continental interiors. The regions of highest pressure are Mongolia in the center of Asia, and the Mackenzie Valley in northwestern Canada. These are regions of intense winter cold, and the high pressure is largely a response to monsoonal influences. In other words, the contrast between the abnormally warm waters of the Bay of Alaska and the north Atlantic, on the one hand, and the cold continents, on the other hand, results in the development of the strongly contrasting areas of high and low pressure in these latitudes.

PREVAILING WESTERLIES

Winds blowing out of the poleward sides of the subtropical belts of high pressure are deflected as they move into higher latitudes and become southwest winds in middle northern latitudes, and northwest or west winds in middle southern latitudes. These are known as the *prevailing westerlies.* They begin about 35° north and south latitudes and extend to the subpolar lows, in the vicinity of the polar circles. Near the surface of the earth, they are subject to many interruptions by storms and irregular, intermittent winds from all directions, but the prevailing direction is from the west. They are often called the *stormy westerlies.* At the Cirrus-cloud level, they come more steadily from a westerly direction. These winds persist throughout the year but are stronger in winter, especially in the north Atlantic and north Pacific, where the deepening of the Aleutian and

Iceland lows and the building up of high pressure over the continental interiors create steep pressure gradients. The area between latitudes 40° south and 50° south is almost entirely water, and the prevailing westerlies are strong and persistent throughout the year. The region is called by sailors the *roaring forties*.

POLAR EASTERLIES

Winds blowing out of the Antarctic cap of high pressure and deflected to the left are known as *polar easterlies*. While there are no winds blowing regularly from the sea around the north pole, there are prevailing outflowing easterly winds from Greenland and, in winter, from the cold centers of Siberia and Canada also, and these may be considered as representing the polar easterlies of the Northern Hemisphere. Recent observations in northern Alaska show that the prevailing winds are from the east below 3,000 meters (about 2 miles), and from the west above that height.

POLAR FRONT

The relatively warm prevailing westerlies meet the cold polar easterlies or the cold air from continental interiors along an irregular shifting boundary which is known as the *polar front*. The polar front is the boundary surface of the cold air as it advances toward warmer latitudes. From day to day, this boundary changes its position, swerving far northward or southward, especially in the Northern Hemisphere in winter. At times warm air swings north in the Atlantic to northern Scandinavia; at other times cold air streams southward from northern Canada or northern Eurasia, chilling the Gulf Coast of the United States or the Mediterranean coast of Europe. Perhaps some of this air from polar regions finally enters the trade winds and reaches the equator. It is along this moving polar front that the storms, or barometric depressions, characteristic of the weather outside the tropics, develop. The polar front will be discussed in greater detail in Chapter 9.

Our direct knowledge of the pressure and movements   **Winds Aloft**
of the upper air comes from observations of cloud
movements, especially of the cirriform clouds, from pilot-balloon observations, and from the records of instruments carried aloft. Additional data are accumulating from these sources, but as yet our knowledge of the normal circulation of the upper air remains incomplete. To get a picture of the distribution of pressure and winds at different levels, it is possible to supplement the observations with calculations based on assumed lapse rates. The increasing number of observations is making these calculations unnecessary, especially over the United States.

UPPER TROPOSPHERE

At upper levels in the atmosphere, the pressure pattern is much simpler than in the surface layers. The migratory highs and lows at the surface are usually shallow and lose their identity within the first mile or two of altitude. The resulting pressure pattern becomes latitudinal as the isobars trend generally east-west in response to the persistent belts of high and low pressures. It may be necessary to point out that winds normally increase in velocity with height above the earth's surface. This is generally true, at least up to the tropopause.

With practically no friction aloft, the winds respond to the existing forces to create gradient winds or geostrophic winds, according to the pressure pattern. Although there is considerable zonal transport of air at high levels as the winds meander over pressure troughs and ridges, the principal air movement is west to east (Fig. 7.6).

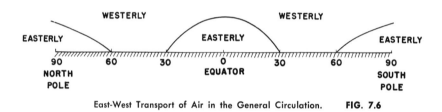

East-West Transport of Air in the General Circulation.   **FIG. 7.6**

ANTITRADES

The height to which the trade winds extend varies in different parts of the world and at the same place at different times of the year. The observed heights range between 3,000 and 13,000 feet (1–4 km). Above the trades, a direct reversal of the wind direction has sometimes been observed. These winds, from the southwest over the northeast trades and from the northwest over the southeast trades, are known as the *antitrades*. It was formerly believed that the antitrades represented a simple pattern of wind flow as a direct counterpart to the surface trades. Recent investigations in the tropics have revealed, however, that the upper-air circulation in the tropics is much more complex than was once supposed. The antitrades are not so constant as the trades, nor are they always present over them.

As the antitrades reach latitudes 30° north and south, they have been cooled by radiation and expansion and they have become deflected by the earth's rotation into a westerly current. This flow of cold air aloft tends to build up the subtropical high-pressure belts and encourage subsidence in these latitudes.

JET STREAM

A recently discovered atmospheric phenomenon, and one that is proving quite valuable in weather forecasting, is the *jet stream*. It is a narrow, meandering band of swift westerly winds that circles the globe in middle latitudes. Evidence of its existence was noted in 1922 when a weather balloon, released in England, came down only four hours later near Leipzig, Germany, some 570 miles (900 km) away.

During World War II, pilots flying bombing missions from Pacific bases to Japan encountered very strong head winds that almost arrested their flight and prevented them from reaching the designated targets. Subsequent research revealed the general characteristics of the jet stream.

The jet stream is a core of extremely swift winds in the prevailing westerlies of middle latitudes. It may range from 25 to 100 miles (40–160 km) in width and up to a mile or two (2–3 km) in depth. Wind speeds of 300 miles per hour have been recorded. The jet stream follows a serpentine path, but the movements are not entirely erratic and seem to follow a definite cycle. The velocity is strongest where north-south temperature contrasts are greatest. This indicates that the jet stream is located along the polar-front boundary and is strongest on the east side of continents during the winter months. It is believed to have much influence in steering air masses, which in turn are responsible for the general surface weather conditions. Because of turbulence along the fringes of the jet stream, it can be dangerous to pilots unfamiliar with it, but it is being successfully utilized for air travel.

It is evident from the foregoing discussion of the general circulation that the air is not completely shut off into separate compartments, but that much transposition and interchange of air occur from one pressure belt to another. **Latitudinal Interchange of Air**

MIXING PROCESSES

Some of the processes by which this mixing is accomplished are: (a) by the shifting of the center of the doldrums north and south of the equator, thus transferring air from one hemisphere to the other; (b) by the circulation of the air around the semipermanent centers of high and low pressure as they gradually change their positions with the changing seasons. For example, the centers of high pressure in the Northern Hemisphere change from the continents in winter to the oceans in summer, involving a change in the direction and the destination of large masses of air; (c) by the movement of great quantities of cold air equatorward and of warm air poleward along the polar front as it rapidly alters its position; (d) by the rising and settling of air in various parts of the world, displacing surface air with air from aloft and involving both in new circulations.

By such processes the air is kept mixed to a considerable extent, and this interchange of air has an important equalizing effect on the temperature. It is true that masses of warm air do accumulate in equatorial regions and cold air in polar regions, and the mixing is not perfect. If it were not for the winds, aided by the ocean currents, the equatorial zone would become unbearably hot, for it receives more heat than it radiates, and the temperature of the polar regions would fall extremely low in the long polar nights.

THE ASIATIC MONSOON

In the coastal region of China and in southeastern Asia and India, there is a complete reversal of wind directions with the seasons. This Asiatic monsoon furnishes a striking example of the transfer of air across the equator with the migration of the sun's rays. See the charts of January and July pressures and winds (Figs. 7.4 and 7.5). In the winter months, pressure is high over the cold interior of Asia, with inflowing air aloft. At the same time, the doldrums are south of the equator, with lowest pressure over northwestern Australia and adjacent islands. During these months the lower air, therefore, moves outward from the interior in an anticyclonic circulation and crosses the equator into the Southern Hemisphere. The wind is from the northwest in northern China, gradually changing to north in southern China, and then to northeast in Indo-China, India, and the northern Indian Ocean. Finally, it becomes northwest again after it crosses the equator and becomes subject to a Coriolis force directed to the left. Where the air does not pass over extensive water surfaces, it is very dry, because it has not been exposed to moisture sources.

This is the northeast (winter) monsoon of India and Indo-China. The coldest air is shut off by the mountains, and the air that reaches this region is warmed and further dried as it moves downslope from the northeast. In this season, therefore, the Indian Peninsula has moderate temperatures, light winds, and very little rain. In the latitude of Japan and eastern China, the winter monsoon is of moderate strength and subject to interruptions by traveling storms.

In the summer, there is a continuous pressure gradient from the high-pressure belt in the southern Indian Ocean to the low-pressure area in heated southwestern Asia. The southeast trades cross the equator and become the southwest monsoons of the northern Indian Ocean and of India and Burma (Fig. 7.5). As the warm, moist, conditionally unstable air from equatorial waters moves northward toward the Himalayas, it is forced upslope, and heavy to excessive rains result. This is the hot, rainy, summer monsoon upon which the crops depend.

Because of the steady, moderate breeze, which is stronger than the winter monsoon in this India-Burma region, the heat is less oppressive than it would otherwise be. Between seasons, in spring and again in autumn, while the pressure distribution is changing, winds are light and variable, and also hot and humid. At these seasons living conditions are rather uncomfortable. North of the mountains there is practically no rain, even in summer. The summer monsoons are from the south in southeastern China and from the southeast in Japan and northeastern China, forming a cyclonic circulation around the interior area of low pressure. They are attended by moderate to heavy, but usually not excessive, rainfall.

AIR MOVEMENT ACROSS THE EQUATOR

Not only in the Asiatic monsoon, but also in the trade winds in the Atlantic and Pacific Oceans, there is movement of air across the equator, northward in the northern summer and southward in the southern summer. This movement of surface air to the warm hemisphere must mean that the pressure is higher in the cold hemisphere, and hence that there is more air over the winter half of the globe than over the summer half. The average pressures obtained by observation show this to be true. While surface air travels to the warmer half of the earth, it is more than replaced by air moving in at higher elevations and settling over the cold continents.

SOURCES OF ENERGY

To move the masses of air involved in the general circulation requires an immense amount of work. Air, like all other material substances, has inertia; force is required to start it moving. After motion begins, friction and turbulence oppose the motion, reducing the speed of the wind and tending to break down the circulation and to make the air flow across the isobars into the areas of low pressure. Despite these opposing forces, such great currents of air as the prevailing westerlies and the trade winds continue without interruption.

The following four factors contribute toward the accomplishment of this work:

1. *Insolation.* The energy received from the sun results in an unequal warming of the air, largely because of an unequal warming of surfaces with which the air comes in contact. This inequality is due in the first place to the differing amounts of insolation received, but the character of a surface also influences its temperature.

2. *Gravitation.* The unequal heating of the air produces differences in its density, and the force of gravity then causes the heavier air to seek the lower level, displacing the lighter air.

3. *Condensation.* The latent heat released by the condensation of water

vapor supplies much energy and is often responsible for vigorous upward convection.

4. *Rotation.* The rotation of the earth results in changing the direction of the moving air and is responsible for the great amount of eastward and westward movement found in the general circulation.

These are the things which produce the movements of the air, and which, as limited by inertia and friction, result in maintaining the general circulation as we find it. The magnitude of the energies of the atmosphere are enormous. It is believed that a single well-developed thunderstorm possesses more energy than can be produced with a present-day thermo-nuclear reaction.

The primary source of energy is the sun, which causes convective movements of the air. Sir Napier Shaw expresses it thus: "There is nothing but thermal convection to act as the motive power for every drop of rain that ever fell and for every wind that ever filled a sail or wrecked a ship since the world began."

PROBLEMS

1.

Seek additional information about the trade winds. How did they get their name? Locate the most probable route that sailing ships once took on voyages from Europe to America and return.

2.

Use a string on a globe to measure the distance a sailing vessel would likely travel in sailing from London to the West Indies. How much farther is this than the most direct route? (A degree of latitude equals 60 nautical miles.)

3.

Why are the winds predominantly from the southwest over the Bay of Bengal in summer? Is it an unusual wind direction for that latitude? Explain.

4.

Describe the characteristic weather of the doldrums. Why does the air not flow in circular patterns near the equator like it does at higher latitudes?

5.

How much stronger is the Coriolis force on a wind of constant velocity at 60° N than at 30° N? What would be the magnitude of the Coriolis force acting on the same wind at the equator?

6.

Compare the locations and magnitudes of the principal low-pressure centers in July with those in January.

7.

Make the same comparisons between the high-pressure centers at the different seasons.

8.

What is the difference in the weight of air over Oklahoma from summer to winter if the average summer pressure is 29.9 inches and the average winter pressure is 30.1 inches? (Oklahoma contains approximately 70,000 square miles.)

9.

The prevailing winds are a fair approximation of the direction of ocean currents. What direction would a life raft drift if it was released on the equator in the middle of the Pacific Ocean?

10.

Toward what direction does the California Current flow? Would you expect it to be a cold or a warm current? Why?

8

the secondary
circulation

The general circulation and the movement of air masses, as discussed
in the preceding chapter, may conveniently be regarded as a background
upon which are superimposed many smaller disturbances and irregularities. It is like the flow of a river, with many eddies and cross currents. The
irregularities to be considered here are traveling disturbances, some of
which originate in high latitudes and others in the tropics. They are
closely associated with air-mass movements and frontal activity in causing the day-by-day weather changes in the temperate latitudes.

Little was known about the characteristics and behavior of moving
wind systems until about 100 years ago. Before discussing them here, it
seems advisable to note the device by which much of our present knowledge about them has been gained.

As the techniques of rapid communication were im-   **Weather Maps**
proved, it became more practical to try to produce a
composite graphical picture of weather conditions at periodic intervals.
Scientists in Germany, England, and America spent much time before
1850 trying to accumulate simultaneous observations of weather conditions

over a wide area. Before these could be collected and entered on a map of the area, several days had passed and weather changes of major proportions had occurred. Soon after the use of the telegraph became widespread, simultaneous weather observations could be quickly collected and charted, permitting inferences to be drawn about future changes in the weather. This was the beginning of weather forecasting on a scientific basis.

SYNOPTIC CHARTS

A synoptic weather chart is designed to present a view of the whole weather situation at one time. Weather observations are made at selected stations over the area to be represented. This information is collected by teletype and plotted on the chart at each station location. Analysis lines and symbols are drawn showing the distribution of pressure, temperature, air masses, fronts, precipitation areas, and the like (Figs. 8.2, 8.3, and 8.4). On a complete surface chart, data are also entered in station-model form showing amounts and types of clouds, wind direction and velocity, visibility, pressure changes, and so forth (Fig. 8.1). Such maps are usually prepared four times daily. Once a student has followed the progression of weather features through several map intervals, he will surely become aware that the synoptic weather chart is a powerful forecasting tool.

FIG. 8.1

Station Model for Plotting Synoptic Weather Data. The information is interpreted as follows: wind, northwest, Beaufort force 4; temperature, 67°F; distant lightning; visibility, 10 miles; dew point, 65°F; towering Cumulus with bases at 1,000 feet and Altostratus; pressure, 1001.7 mb, having risen 0.4 mb in an unsteady fashion during the last three hours; there has been a thunderstorm at the station during the past six hours.

Charts may also be drawn for levels other than the surface when upper-air data are available. Such charts are usually prepared for the 850-, 700-, 500-, and 300-mb surfaces. They do not show all the details of the surface chart, but they give a good picture of the distribution of pressure, temperature, humidity, and wind at those levels.

MAKING A WEATHER MAP

The making of a weather map requires the work of a large organization. First, there must be, over a large area, a well-distributed network of meteorological stations at which competent trained observers make synchronous observations of the weather. Second, the data so obtained must be collected rapidly by wire or radio at the centers where maps are to be prepared. Third, the information so collected must be quickly mapped to

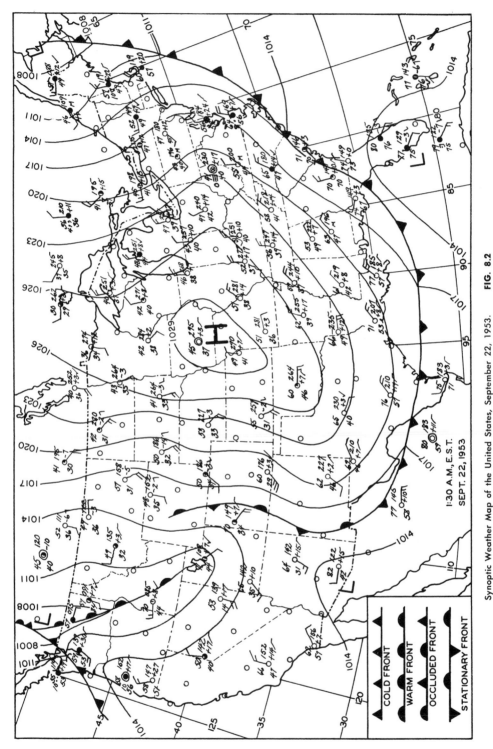

1:30 A.M., E.S.T.
SEPT. 22, 1953

Synoptic Weather Map of the United States, September 22, 1953. FIG. 8.2

COLD FRONT
WARM FRONT
OCCLUDED FRONT
STATIONARY FRONT

154

show the distribution and intensity of the weather elements. Fourth, from this picture of the weather, the forecaster must make his interpretations and inferences. Finally, the forecasts must be promptly distributed if they are to serve their purpose of informing the public and giving the news of the weather to those interested.

Numerous symbols have been adopted for use in the preparation of weather maps. We have already observed the symbols used in reporting wind direction and speed. Other symbols are used for high, middle, and low clouds and for present weather, past weather, barometric tendency, and cloud cover. The use of these symbols with several numerals permits entry on the map of much detailed information in quick order. To record the present weather at a station there are 100 different symbols from which to choose. There are ten symbols each to identify past weather, barometric tendency, and for each of the three cloud *etages*.

VALUE OF WEATHER MAPS

The entire system of short-period weather forecasting is dependent on the synoptic chart and the supplementary charts. From the picture of the existing weather thus set before him, the meteorologist is able to estimate with fair accuracy the changes that will occur in a given area during the next twenty-four to forty-eight hours. He can do this for a distant area about as well as for his own locality if he has become thoroughly familiar with the behavior of the weather in the area. This is true because he makes his forecast primarily from a study of the map. His inferences are based partly upon known physical laws governing the behavior of the atmosphere and partly upon familiarity with previous maps, that is, upon a knowledge of how the weather has behaved before under similar conditions.

During the time that weather maps have been available, they have been carefully examined, studied, and classified by many students. They have been proven indispensable in the making of weather forecasts and in the scientific study of many meteorological problems. They have not, however, completely fulfilled early expectations. They have not led to the explanation of all the phenomena of the air nor to the development of perfect weather forecasting. Much has been accomplished by their aid, but much remains to be done before a complete understanding of the atmosphere is reached.

If we examine even a short series of weather maps, we find that the isobars do not have the same regularity of spacing and direction that is shown on the charts of the **Low-pressure Centers** general circulation. Instead, the isobars are disturbed by irregularities of pressure and assume various shapes and patterns which change their loca-

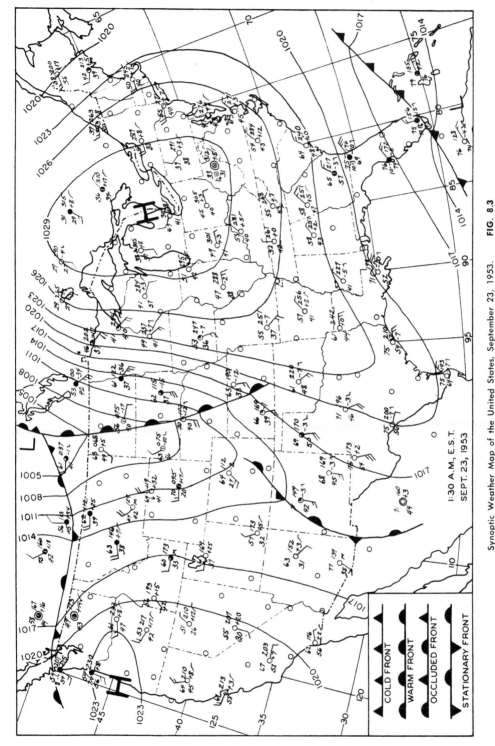

Synoptic Weather Map of the United States, September 23, 1953.   **FIG. 8.3**

1:30 A.M., E.S.T.
SEPT. 23, 1953

COLD FRONT

WARM FRONT

OCCLUDED FRONT

STATIONARY FRONT

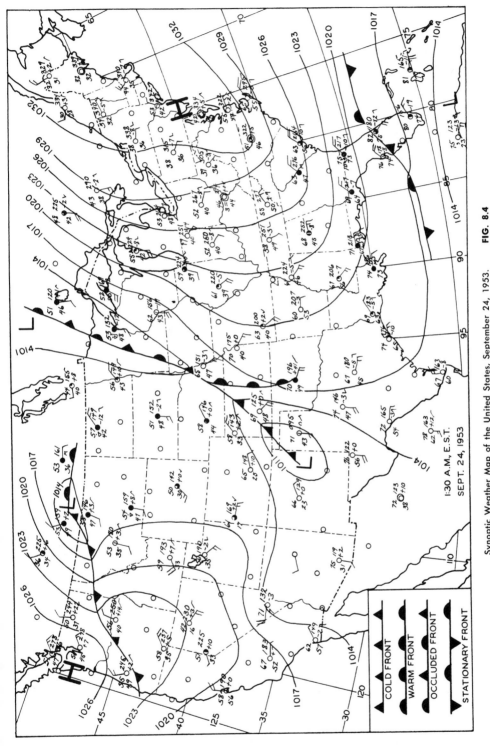

Synoptic Weather Map of the United States, September 24, 1953.

FIG. 8.4

1:30 A.M., E.S.T.

SEPT. 24, 1953

COLD FRONT

WARM FRONT

OCCLUDED FRONT

STATIONARY FRONT

157

tions and alter their shapes and patterns from day to day. Two patterns most easily recognized and of great importance in understanding the weather are those which enclose areas of low or high barometric pressure. A low-pressure center which is enclosed by one or more isobars is often called a *cyclone*.

CHARACTERISTICS OF CYCLONES

The cyclone is a barometric depression marked by a series of roughly circular or oval isobars inclosing an area of low pressure, that is, where pressure decreases from its outer rim to its center (Fig. 8.5). Such a system has long been known in meteorology as a *cyclone* or an *extratropical cyclone*. The word *cyclone* carries the idea of a revolving storm. The names *depression, cyclonic depression,* and *low* seem preferable, because it is now known that such a traveling disturbance is not always composed of a revolving mass of air, and also because the name *cyclone* has been applied to storms of a different nature (the tropical disturbance and the tornado, to be noted later). However, the name *cyclone* is well established to designate the type of pressure pattern discussed in this section.

Individual lows differ greatly in size, ranging in diameter from 100 to 2,000 miles, the average diameter in the United States being 1,000 miles or more. They also vary in form from approximate circles to much elongated ovals. The ovals are sometimes so much flattened at one end as to receive the name of *V-shaped depressions* and sometimes become so broad and shallow that they are called *troughs of low pressure*. When thus greatly elongated, they lose some of the features generally regarded as characteristic of cyclones. The typical round or elliptical low has, near the surface of the earth, moderate winds directed inward and around the center of low pressure, making an angle of from 20° to 40° with the isobars. The direction of movement is counterclockwise in

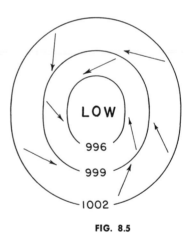

FIG. 8.5

Barometric Depression Showing Cyclonic Circulation in the Northern Hemisphere.

the Northern Hemisphere, responding to the influence of the earth's rotation and the pressure gradient. Such a movement of air around a center of low pressure is called a *cyclonic circulation* (Fig. 8.5). Cloudiness and precipitation are usually associated with a cyclone.

SOURCE REGIONS

Low-pressure systems are associated with the equatorward movements of the polar front and usually originate outside of the tropics, more frequently in high latitudes. They are more numerous and better developed in winter than in summer. In the Northern Hemisphere, many begin in the North Pacific and the North Atlantic oceans—most frequently in the regions extending from their western borders eastward to the Aleutian and Iceland lows. Many have their origin in the region of China and the Philippines. Others that affect the United States begin in western Canada, or in western and southern portions of the United States. In the United States, lows are given names indicating their place of origin or first appearance on the weather map: Alberta, North Pacific, South Pacific, northern Rocky Mountain, Colorado, Texas, East Gulf, South Atlantic, and central. Of these, the Alberta low is the most frequent, and those that come from the East Gulf and South Atlantic regions are the least numerous. Lows from the different regions have somewhat different characteristics and paths. A *secondary low*, having the same general characteristics, frequently develops on the equatorward side of the primary depression. This is especially likely to occur in elongated-oval or V-shaped depressions.

MOVEMENT OF LOWS

The general direction of motion is from west to east, with frequent trends to southeast or northeast. Each individual depression, in fact, seems to select its own path as it makes its way eastward. There is no fixed path which all follow, but there are general tracks more frequented than others. The lows originating in the western Pacific move northeastward by way of Japan and the Kurile Islands to the Bay of Alaska. From there they move southeastward, as do those that have their beginning in the Aleutian low, to enter the continent as North Pacific or Alberta lows. Across North America, there are three predominant paths: (a) eastward along the border of the United States and Canada; (b) from western Canada or the North Pacific southeastward into the Mississippi Valley, and thence northeastward to the Great Lakes, The New England states, or the St. Lawrence Valley; (c) from the southwestern region eastward to the Mississippi Valley and then northeastward to New England. Typical paths of the nine named types are shown in Fig. 8.6.

Some of the cyclones from North America cross the Atlantic Ocean to Europe. Most of these, together with those that begin in the North Atlantic, move northeastward across or north of the British Isles into Russia. Some curve farther south and enter Europe by way of France. The rates

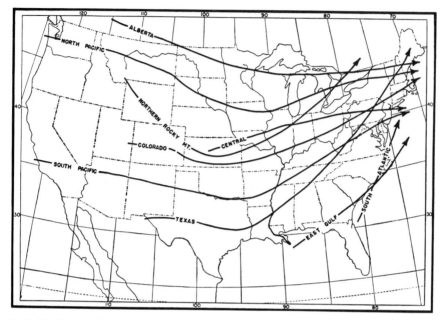

Typical Paths of Cyclones Appearing in Various Regions of the United   **FIG. 8.6**
States. *After Bowie and Weightman.*

at which the cyclones advance are variable and individual, like their paths. The average movement is 20 to 30 miles (30–40 km) per hour. The higher averages occur in winter and the lower in summer.

By thus giving different names to the cyclones originating in different regions, and by following individual disturbances for considerable distances, we seem to treat them as independent entities; but the fact should be kept in mind that they are comparatively small irregularities in the larger, more orderly movements of the air. They are not independent of the general circulation but are interruptions in its symmetry. They are found along the boundaries (fronts) between adjacent air masses and move somewhat as the air masses move. The air in a low-pressure center usually consists of the air along the edges of two or three adjacent air masses. (See Chapter 9 for a more detailed discussion of air masses). In this case, the different air masses are separated from each other by frontal surfaces. The apparent circular wind flow, characteristic of moving cyclones, is the result of separate wind movements in each of the contributing air masses.

The other characteristic pattern of isobars to be ob-   **High-pressure**
served on almost any weather map is the *high-pressure*   **Centers**
area or *anticyclone*, sometimes simply called a *high*.

CHARACTERISTICS OF ANTICYCLONES

Isobars enclose an anticyclone in circular or elliptical fashion. Winds spiral outward around the center, clockwise in the Northern Hemisphere, gradually crossing the isobars toward low pressure. This system of diverging winds constitutes an *anticyclone circulation* (Fig. 8.7). The area within the closed isobars is often larger than in a cyclone, and the pressure gradient is smaller (the isobars are farther apart). Winds are generally light in conformity with the pressure gradient, and calms are common near the center. There is usually little cloudiness, although heavy clouds and precipitation may characterize the advancing edge of a moving anticyclone in the area near the frontal boundary. In the Northern Hemisphere, the eastern half of a traveling high is cool or cold at the surface with northerly winds, while the western half is relatively warm with southerly winds.

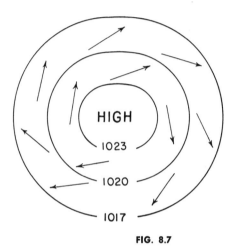

FIG. 8.7

Anticyclone and Clockwise Circulation in the Northern Hemisphere.

Unlike a low-pressure center, which may be composed of two or more air masses, an anticyclone usually consists of a single air mass with more or less homogeneous properties. Identifying characteristics of temperature and humidity can be traced to the life cycle of the circulation, including its source region and trajectory.

TRACKS AND VELOCITIES

The movement of anticyclones is similar in general to that of cyclones, highs and lows often following each other in regular succession. This is particularly true in middle latitudes of the Southern Hemisphere, where the surface is largely a water surface. There, the regularity is such as to form a wavelike procession around the earth. Over the large land areas of the Northern Hemisphere, highs are more likely to become stationary, or nearly so, than are lows, and their progress sometimes comes to resemble spreading rather than traveling. They then become isolated areas of high pressure with lows moving past them on either side. Such stagnation occurs more frequently in Europe than in America.

The principal types of American highs, named according to the regions

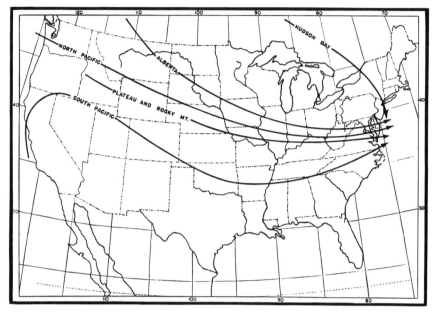

Typical Paths of Anticyclones Appearing in Various Regions of the United   **FIG. 8.8**
States. *After Bowie and Weightman.*

where they develop are: Alberta, North Pacific, South Pacific, Plateau and
Rocky Mountain, and Hudson Bay. It will be noted in Fig. 8.8 that their
average paths differ somewhat from those of cyclones, and in particular
that they enter the Atlantic Ocean farther south. The cyclones appear to
be attracted by the Iceland low; the anticyclones remain south of it.

In connection with the formation and maintenance of   **Nature and Origin**
cyclones and anticyclones, two primary facts about   **of Highs and Lows**
their nature are to be kept in mind: (*a*) in a low, air is
moving inward toward a center, and some of it is being carried up and
removed at the top; (*b*) in a high, air is added at the top and is slowly
flowing out at the bottom. Any theory of their origin must account for
these facts and for the supply of energy which maintains and moves them.

CONVECTION THEORY

Early attempts to explain the genesis of cyclones were along the lines of
convection. It was assumed that a low was a mass of warm, moist air, rotating around a center where the air was rising by thermal convection, and
that the overflow formed the adjacent high. Further knowledge of the actual conditions obtaining in lows and highs shows that this explanation is

inadequate and not in agreement with the facts. Some of the reasons for the rejection of this theory are: (*a*) lows are more frequent and better developed in winter, when convection is less active, than in summer; (*b*) they frequently begin over oceans, where surface heating is negligible; (*c*) the depression or low-pressure system as a whole usually is not a single body of warm air revolving around a center.

These facts seem to exclude local heating of the surface air as a primary cause of cyclonic depressions. Brunt has pointed out, however, certain special conditions under which the origin of a moving low may be ascribed to surface warming. When a mass of cold air moves from polar regions into warmer latitudes and passes over progressively warmer land or ocean surfaces, the lower layers are warmed. Thus convection may begin over a large area. If the rising air is soon saturated and if the lapse rate is between the dry and the saturated adiabatic rates, the upward motion thus begun may continue to great heights and over a large enough area to initiate a characteristic cyclone. It should be noted, also, that *stationary* areas of low pressure frequently form over heated regions, as in Arizona in summer, and are properly called *heat* or *convection lows* but may not have cyclonic circulations.

POLAR-FRONT THEORY

Originating with the Norwegian meteorologist V. Bjerknes, a more definite explanation of the origin of cyclones and anticyclones has been developed since about 1915. Instead of a gradual, uniform change of temperature from equatorial to polar regions, Bjerknes envisages masses of cold air accumulating in polar regions and masses of warm air in equatorial and tropical regions. In the region of the prevailing westerlies, these masses of cold and warm air meet and thereby form a *surface of discontinuity*, a well-marked and distinct surface of separation between the two masses. This surface is the *polar front* (see Chapter 9), across which there is a sudden change in the temperature of the air and often in its humidity. Irregularities of flow along the polar front are thought to initiate depressions, and the energy of flow of the two masses of air combines with the instability due to their difference in density to develop and maintain them.

The essential condition for the formation of a cyclone is the existence of bodies of warm and cold air adjacent to each other. The meeting of large masses of air of different temperatures and humidities and moving in different directions is the best available basis for the study and interpretation of the weather phenomena attending cyclones.

ORIGIN OF ANTICYCLONES

An examination of the paths of typical highs originating in Canada and the United States shows that most of them follow closely in the rear of well-developed lows. The active circulation engendered by the depression, with northerly winds on its western side, brings down a surge of cold air from northerly regions. Because the pressure is high in this cold, dense air, the surface air is forced out at the bottom, thus starting an anticyclonic circulation.

At other times we may have a single large mass of cold air moving southward, irrespective of the presence of a preceding low. In polar regions, in the area between the prevailing westerlies and the polar easterlies, there are often large masses of air having little movement. This quiet air becomes continually colder by radiating its heat to the cold earth and the clear skies. Consequently, it settles, the isobaric surfaces bend downward, other air moves in above it, and the pressure increases. When the pressure becomes too great, a portion of this cold air breaks off and flows southward, forming a tongue or wedge of cold air protruding into the warm westerly winds. (See Fig. 8.9.) This puts an obstruction across the flow of the westerlies, reducing the

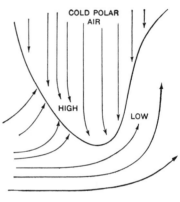

FIG. 8.9

Wedge of Cold Air Invading a Warm Current. A cyclonic circulation is beginning on the east, and an anticyclonic circulation on the west.

pressure on the eastern side of the wedge, forming a depression there, and piling up the air on its western side to form an anticyclone.

TWO TYPES OF ANTICYCLONES

Highs crossing the United States and Canada begin as surges or wedges moving southward from polar regions and may be regarded as moving masses of cold air in the lower troposphere. Their depth is ordinarily only 1 or 2 miles (1 1/2–3 km) but is sometimes greater. In winter there is frequently a stagnant high over the plateau region of western United States, but the typical anticyclone of North America is a shallow, moving high. Such highs are the result of the presence of cold air near the surface of the earth. Hence, they are called *cold* or *shallow anticyclones*. There is subsidence in the cold air with divergence near the surface and inflowing warmer air aloft.

Sometimes, the highs originate as shallow anticyclones and then develop into large and relatively warm high-pressure areas. These are known as *warm* or *deep anticyclones* and more nearly resemble the semipermanent high-pressure systems of the subtropics. Deep anticyclones are not as mobile as the shallow type, and when one becomes established over a continental area in summer, prolonged "heat-wave" and "drought" conditions may result.

Unlike the oscillating surges of pressure with the **Atmospheric** frequent passage of highs and lows in middle lati- **Circulation** tudes, the pressure pattern of the tropics is more **in the Tropics** persistent. A low-pressure belt, or *equatorial trough,* extends latitudinally around the earth and is flanked on either side by semipermanent high-pressure belts, or *subtropical ridges,* with characteristics similarly persistent. The equatorial trough and the subtropical ridges migrate north and south with the change of seasons, the former shifting through 20 degrees of latitude while the ridges shift only 5 or 6 degrees.

PRESSURE, WINDS, AND WEATHER

The mean pressure of the equatorial trough is from about 1,010 to 1,012 mb, with a very flat pressure gradient increasing gradually toward the subtropical ridges (Fig. 8.10). Isobars trend east-west, but may meander considerably owing to the flatness of the pressure field or to tropical disturbances. Diurnal variations in pressure at a given station may exceed the daily variations over a much longer period of time. As a result, meteorologists have found isobars to be a less useful tool for weather analysis in the tropics than in higher latitudes.

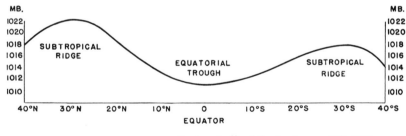

Pressure Profile of the Tropics.   **FIG. 8.10**

Streamlines are used in tropical weather analysis to examine the horizontal wind field. To a degree, they will also represent the pressure distribution; but, since streamlines have no numerical values, they can give no quantitative measure of pressure. They are drawn parallel to the wind direction everywhere and give a qualitative picture of wind direction and speed (Fig. 8.11). Like most other weather charts, a

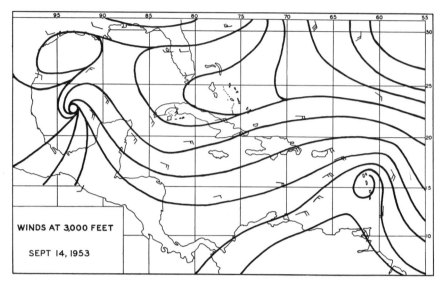

Streamline Chart of the Caribbean Area. After Herbert Riehl.   **FIG. 8.11**

reliable streamline analysis requires a fairly dense network of reporting stations. Lack of data is one of the principal handicaps of the synoptic meteorologist in the tropics.

The equatorial trough is flanked by the easterly trade winds which converge from the northeast and the southeast. (Fig. 7.2 on page 138). This converging air convectively rises above the equatorial trough; otherwise, the trough would necessarily fill. The convection gives rise to Cumulus and thundershowers, which are typical of that region.

Convergence of the trades from the two hemispheres often sets up one or more lines of squalls or thunderstorms which many meteorologists have called an *intertropical front*. This concept was especially prevalent during World War II. It is more commonly agreed today, however, that a front in the true sense seldom exists in the equatorial trough because the two converging air streams usually lack the necessary temperature contrast. Furthermore, the bands of weather sometimes shift erratically, jump, or completely disappear in a fashion that is not characteristic of frontal activity. A more satisfactory name for this equatorial phenomenon is *intertropical convergence*.

EASTERLY WAVES

Waves have been recognized and studied in the westerlies of middle latitudes for many years. The *easterly wave* is a more recently discovered phenomenon of the trade winds. It may be detected by an area of squally weather, a poleward bulge in the surface isobars or streamlines, or by careful analysis of the upper-air data.

The cause of the easterly wave is somewhat obscure, but undoubtedly it is related to perturbations or large eddies in the general circulation of the atmosphere. Once developed, an easterly wave tends to perpetuate itself and move along the equatorward boundary of the subtropical ridge from east to west. The typical wave is about 15 degrees of longitude in length, has an amplitude of from 1 to 5 degrees of latitude, and moves toward the west at from 10 to 20 miles (15–30 km) per hour. It brings cloudiness and precipitation to the area over which it passes and sometimes moves out of the tropics by curving north, then east. In this case, the easterly wave may become associated with a pressure trough and move northeastward as an *extratropical cyclone*. The most important characteristic of the easterly wave, however, is its tendency to incubate or propagate hurricanes and typhoons.

PROBLEMS

The maps on pages 154, 156, 157, 231, 232, and 233 make up a six-day series of synoptic charts at twenty-four-hour intervals. Use this or any other six-day series of weather charts to answer problems 1–7.

1.

Determine the size of the highs and lows within the closed isobars, noting the length and direction of the longest and shortest diameters.

2.

Determine the direction and speed of motion of the individual highs and lows.

3.

Determine the distribution of temperature about the centers. Where is its highest? Where is its lowest? Where are the sharp discontinuities of temperature?

4.

Determine the distribution of cloudiness.

5.

Where, with reference to the centers of the depressions, is rain falling at the time of observations?

6.

Determine the direction and velocity of the winds in the different quadrants of the lows and highs, and note their relation to the pressure gradient.

7.

Note the locations where significant weather changes seem to be occurring. In these locations, can you detect any relationship between sharp temperature differences and such things as wind shifts, clouds, and precipitation?

8.

Why are streamlines sometimes more practical than isobars for analyzing surface weather maps in the tropics?

9.

Are clouds more commonly associated with cyclones or anticyclones? Explain your answer.

10.

You will note that only the last three digits are used to plot station pressure to the nearest tenth of a millibar on the synoptic weather maps. How is it possible to know that a station plot of 122 means 1,012.2 mb instead of 912.2 mb?

9

air masses
and fronts

As noted in the previous chapter, there is a general circulation pattern which tends to persist from season to season over the earth. This pattern obviously does not remain fixed in all its details, even for a short period of days, or the weather would tend toward monotony in all parts of the world.

Variations of intensity in the high- and low-pressure belts permit the accumulation of large masses of air over certain geographical regions. As a mass of air lingers over a single region without being replaced by new air, it tends to assume the temperature and humidity characteristics of that region. Conflict results when two such air masses finally move together from different source regions. Some of the principal weather characteristics of the middle latitudes are created in this manner. Air masses take a leading role in the weather drama. Present-day weather analysis and forecasting consist, too a large degree, of studying the structure and characteristics of air masses and their interactions when they converge.

An *air mass* may be defined as a large body of air of   **Air Masses**
considerable depth which is approximately homoge-
nous horizontally. At the same level it has nearly uniform physical properties, especially as regards its temperature and its moisture con-

tent. Such masses are formed over large uniform areas of land or water surface where the wind movement is light. Under these conditions, the air near the surface gradually takes on uniform characteristics, approaching those of the surface over which it lies, and the air above adjusts itself to the temperature and moisture conditions at the surface. The principal processes bringing about this adjustment are radiation to and from the air, vertical convection, turbulence, and horizontal movement (advection).

The warm waters of the Gulf of Mexico and the Caribbean Sea and similar areas in the Pacific Ocean between Mexico and Hawaii are areas over which great masses of warm air accumulate. These are regions of light winds on the edge of the trade-wind belt. The snow- and ice-covered areas comprising northern North America and the adjacent portions of the Arctic Ocean are sources of extremely cold air masses. Observations show that the movement of air in northern Alaska is from 30 to 40 per cent less than in the United States. The same is probably true for the Mackenzie River Valley of northwest Canada. This region is therefore favorable for the accumulation of masses of cold air.

Eventually the air masses are carried in the general circulation from their *source regions* to other parts of the world. Thus, warm, moist, tropical air is transported northward, and cold, dry, polar air southward. As they move, they tend to retain their properties, especially in their upper portions. The surface layers are more or less modified by the surfaces over which they move. After the two masses from different sources meet, they tend to preserve their identities. Instead of mixing freely, "fronts" or "discontinuities" develop along the boundary zone. As a front crosses a given place on the earth, there is an abrupt change in the properties of the air due to one air mass replacing another. It is along these fronts that the principal changes in weather occur. Of primary importance to the weather is the distribution of temperature and moisture in the two air masses.

CLASSIFICATION OF AIR MASSES

There is some lack of uniformity in the classification of air masses, but the following conforms to present American usage and includes the air masses that affect the weather of the United States. With reference to latitude of origin, air masses are divided into four types, namely: *arctic* (A), *polar* (P), *tropical* (T), and *equatorial* (E). The differences between arctic and polar air and between equatorial and tropical air are relatively small. Arctic and equatorial serve as superlatives to emphasize the degree of coldness and warmness of the air masses, respectively, as well as to emphasize the extremes of place of origin.

Air-mass types are subdivided with reference to the nature of the surface over which they originate into *continental* (*c*) if the air mass originates over land, and *maritime* (*m*) if it has its origin over water. An air mass is further classified according to its low-level temperature relative to the surface over which it is passing. It is important to the meteorologist to know whether the air mass is being heated or cooled by the earth's surface. Cooling from below favors stability, and heating favors instability. From surface observations, then, the air mass can be classified as *warm* (*w*) or *cold* (*k*), meaning, respectively, that it is warmer or colder than the surface with which it is in contact. One additional type of air mass is generally recognized. It is composed of very dry air descending from aloft and is known as a *superior* (*S*) or *subsidence* air mass.

TABLE 9.1   Air Masses of North America

TYPE	SYMBOL	SOURCE REGIONS
Polar continental	*cPk* *cPw*	Canada, Alaska, Arctic region.
Polar maritime	*mPk* *mPw*	Northwestern Atlantic, North Pacific, particularly in vicinity of Aleutian low.
Tropical continental	*cTk* *cTw*	Southwestern United States and northern Mexico, in summer only.
Tropical maritime	*mTk* *mTw*	Sargasso Sea, Caribbean Sea, Gulf of Mexico, subtropical North Pacific.
Superior	*S*	Upper levels of troposphere in region of subtropical highs.

MODIFICATIONS OF AIR MASSES

When any one of these air masses moves from the area in which it acquired its characteristic properties to a region of different surface conditions, it immediately begins to be modified by the new influences to which it is subjected; and the longer it remains under the new conditions, the more the original characteristics are modified. The lower layers, especially, undergo a gradual transition in temperature and humidity, while the upper layers remain relatively unchanged unless the mass becomes unstable. The most significant changes in their effect upon the weather are changes in stability, resulting from changes in temperature and in moisture content.

It can be seen that the properties of an air mass depend upon its history. We need to know, first, the fundamental properties of the mass, as acquired at its source. Then we should know by what path it has reached its present position and the nature of the surfaces over which it has moved, and finally, how long it has been away from its source and subjected to modifying influences. Air may reach the Ohio Valley, for example, as a southwest wind which a few days earlier moved southward from Canada as true polar air. The weather that it brings will be quite different from that brought by a southwest wind originating as tropical Gulf air. The direction of the wind is not always a true indication of the history, nor, therefore, of the properties of the air.

One of the most frequent and most important modifications of air masses is that indicated by the addition of the letters *w* and *k* to air-mass designations. For example, when a cold, stable *mP* air mass moves southward over the heated interior of the United States in summer, it is much colder than the surface over which it is moving, and is designated *mPk*. It is thus heated from below, rather rapidly near the surface and more slowly and to a lesser degree aloft. This heating increases the lapse rate, decreases the stability, and favors turbulence and convection. Thus the original character of the air mass and the kind of weather attending it are considerably modified. Similarly, a mass of warm, tropical air moving northward over land in winter is cooled at its surface and made more stable. It is obvious, then, that heating and cooling of an air mass from below are important modifying influences. In general, *w* indicates a stable air mass and *k* an unstable air mass.

Vertical movements are also important modifiers of air masses. Downward movement of stable air increases both the temperature and the stability, whether the descent is by movement downslope, or by direct subsidence from aloft. Lifting of an air mass results in adiabatic cooling, an increased lapse rate, and active convection in case convective instability is possible. Addition and removal of water vapor are other processes by which air masses are modified. Water may be added by evaporation from a moist surface or from falling rain. Removal of water by condensation and precipitation adds latent heat, decreases the lapse rate, and makes future condensation less probable. Mixing, either by turbulence or by the convergence of air currents, is another process by which the properties of air masses are modified. Thus, in studying the characteristics of air masses, it is to be remembered that they are subject to constant change as they move from their source regions. Hence, it is important to know their path and history.

The weather that we experience from day to day depends primarily upon the characteristics of the air masses that move over us. By characteristics we mean specifically the temperature, the lapse rate, **Characteristics of North American Air Masses** and the moisture content of the air masses. The aviator is especially interested, also, in such properties as dew point, visibility, ceiling, and kind of clouds. The characteristics are determined by the temperature and moisture conditions of the source regions over which the air masses were formed and by their subsequent histories. We shall now discuss briefly the characteristics of the principal North American air masses and how they differ from winter to summer.

POLAR CONTINENTAL (cP) AIR MASSES IN WINTER

The source regions for cP air in winter are Canada, the ice-covered Arctic Ocean, and northeastern Siberia. Such of these air masses as affect the United States usually originate in the high-pressure center over northwestern Canada. For a considerable period, this air has overlain a frozen or snow-covered surface and has become very cold in its lower levels by radiation cooling in the long winter nights of high latitudes. Since cooling in the free air is not so rapid as at the surface, and also since the air is, in general, subsiding, the temperature usually increases from the ground up to a considerable elevation. This inversion of temperature means marked stability; convection is impossible and turbulence is reduced. In such cold air the moisture content (specific humidity) is necessarily very low, but relative humidity may be high. Generally, cP air brings clear, cold weather and good visibility to the United States. As these air masses move southward, they usually move over warmer surfaces and become cPk air masses. The consequent warming of the lower air is sometimes sufficient to cause instability, resulting in convective movements attended by cloudiness and precipitation.

POLAR CONTINENTAL (cP) AIR MASSES IN SUMMER

The source regions of summer cP air are in Alaska and in central and northern Canada. The ground is not snow-covered, and there is some heating of the surface in the long hours of summer sunshine, sometimes resulting in conditional instability. But the air usually remains cool as compared with surface temperatures farther south. The moisture content is small and the relative humidity usually not over 45 per cent. Hence, such air reaches the United States with temperature and humidity both moderately low. It becomes cPk air and may become unstable, but the condensation level is high and the air usually remains cloudless.

POLAR MARITIME (mP) AIR MASSES IN WINTER

There are two source regions of the mP air masses that occur in the United States in winter. One of these is the North Pacific Ocean in the region of the Aleutian low, and the other is the cold northwestern Atlantic off the coasts of Newfoundland, Labrador, and Greenland. In the main, the Pacific air masses were formed originally as stable cP air in Siberia; but as they move eastward over the relatively warm water, from which there is active evaporation, they become warm and humid in their lower levels. Thus they develop a steep lapse rate and conditional and convective instability. The condensation level is low, and Cumulus and showers may develop.

The degree of instability developed depends upon the length of time the air has overlain the ocean. Some of the air masses move in a short path across the narrow North Pacific and retain many of their cP characteristics. In general they reach the West Coast of North America as mPk air masses, but as they move inland they become mPw, because the land surface is cold. The air is cooled at the surface and becomes more stable, with little cloudiness and little turbulence. When such air moves against the western mountain ranges, however, the orographic uplift results in heavy rain or snow on the western slopes of the mountains.

Some Atlantic air masses originating in the northwestern Atlantic invade the eastern coastal region of North America as far south as Virginia, giving raw, northeast winds. They are not numerous because of the prevailing west-to-east movement of the air in the general circulation. The air on the Atlantic Coast differs from the air reaching the Pacific Coast by being colder near the ground and stable aloft. In their lower levels, both have conditional instability and high humidity.

POLAR MARITIME (mP) AIR MASSES IN SUMMER

The source regions of mP air are the same in summer as in winter. Along the West Coast in summer, there is an almost continuous southward flow of air of moderate temperatures. There is subsidence and marked stability in the dry air aloft, but there is conditional instability in a shallow lower layer. This situation results in low Stratus and summer fogs characteristic of much of the Pacific Coast. This air moves inland as mPk air. It is quickly heated at the surface over the hot and dry interior, but the upper layers remain dry and stable. The heating and the turbulent mixing reduce the relative humidity of the lower layer and dissolve the low clouds. The air is dry and generally clear, and remains cooler than the surface over which it is moving. After it has crossed the Rocky Mountains, this mP air is indistinguishable from cP air.

Along the East Coast, air occasionally moves inland out of a high-pressure area over the cold water of the northwestern Atlantic. This westward movement occurs more frequently in summer than in winter because of the change in the general pressure distribution with the seasons. The upper air is stable because of subsidence over the high-pressure area, and the lower air is cool, dry, and stable because of the cold water. It is stable *mP* or *mPw* air over the water and becomes *mPk* over land. Because of the stability of the mass as a whole and its low humidity, there are no clouds, or only thin Stratocumulus, which are dissolved by insolational heating as the air proceeds inland. Hence, summer *mP* air from the Atlantic often brings clear and cool weather and good visibility to the New England states and occasionally to the coastal states as far south as Virginia.

TROPICAL CONTINENTAL (cT) AIR MASSES

Because the North American continent narrows rapidly as it extends southward through Mexico into tropical regions, little true *cT* air ever invades the United States. During the winter months there are no *cT* air masses in North America. The only source of such air in the Northern Hemisphere in winter is over North Africa. In summer, northern interior Mexico and adjacent portions of our arid Southwest are in the subtropical belt of light winds and light rainfall, and in consequence, hot and dry masses of air accumulate in those regions. These may properly be called *cT* air masses.

Owing to the intense heating of the surface, there is turbulence and convection to a considerable height (2 miles or 3 km), resulting in a lapse rate approximating the dry adiabatic rate. Notwithstanding this steep lapse rate, the air remains cloudless because of its extreme dryness. The dryness results also in rapid insolational heating by day and rapid radiational cooling by night. Accordingly, the weather is hot, dry, and clear, with large diurnal ranges of temperature. These air masses are confined to the region of their origin. When they move away from this region, they become mixed with *mT* air masses and lose their identity.

TROPICAL MARITIME (mT) AIR MASSES IN WINTER

The tropical maritime air that affects the weather of North America has its sources in the subtropical high-pressure belt, either in the Pacific Ocean between Baja, California and Hawaii, or in the Gulf and Caribbean regions and the region of the Sargasso Sea. In winter, the temperature and humidity of the Pacific *mT* air masses are moderate. Subsidence is characteristic of the warm dry air. The surface turbulence layer is cool and moist. When this air moves northward into colder latitudes, it becomes *mTw* air. The cooling and convergence as it moves northward cause the lower layers to become more stable and often cause decreasing visibility, fog, and drizzle, particularly at night. These conditions favor convective instability, and when such air is forced upward by colder air masses along a front or by moving inland and upslope, there is often steady, moderate to heavy precipitation. These are the conditions under which the winter rains of the Pacific Coast occur. These mT air masses are greatly modified before they cross the continental divide.

The waters of the Gulf of Mexico and the subtropical western Atlantic are exceptionally warm in winter and evaporation from their surfaces is active. Hence, they are both warm and humid in their lower layers, and thus their specific humidity is unusually high. The upper levels of these air masses are like those of tropical Pacific air, warm, dry, and stable, owing to subsidence. As they move northward, there is rapid surface cooling and, hence, condensation in the humid lower levels. These happenings produce poor visibility, fog, drizzle, and low Stratus, resulting in very poor flying weather. The air continues warm (mTw) compared to the surface, especially over northern land areas, where it often causes winter thaws. The upper levels become colder and less stable northward, resulting in convective instability and considerable precipitation. When there is frontal or orographic uplift, the rains become heavy and widespread. The mT air masses of the Atlantic and Pacific Oceans have essentially the same tropical maritime properties, and, taken together, they are responsible for the warm and rainy winter weather of the entire central and eastern portions of the United States and of southeastern Canada.

TROPICAL MARITIME (mT) AIR MASSES IN SUMMER

There are practically no mT air masses moving over the United States from the Pacific Ocean in summer. On the other hand, Atlantic and Gulf air masses are more numerous in summer and cover a wider area. Temperature, specific humidity, and relative humidity are all high in these air masses at their sources in the Gulf and western Atlantic. There is conditional instability; a small uplift causes strong convective currents and frequent thundershowers. As they move over land, they become mTk air masses. Stratus and Stratocumulus frequently form by radiational cooling of the humid air at night. These disappear in the forenoon, to be followed in the afternoon by Cumulus and thundershowers, due to insolational heating of the surface.

Where there is convergence and uplift, as in frontal zones, the mT air becomes definitely unstable aloft, resulting in active convection and heavy showers or widespread heavy rain. There is little change in this air as it moves northward over land, and when it crosses the Great Lakes, it is warmer than the water. Fogs and low Stratus frequently result on the northern shores of the lakes. Over the cold water off the northeastern United States and the maritime provinces of Canada there are deep and dense fogs. These air masses largely dominate the sum-

mer weather of the eastern half of the continent, where they are responsible for much hot, humid, and oppressive weather, as well as for most
of the rainfall. Most thunderstorms in the United States take place in
mT air.

SUPERIOR (S) AIR MASSES

Masses of warm and dry air, known as *Superior* air, are common at
middle and upper levels, 6,500 feet (2 km) and upward, over most of the
United States at all seasons. This air is especially common over *mT* air,
but it occurs also over air of polar origin. Its extreme dryness is evidently
due to subsidence. The name *Superior* is now often applied to all warm
air masses having a relative humidity of less than 40 per cent, under the
assumption that they have become warm and dry by subsidence from
aloft. The source regions of the warm, dry air aloft are not definitely
known. It is probable that the greater part of such air develops slowly in
the upper levels of the subtropical high-pressure cells. Much of it reaches
North America from the eastern side of the Pacific high in great tongues
of dry air moving out of the prevailing westerlies.

Superior air has a steep lapse rate, approaching the dry adiabatic, but
it remains stable because of its extreme dryness. It is usually warmer at its
base than the air which it overlies; that is, there is a temperature inversion
at its lower boundary, stopping convective movements from below. It is
essentially a high-level air mass, but at times, especially in summer, it
sometimes appears at the surface, attended by hot and dry weather. The
Great Plains and the southwestern states are subject to such periods of
heat and drought, due to the continued presence of *S* air at or near the
surface. It is present much of the time at all seasons over *mT* air in central
and southern United States.

Fronts

A *front* is a boundary surface, or, more correctly, a
transition zone, separating air masses of differing character, especially of markedly different temperatures. It is a sloping boundary and comparatively narrow, varying from 50 to 500 miles in width.

When differing air masses are brought together by converging movements in the general circulation, they ordinarily do not mix freely but
form a transition zone, across which there is a rapid change in temperature. The cold air underlies the warm air in a sloping wedgelike mass.
The natural tendency is for the warm air to lie above the colder air in a
horizontal layer, but continuous forces of pressure and the earth's rotation never permit this state of equilibrium to be reached. The front
shown on a weather map is the line along which an inclined boundary
surface between two air masses reaches the ground. A wedge-shaped,

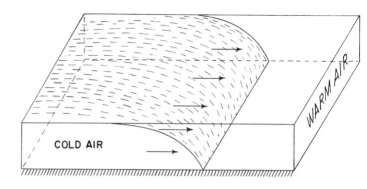

FIG. 9.1

Three-dimensional Representation of a Cold Front.

COLD AIR

WARM AIR

cold air mass is shown invading a region of warmer air in the three-dimensional sketch of Fig. 9.1.

If a cold air mass is replacing a warm air mass at the surface, the front between them is said to be a *cold front*. If warm air is replacing cold air, the front between the two air masses is a *warm front*.

FRONTOGENESIS AND FRONTOLYSIS

The formation of new fronts or the regeneration and strengthening of weak and decaying fronts is called *frontogenesis*. The opposite process, that of the weakening or dissipation of existing fronts, is *frontolysis*. Frontogenesis occurs where the wind system causes a convergence of cold polar air and warm tropical air. A contrast in temperature is a necessary condition, and any process that causes and maintains an increasing temperature gradient tends to produce a front. Similarly, any distribution of winds that causes a decrease in the temperature gradient across a frontal boundary is a process of frontolysis.

The two most active regions of frontogenesis in the Northern Hemisphere in winter are: (*a*) the North Atlantic Ocean from the region of the Iceland low westward to the coast of North America and (*b*) the North Pacific from the region of the Aleutian low westward to the coast of Asia. In summer there is active frontal development in the Bering Sea region and across central Canada. These are regions in which the zonal and cellular wind systems bring together air masses of strongly contrasting characteristics.

CHARACTERISTICS OF WARM FRONTS

At a warm front, warm air is advancing against cold air and being forced upward over a retreating wedge of the cold air. The slope of a warm front is generally about 1:300. The resulting adiabatic cooling of the warm air takes place slowly because the upslope is gentle. The amount and type of cloudiness and precipitation resulting from this upward movement depend upon the existing humidity and lapse rate in the warm air. If the air is stable and dry, there may be little cloudiness and no precipi-

178

tation. In most cases in the United States, however, the warm air is a tropical maritime air mass, either from the Pacific or from the Gulf or Atlantic source regions. Such air is humid and normally conditionally and convectively unstable. Hence, the initial uplift usually leads also to convective ascent.

In advance of an approaching warm front of this character, we find first a slowly falling barometer and the formation of high clouds. The clouds may begin as much as 1,000 miles in advance of the surface front. They are Cirrus, thickening into Cirrostratus (Fig. 9.2). As the front approaches, cloudiness begins at intermediate levels, the sky becoming overcast with Altostratus and Altocumulus. Slow, steady rain may begin from the Altostratus. The temperature is constant or slowly rising, unless lowered by falling rain. As the front draws near, there is an increasing fall in pressure, and the clouds lower and thicken into Stratocumulus and Nimbostratus, attended by steady, moderate rain or snow. Sometimes there is suffi-

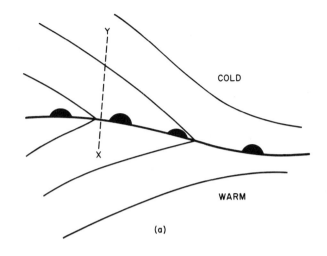

(a)

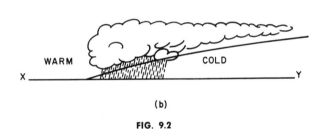

(b)

FIG. 9.2

(a) Surface and (b) Vertical Sections of a Warm Front.

cient instability to produce Cumulonimbus and thunderstorms. As the warm rain falls through the underlying cold air, evaporation of the raindrops, combined with movements of the lower air, may result in low Stratus and fog. In winter, there may also be icing from supercooled drops. With the passage of the front, there is a gradual rise in temperature, a change in wind direction, and generally clearing weather, although some cloudiness may continue throughout the warm-sector air mass.

CHARACTERISTICS OF COLD FRONTS

In a cold front, warm air is being replaced by an advancing wedge of cold air. As in the case of the warm front, the vertical structure of the warm air determines the reactions with reference to cloudiness and rainfall. A cold front differs from a warm front in the following particulars:

(*a*) it is steeper, giving the same uplift in a shorter distance (the slope of a cold front is generally about 1:50); (*b*) it slopes backward instead of forward; and (*c*) the warm air is being removed. There is usually no warning far in advance of an approaching cold front unless thunderstorms are especially active along the front. In the latter case, Cirrus or thin Cirrostratus from the anvil tops of the Cumulonimbus may be carried by strong westerlies aloft and precede the front by several hours. There is only a narrow band of cloudiness and precipitation and the reactions are sharper and more violent.

As the typical active cold front draws near, there is some increase of wind in the warm sector and Cirrus or Cirrostratus appear. These are quickly followed by lower and denser Altocumulus and Altostratus, and then at the actual front by Nimbostratus and Cumulonimbus, with heavy show-

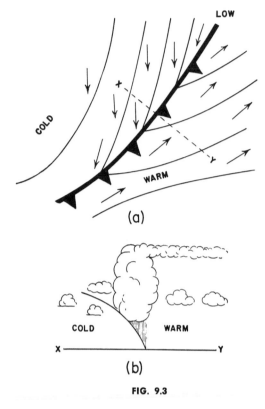

FIG. 9.3

(a) Surface and (b) Vertical Sections of a Cold Front.

ers. These changes take place within an hour or two. As the front passes, there is a rise in pressure, an abrupt and often large drop in temperature, an increase in wind force, and a change in wind direction from southwesterly to northwesterly. These events are usually followed by fairly rapid clearing, but scattered Cumulus or Stratocumulus may persist for some time (Fig. 9.3).

There are, of course, many individual variations from the typical conditions, depending upon the characteristics of both air masses, hence the importance of upper-air soundings in analyzing an individual front. Sometimes most of the rain comes just ahead of the front; sometimes, a little behind it. If the front moves very slowly, or if the slope of the frontal surface is not very steep, clouds and precipitation extend backward a considerable distance.

When the cold air moves over a warm surface, especially a warm water surface, evaporation often produces low clouds or fog. In other cases, the falling raindrops freeze, forming sleet, or they become supercooled and deposit a layer of ice when they strike surface objects. When the cold front is moving rapidly and increasing its speed, one or two *secondary cold fronts* sometimes develop some distance behind the main front.

Along the cold front of an advancing high, where polar air quickly replaces tropical air, there is a sudden change from warm to much colder weather. This occurs especially in winter in interior and eastern North America and is known as a *cold wave*. As a great drop in temperature advances rapidly eastward and southward, its movement suggests an oncoming flood or large ocean wave. The definition of a cold wave varies with the season and the locality. Cold-wave warnings are issued as far in advance as practicable in order that preparations may be made for these sudden changes.

SQUALL LINES

One of the most respected features on the weather map and one of the most difficult to predict is the *pre-cold-frontal squall line*. It is characterized by a line of heavy showers and thunderstorms aligned parallel with the cold front and advancing ahead of it.

Squall lines are commonly identified with cold fronts moving across the United States in the spring but may occur during all seasons. Storminess along a squall line intensifies and dissipates more or less erratically. The line forms from 50 to 150 miles (80–240 km) in advance of a cold front which is pushing into warm, conditionally unstable air. Once formed, a squall line usually travels faster than the parent front and dissipates when the distance between them approaches 200 or 300 miles (320–480 km). When convective activity along the squall line increases, there is a corresponding decrease in activity along the main front, thus indicating that the dynamics of the two lines of weather are closely related.

The exact cause of pre-cold-frontal squall lines is not known. One theory holds that outrushing cold air from the downdrafts of thunderstorms along the main front creates a secondary frontal situation in the warm air mass. Another advocates that surface friction may retard the advance of cold air near the ground, causing an almost vertical frontal surface at lower levels. The free movement of warm air up the frontal surface would thus be impaired and result in a band of convection ahead of the frontal surface. Convection is present along a squall line, as most any aviator can testify, sometimes creating weather conditions more commonly associated with a very active cold front.

OTHER TYPES OF FRONTS

Basically, all fronts are either warm or cold; but when a front ceases to move in either direction, it is called a *stationary front*. This is not an

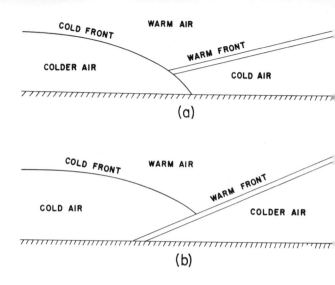

FIG. 9.4

(a) Cold Front and (b) Warm Front
Types of Occlusion.

(a)

(b)

uncommon occurrence, especially along the eastern edge of the Rocky Mountains where the physical barrier hinders free movement of the air masses. Cold fronts often become stationary along the Gulf Coast and across Texas or Mexico as the cold air ceases to advance further southward and the main body of cold air moves off to the east. A front may remain stationary for several hours or days before it dissipates or begins to move again as a cold front or a warm front.

It sometimes happens that one front overtakes another front, bringing into close proximity three different air masses. This situation becomes possible when the middle air mass is warmer (and lighter) than the other two. As the fronts meet, the air masses are displaced vertically according to their densities. The warmest air mass is completely occluded from the ground and the frontal structure becomes known as an *occluded front* or an *occlusion*. Occluded fronts are generally associated with wave cyclones. In an occlusion, one of the fronts no longer touches the ground (Fig. 9.4). Its lower boundary terminates along the frontal surface which separates the coldest air from the other two air masses.

A frontal surface which does not extend to the ground is called an *upper front*. It may be classed as either warm or cold depending on the characteristics of the two interacting air masses and the direction of its movement. An upper front may be associated with an occlusion, or it may move along above a cold layer of air which is marked at the top by a strong temperature inversion. The passage of a front aloft will generally cause pressure changes at the surface which shows up as a troughing of the isobars and its effect on clouds and precipitation may be quite significant.

WAVE CYCLONE

The cold front along the leading edge of an advancing polar air mass is the principal breeding place for a migrating extratropical storm called

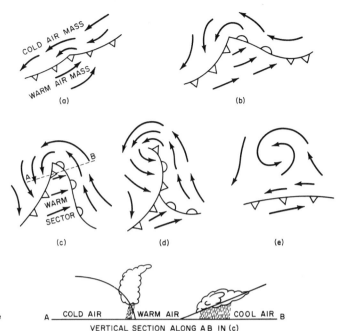

FIG. 9.5

Stages in the Life Cycle of a Wave Cyclone.

A ___ COLD AIR ___ WARM AIR ___ COOL AIR ___ B

VERTICAL SECTION ALONG A B IN (c)

a *wave cyclone*. It plays an important part in the weather of middle latitudes. The formation of a wave cyclone is called *cyclogenesis*. When some disturbance or topographical irregularity occurs along the frontal boundary between two air masses, a wave may develop in the front. The pressure in the vicinity of the wave begins to fall and the winds on either side of the wave shift into a cyclonic pattern (Fig. 9.5a).

Within a few hours the pressure may drop several millibars while the winds increase and the wave in the front becomes more acute (Fig. 9.5b). This causes a change in the relative motion and direction of the two segments of the wave. Although the entire wave moves along with the movement of the original frontal surface, the leading segment becomes oriented in such a way that it becomes a warm front while the trailing segment continues to advance as a cold front and overtakes the warm front (Fig. 9.5c). The final stage of the wave cyclone is an occlusion (Fig. 9.5d). It finally dissipates in a swirl of air, but usually not before it has caused much significant weather over a broad area along the frontal zone (Fig. 9.5e).

PROBLEMS

1.

Assuming a cold-front slope of 1:50, how high will the frontal surface be over Little Rock when the leading edge extends through Indianapolis, Memphis, and Dallas?

2.

What would be the depth of the advancing wedge of cold air at Oklahoma City at the time of the situation in problem 1?

3.

If a warm front with a slope of 1:300 was oriented east-west through Kansas City, what kind of clouds could be expected at Lincoln, Nebraska? Explain your answer.

4.

Based on the conditions of problem 3, what can you surmise about the past and present weather at Wichita, Kansas?

5.

Name four principal air-mass source regions that affect the weather over the continental United States.

6.

List the various factors that influence the characteristics of an air mass at any given time.

7.

In what season of the year will an *mPk* air mass likely become *mPw* as it moves on to the West Coast of North America? Explain your answer.

8.

Under what circumstances can a *cPk* air mass in winter become *cPw?* Identify a geographical situation where this might happen.

9.

The wind has been gradually increasing in velocity from the south and southwest for two days at Kansas City. On the second afternoon, a high veil of Cirrostratus began moving across the sky from the northwest. What is the probable weather situation and what changes are likely to occur within the next twenty-four hours?

10.

How does a "cold wave" warning help the rancher? citrus-fruit grower? natural-gas company? ready-to-wear merchant? cement contractor?

11.

A rather spectacular demonstration of simulated air mass and frontal activity can be accomplished by following these directions. Prepare a reasonably tight, but removable, vertical partition to separate a rectangular aquarium into two equal compartments. Fill the aquarium almost full with water. Then with the partition in place, add some salt and blue coloring to the water in one compartment and some red coloring (but no salt) to the other compartment. Stir the contents of both compartments to distribute the respective colors uniformly and to dissolve the salt. Now remove the partition and watch the two fluid masses interact because of their difference in density. What is the least amount of salt that one can use per gallon of water and still get a significant interaction between the two fluid masses?

12.

What is the maximum difference in density that can be attained by the procedure in problem 11 when common table salt is used? Is the rate of interaction between the two masses dependent on the amount of salt used? How? Apply this reasoning to the interaction of cold and warm air masses.

10

special storms
and lesser
atmospheric
disturbances

There are several air disturbances which, though smaller or less frequent than the cyclones and anticyclones of middle latitudes, are attended by characteristic and striking phenomena of major importance wherever they occur. The largest of these is the *tropical cyclone*, seasonally familiar to certain ocean areas and coastal locations in the low latitudes. More common to the interior locations of the United States are the *thunderstorm* and the *tornado*. In addition, certain winds which are not independent disturbances but are parts of larger air movements acquire distinguishing properties in some regions and at times have received special names. Those to be discussed briefly in this chapter are the *foehn* or *chinook, sirocco, blizzard,* and *dust storm*. Special characteristics are acquired by these winds because of geographic situation, local topography, or conditions of the earth's surface.

Tropical Cyclones

A study of weather maps of the West Indies in summer and autumn shows an occasional low-pressure area, differing in a number of ways from the barometric depressions of higher latitudes, and traveling westward instead of eastward. Similar storms occur in low latitudes in other parts of the world, and the general name for them is *tropical cyclone*. Local names are *hurricane* in the West Indies, *typhoon* in the general western Pacific area, *baguio* in the South China Sea, and *cyclone* in the Indian Ocean.

CHARACTERISTICS

A tropical cyclone is a true revolving storm, a vast cyclonic whirl with a calm central core, or *eye*, resulting from the rapidity of the whirling motion. There are no fronts separating masses of warm and cold air; temperature, pressure, winds, and cloudiness may be more or less symmetrical around the center. Pressure gradients are steep, and winds often reach destructive velocities of from 75 to 200 miles (120–320 km) per hour. For the storm to be classed as a true hurricane, the wind must reach a velocity of at least 75 miles (120 km) per hour. Winds are directed counterclockwise in the Northern Hemisphere and clockwise in the Southern Hemisphere.

In well-developed hurricanes, the pressure at the center is below 28.50 inches (965 mb)—often, much below. In 1933, four storms with minimum pressures between 27.40 and 27.99 inches (928 and 948 mb) occurred in the region of the West Indies. A tropical cyclone is an area of active convection, the air moving upward in spirals around the core. The closed cyclonic circulation usually begins at heights of 1 to 2 miles and builds down to the surface and up to heights of from 4 to 7 miles. Its diameter is usually from 300 to 600 miles (480–960 km). Details of the structure of tropical cyclones have recently been obtained by airplane flights in and around them at various levels (Fig. 10.1), and by the use of radar, with raindrops echoing the microwaves. The Army radar station near Orlando, Florida obtained an excellent record of the Florida hurricane of September 15, 1945. It found that the eye of the storm was 12 miles (19 km) in

Panorama Inside the Eye of a Typhoon. Photographs by Paul A. Humphrey on August 7, 1945, in the South China Sea. *U.S. Navy Photo.*   **FIG. 10.1**

diameter, that the dense clouds of the whirling storm extended to an average height of 18,000 feet (5.5 km), and that long "tails" or rain-bearing clouds spiraled around the storm center. This is somewhat typical of most hurricanes.

As such a storm approaches, the barometer begins falling, slowly at first and then more and more rapidly, while the wind increases from a gentle breeze to hurricane force, and the clouds thicken from Cirrus and Cirrostratus to dense Cumulonimbus, attended by thunder and lightning and excessive rain. These conditions continue for several hours, spreading destruction in their course. Then suddenly the eye of the storm arrives, the wind and the rain cease, the sky clears, or partly so, and the pressure no longer falls but remains at its lowest. This phase may last thirty minutes or longer, and then the storm begins again in all its severity, as before, except that the wind is from the opposite direction and the pressure is rising rapidly. As this continues, the wind gradually decreases in violence until the tempest is passed and the tropical oceans resume their normal repose. The violent portion of the storm may last from twelve to twenty-four hours.

THE FLORIDA KEYS STORM OF SEPTEMBER 1935

A hurricane of great intensity devastated some of the Florida Keys on the afternoon and night of September 2, 1935. The center passed over Long Key, where a cooperative observer of the Weather Bureau, J. E. Duane, and nineteen other persons were living at a fishing camp. The following is paraphrased from Mr. Duane's graphic and complete description of the storm:

September 2:
2 P.M.—Barometer falling; heavy sea swell and high tide; heavy rain squalls continue; wind from N or NNE, force 6.

3 P.M.—Ocean swells changed; large waves now rolling in from SE, somewhat against winds, which are still in N or NE.

4 P.M.—Wind still N, force 9; barometer dropping 0.01 inch every five minutes; rain continues.

5 P.M.—Wind N, hurricane force; swells from SE.

6 P.M.—Barometer 28.04, still falling; heavy rains; wind still N, hurricane force and increasing; water rising on N side of island.

6:45 P.M.—Barometer 27.90; wind backing to NW, increasing; heavy timbers flying; beam 6 by 8 inches, 18 feet long, blown through observer's house.

7 P.M.—Now in main lodge building, which is shaking with every blast and being wrecked by flying timbers; water piling up on north side of camp.

9 P.M.—No signs of storm letting up; barometer still falling very fast.

9:20 P.M.—Barometer 27.22; wind abated. During this lull all hands gather in the last cottage. Sky is clear to northward, stars shining brightly and a very light breeze continues; no flat calm. About the middle of the lull, which lasted 55 minutes, the sea began to rise very fast from ocean side of camp. Water lifted the cottage from its foundations and it floated.

10:10 P.M.—Barometer 27.02; wind beginning to blow from SSW.

10:15 P.M.—First blast from SSW, full force. House is now breaking up; wind seems stronger than at any time during storm. Barometer reads 26.98 inches. I was blown outside into sea; got hung up in broken fronds of coconut tree and hung on for dear life; was then struck by some object and knocked unconscious.

September 3:

2:25 A.M.—Became conscious in tree and found I was lodged about 20 feet above the ground. The cottage had been blown back on the island, from whence the sea had receded and left it with all people safe.

Hurricane winds continued till 5 A.M. and terrific lightning flashes were seen. After 5 A.M. strong gales continued throughout the day with very heavy rain.

It is estimated that in this storm, wind velocities were 150 to 200 miles per hour. Destruction was practically complete over a path 30 miles wide, extending considerably farther to the right than to the left of the path of the center. The destructive storm tide had the same direction of advance as the storm center, flowing from southeast to northwest. The rate of advance of the storm was about 10 miles per hour, and the calm center was perhaps 8 miles in diameter.[1]

LOWEST OBSERVED PRESSURES

It is not known how low the pressure may fall at the centers of severe hurricanes, because in the greater number of such storms no records are obtained. The lowest barometer readings of which there are reliable records are given by McDonald as follows:

> In the Florida Keys storm just described, an aneroid barometer in a boat tied up near the north end of Long Key indicated a barometric pressure of 892.2 mb (26.35 inches) at the center of the storm. This pressure was arrived at after careful tests of the aneroid with standard mercurial instruments under reduced pressure in the laboratory. It is the lowest sea level pressure ever observed in the Western Hemisphere. The lowest previous record was 914.7 mb in the Caribbean hurricane of November 5, 1932, and the previous record in the United States was 929.6 mb, September 16, 1928, at West Palm Beach, Florida. Only one reading lower than the Florida Keys storm has been reported at sea level anywhere in the world. This was a pressure of 886.8 mb (26.185 inches), observed in a typhoon about 460 miles east of Luzon on August 18, 1927.[2]

REGIONS AND TIMES OF OCCURRENCE

Tropical cyclones begin over the oceans in the equatorial trough when it is some distance from the equator. They are more frequent on the west-

---

[1] W. F. McDonald, "The Hurricane of August 31 to September 6, 1935," *Monthly Weather Review*, LXIII (1935), 269-271.

[2] W. F. McDonald, "Lowest Barometer Reading in the Florida Keys Storm of September 2, 1935," *Monthly Weather Review*, LXIII (1935), 295.

ern sides of the oceans, but some originate toward the eastern boundaries, as, for example, near the Cape Verde Islands in the North Atlantic and off the coast of Mexico in the Pacific. The six general regions of the world where most tropical cyclones occur are: (*a*) from the Bahamas to the Caribbean Sea and the Gulf of Mexico; (*b*) in the Pacific Ocean west of Mexico and Central America; (*c*) in the neighborhood of the Philippines and the China Sea; (*d*) in the Bay of Bengal and, less frequently, in the Arabian Sea; (*e*) in the southern Indian Ocean east of Madagascar; (*f*) in the South Pacific from the vicinity of Samoa and the Fiji Islands westward to the north and west coasts of Australia. Some tropical cyclones occur outside of these regions. None are known to occur in the South Atlantic Ocean. The regions of frequent occurrence and the normal paths are shown in Fig. 10.2.

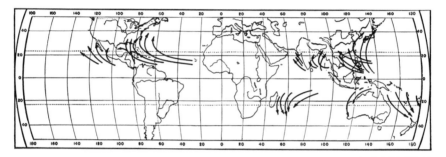

Regions and Generalized Paths of Tropical Cyclones. Individual paths are   **FIG. 10.2**
extremely variable, and occasional storms of this type develop or travel
far outside of these areas.

These disturbances occur almost exclusively in summer and autumn, in contrast to the depressions occurring within the prevailing westerlies. The latter are present at all seasons of the year but are most active in winter. In the Northern Hemisphere, tropical cyclones occur from May to November, but the months of greatest frequency are September and October, except in the Arabian Sea. There they are most frequent in the calm seasons between the monsoons, that is, in June and again in October. The average number in the North Atlantic is from six to ten per year but not all of these reach land or develop full hurricane strength.

ORIGIN AND PATH

Tropical cyclones originate in the warm, moist air of the equatorial trough. The winds are light and usually drifting lazily from east to west. A wave appears in the easterly flow and proceeds westward at from 10 to 15 miles (15–25 km) per hour. Why some easterly waves develop into raging tropical cyclones and others remain relatively stable disturbances is not fully understood. They seldom have been known to form nearer than 5° nor more than 20° from the equator. Some believe the Coriolis force is a necessary contributing factor to formation; hence no storms would form immediately at the equator, because there the Coriolis force is zero. Riehl and others have shown that tropical cyclones are frequent only over very warm oceans and are extremely rare when the sea-surface temperatures are below 79°F (26°C). There are no storms in the South Atlantic nor in the eastern part of the South Pacific, where cold ocean currents keep the surface-water temperatures continually below 79°F. Nor do storms form in the regular source regions when the water temperatures are much below normal.

Tropical cyclones, once started, move westward in the prevailing westward drift of the easterlies and curve gradually to the right in the Northern Hemisphere and to the left in the Southern. They travel at the moderate speed of from 10 to 30 miles (15–50 km) per hour, but occasionally remain stationary for a time or veer from their normal course. Finally, if they persist long enough, they move into the prevailing westerlies, often curving around the western sides of the summer oceanic highs, and then travel northeastward with decreasing energy, becoming like ordinary extratropical lows. The typical path is parabolic, but the actual path of any given storm appears to be governed by the winds existing above it at the time.

Since hurricanes and typhoons always develop over oceans, weather observations at the points of origin are limited indeed. It is known that most of them form along easterly waves over the tropical oceans a few degrees north or south of the equator.

Regular airplane reconnaissance of known storms, to determine path and intensity, has been a common practice in some areas for more than twenty years. More recently, weather satellites offer great promise in locating and tracking these tropical storms. Figure 10.3 shows cloud photographs of the first five hurricanes of the 1961 season. All were successfully located and tracked by Tiros III. It is safe to assume that the use of satellites for this type of reconnaissance will continue and increase in usefulness.

A tropical cyclone moving over land soon becomes larger and weaker and ceases to be of destructive intensity. Evidently, this is because of the diminished supply of warm, moisture-laden air, and because of the increased friction over land. There are many storms over the oceans in the usual tracks of tropical cyclones that resemble hurricanes in many respects except that they fail to reach hurricane intensity. These have varying intensities from near-hurricane to moderate wind velocities. All are attended by rain. These facts indicate that favorable convective conditions must exist to a considerable height above the surface for the formation

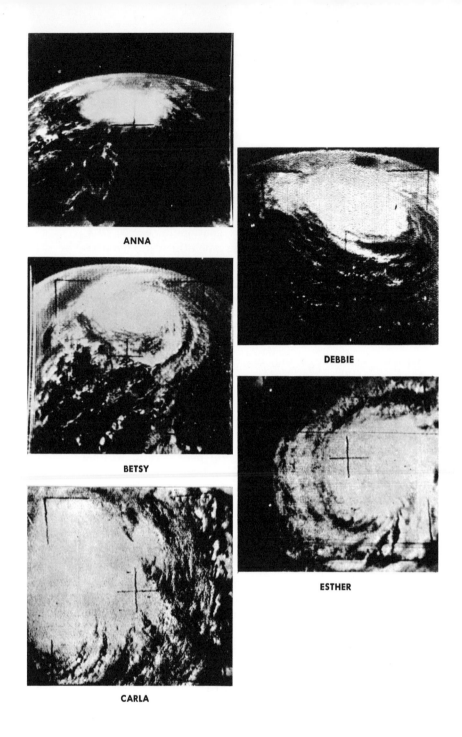

ANNA

DEBBIE

BETSY

ESTHER

CARLA

Five Hurricanes Photographed by Tiros III. Hurricane reconnaissance by   **FIG. 10.3**
satellite represents a great advancement in our ability to locate and track
these storms over the oceans. The five storms pictured here were the first five of the hurricane season as can be noted by the alphabetical order of the names assigned to them. *Courtesy, National
Aeronautics and Space Administration.*

of a true hurricane. There are also many minor tropical disturbances, weak and poorly developed cyclones, over both land and water areas in the tropics, attended by squalls and thunderstorms.

EFFECTS OF TROPICAL CYCLONES

Tropical cyclones are destructive in their violence and are avoided if possible by ships at sea (Fig. 10.4). The islands of the West Indies have been struck by hurricanes at various times, and paths of differing widths up to a few hundred miles have been laid waste, often with great loss of life. Storms of equal violence, killing large numbers of people, have also occurred in China, the Philippines, and Samoa. Occasionally storms of destructive severity reach Florida and the Gulf Coast of the United States. There was such a storm at Galveston, Texas in September, 1900, with a loss of 6,000 lives, and in Florida in September, 1928, resulting in about 2,000 deaths. In the Florida storm, a large part of the loss of life and property was caused by the overflowing of Lake Okeechobee; strong north winds, estimated at 150 miles (244 km) per hour, raised the water level on the south shore by 10 to 15 feet and drowned many people. At Galveston, also, the loss of life was largely due to flooding of the low lands on which the city is built. (The city is now protected by a sea wall.)

The violence of these storms creates great ocean swells, which out-travel the storm and precede it by some distance. Along the Gulf Coast, the water begins to rise when the hurricane is from 300 to 500 miles (500–800 km) distant, that is, one or two days before the storm arrives, and often rises from 8 to 15 feet above the normal level of the Gulf. Observations of the direction and character of the waves as they reach the coast, and of the amount of the rise at different places, afford a basis of forecasting the time and point at which the hurricane will arrive.

The United States weather services follow as closely as possible the development and path of each West Indies hurricane and forecast its future movement and severity. They make use of reports from merchant ships, island stations, reconnaissance aircraft, and weather satellites. With the development of radiosonde and rawin soundings and their extension to great heights, upper-air reports have become of primary importance. From them, two methods of estimating with considerable accuracy the future movement of tropical cyclones have been developed. First, the direction and force of the wind at the steering level, that is, at the top of the closed circulation, give a reliable indication of future movement. The objection to the use of this method is that the height of the steering level varies greatly in different storms and in the same storm from day to day. This fact makes it difficult to determine winds at the steering level without numerous soundings from many heights.

During World War II, ships traveled in convoys, and ship radio reports ceased for security reasons, leaving vast areas of the hurricane region

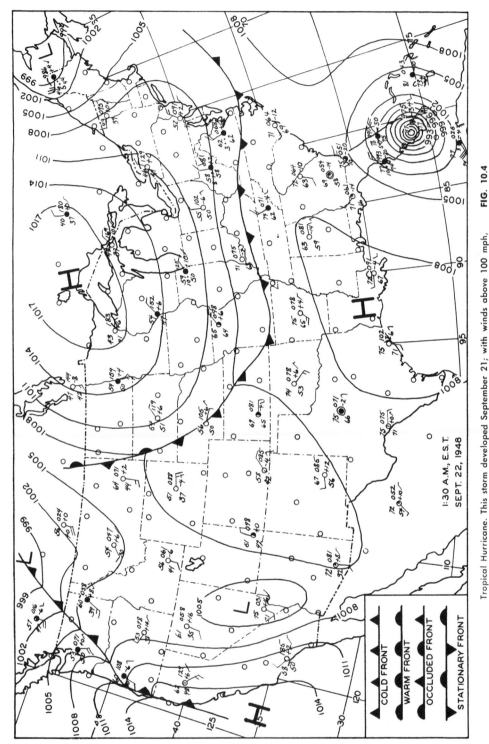

FIG. 10.4

Tropical Hurricane. This storm developed September 21; with winds above 100 mph, it moved slowly across Cuba and Florida, then northeastward. Rough seas and heavy swells were experienced in the Newfoundland-Nova Scotia area on September 26.

1:30 A.M., E.S.T.
SEPT. 22, 1948

COLD FRONT
WARM FRONT
OCCLUDED FRONT
STATIONARY FRONT

unreported. The United States Navy developed three methods of meeting this situation: (*a*) aircraft reconnaissance methods were used to search out the storms; (*b*) radar was utilized to locate the storm centers, as explained later; (*c*) special instruments were designed to determine the direction and amplitude of microseisms originating at the storm center. *Microseisms* are feeble earth tremors detected only by specially constructed apparatus. Some of these tremors originated at the centers of intense lows and move outward in all directions with decreasing amplitude. By observing the direction and amplitude of these earth tremblings at two or three coastal stations, it is possible to follow the path of a hurricane and estimate its intensity, and thereby to forecast its future movement and destructive force with some accuracy. None of the forecast methods have proved entirely satisfactory.

Broadly speaking, a thunderstorm is any storm in **Thunderstorms** which thunder is heard. Thunder often occurs in tropical cyclones, general cyclonic storms, and tornadoes, but a typical thunderstorm, as distinguished from these storms in which thunder is incidental, is a local storm of short duration and of convective origin, proceeding from a large, anvil-shaped Cumulonimbus, often attended by heavy rain for short periods and sometimes by hail.

DESCRIPTION OF A LOCAL THUNDERSTORM

On a quiet summer afternoon with gentle southern winds, a Cumulonimbus sometimes approaches from the west or southwest, drifting east or northeast with the wind aloft while the surface air is moving slowly toward the cloud. The black, suspicious, threatening cloud draws near, and "Heaven's artillery thunders in the skies." About the time the first rain reaches the earth, there is a sudden strong and chilly gust of wind directly out of the storm and preceding it by several thousand feet. (Fig. 10.5). This out-blow may continue strong until the rain reaches the observer, then diminish quickly. The rain comes down in "sheets" for a time; then it also gradually diminishes, and in half an hour or so the storm is past, the sky clears, and a gentle wind again blows from the south. Such a storm is normally only a few miles wide, sometimes spreading over 30 or 40 miles if it continues over a path 100 miles or more in length, as occasionally happens. The edges of the storm are well marked; the rainfall may be heavy within the path and diminish to nothing within a few hundred feet.

VIOLENT MOVEMENTS IN A THUNDERSTORM

If one watches for a time the growth of Cumulus with their flat bases and irregular, towering summits, one sees evidence of much turbulence

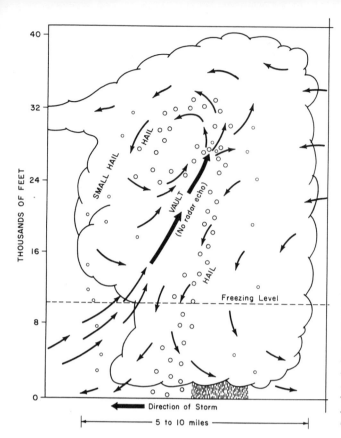

40 —

32 —

24 —

THOUSANDS OF FEET

16 —

8 —

0 —

SMALL HAIL

HAIL

VAULT (No radar echo)

HAIL

Freezing Level

Direction of Storm

5 to 10 miles

FIG. 10.5

A Mature Thunderstorm. The "vault" associated with the principal updraft may not be present in all thunderstorms, but it can occasionally be identified on a radar scope. This schematic representation is partially theoretical, but it agrees with observed characteristic phenomena of most thunderstorms. (See Browning and Ludlam, "Airflow in Convective Storms," *Quarterly Journal of the Royal Meteorological Society*, April 1962.)

and active vertical motion. Aviators are vividly aware of the dangers lurking within these billowing clouds, especially after a firsthand encounter with one.

Because Cumulonimbus is always a hazard to aviation, the United States Air Force, in cooperation with the Navy, the National Advisory Committee on Aeronautics, and the United States Weather Bureau, conducted a research project in 1946–1947 to determine more of the thunderstorm's characteristics. In Florida during the summer of 1946, more than five hundred penetrations of Cumulonimbus were made by skilled pilots at levels ranging from 5,000 to 25,000 feet. More than eight hundred similar penetrations were made of thunderstorms of Ohio in 1947.

Violent updrafts and downdrafts exist side by side in the mature thunderstorms. The updrafts apparently reach greater velocities, up to 100 feet per second or about 70 miles per hour. Severe turbulence, including short, choppy gusts, together with the more steady vertical drafts, create flying conditions so hazardous to aircraft that the storms should always be avoided whenever possible.

THUNDERSTORM STRUCTURE

Thunderstorms are made up of *cells* of circulation, each having its own vertical drafts operating independently of the other cells. They are joined by "connective tissue" of static clouds. When thunderstorms persist over long periods of time, it is probable that new cells are forming and developing as old cells dissipate.

Three stages are recognized in the life cycle of a thunderstorm cell. First, the *Cumulus stage* represents the early period of development when the entire cell is a single updraft current. The cloud is building vertically at a rapid pace, but no precipitation is possible. Occurrence of precipitation at the ground marks the beginning of the *mature stage*. Downdrafts, probably started by the drag of hydrometers within the cloud, develop first in the lower portion and build upward through the cell. Throughout the mature stage, updrafts and downdrafts persist in close proximity. Maximum intensities of all aspects of the storm may be expected during this stage. Vertical development always extends well above the freezing level, and in some cases to a height of 65,000 to 70,000 feet (20,000–25,000 m) above sea level. The *dispersal stage* begins as the downdraft spreads over the entire cell. With the updraft cut off, the cell is no longer fed additional water vapor. The precipitation necessarily diminishes and then stops altogether. Much of the cloud structure is shortly evaporated owing to the increasing mixing ratio resulting from the downdrafts.

Individual thunderstorm cells may range in diameter from half a mile to 5 or 6 miles (1–10 km); however, measurements by the project sited above showed the average cell to be about 5,000 feet (1.8 km) in diameter.

To produce the strong convectional activity necessary to the development of a thunderstorm, both an adequate supply of moisture and a large lapse rate are necessary. In order that the clouds may grow to sufficient height to produce a thunderstorm, an unstable condition must be created through a vertical distance of from 2 to 5 miles. This requires a lapse rate greater than the dry adiabatic up to the lifting condensation level, and greater than the wet adiabatic for a considerable distance beyond the freezing level.

DEVELOPMENT OF CONVECTIVE INSTABILITY

There are several ways by which convective instability may be brought about. First, *heating of surface air,* such as occurs over land areas in summer, may create a large temperature difference between the lower air and the air above it. If the air is moist and conditionally unstable aloft, this gives rise to the typical thunderstorm described above, often called a *heat thunderstorm.* Such storms occur most frequently over land and on summer afternoons when the humidity is high. Although the air is cooled during the time of cloudiness and rainfall, it again becomes hot and oppressive after the storm has passed, for such storms occur within warm air masses. What may be called *artificial heat thunderstorms* sometimes occur over forest fires and active volcanoes, but only if the lapse rate above them is favorable.

Second, the presence of abnormally *cold air aloft,* aided by convergence, may produce the necessary steep temperature gradient and instability. Such thunderstorms occur especially in the southern quadrants of depressions, where there are converging warm surface currents from the south or southeast and much colder upper currents from the southwest or west. They may occur by night and in winter, but over continental areas they are more frequent in summer and by day, when local surface heating helps to create the necessary temperature contrast and when, also, absolute humidity is greater.

Over the oceans, convective thunderstorms occur mostly in winter and in the latter half of the night. There is little heating of the ocean surface by day—not enough to produce strong convection currents. At night the ocean surface and the moist lower air cool slowly, while the upper air cools more rapidly by radiation. The difference in temperature becomes greater as the night progresses, and hence the lapse rates necessary for convection are most frequent late at night. Similarly, in winter the lower air over the oceans is relatively warm, because the water cools slowly, while the upper air is cold.

The forcing of warm, moist air upward by its movement upslope or by the underrunning of cold air often furnishes the initial impulse in the formation of thunderstorms, when the lapse rate aloft is sufficient to continue active convection. Thunderstorms due to underrunning cold air occur along an active cold front, sometimes in connection with general rains attending the passage of the front.

Frontal and prefrontal thunderstorms may occur at any time of day and any season of the year but are rare over land areas in winter. Cold-front thunderstorms are followed by lower temperatures because of the advancing cool air that causes them. When they follow a hot spell in summer, the newspaper headlines often say, "Showers bring cooler weather," when the correct heading should be, "Cooler air brings showers." Another popular error is the assumption that hail has caused the cooler weather. The cooling by hail is slight, temporary, and local. The change to cooler weather is due to the arrival of a cool air mass.

THUNDERSTORM TYPES

Thunderstorms are often classified in two main types, namely, *air mass* and *frontal. Air mass thunderstorms* are those occurring as a result of vertical displacement of the air within a single air mass. The type includes local heat thunderstorms induced by thermal convection, orographic thunderstorms due to movement of air against rising ground, and upper-level thunderstorms caused by advection of warm air at low levels or by overrunning of cold air aloft. *Frontal thunderstorms* are the result of the interaction of two air masses in connection with the passage of a front. They are particularly characteristic of cold fronts.

GEOGRAPHIC DISTRIBUTION

Thunderstorms are most frequent in the rainy regions of the tropics where heat and moisture are abundant and where, also, light winds favor convection. At some places within the tropics, as in Panama, Java, and equatorial Africa, the average number of days with thunderstorms is as great as 200 per year. They are rare in polar regions and in cold areas generally. In the United States they are most frequent along the eastern Gulf Coast, where they occur on more than seventy days per year, mostly from June to September, inclusive, reaching an average of ninety-four a year at Tampa, Florida (Fig. 10.6). There is a secondary maximum for the United States in the southern Rocky Mountain region, Santa Fe, New Mexico, averaging seventy-three thunderstorm days per year. Here orographic influences are the most important factor, because mountainsides facing the wind force air upward, and mountainsides facing the sun are great aids to convection. The region of minimum frequency in the United States

Average Annual Number of Days with Thunderstorms in the United   **FIG. 10.6**
States. *From "Climate and Man,"* U.S.D.A. Yearbook, 1941.

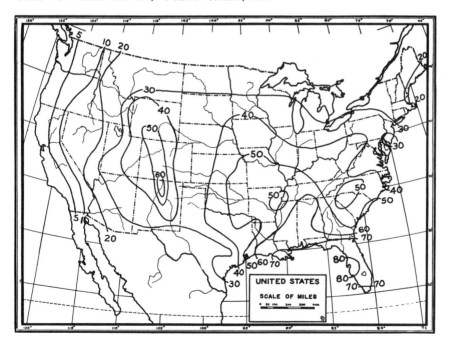

is in the Pacific Coast states, where thunderstorms average from one to four a year, not including the mountain regions.

It has been estimated that over the earth as a whole an average of 44,000 thunderstorms occur each day, and an average of 1,800 are in progress at all times. Because of their small size and local character, it is usually not possible to foresee the precise time and place of occurrence of thunderstorms, but their development and progress can be detected at a distance by the use of radar. The hour of fall and area covered by the rain seem to be matters of chance, especially for those storms in which local heating plays a large part. Thunderstorms occurring along a cold front can be predicted more accurately if the front is followed closely.

Although thunderstorms over land areas are more likely to occur during the day than at night, because of the heating of the air by day, a large part of the United States receives more than half its precipitation at night during the warm season, April to September, inclusive. This is the region of the Great Plains, the Missouri Valley, and the upper Mississippi Valley. In this area of generally light rainfall, the occurrence of most of the precipitation at night is of some economic value in conserving the moisture. It is also of value in harvesting and threshing small grains and curing hay, because it permits drying by day.

In this region of rather low average humidity, heating of the surface air is often not sufficient of itself to cause thunderstorms, but such storms are frequent when the lapse rate is increased by an inflow of cold air aloft. This inflow occurs more often at night according to Humphreys. Most of the summer thunderstorms of this region occur when there is a cool anticyclone along the northern border of the country between Montana and the Great Lakes, and when there is either low pressure in the southwest or a trough of low pressure across the central portion of the country from north to south, or from northeast to southwest. Under such conditions high daytime temperatures often prevail in the Great Plains and the Missouri and Upper Mississippi valleys. Hence, the lower air expands, and the pressure at an elevation of a half-mile and higher is increased until it may be approximately equal to that over the cold anticyclone to the north, at corresponding altitudes. This situation prevents the inflow by day of much cold air at these heights. At night the warmer region normally loses heat more rapidly than the cooler region; the pressure at moderate heights accordingly tends to fall more over the warm region than over the cold, and this allows the cooler air to flow southward over the warm lower air. This results in instability which is essential to the genesis of the thunderstorm.

It is believed, also, that many nocturnal thunderstorms in this region are due to an increased inflow (advection) of warm air at night at altitudes between 3,000 and 6,000 feet (1 and 2 km). The reaction occurs between the warm air and the cold air above it, while the surface air cools by radiation and contracts.

THE ELECTRIC CHARGE

For two centuries since Benjamin Franklin made his famous "kite experiments," the mysteries of thunderstorm electricity have remained largely unsolved. It has become evident, however, that the Cumulonimbus is a huge static-electricity generator capable of building potentials of millions of volts within very short distances. The scientist, studying this phenomenon, is handicapped by being unable to create a working model of a thunderstorm in the laboratory, but ingenious instruments have been devised to measure the electrical characteristics within the actual thunderstorm.

Experiments have shown that, when drops of water are broken into spray by a current of air, the spray particles gain a small positive charge, and the drops that remain gain an equal negative charge. This may explain the positive charge observed in the lower front portion of the cloud, where rain is falling heavily through a rapid updraft of air. In the upper portion of the cloud, where temperatures are below freezing, it is thought that collision between ice particles causes the crystals to become negatively charged and the air positively charged. As the air ascends, it carries the positive charge to the top of the Cumulonimbus. These suggestions appear to offer partial explanation for the separation of electrical charges in a thundercloud. Other forms of cloud do not become so highly charged because of the absence of the rapid uprush characteristic of Cumulonimbus.

NATURE OF LIGHTNING

Lightning is the flash of light caused by a discharge of atmospheric electricity. The discharge may be (*a*) between two parts of the same cloud, (*b*) from one cloud to another, or (*c*) between a cloud and the earth. Thunder is the sound of the discharge, which is caused by the sudden expansion of the air due to heating. Air offers a high resistance to an electric current, and the passage of current through it produces rapid heating. Lightning is a direct, not alternating, discharge, and its duration is from 0.0002 second up to perhaps 1 second or more in a multiple discharge (successive flashes along the same path). The current varies from a few thousand to 100,000 amperes, and the potential difference is of the order of 100,000,000 volts.

The common names *forked, zigzag,* and *streak* lightning are used when the path of the discharge is visible, whether between cloud and earth or from one cloud to another (Fig. 10.7). The path of a discharge is never really a zigzag but is often variously curved and frequently branched. *Sheet* lightning is the sudden lighting up of clouds and sky by a discharge whose path is not seen. In this case the storm is usually distant, as indicated in Kipling's description, "Sheet lightning was dancing on the horizon to a broken tune played by far-off thunder." Often the thunder is not

Direct Lightning Discharge. Courtesy, U.S. Department of Commerce,   **FIG. 10.7**
Weather Bureau.

audible. A rare and curious form of lightning, not fully explained, is known as *ball lightning* and consists of luminous balls or masses, usually moving at moderate speed and lasting a few seconds (Fig. 10.8). The disturbing effects in radio-receiving apparatus, known as *atmospherics, sferics,* or *static,* originate largely in lightning strokes, and thus the positions of large, distant thunderstorms can be determined by the use of two or more radio-direction recorders (oscillographs) placed at known distances from each other.

Ball Lightning. Three stages; about 2 1/2 minutes elapsed between the first and last stages. Courtesy, Dr. John C. Jensen, Nebraska Wesleyan University.

FIG. 10.8

PROTECTION AGAINST LIGHTNING

Lightning rods, if properly installed, carry the electric current to the earth and afford good protection to a building and its occupants. Proper installation requires that the conductors be of sufficient size, extend to every high point of the building, be cross connected into one system with good joints and no sharp angles, and be well grounded at several places. Steel buildings are safe places to be in during a thunderstorm, and any house is safer than out-of-doors. Low places are safer than hills. Wire fences and trees standing alone are especially to be avoided.

Tornadoes

A small storm which is rare in its occurrence at any one place but which is much feared because of its destructive violence is the tornado, meaning, in its derivation, a turning or whirling wind, and often coloquially called a *twister*.

TORNADO CHARACTERISTICS

Tornadoes are revolving storms, turning counterclockwise in the Northern Hemisphere. They are violent storms with small diameter and have rapidly rising air at the center. They are barometric depressions resembling tropical cyclones but much smaller, of much shorter life, and with much steeper pressure gradients. A funnel-shaped cloud develops in a low, heavy Cumulonimbus and extends toward the earth. The funnel rises and falls, turns and swings in various directions. Where it reaches the earth, there is almost total destruction attended by a deafening roar and by semi-darkness; where it fails to reach the earth, there is little damage. It is estimated that winds near the center attain velocities of from 200 to 500 miles per hour (100–250 mps), and the updraft at the center reaches very high velocities. The strongest natural winds that ever occur near the surface of the earth are associated with tornadoes. The funnel always develops in association with the lower portion of an exceptionally violent thunderstorm. Heavy rain or hail may precede and follow the storm passage, although some destructive tornadoes have been officially recorded with no form of precipitation in the area.

The pendant cloud develops downward from the base of the Cumulonimbus as seen in Fig. 10.9. It is a real cloud of water droplets formed by rapid expansional cooling of air entrained in the circulation. Dust and other debris are pulled into the cloud as the funnel reaches the earth. The diameter of the destructive portion is generally less than a quarter of a mile, but paths of destruction range from a hundred yards to more than a mile in width. All funnels do not look the same. Many are clearly visible for several miles, as the one in Fig. 10.9; others are obscured by turbulent *scud clouds* extending down to the ground.

The speed of a tornado over the ground varies between different storms and with time during a single storm. The average cross-country movement is usually in a northeasterly direction at the rate of 35 to 45 miles per hour (18–23 mps). While the average hourly speed of some tornadoes has been as low as 5 miles, at least one storm was clocked at 65 miles per hour over a distance of 17 miles. Although, in rare cases, the funnel cloud has been reported to "stand still" for a few minutes, normally a tornado at a given place is all over in about thirty seconds. The path ranges in length from a few hundred feet to more than 100 miles. The length of path of more than a thousand tornadoes, however, averages about 10 or 15 miles. The average tornado path covers an area of about 3 square miles.

DESTRUCTIVE FORCES IN A TORNADO

There are three damaging forces active in a tornado. First, the "hideous tempest" wrecks buildings and blows down trees. Using the simple wind formula given on page 29, the pressure exerted against a vertical wall arranged normal to the wind direction of a tornado would range from 160 to 1,000 pounds per square foot. Second, there is an explosive effect within buildings because of the sudden reduction of pressure on the outside. Very few measurements have ever been recorded of pressures within the tornado funnel. A few observations have given the indication that sudden atmospheric pressure drops, ranging from 1 to 5 inches of mercury, can be expected. This would leave an instantaneous net excess pressure within a tight building of from 70 to 400 pounds per square foot. A building may literally "explode" if it is not constructed to withstand such internal pressures. Third, the lifting effect of the violent updraft may raise even heavy objects and carry them considerable distances before hurling them back to the earth, or sometimes set them down gently without damage.

PLACE AND TIME OF OCCURRENCE

Every state in the United States has experienced one or more tornadoes. They are primarily an atmospheric phenomenon of North America and Australia, and more especially of the central part of the United States, although they have occurred at irregular intervals on every continent of the globe. Conditions peculiarly favorable to tornado formation especially frequent those states east of the Rocky Mountains.

The greatest tornado frequency per unit area during a recent thirty-five year period occurred in Iowa, which averaged 2.8 tornadoes per year per 10,000 square miles. Not far behind were Kansas, Arkansas, Oklahoma, and Mississippi. Texas has recorded more tornadoes than any other state because of its size, but the frequency per unit area is small. Tornadoes also occur rather frequently in Illinois, Indiana, Missouri, Nebraska, Alabama, Georgia, Ohio, Minnesota, Wisconsin, and southern Michigan. The number reported in the United States averages about 150 per year. The number recorded has been increasing recently, probably owing to an increasing population density and to improved methods of communication. There is no indication that tornadoes are actually becoming more frequent. Sometimes there is a concentration of storms in a given year or even on a given day in a single area. For example, twenty-nine confirmed tornadoes occurred along a cold front across Oklahoma during the single afternoon of May 1, 1954.

Most tornadoes occur during the spring months and during the afternoon hours of the day, but no month of the year or hour of the day has been completely free of storms. In fact, some of the more destructive storms have occurred out of season or at night when the people were caught completely off guard. Because of the small size and unusually short path of a tornado, the chances of a given building being wrecked by one are extremely small even in areas where these storms are most numerous. The same is true regarding the loss of life.

TORNADO WARNING

Forecasting tornadoes has been an extremely difficult task. The storm represents a local violent convection in the atmosphere which lasts only a short time. Even today, the exact requisites for tornado formation are not

(a) Heavy, dark cloud with ragged undersurface. The funnel has just extended to the ground. Note the lightning discharge just above the tower at right center.

(b) The funnel is well-defined and moving eastward. A long, vertical lightning discharge in the upper right quadrant was barely caught in the photograph.

Tornado at Wichita Falls, Texas, April 3, 1964. *All photos, courtesy of the Times Publishing Company of Wichita Falls.*   **FIG. 10.9**

(c) Debris from the surface gives the funnel a massive appearance. A short lightning discharge can be seen near the horizon to the rear of the funnel's path.

(d) The wake of the tornado. This storm took seven lives and left scores injured. Damage to personal property was estimated at more than $3,000,000.

fully known. Accurate atmospheric measurements in and around the storm are most difficult to obtain. Until recently, official warnings were restricted to those occasions when a funnel was actually sighted in order to avoid the possibility of unnecessary alarm and possible hysteria among the populace.

Two unusual tornadoes on March 20 and March 25, 1948 struck Tinker Air Force Base near Oklahoma City and inflicted property damage of $10,000,000 and $6,000,000, respectively. As a result, the Air Weather Service set up a tornado research unit at the base, where Fawbush and Miller developed a workable method of forecasting tornadoes. Modifications of their method are widely used for recognizing probable regions of occurrence. Criteria for the forecast consist of the recognition of an active cold front separating polar air from maritime tropical air in the same vicinity that a strong high-altitude jet of cold air from the west crosses a moisture tongue which is invading from the Gulf of Mexico or the Atlantic Ocean. Tornado-producing weather conditions can now be reliably identified in advance of the storm and the limits of possible tornado occurrence determined. The U.S. Weather Bureau inaugurated a public tornado-warning service in 1952. It consists of a "tornado alert" released through radio and television mediums for a definite area during a specified time.

WATERSPOUTS

When tornadoes occur at sea they are known as *waterspouts*. The funnel cloud is formed in the same way, by unstable atmospheric conditions and is generally associated with a thunderstorm. When it reaches the water surface, it picks up spray. Such waterspouts are known to occur in the United States off the East Coast and in the Gulf of Mexico, and off the coasts of China and Japan, in regions where cold, continental air extends over warm water. They have a cyclonic circulation like that of tornadoes (Fig. 10.10). Another type of storm that is also called a waterspout begins in fair weather instead of with a thunderstorm and is observed mostly in tropical waters. Such storms begin at the ground and grow upward, are small in diameter, are not much affected by the earth's deflective force, and may turn in either direction. There can hardly be strong enough contrasts of temperature in tropical waters to start these whirls, but it is thought that strong convection begins at the ground because the surface layer of air in contact with warm water becomes very moist and hence lighter than the drier air above it. This convective rising is probably caused more by humidity differences than by temperature differences.

WHIRLWINDS

Whirlwinds, or dust whirls, occur over land on hot days when the surface air becomes much warmer than that a few hundred feet above it, thus starting these small, shallow whirls of upflowing and inflowing air. By mix-

Small Waterspout. Photographed near Hong Kong along a cold front by
R. C. Fite. Note the line of wind shift, as evidenced on the sea surface.
U.S. Navy Photo.

FIG. 10.10

ing the air to an increased depth, they prevent the surface air from getting as hot as it otherwise would. Unlike tornadoes, the whirls begin at the ground and may turn in either direction. They are common in many parts of the world, but especially in desert and semiarid regions, where they sometimes reach sufficient force to do some damage.

Many local winds in various parts of the world have **Some Special Winds** been given special names because they blow from certain directions or have some easily recognizable characteristic. Often these winds have no general meteorological interest, but a few of them have special properties worth noting.

FOEHN OR CHINOOK

There is a warm, dry, gusty type of wind of moderate to strong velocity which comes down the slope of a mountain. The movement is the result of pressure differences on opposite sides of the mountain chain. On the windward side, pressure is relatively high, and air is forced to rise over the mountain, with consequent expansion and cooling at least during part of the ascent at the wet adiabatic rate. On the leeward side, there is descent of air, compression, and warming at the dry adiabatic rate for the entire

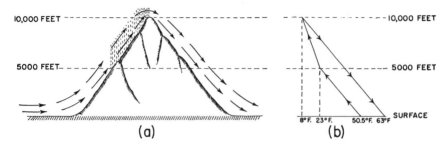

Diagram of Foehn Wind and Resulting Changes in Air Condition. Con-   **FIG. 10.11**
densation begins at 5,000 feet, and the air cools at the wet adiabatic
rate to the top of the mountain. Condensation and precipitation do not occur on the lee side, so the
air warms at the dry adiabatic rate, returning to the base level much warmer than before.

distance. Therefore, when the air reaches the same elevation from which it started on the other side, it has become both warmer and drier (Fig. 10.11). Winds of this kind are local and intermittent in character. They are especially common on the northern side of the Alps in Switzerland, where they are called *foehn winds*, and on the eastern slope of the Rocky Mountains in Wyoming and Montana, where they are called *chinooks*. There is frequently a marked contrast between the air in these winds and the surrounding air, especially in winter, and the chinooks are capable of causing the quick disappearance, by melting and evaporation, of a deep snow cover. With the arrival of a chinook, a great and rapid rise in temperature may occur. At Rapid City, South Dakota, on January 13, 1913, the temperature rose from −17° at 8 A.M. to 47° at 10 P.M.

SIROCCO

Warm cyclonic winds have received local names in many parts of the world. A *sirocco* is a south wind coming from the Sahara Desert and is hot, dry, and dusty when it reaches North Africa. Sometimes it extends to the northern shores of the Mediterranean Sea in advance of a low center moving eastward. Crossing the sea, it picks up enough moisture in the lower levels to become uncomfortably muggy. This condition may be intensified by the foehn effect on the lee shores of Sicily and Italy. Sirocco has sometimes been applied more generally to any hot, dry wind occurring in the warm sector of a moving depression which has been heated by blowing over a hot and arid land surface. Such hot winds occur over the Great Plains of the United States in the summer.

NORTHERS AND BLIZZARDS

One of the most outstanding special winds of the central and southern parts of the United States, Mexico, and the Caribbean area is the *norther*.

It is a strong, cold wind from a northerly direction in winter, caused by the rapid advance of a polar anticyclone. Its arrival is accompanied by rapid temperature falls, sometimes as much as from 20°F to 30°F in one hour, and at times by snow, sleet, or rain. Severe northers are sometimes referred to as *cold waves*. Occasionally, severe northers bring freezing conditions and resulting damage to the truck-gardening and citrus industries of the Gulf Coast and the Rio Grande Valley. A similar wind in South America is called the *pampero*.

Blizzard is a term originating in America and refers to a violent cold wind (usually a norther) which is laden with snow, partially or entirely picked up from the ground. The snow usually consists of fine, powdery particles whipped by the wind in such great density that one can see only a few yards through it. The snow particles often are so fine and dense that they give the appearance of dense fog. Officially, the blizzard is defined as having wind velocities of 32 miles per hour or more, accompanied by a temperature in the twenties or lower and much snow in the air, from either falling snow or from blowing snow originating on the ground, or both, reducing the visibility to less than 500 feet and occasionally to zero. Blizzards have been reported in Antarctica with velocities of from 75 to 100 miles per hour.

DUST STORMS AND DUST FALLS

Moderate to strong winds blowing over a soil that is dry, loose, and unprotected by vegetation often raise clouds of dust which are carried along in the lower air by the wind. These are frequent in the southern Great Plains but are usually local in their incidence. However, when great areas become extremely dry, as happened in the early 1930's from North Dakota to Texas, and to a lesser degree in the early 1950's over the southern part of the same area, the entire lower atmosphere over large regions may be filled with dust. When the air has a stable lapse rate, the dust remains near the ground, and clear sky can be seen overhead. When the air mass is unstable, turbulence and convection lift the dust to greater heights, and a thick layer of the lower air becomes so dust laden that the sky is overcast with a gray dust cloud and the sun becomes a pale disk or is completely hidden. Sometimes in the Great Plains region the cloud is so dense and dark in limited areas that artificial lighting is required at midday. Along a distinct front having a sharp increase in wind velocity, the cloud of dust may advance like a moving wall, and the very minute of its arrival at a given place may be observed (Fig. 10.12). At other times the dust diffuses and thickens slowly and imperceptibly.

Dust which is thus lifted into the air is composed of fine particles which may be carried great distances, usually moving eastward before settling to the earth. Thus, in the summer of 1934, dust originating in the Great

Dust Storm, Johnson, Kansas, April 14, 1935. Courtesy, U.S. Department   **FIG. 10.12**
of Commerce, Weather Bureau.

Plains was observed and collected in Washington, D.C. In the airway meteorological service of the Weather Bureau the condition is recorded as "dust" when dust is present and the visibility is from 1 to 6 miles, and "thick dust" when the visibility is less than 1 mile. In addition to producing disagreeable dust storms, turbulent winds over loose, bare soil cause much damage by drifting and by loss of fertile topsoil. Dust storms similar to those originating in our Great Plains are frequent in the dry plains of northern China and in other parts of the world.

When precipitation begins in an air mass carrying large amounts of dust, or falls through such a mass, the rain or snow gathers the particles as it falls and reaches the earth as "muddy" rain or discolored snow, leaving a coating of soil on exposed surfaces. Noticeable dust falls usually occur in this way, mixed with falling rain or snow. At Cheney, Nebraska, on May 12, 1934, there was a fall of colored hail, the stones looking much like small balls of clay, owing to the accumulation of yellowish dust. At Madison, Wisconsin, on March 9, 1918, dust amounting to 13.5 tons per square mile was deposited with snow and sleet, giving it a light-yellow tint. Microscopic examination of this dust showed that much the greater part of it was of mineral particles, ranging from 0.008 to 0.025 millimeter in size, but it also contained fragments of leaves and other vegetable matter, including fungi and spores. Its origin was probably in Oklahoma or Kansas.

Occasionally a slackening of the dust-bearing currents permits a rapid settling of the dust, without accompanying condensation, resulting in a dry dust fall. At Lincoln, Nebraska, on April 29, 1933, there was a fall of dry, reddish-brown dust that continued for four hours, discoloring all horizontal objects and probably amounting to about 30 tons per square mile. Earlier in the day there were several showers of rain without any perceptible dust content, but four hours after the last rain, the dust began settling of its own weight, through quiet air, possibly aided by subsidence.

PROBLEMS

1.

Air starts at an elevation of 1,000 feet and a temperature of 65° and rises over a mountain at 7,000 feet, condensation beginning at 4,000 feet. What is the temperature of the air when it has descended on the other side to an elevation of 1,000 feet, assuming that the gain of heat by radiation and conduction is equal to the loss?

2.

If the air, before ascent in problem 1, has a specific humidity of 7 grams per kilogram and a mixing ratio of 14 grams per kilogram, what is the relative humidity?

3.

How much heat is imparted to the air for each gram of water precipitated in problem 1 if the specific humidity at the top of the mountain is 5 grams per kilogram?

4.

If the mixing ratio is 16 g/kg at 1,000 feet on the lee side of the mountain in problem 1, what is the relative humidity at that point?

5.

Tampa, Florida and Santa Fe, New Mexico each has a high concentration of thunderstorms. Explain the high thunderstorm frequencies at these two places.

6.

Describe the similarities and differences between foehn and katabatic winds.

7.

Make a list of precautionary measures that would be valuable to remember in the case of an approaching tornado.

8.

If the pressure inside the funnel of a tornado is 2 pounds per square inch less than surrounding pressure, what would be the total force on the walls and ceiling of a 10 x 10 x 10 ft. structure inside this funnel as a result of the pressure differential?

9.

Would the force in problem 8 tend to crush or explode the structure? Explain.

10.

The following storm advisories were issued by the Miami Weather Bureau Office regarding the location of the hurricane shown in Fig. 10.4 on page 194:

> 4:45 A.M., Sept. 19, 19.0°N, 82.0°W
> 4:45 A.M., Sept. 20, 20.7°N, 82.4°W
> 2:45 A.M., Sept. 21, 23.6°N, 81.6°W
> 4:30 A.M., Sept. 22, 25.8°N, 81.0°W
> 5:00 A.M., Sept. 23, 28.7°N, 76.7°W
> 11:45 P.M., Sept. 23, 34.5°N, 70.4°W
> 11:00 P.M., Sept. 24, 42.6°N, 56.2°W

Plot these positions on graph paper or on a map and draw the path of the hurricane. Compute the speed of the hurricane for each time interval.

11

weather analysis and forecasting

A primary object of weather study is to understand why the weather is as it is today and what it will be like tomorrow. The hope of being able to foresee future weather conditions furnishes the principal incentive for maintaining meteorological services by the government, armed forces, and private organizations. The practical value of accurate weather prediction is evident.

The basic tool of a forecaster is the surface weather map. It makes possible the visualization of weather conditions over large areas. The interaction of different air masses and the resulting development and motion of cyclones and anticyclones become evident. As one traces the weather from day to day on a series of weather maps, he will surely become aware that *weather travels*. This fact is of primary importance in weather forecasting. Forecasting is a matter of charting atmospheric conditions and interpreting them in such a way as to be able to foresee the state of the weather in the future, usually for a short period of time. The aim in the following discussion is to indicate briefly the nature of the problems involved in forecasting the weather and the means thus far developed to solve these problems. No attempt is made to give a complete exposition of forecasting techniques.

From the beginning of the use of weather maps until **Analysis** recently, the chief attention of forecasters was centered **of Synoptic Charts** upon the moving cyclones and anticyclones of the weather map as revealed by the pattern of isobars. The chief effort was given to estimating the paths and velocities of these highs and lows and their influence on the weather as they passed. Since the forces controlling their movement and changing intensity were unknown in detail, rules for forecasting were necessarily empirical. After a long and intimate familiarity with weather maps, the forecaster developed the ability to judge with considerable accuracy what changes in existing weather to expect under given conditions. With increasing daily exploration of the upper air, there is increasing knowledge of the physics of the air and an increasingly definite and scientific basis for forecasting.

ESTIMATING MOVEMENTS OF LOWS AND HIGHS

In deciding where a cyclone or anticyclone will be at a later time, twelve to forty-eight hours in the future, consideration is given to the normal or average direction and rate of movement of a disturbance in that position, and then to any reasons that may appear for a deviation from the normal. Usually the lows and highs move with the prevailing westerlies at an average velocity of about 30 to 35 miles per hour in winter and about 20 to 25 miles per hour in summer, and the normal movement always has an easterly component. There are large individual variations from the average, however, and each case must be considered separately.

These are some of the more general criteria used in forecasting the movement of a depression. It tends to move with the same velocity and direction as during the past twelve to twenty-four hours, in the absence of other indications. Strong winds in front of a low retard it. A low tends to move parallel to the isobars in the warm sector, but to cross the isotherms, that is, to move toward an area of high temperature. It tends to travel toward the area where the greatest fall in pressure is occurring, as indicated by the barometric tendency, that is, by the amount and sign of the pressure change during the past three hours. Highs move toward the area where the greatest rise in pressure is occurring.

As an aid in visualizing the pressure changes that are in progress, the three-hour pressure tendencies may be entered on the weather map, or on a separate map, and lines drawn connecting points of equal change. Such lines are called *isallobars*. A similar *pressure-change chart* may be drawn to show the changes in pressure that have occurred during the past twelve to twenty-four hours. Such charts make visible the areas of rising and falling pressure and the amount of rise or fall, thus indicating the current direction and speed of movement of the pressure systems. They are regularly used by forecasters in estimating future changes for short periods.

The distribution of pressure around the system under consideration influences its movement; the tendency is to move toward a region of small gradient and away from a region of steep gradient. A strong high east of a low, especially if the high is increasing in intensity or is nearly stationary, will retard the low or deflect it to the right or left. Two lows close together tend to unite. Consideration must also be given to the question of whether the low is increasing or decreasing in intensity or is likely to do so within the forecast period. A low with a marked pressure gradient but with weak winds around it will increase in intensity. There are other such precepts, but these will serve to illustrate the nature of the problems presented to the forecaster.

ESTIMATING THE RESULTING WEATHER

Having decided where the highs and lows on the map will be on the following day and how they will change, the question remains of how the new distribution of pressure will affect the weather. What will be the direction and force of the wind? What changes in temperature will occur? Will there be cloudiness or rain? In answering these questions, the following fundamental facts are kept in mind:

1. The wind has a direct relation to the pressure distribution. If the latter is correctly foreseen, the wind forecast should be correct both as to direction and approximate speed.

2. Temperature changes are largely controlled by the wind: "Every wind hath its weather"—more especially, its temperature. These are questions to be answered. What is the temperature of the air that is expected to arrive, and how will it be modified as it moves? How much cooler or warmer is it than is normal for the season, or than the air now in the area for which the forecast is being made?

3. Will cloudiness and precipitation likely be associated with the anticipated situation?

The occurrence of rain in any given pressure situation is related to the topography and slope of the region and its position relative to mountain chains and bodies of water. These affect the amount of moisture in the air and the amount and rate of the upward movement of the air. The question of where the moisture comes from is not always obvious because of our lack of complete knowledge of the movements of the upper air. In most cases, however, the source is evident.

PLACING OF FRONTS

A major problem in the analysis of the weather situation at a given time is the placing of fronts in their proper positions on the weather map, the identification of air masses, and the determination of their physical characteristics. It is first necessary to be familiar with the general characteristics of air masses and fronts, as outlined in Chapters 8 and 9. In the placing of fronts from surface data, the following considerations should also be kept in mind: Fronts persist from day to day, and the position of a front on any one map should be a consistent development from its position on the previous map. The change in wind direction at a front is usually well marked, especially along cold and occluded fronts.

A well-developed front is usually marked by an area of clouds and precipitation more or less parallel to it. The types and areas of clouds and precipitation are significant in locating a front, as, for example, the succession of cloud forms from Cirrus to Stratus preceding a warm front, and the relatively thin band of cumuliform clouds attending a cold front. The dew point usually shows an abrupt change on the passage of a front. The front lies in a pressure trough and the isobars make an abrupt change in direction at the front. In the warm sector of an active depression, the isobars are nearly straight lines and uniformly spaced. The character and magnitude of the pressure change in the past three hours are significantly different on the opposite sides of a front.

As previously stated, the properties of an air mass change as it moves away from the influences that have given it its characteristics. The modification is greatest in the lower layers, where there is interchange of heat to or from the earth and much turbulent mixing of the air, and where evaporation and condensation alter the moisture content. These influences so change the lower air that it is sometimes impossible to recognize its source by its surface properties, particularly by its temperature. Usually, however, there is a definite temperature discontinuity at a front, more pronounced in winter than in summer.

The primary role of air masses in the control of the   **Upper-air Analysis**
weather having been recognized, the necessity of frequent and well-distributed upper-air observations is evident. It is only by such observations that the characteristics, alterations, and movements of air masses can be known and their effects on the weather foreseen. Much of the progress in scientific meteorology has been wholly dependent upon the addition of this third dimension to weather observations.

The data for upper-air analysis are obtained from radiosonde recordings of pressure, temperature, and humidity at computed elevations. Also pilot balloon or rawin observations give wind direction and force at known elevations, and aircraft reconnaissance often provides information from otherwise inaccessible areas. In the absence of wind observations, the geostrophic and gradient winds are computed from the pressure gradient. The data thus obtained are used to construct maps representing atmospheric conditions at various elevations above sea level. It is found that, with increasing height, the surface irregularities and abrupt changes in pressure, temperature, and wind tend to disappear and the large-scale features of the circulation become more evident and are characterized by more gradual changes. Moreover, the circulation in these large-scale features at the higher levels largely governs the movement and behavior of disturbances in the lower levels. These facts indicate the fundamental importance of upper-air soundings and upper-air charts.

ANALYSIS OF AIR MASSES

In the analysis of air masses, an effort is made to ascertain (*a*) the extent and physical properties of each air mass, (*b*) the relations of the different masses to each other, and (*c*) the location, structure, and movement of the fronts along which the different masses meet. Structure of an air mass includes such properties as the temperature, humidity, and lapse rate at different levels; the degree of stability or instability of the air; whether it is stratified or well mixed; the existence of inversions, and whether these are due to warm currents of a different air mass or to subsidence of the upper air. A knowledge of the structure along the front involves ascertaining the slope of the front, the difference in temperature between the two masses, and the extent of mixing and turbulence at their surface of contact. Air-mass analysis, then, consists of a detailed study of the structure of the air. For successful application to forecasting, frequent observations at the surface and aloft are required.

IDENTIFYING AIR MASSES

The part of an air mass that is above surface influences is slower and more conservative in its changes than is the surface air. That is one reason why upper-air observations are more valuable than surface observations in identifying air masses. But even in the upper air, temperature and relative humidity may change greatly within a short period. A general uplift or subsidence of an air mass is a frequent occurrence; it results in dynamic cooling or warming and a consequent increase or decrease in the relative humidity. Hence, upper-air observations on successive days may give quite different temperatures and humidities in the same air mass and mislead the forecaster into thinking that one mass has been replaced by another.

The potential temperature remains the same with changing elevation as long as there is no condensation or evaporation, and the *equivalent potential temperature* is unchanged even by condensation or precipitation. The equivalent potential temperature is therefore called a *conservative property* of the air. It changes very slowly. (See page 86.) It is altered slightly by the evaporation of rain or fog and may be changed by the absorption or radiation of heat or by mixing with other air. These processes act slowly on large air masses above the surface layers. Accordingly, an air mass can be identified more definitely by its equivalent potential temperature than by its actual temperature or by even its potential temperature.

Similarly, *specific humidity* is a much more conservative property of an air mass than is relative humidity. The latter changes rapidly when the temperature changes, but temperature differences in themselves have no effect on specific humidity. The only processes that alter the specific humidity are the actual addition or removal of water vapor. The *mixing ratio* is conservative in the same way as the specific humidity. Dew point is also a more conservative element than relative humidity, because dew point is a function of absolute humidity, which changes more slowly than relative humidity. But absolute humidity and dew point both change when pressure changes.

Another property, more conservative than dew point or specific humidity, is the *wet-bulb potential temperature*, which is the wet-bulb temperature that a parcel of air will have when brought adiabatically to the standard pressure of 1,000 millibars. The wet-bulb temperature is the lowest temperature to which air can be cooled by evaporation of water into it. Hence, although evaporation reduces the temperature of the air, it leaves its wet-bulb temperature unchanged. In like manner, the condensation of moisture releases latent heat but does not alter the wet-bulb temperature. Accordingly, the wet-bulb potential temperature is not changed by adiabatic processes nor by the gain or loss of moisture. It varies only by acquiring heat from the outside or by losing heat by conduction, radiation, or mixing. Emphasis upon these conservative physical properties has come with the development of upper-air observations and air-mass analysis.

As was pointed out in Chapter 4, the basic tool for upper-air analysis is the adiabatic chart. From it can be read the degree of stability, mixing ratio, specific humidity, dew point, lifting condensation level, temperature, potential temperature, equivalent potential temperature, pressure, and height of all levels included in the sounding. These values are not only important in the analysis of atmospheric characteristics above a given station, but they may be transposed to several other specialized charts to provide regional, continental, or even hemispheric coverage of the selected characteristics.

CROSS SECTIONS

A vertical cross section of the atmosphere may be prepared by plotting the data obtained from radiosonde flights at stations in an approximate line across the country (Fig. 11.1). The values at the several elevations for each station are entered on a vertical scale at that station which extends from the base line representing the surface up to heights of 3 or 4 miles.

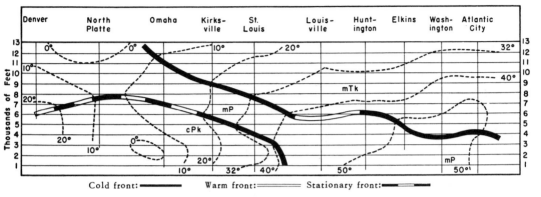

Atmospheric Cross Section from Denver to Atlantic City. Dashed lines are   **FIG. 11.1**
isotherms of actual temperature in degrees Fahrenheit.

Isopleths can then be drawn for temperature, potential temperature, mixing ratio, or other elements shown by the soundings. Sometimes it is helpful to construct more than one cross section along different base lines. Such cross sections show the condition of the air at the time of the soundings and may be of much value to the forecaster. They are especially helpful in fixing the position and slope of fronts and in making route forecasts for aircraft.

CONSTANT-PRESSURE CHARTS

The *constant-pressure chart*, also called the *pressure-contour chart,* has become the most commonly used type of synoptic upper-air chart (Fig. 11.2). Charts are prepared for several selected pressure surfaces. The most common ones used are the 850-, 700-, 500-, and 300-millibar surfaces. Height (in feet),[1] temperature (in degrees centigrade), and dew point are obtained from the radiosonde reports for each station at the chosen pressure surfaces. These data are entered on a chart at the geographical location of the appropriate stations. If upper-air wind data are available for these elevations, wind direction and force may be plotted also. Isotherms are then drawn which show the distribution of temperature characteristics on the isobaric surface. Along such an isotherm, pressure, temperature, potential temperature, and density are constant (neglecting the slight influence of moisture content on density). *Contour lines* are also drawn, connecting points of equal elevation. These lines show how the height of the chosen pressure surface varies from place to place. See Fig. 11.2, where

---

[1] In meteorology, height is usually determined by computation from the distribution of temperature and pressure through the atmosphere. Heights are therefore expressed in "geopotential" or "dynamic" units, which are almost the equivalent of linear units.

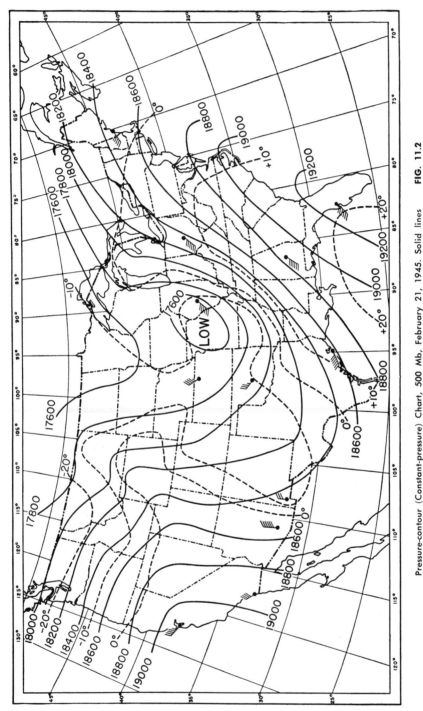

Pressure-contour (Constant-pressure) Chart, 500 Mb, February 21, 1945. Solid lines are contours showing height of constant pressure in feet. Dashed lines are isotherms.

FIG. 11.2

contour lines are drawn for each 200 feet of difference in elevation of the 500-millibar pressure surface.

Since they are all on the 500-millibar surface, each contour line is also a 500-millibar isobar. Thus the 18,000-foot contour on the constant-pressure surface is also a 500-millibar isobar on the 18,000-foot elevation surface. It follows, then, that the contour lines show the horizontal variation of pressure. For example, Fig. 11.2 shows an area inclosed by the contour of 17,600 feet. If we rose 400 feet above this area to a height of 18,000 feet, the pressure there would evidently be less than 500 millibars, for pressure decreases upward. Therefore, a low level of the contour lines indicates low pressure, considered horizontally, and a high level indicates high pressure.

At this altitude, the highs and lows and the irregularities of the isobars, as found at the ground, give way to a smooth, wavelike succession of troughs of low pressure and ridges (or wedges) of high pressure. There is a mathematical relation between wave length and speed of advance, and a formula has been developed for calculating the movements of the series of troughs and ridges. There is also a theoretical relation between the speed and the relative positions of isobars and isotherms in such wavelike motions. The movements of these troughs and ridges can thus be anticipated with fair accuracy for some days in advance. They are closely related to the movements of air masses and fronts at the earth's surface. In general, surface disturbances move along the isobars between the principal troughs and ridges shown on the upper-air chart and at a rate proportional to the pressure gradient between them. This chart is therefore of direct use to meteorologists for daily forecasting and especially in the preparation of forecasts for periods of two to five days in advance.

Constant-pressure charts are usually drawn for several different pressure values. The pressures of 500, 700, and 850 millibars correspond approximately to altitudes of 18,000, 10,000, and 5,000 feet, respectively. Charts are also in use for pressures of 1,000 millibars (very near the surface) and for 300 millibars (about 10 km or 30,000 ft), and sometimes for even smaller pressure values, extending into the stratosphere.

On a pressure-contour chart, the geostrophic wind is a function only of the spacing between contour lines, that is, of change of height with change of horizontal distance (neglecting local differences in gravity and in the Coriolis force). No correction for density is required. The direction and force of the wind at various pressure levels can thus be readily determined by the use of a single geostrophic wind scale, the same scale for all pressure-contour charts. The relative values of the wind at different levels are visible on the map. This is of direct value to the airplane pilot, and a knowledge of geostrophic wind values is important in forecasting the future movement of pressure systems.

By comparing two charts at different pressure levels, the thickness of the layer between them can be determined. This thickness is a measure of the *mean virtual temperature* of the layer. (Virtual temperature is affected by the moisture content of the air and may be defined as the temperature of dry air having the same pressure and same density as the existing air with moisture present.) The warmer the layer, the greater the thickness. A further comparison is obtained by superimposing successive surfaces one upon another. This procedure furnishes a check upon the accuracy and consistency of the analyses of the individual levels and brings out the relations between the various elements within the layer. Such an analysis of the atmosphere, layer by layer, is known as *differential analysis*. There is a shear of the geostrophic wind with height, that is, a change in direction and speed due to differences in temperature along isobaric surfaces. This is called the *thermal wind component* of the geostrophic wind aloft. It is determined in direction and magnitude by the distribution of the mean temperature. Hence, it may be obtained from the varying thickness of the layers between isobaric surfaces.

Knowing the winds and the mean virtual temperatures at various pressure levels in the free air helps meteorologists to estimate future pressure and temperature changes at the earth's surface. For example, it is found that there is a tendency for low-pressure centers to move along isotherms of mean virtual temperature between the 1,000- and the 700-millibar surfaces at a speed proportional to the speed of the geostrophic wind. The temperature differences on an isobaric surface are obviously not due to differences of pressure. They are "real" and of real significance to the forecaster. Where the isotherms cut across the contour lines, there is an active movement of masses of warm and cold air, and a change of pressure is in progress. The direction of the thermal winds in relation to the contours has a "steering" effect upon these pressure changes; it indicates areas of pressure rise and pressure fall.

ISENTROPIC ANALYSIS

Another method of charting upper-air conditions is to select a surface having the same potential temperature throughout (called an *isentropic surface*), and enter on the map at each station the pressure and the condensation pressure existing at the chosen potential temperature. *Condensation pressure* (also called *saturation pressure*) is the pressure at which saturation is attained in air ascending adiabatically. It can be readily obtained from the radiosonde observations. Lines may then be drawn (isobars) connecting points of equal pressure, and other lines (condensation isobars) connecting points of equal condensation pressure (Fig. 11.3). Where corresponding isobars and condensation isobars are near each other, the air is moist; where they are far apart, the air is dry.

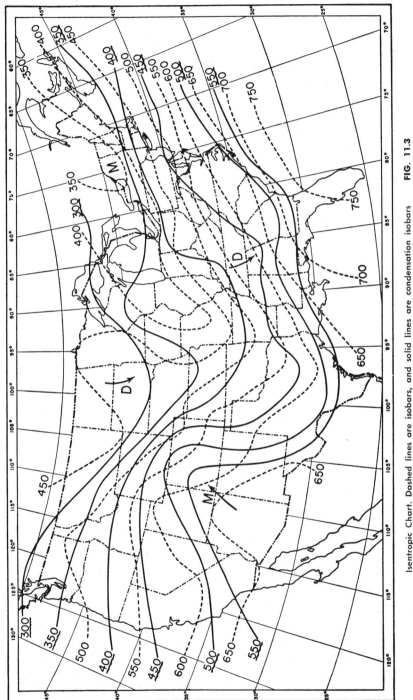

Isentropic Chart. Dashed lines are isobars, and solid lines are condensation isobars on an isentropic surface of potential temperature (302° A). D indicates dry area and M, moist area.

FIG. 11.3

The isentropic chart represents an attempt to study one of the most conservative properties of the atmosphere, namely, potential temperature. It is seldom used as a forecast tool, however, because similar information can be obtained from the constant-pressure charts.

CIRCULATION INDEX

As has been noted in Chapter 7, the prevailing westerly zonal circulation of middle latitudes results from the difference in pressure between the subtropical belts of high pressure and the subpolar low-pressure areas, and is modified by the cellular circulations around centers of action. These centers of action vary in intensity and position not only with the seasons, but also in short periods of irregular length, usually of a few weeks. The varying intensity of this zonal circulation in the prevailing westerlies of the Northern Hemisphere is expressed in terms of a *circulation index.* This index is obtained by taking the difference in sea-level pressure between latitudes 35°N and 55°N along several meridians around the hemisphere, and averaging these differences. If the average difference is 8 millibars or more, the circulation is said to have a *high index;* if the difference is less than 3 millibars, it has a *low index.* The higher the index is, the stronger are the prevailing westerlies.

The index thus obtained is in terms of sea-level pressures, but the different index values are most easily and quickly recognized on the 700-millibar pressure-contour chart, where they form distinctive patterns. When the index is high, the 700-millibar map shows nearly straight contours or long waves, and the troughs are small and move rapidly. At the same time, the centers of action in the lower air are large and few, the westerlies are strong, and there is little cyclonic activity.

When the index is low, the waves are short and move slowly. The centers of action break up into numerous small centers, the westerlies become weak and there is much cyclonic activity. Fast-moving waves on the upper-level charts indicate a high index and slow-moving waves indicate a low index. When values of the index are intermediate, lying between about 3 millibars and 8 millibars, the conditions shown on the charts are also intermediate. A low-index pattern is indicated in Fig. 11.4, which shows marked cyclonic activity and much north-south air movement. Severe blizzards and dust storms occurred in the Middle West and Great Plains concurrently with this synoptic situation.

Both high and low indexes occur characteristically in winter; summer values are usually intermediate. A particular index may persist for from three to eight weeks and then give place to an index of the opposite type. Changes in the value of the index are evidence of variations in the zonal circulation; such variations largely determine the formation and movement of air masses and fronts, and hence, the general character of the

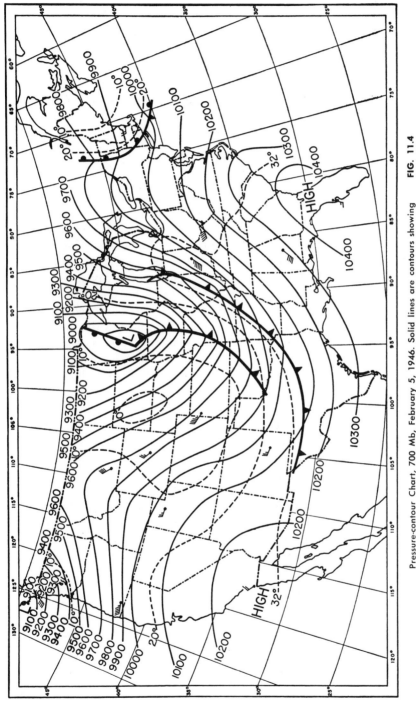

Pressure-contour Chart, 700 Mb, February 5, 1946. Solid lines are contours showing height of constant pressure in feet. Dashed lines are isotherms.

FIG. 11.4

weather. Therefore, the meteorologist must have in mind the existing index and its recent history. This is especially necessary in winter and in the preparation of forecasts for several days in advance.

MEAN WEATHER CHARTS

Averaging values to obtain more representative results is not new; however, its application to weather analysis is fairly recent. Mean charts tend to eliminate lesser perturbations in the atmosphere and to reveal only the larger or long-range trends. The technique has been used in climatology for many years. It promises to be of much value to meteorologists also, especially for long-range forecasting.

A five-day *time mean chart,* developed by Jerome Namias, can be drawn for the entire Northern Hemisphere on the basis of the five-day average height of a selected pressure surface (usually 500 millibars) over predetermined stations. This reveals a simplified pattern of slow-moving, long waves about the hemisphere which could definitely be associated with regional weather characteristics. Since the most current five-day mean chart is necessarily two and one-half days old, its value for operational forecasts is seriously impaired. The *space mean chart* was developed to overcome this handicap. It is obtained by averaging the values at the four points of a diamond and plotting the result at the center. The space mean chart seems to possess all the merits of the time mean chart plus the fact that it can be analyzed and ready for forecasting use within a few hours of the actual observations.

Forecasting the Weather

The first step in making a weather forecast is the collection of available weather information. Most of the countries of the world maintain a grid of observation stations and a teletype network for the collection and distribution of regular weather reports. These reports are transmitted in numerical weather codes which can be decoded into the various languages of the world. In other words, the *international meteorological code* is a kind of international language which permits meteorologists in various countries to communicate freely about the weather in spite of a language barrier.

From the moment a series of standard observations begin to pour into a forecast station, a race with the clock begins. Plotters and analysts must do their work quickly if a reliable forecast is to be made in time to be of value to the public. A typical weather station in the United States is now relieved of much of this "organized bedlam" through the use of facsimile machines and circuits for the transmission of weather maps and charts. Other countries of the world as well as the military services make use of this ingenious communication medium (Fig. 11.5).

Facsimile. This instrument reproduces weather maps and charts transmitted   **FIG. 11.5**
via wire line from Washington, D.C. The addition of auxiliary radio
equipment allows reception over radio circuits. *Courtesy, Adler/Westrex Communications Division,
Amecom/Litton Systems, Inc.*

Facsimile equipment permits highly skilled specialists at a single
weather office to produce charts and maps for the entire country. With
these charts in hand the local forecaster must, in relatively short order,
integrate a mass of data and analyses with local observations and geographical considerations. The race with the clock is always present, for
the meteorologist must try to prepare the best possible forecast in the
least possible time. There always seems to be more information available
than one can digest and assimilate into usable form before a forecast is
due. Literally tens of thousands of items of information must be dealt
with on each forecast. An ordinary surface map of the United States and
Canada alone may contain upwards of 10,000 items. This does not take
into account a similar amount of upper-air information and a host of airways hourly sequence reports. Finally, all of this information must be cor-
related with similar information on previous charts and then projected
into the future. It is no wonder that weather forecasts are not always
perfect.

For forecasting in the United States, an area including the whole of
North America, the North Pacific Ocean, and the western part of the
North Atlantic Ocean should be charted. Reports are received from points

in Alaska and Canada as well as from weather ships in the two oceans. The primary purpose for collecting and plotting all of this information is to be able to foresee future weather conditions by understanding the present situation and the physical processes which will cause changes in the future.

CHARTING OF DATA

The following types of data are available for charting at the forecast centers: (a) the simultaneous surface observations from which are prepared the synoptic weather map and supplementary charts, such as pressure-change charts; (b) radiosonde observations, giving pressure, temperature, and humidity of the air at various levels above the stations; (c) pilot-balloon observations and rawins, giving wind direction and force at known elevations. These upper-air data are the basis for the construction of constant-pressure charts, winds-aloft charts, isentropic charts, vertical cross sections, and mean pressure charts of the atmosphere. Not all of these facilities, but sometimes a few additional ones, are available for every forecaster. Making use of all the relevant information thus collected and charted, the meteorologist identifies the air masses and places the fronts properly on the weather map. Areas of precipitation and other special weather conditions are carefully analyzed and related to their causes. This is the modern method of analyzing the weather situation at a given time, and is known as *weather analysis* or *air-mass analysis*.

DAILY FORECASTS

Having charted the data, the next step in the preparation of the forecast is to estimate the movement, future position, and development of patterns such as shown on the charts of Figs. 11.6, 11.7, and 11.8. The simplest procedure is to assume that the isobars, the fronts, and the areas of high and low pressure will move without change in the same direction and at the same speed as they are currently moving, as shown by the pressure-change chart. This procedure will usually give fairly accurate results for twelve hours in advance, but beyond that period there is increasing error, and the meteorologist must look for indications of change. Here, the circulation index and the upper-air charts, especially the pressure-contour charts for 500 and 700 millibars, give valuable information. *Prognostic charts* for various constant-pressure levels are drawn by the meteorologist as he thinks the pressure patterns will appear at a selected hour in the future, usually twenty-four hours in advance. These serve to check the indications shown on the surface weather map concerning the movements of pressure systems and fronts.

Since fronts have a more or less definite association with centers of high and low pressure, the general rules applying to the movement of cyclones and anticyclones may be applied also with little modification to the movement of the discontinuities attending them. A few precepts relative to the

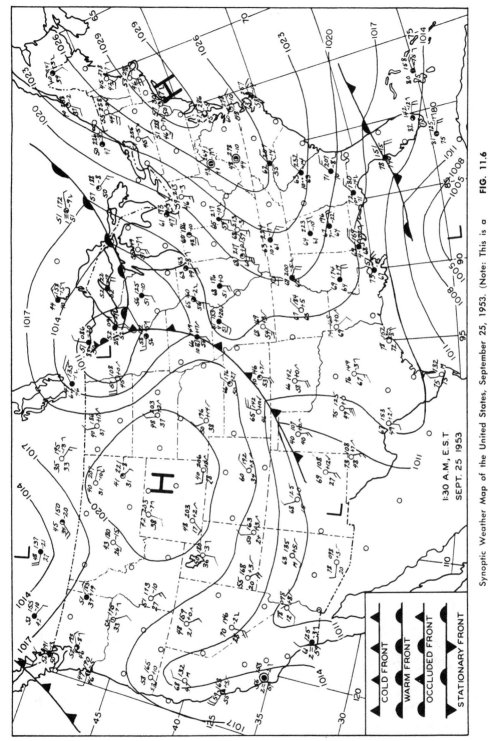

COLD FRONT
WARM FRONT
OCCLUDED FRONT
STATIONARY FRONT

1:30 A.M., E.S.T
SEPT. 25 1953

Synoptic Weather Map of the United States, September 25, 1953. (Note: This is a continuation of the series shown in Figs. 8.2, 8.3, and 8.4 on pages 154, 156, and 157.)

FIG. 11.6

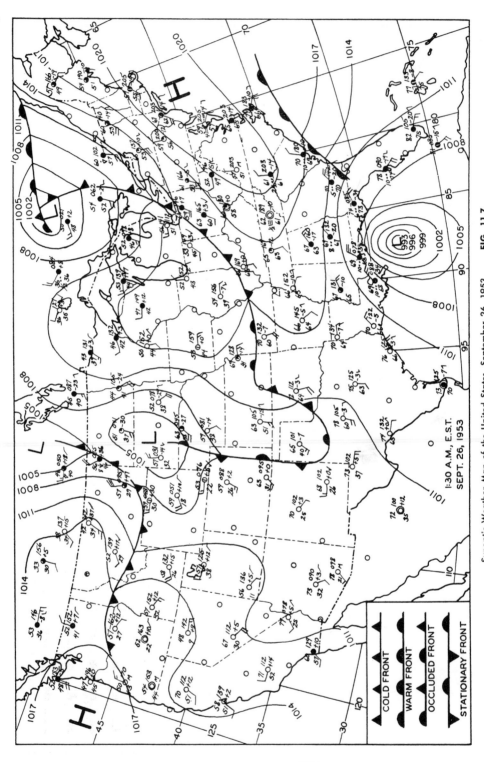

COLD FRONT

WARM FRONT

OCCLUDED FRONT

STATIONARY FRONT

1:30 A.M., E.S.T.
SEPT. 26, 1953

Synoptic Weather Map of the United States, September 26, 1953.   FIG. 11.7

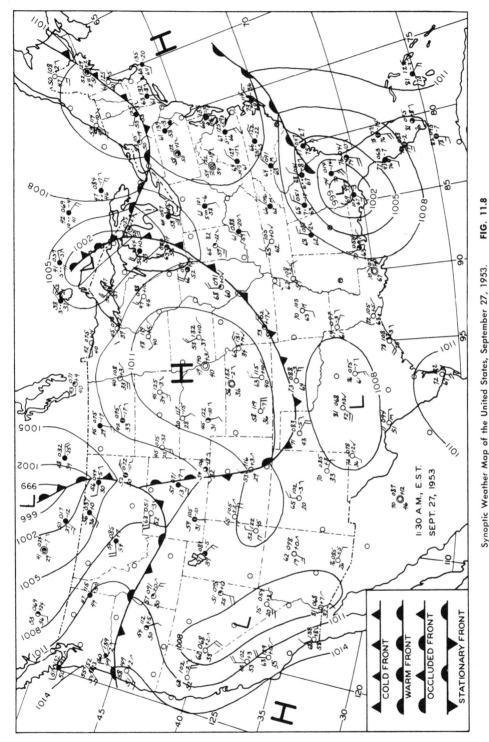

Synoptic Weather Map of the United States, September 27, 1953.   **FIG. 11.8**

1:30 A.M., E.S.T.
SEPT. 27, 1953

COLD FRONT
WARM FRONT
OCCLUDED FRONT
STATIONARY FRONT

movement of fronts may be summarized. The movement of fronts, as well as of pressure systems, is more or less clearly indicated by the existing differences in pressure around them and by the rate of change of this pressure. More specifically, a warm front moves faster, the greater the fall in pressure in front of it within the preceding three hours, and a cold front moves faster, the greater the rise in pressure behind it. A front moves slowly when it is nearly parallel to the isobars and increases in velocity as the number of isobars intersecting it increases. Fronts are retarded by high mountain ranges and by large, slow-moving anticyclones.

A method of computing the movement of isobars and of pressure troughs and wedges on the surface map has been developed by S. Petterssen. The method is based on the pressure tendencies as shown on the surface map. If we take, for example, a station on the forward side of an advancing trough of low pressure, it is evident that the fall in pressure at that station during the past three hours is an indication of the speed of advance of the low, provided the low is not changing in shape nor in intensity. Similarly, a station at the rear of the trough will show a rise in pressure due to the movement of the trough. If there has been no change in intensity, the fall in pressure at the station in front should equal the rise at a station an equal distance in the rear. This value, the same on each side, is therefore a measure of the speed of displacement of the trough.

A change in intensity is indicated by a *deepening* of the low (pressure lower at the center than it was at the previous observation), or by a *filling* of the low (pressure becoming higher at the center). If there has been deepening, the station ahead of the front will show a pressure fall greater than the pressure rise at the rear. Similarly, if there has been filling, the advance station will indicate a smaller pressure fall than the pressure rise at the rear station. From these considerations, Petterssen developed a simple equation for computing in miles per hour the movement of isobars and pressure systems. His equation has proved valuable and is being used, although it does not take account of all possibilities of change and, therefore, sometimes gives erroneous results.

A more recently developed technique for computing movement and intensity of surface weather features has been developed by J. J. George and associates. This method is now being widely tested by forecasters and has become known as the *George method.* It is an empirical manipulation of pressure, temperature, and wind values, taken from the synoptic weather chart and the 850-, 700-, and 500-millibar constant-pressure charts, to obtain a twenty-four hour forecast of movement and intensity of highs, lows, and fronts.

Making use of all such prognostic precepts and rules, the meteorologist next makes a prognostic chart of surface conditions, placing isobars and fronts as he thinks they will appear at the end of the forecast period and perhaps, also, at intermediate intervals. He is then ready to prepare the detailed forecast for a given station or a given area. A daily forecast is generally concerned with winds, temperatures, cloud cover, and precipitation, if any is expected. To be most effective, it must state the time during the period when changes or variations are expected to take place.

SHORT-RANGE FORECASTS

Ordinarily, the making of short-range forecasts consists in extrapolating for a few hours in advance the conditions shown on the current synoptic map. In doing this, attention is given to the general trend of the weather situation and to any specific indications of change. For example, the Petterssen method of computing displacements is especially applicable to short-range forecasts. By applying these methods as they are used in making daily forecasts, short-range forecasts can usually be made without serious error and with greater accuracy in detail and in timing than is possible for longer periods. For this reason, air-transport companies depend very largely on short-range forecasts in the operation of airports and the maintenance of flight schedules. In the case of the development of dangerous storms of small area, such as hurricanes, tornadoes, or severe thunderstorms, these methods do not make it possible to foresee with the desired precision the severity, path, and time of arrival of such storms. In these cases, aircraft reconnaissance and radar storm detection have proved of great value.

Radar storm detection. The development of radar and its adaptability to the detection of severe weather phenomena represents one of the greatest advances in the last quarter of a century in our ability to pinpoint intense storms and to provide adequate forecasts and warnings. *Radar* is a contraction of "radio detection and ranging." It depends on the emission of short, sharp pulses of electromagnetic energy in a known direction. These pulses intercept targets which cause the energy waves to scatter in all directions. That small part of the energy which is reflected back in the direction of the radar is picked up by an antenna and recorded as an echo or "blip" on a receiver scope (Fig. 11.9). The time taken for the pulse to travel to the target and back again determines the distance to the target. This time interval must be measured very accurately since a pulse travels at the speed of light.

The principal of radar was first discovered in 1887 by a physicist named Hertz. In 1922, Dr. H. A. Taylor first attempted to develop it for a practical use, but not until 1942, after the United States and England had pooled their research and development efforts, did radar become an important detection device.

Two radar sets have been specifically designed for weather detection. The first, the CPS-9 set, was developed by the U.S. Air Force and is being widely used. The second weather radar set is the WSR-57, developed by the U.S. Weather Bureau and the Navy, has numerous desirable features.

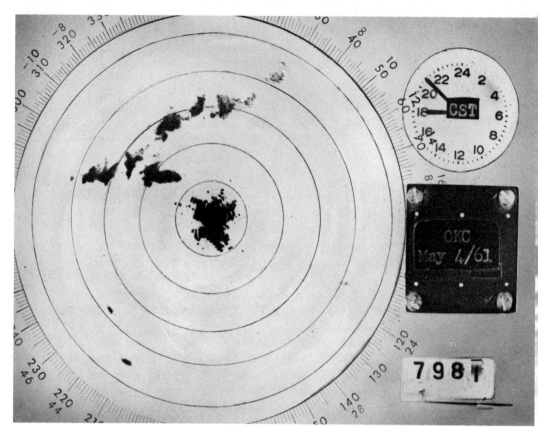

Radar PPI Scope. This WSR-57 radar PPI scope photograph showed a **FIG. 11.9**
tornado 20 miles northwest of Oklahoma City on May 4, 1961. The cloud
sustaining the tornado was moving slightly in advance of a general line of thunderstorms oriented
from the Southwest to the Northeast. A transparent map overlay allows the observer to pinpoint the
exact locations of the thunderstorms. *Courtesy, U.S. Department of Commerce, Weather Bureau.*

In addition to the PPI (plan-position indicator) scope, it has a RHI (range-height indicator) scope which allows investigation of the location, height, and intensity of storms within a range of about 250 miles (400 km).

Echoes returned by weather phenomena can usually be easily distinguished from those of other targets, and different types of storms give distinctive echo patterns. Hurricanes, tornadoes, thunderstorms, cold fronts, squall lines—in fact, about any type of storm that is accompanied by significant precipitation—can be located with great accuracy and tracked with precision. Also helpful is a feature permitting variation in wave length of the energy pulse which permits an examination of the intensity of the storm. It is evident that weather radar improves local forecasts and helps protect life and property on land, on sea, and in the air.

EXTENDED FORECASTS

In the preparation of extended forecasts for periods of from five to seven days in the future, three somewhat different methods of approach have been used by different groups of forecasters. These are discussed briefly in the following paragraphs.

Method of five-day means. In forecasting by the use of five-day averages, reliance is placed mainly on the 700-millibar pressure-contour chart and the circulation index to enable the forecaster to foresee the pressure pattern that will exist during the next five to seven days. First, a chart is prepared on which the isobars show the average pressure at sea level for the five-day period ending the day before the forecasts are made. Next, a similar chart is made on which the contour lines show the average height of the 700-millibar surface for the same period. These charts obscure the small and irregular fluctuations in pressure distribution and circulation index, but emphasize their general trends and bring out the position and intensity of the centers of action. A comparison of these five-day means with the corresponding normals for the time of year is then made.

From a study of these charts, the forecaster first makes a forecast of the index in the westerlies for the coming week and then prepares prognostic charts of the upper-air and surface mean-pressure distribution for the five-day period ending a week ahead. Finally, prognostic charts of surface-pressure distribution are drawn for each day of the forecast period, and daily forecasts are made from these as from the usual daily synoptic charts.

Method of extrapolation. An extrapolation method has been used in the preparation of daily forecasts for a six-day period beginning with the day following that on which the forecasts are made. In this method, a thorough study is made of existing conditions and tendencies as shown by the surface charts, and in particular by pressure-contour charts at various surfaces in the upper air, extending into the stratosphere. Special attention is given to the two main types of circulation in the westerlies, corresponding to high and low values of the circulation index. Change charts are prepared to show past movements, both at the surface and in the upper air. Then the expected positions of pressure centers, ridges, and troughs at the various levels at stated times in the future are extrapolated by extending previous movements and trends, step by step. Lastly, for each of the six days, the frontal systems and isobars are drawn, the air masses named, the areas of expected precipitation outlined, and the forecasts stated.

Method of weather types. A third approach in the preparation of extended forecasts is called the *weather-type* method. By this method future *weather analogues* are determined by a study of past cases where similar conditions prevailed. The method makes use of the fact that the weather in the zone of the westerlies is largely controlled by the irregular outbreaks of polar air along the polar front and by the varying position and character of the subtropical cells of high pressure.

A large outbreak of polar air, for example, produces a typical meridional (north-south) circulation, which gradually becomes more and more zonal (westerly) as the polar air moves from its source and warms and merges with other air. This is the usual behavior of the circulation in the zone of the prevailing westerlies—an occasional abrupt change from zonal to meridional flow, and then a gradual trend back to zonal in a period of a few weeks. A study of a long series of daily weather maps has shown, also, that three days is the most frequent interval between successive cyclone families or frontal passages, and that the principal troughs and ridges in the heart of the westerlies travel an average of 15° of longitude a day.

In applying these principles, the zone of the westerlies is divided into geographical regions in each of which the major controlling factor is either in the subtropical cells or in the polar outbreaks. In each of these regions, various types of pressure distribution and frontal activity are set up. This is done by a study of past weather maps for a long series of years and by classifying them into types in which similar conditions obtain and similar weather is observed. In the North American region, about twelve principal types have been catalogued.

Making use of these types and of such longer-term trends or tendencies as may appear, the forecaster proceeds to determine the current type and then to predict the succeeding type on the assumption that past analogous situations will be repeated. Having done this, he prepares prognostic charts for each day of the forecast period, and from these prepares the daily forecasts. This method is not limited to a forecast period of a fixed number of days, but there is increasing error beyond five or six days.

The preparation of the long series of weather maps of the Northern Hemisphere, upon which this method of extended forecasting depends, occurred during World War II. It resulted in the accumulation of a file of modern daily surface weather maps of the Northern Hemisphere covering a period of forty years. These maps were carefully classified and separated into types in terms of fundamental atmospheric processes and were then indexed and catalogued. An archive of classified weather maps, convenient for reference and research, was thus created. It was put to immediate use in the making of extended forecasts by the weather-type method, and has also been found useful in affording some indication of monthly and seasonal weather trends. It may well be the source of additional information and new concepts, as the effort to interpret atmospheric processes continues.

LONG-RANGE FORECASTS

Attention has been given for many years to the possibility of foreseeing weather conditions for a month or more in advance. Several different approaches to the problem have been developed. Attempts have been made to determine the general character of the weather a month, a season, or a year in advance by various statistical and physical approaches. These are discussed in Chapter 15 under the head of *seasonal forecasting*. In the present connection, we shall consider briefly the more strictly meteorological method of attacking the problem. This method in the main is an attempt to find types and analogues.

Making use of methods similar to those used in the preparation of extended forecasts for a few days by the study of weather types, attempts have been made to extend the period farther into the future. In the classification of weather types, it is found that there are certain trends, tendencies, or oscillations that show themselves as a repetition of a given type or a series of closely related types. For example, the cycle that follows an outbreak of polar air, from zonal to meridional flow and back again to zonal, is usually completed in from twenty-five to forty days, averaging about thirty-five days. This has been called the *polar sequence,* or *polar cycle.* Such trends and oscillations are used in estimating future developments.

However, in making such estimates, chief reliance is placed upon pressure and wind conditions in the upper troposphere and the lower stratosphere, as shown by upper-air charts. At these heights, conditions change slowly and, therefore, are more predictable. It is assumed that these upper-air conditions steer or control surface conditions. The assumption is made also that future weather for a month or more will follow a course like that followed in similar situations in the past, that the same weather sequences will occur. This is the essence of the method of analogues.

By such means, attempts have been made, not only to predict the general character of the weather or the average weather for a month to a year in the future, but even to forecast the weather for each day for a month or more. This method of analogues has been used to some extent by our military forces, but it must still be regarded as in a preliminary, experimental stage, especially in the forecasting of daily weather for more than ten days in advance. No sufficient basis has been established for the assumption that one weather situation, which at best can be only partially defined, always leads to the same subsequent weather, nor for the assumption that the course of events can be timed accurately. Continuous progress is being made, however, in measuring and interpreting the physical reactions of the atmosphere, and this advance keeps alive the hope for an ultimate understanding that will permit accurate long-range prognosis.

NUMERICAL WEATHER PREDICTION

As early as 1910, L. F. Richardson believed that weather forecasts could be made by solving the hydrodynamical equations of the atmosphere, thus eliminating the empirical aspects of synoptic meteorology. The calculations were laborious, however, and about ten years were required for Richardson to complete a twenty-four-hour forecast. Richardson's forecast results proved to be in error by a considerable degree, thus discouraging any further investigations into this technique of weather forecasting for several years. The development of high-speed electronic computers has more recently allowed Richardson's efforts to be duplicated and checked. It has been concluded that the idea is sound but that Richardson was doomed to fail from the start because of the limitations of the science at the time he was doing his experiment. Numerical weather prediction has now been developed to a degree of accuracy comparable to other existing forecast methods. The forecasting success of the electronic computer depends on the accuracy of the data it receives and its ability to integrate, within a relatively short time, the interrelationships of atmospheric variables over the forecast period. The numerical prediction technique is most promising for increasing the accuracy of short-range weather forecasts of forty-eight hours or less. If it is ever to be useful for long-range forecasting, the short-range forecast must increase in accuracy to near 100 per cent.

The value of numerical weather analysis should not be underestimated. Already machines have been developed and are in regular use which can take raw weather data and produce finished prognostic charts without further aid from the plotter, analyst, or forecaster. These charts are produced at a center in Suitland, Maryland and distributed nationally by means of facsimile transmission equipment. One should not be misled into thinking, however, that we are on the threshold of perfect and exact forecasts. There are too many variables and interrelated influences with non-linear relationships affecting the weather to hope for such a panacea in the near future.

"Men judge by the complexion of the sky
The state and inclination of the day."

**Local Forecasts
and Weather Lore**

Forecasts for a few hours in advance may be made without instruments or maps from the appearance of the sky, from the wind, and from the "feel" of the air. They are made by everyone who looks out in the morning and decides whether to carry a raincoat or not. "When clouds appear, wise men put on their cloaks." Farmers, sailors, and others who watch the weather closely may become quite adept in such forecasting.

WIND-BAROMETER INDICATIONS

A barometer will help in making such local, short-period forecasts, but its indications are not simple. The words on the dial of an aneroid barometer mean little. It is not the actual reading of the barometer so much as the kind and rate of change of pressure that are of importance. The following rules for interpreting changes in wind and pressure are useful in the absence of additional information and official forecasts:

When the wind sets in from points between south and southeast and the barometer falls steadily, a storm is approaching from the west or northwest, and its center will pass near or north of the observer within twelve to twenty-four hours with wind shifting to northwest by way of southwest and west.

When the wind sets in from points between east and northeast and the barometer falls steadily, a storm is approaching from the south or southwest, and its center will pass near or to the south or east of the observer within twelve to twenty-four hours with wind shifting to northwest by way of north. The rapidity of the storm's approach and its intensity will be indicated by the rate and the amount of the fall in the barometer.

STATISTICAL INDICATIONS

From a long series of observations, tables or graphs may be prepared showing the probability of rain or other weather occurrences under certain conditions of pressure, temperature, or wind direction. Thus, it was found at Dubuque, Iowa, that during the summer months rain fell within twelve hours in 93 per cent of the cases when the following conditions were recorded at the morning observation, namely, pressure between 29.75 and 29.85 inches (1,008 and 1,011 mb) and falling, temperature also falling and sky cloudy. The percentage was only 33 under conditions which were the same except that the pressure was rising and the sky clear. It was also found that the probability of rain within twenty-four hours was 72 in 100 in all cases when the wind was from the east and the barometer falling, and only 44 in 100 when the wind was from the northwest.

Such results are local in their application, and studies of this character cannot hope to take the place of synoptic charts in forecasting. They may, however, furnish supplementary information and suggestion, and, in the absence of a weather map, are of value in indicating probable local weather conditions. The best results for short periods in advance are obtained by combining the use of the weather map with a knowledge of local signs, such as are furnished by clouds, wind directions, and pressure changes. This is true for short periods only. For forecasts for twelve or more hours in advance, dependence must be placed on the weather map, for the weather can change greatly in that period, and it is often misleading to look out of the window and try to anticipate tomorrow's weather from today's.

SINGLE-STATION FORECASTING

It happens often in war and sometimes in peace that there are isolated units on land or on ships at sea to whom a knowledge of coming weather is of much importance but to whom synoptic reports are not available. A meteorologist in such a situation can gain valuable information from a study of the clouds if he is thoroughly familiar with their various types and subtypes and the details of their structure. The amount of cloudiness and whether it is increasing or decreasing, and the shapes and character-istics of the clouds, tell him much concerning the structure of the air masses in which the clouds lie. They help to identify the air masses and to indicate their degree of stability, and thus give an indication of the coming weather. A detailed knowledge of cloud characteristics is of importance at all times to the forecaster and the pilot, but especially when only local data are at hand.

If the isolated unit is equipped with pilot balloons and radiosondes, or airplanes with recording instruments, additional information valuable in forecasting may be obtained. The pilot-balloon records of the direction and force of the wind at different levels give an indication of the positions of the centers of areas of high and low pressure, and the direction of the isobars and isotherms, at upper levels. From these indications, inferences may be drawn concerning the movement of pressure systems at the earth's surface. Radiosonde or airplane observations, especially if they extend to the tropopause, give information as to the value of the circulation index, the types of air masses at different levels, and the location of fronts. Clouds and local free-air soundings thus help the meteorologist to get a fairly authentic picture of existing local weather conditions and probable future conditions, even in the absence of an extensive network of observations.

Remembering that weather normally travels from west to east in middle latitudes, a single station may take frequent detailed observations of the weather and plot each succeeding observation to the west of the preceding one. In the trade-wind belt of low latitudes, where weather moves from east to west, the plotting should be done in reverse order. After several entries have been made, the forecaster has an approximate cross section of the atmosphere in one direction from his station. Thus he has a better concept of the pressure pattern, wind field, and general weather conditions than would otherwise be possible. This technique is especially useful on ships and small island stations where local orographic effects are negligible.

WEATHER PROVERBS

Some of the weather proverbs relating to the appearance of the sky, the direction of the winds, and the humidity of the air are the result of long experience and have a certain validity, similar to the statistical results mentioned above; but, many of them lose their application when transplanted from the part of the world where they developed. None of them are "sure signs." For example, Cirrus often develop far in advance of a warm front, and when they thicken into Cirrostratus, it is a good indication that the warm-front rain is approaching; but rain does not fall in the entire area over which the cirriform clouds appear.

The conditions of plants and the condition and behavior of animals are largely responses to past and present weather influences, but probably they furnish no indication of future weather. The belief in such omens is suggestive of the superstitious practices of the augurs of ancient Rome. It may be true that certain plants and animals are sensitive to changes in pressure, temperature, and humidity, and for that reason their actions just before a storm may give a few minutes' warning of an approaching change. There is no "equinoctial storm" except in the sense that the equinoxes mark transition periods between winter and summer conditions, and storms often occur in the regular progress of the seasons during the latter part of March and of September. The long-range "forecasts" published in almanacs are generalized statements for large areas based on normals and normal variations and are confirmed only by chance.

PROBLEMS

1.

Make a list of the weather proverbs you have heard. Try to trace them to their probable origins. In each case, can you recognize any scientific basis for the proverb?

2.

Using Figs. 11.7 and 11.8, compute the twenty-four-hour movement of the incipient hurricane from 1:30 A.M., Sept. 26 to the same time the following day. What was the hourly speed of the system?

3.

Was the storm in problem 2 increasing or decreasing in intensity? How can you tell?

4.

Study the wave cyclone in the vicinity of the Great Lakes in Figs. 11.6, 11.7, and 11.8. If the positions on Sept. 25 and 27 are correct, what is probably wrong with the analysis on Sept. 26?

5.

By looking at the map of Sept. 26, can you explain why it was easy to not locate the warm front in the wave cyclone correctly?

6.

Make a list of rules that might help you predict the weather without the aid of a weather map.

7.

What are the criteria to look for in deciding where to place a cold front on a weather map?

8.

Explain why a contour line on a constant-pressure chart is also an isobar on a constant-level chart.

9.

If the average surface pressure across southern Canada was 1,002 mb while the average surface pressure was 1,012 mb across the southern United States, would the circulation index be high or low? Explain your answer.

10.

Compute the distance to a target thunderstorm if the round trip time for a radar pulse is 6.1 microseconds; 10.74 microseconds; 12.36 microseconds; 537 microseconds. (*Note:* Light travels 984 feet in one microsecond.)

12

aviation
and the weather

In the use of the air as a medium through which to propel great ships of many tons' weight, some knowledge of the properties and behavior of the air is obviously necessary. The operation and safety of airplanes are not independent of atmospheric conditions, in spite of the fact that modern methods, instruments, and flying aids have greatly reduced flying hazards.

Airways Service

With the development of aviation has come a more intensive and extensive use of weather data. The U.S. Weather Bureau and the Federal Aviation Agency have developed, along the principal airways of the country, a service by means of which the officials at the airports and the pilots in flight are kept constantly informed of weather conditions along the routes traveled and are provided with specific forecasts of conditions to be expected during the next few hours.

AIRWAYS OBSERVATIONS

Weather observations are made and recorded hourly at hundreds of airways weather stations situated at airports in all parts of the country and at stations a considerable distance from the airways on both sides. At most stations, this service is continued for twenty-four hours each day. In addition, special observations are made whenever marked changes in weather conditions occur. All these observations are transmitted over teletype circuits to regional centers and become available to all intermediate stations equipped with teletype service. They are known as *sequence reports,* or *hourly sequences.* From the regional centers, the existing weather conditions along the airways, as shown by these reports, are broadcast at frequent intervals for the information of all, but especially for aviators in flight. Thus, both officials and aviators are kept continuously informed of current weather conditions. The broadcasts are available to all planes equipped with radio-receiving facilities. A network of weather-reporting stations is indispensable in the regular operation of airways.

The elements of the sequence reports are:

Station identification. Identifying code letters are assigned each reporting station by the Federal Aviation Agency.

Type of report. This group is omitted except for a special report which indicates important weather changes.

Ceiling. Ceiling and cloud heights are expressed in hundreds of feet. The manner in which the ceiling was determined is indicated by A, aircraft; B, balloon; E, estimated; M, measured; and W, indefinite.

Sky condition. Sky condition is reported as clear, scattered clouds, broken, or overcast. The sky may also be reported as obscured by dust, fog, haze, or smoke.

Visibility. Visibility is reported in statute miles and fractions.

Weather. Letter symbols are assigned to indicate prevailing weather conditions and obstructions to vision.

Sea-level pressure. Three coded digits indicate tens, units, and tenths of millibars.

Temperature. Temperature is reported in degrees Fahrenheit. A minus sign (—) is prefixed when the temperature is below zero.

Dew point. Dew point is reported in the same manner as temperature and is especially valuable when fog or icing conditions are anticipated.

Wind direction and speed. The wind is reported by arrows indicating direction, followed by its speed in knots.

Altimeter setting. Three coded digits expressing units, tenths, and hundredths of inches allows the pilot to adjust his pressure altimeter so that it will read the proper elevation above mean sea level.

Remarks. Used to report in plain language, symbols, or contractions significant weather phenomena not included elsewhere in the message.

A sample sequence report is decoded below:

PIT S1 M3V ⊕ 7 ⊕ 1 1/2 V L–FK 146/72/68 → 11/989/CIG 2V4 VSBY 1V2   Pittsburgh, Pa., special report no. 1, measured ceiling 300 feet and variable, broken clouds with overcast at 700 feet, visibility 1 1/2 miles and variable, light drizzle with fog and smoke, pressure is

1,014.6 millibars, temperature is 72°F, dew point is 68°F, west wind at 11 nautical miles per hour, altimeter setting is 29.89 inches, ceiling variable from 200 to 400 feet, and visibility variable from 1 to 2 miles.

AIRWAYS FORECASTS

Weather service to aviation was made a primary responsibility of the Weather Bureau by federal legislation in 1938. The service was reorganized in 1952 as the Flight Advisory Weather Service, whose function includes all weather forecast and warning services to air navigation, provided by twenty-six FAWS forecast centers. Forecasts contain information on clouds, cloud heights, visibilities, fog, haze, smoke, wind conditions, icing, turbulence, the location and intensity of local storms and frontal systems, and other weather elements of particular interest to aviation.

Aviation forecasts are of four types: (*a*) *regional* forecasts, which cover large geographical areas; (*b*) *terminal* forecasts, which are individual forecasts of probable weather conditions at air terminals; (*c*) *trip* forecasts issued upon request to cover an individual flight (Fig. 12.1); and (*d*) *advisory* service to Federal Aviation Agency traffic controllers. In addition, special international forecasts are prepared to serve planes flying beyond the boundaries of the United States.

The principal air-transport companies employ their own meteorologists, who cooperate with the government officials and supplement the official forecasts by special advice to their own aviators at the beginning of each

Flight Forecast Cross Section. Much information of value to an aviator in cross-country flight can best be portrayed pictorially on a flight forecast cross section.   **FIG. 12.1**

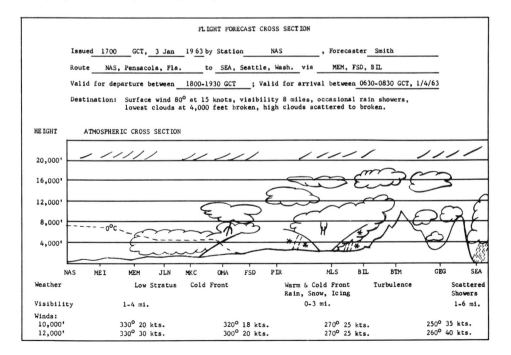

flight. Clearance must be given to the aviator by the company meteorologist and is given only when he knows the weather conditions and thinks them safe not only at the destination, but also at intermediate and surrounding airports. In the making of forecasts, use is also made of observations received from airplanes in flight and of the regular upper-air observations. The United States Air Force and Navy make similar airways forecasts for the guidance of their own personnel in addition to making use of the regular forecasts.

Besides the hourly sequence reports and the six-hourly forecasts and summaries, the aviator has access before take-off to direct information concerning conditions above the surface. Pilot-balloon and rawin observations give him the direction and speed of the wind at various levels in the atmosphere. Radiosonde observations provide data on the temperature, pressure, and relative humidity of the air at short intervals from the surface up to the stratosphere. Graphs, or *sounding curves,* showing the vertical structure of the air, are constructed on adiabatic charts from these radiosonde reports. They supply the data also for upper-air charts showing temperature and pressure distribution and wind conditions at fixed levels above the surface and for charts showing weather conditions at constant pressure levels.

The existence of such a complete organization for the   **Flying Weather**
collection and distribution of weather information is
evidence of the importance of weather in aircraft operation. It follows that the aviator should have enough knowledge of meteorology to interpret properly the reports and forecasts and to understand the significance of any changes that he may encounter while in the air. He needs to know the characteristics of air masses, of warm and cold fronts, and of cyclones and anticyclones. He should know under what conditions to expect unusual turbulence and when ice is likely to form on exposed surfaces. He should recognize quickly the various cloud types and their methods of formation, and know when to attempt to fly over them, under them, or through them. A knowledge of the average frequency of different wind directions and speeds and their changes with altitude is important to the aviator. The wind may be used to advantage in flying, since it is frequently from different directions at different levels. Some of the more important weather conditions that are sources of danger to aviators are discussed briefly in the following paragraphs.

THUNDERSTORMS

Thunderstorms present a major hazard in flying because of the violent vertical movements of the air—up-and-down movements in close proximity to each other. Upward velocities sometimes reach 100 miles per hour. When a plane passes from such an updraft to a strong downdraft, there is danger of structural damage and damage to flight instruments. Under such circumstances, it is extremely difficult to maintain control of the plane. Turbulence may cause the instruments to oscillate so much as to make accurate readings impossible. For these reasons, thunderstorms are to be avoided if at all possible. The turbulence danger is worst in the lower forward portion of the Cumulonimbus, and it is particularly important to avoid the squall cloud. High wind velocities extend to the top portion. The top is often from 25,000 to 35,000 feet (8–10 km) in height and sometimes penetrates to 70,000 or 80,000 feet (22–25 km) above sea level. Many planes are not designed to fly over the tops of Cumulonimbus, nor are they equipped with the necessary oxygen supply to fly at these altitudes.

Air-mass thunderstorms are generally scattered and occur more frequently by day. They can usually be avoided. Frontal and prefrontal thunderstorms are harder to avoid because they frequently occur in long, continuous squall lines. They are usually more severe, also, especially along and ahead of a strong cold front. Cold-front thunderstorms are low-level storms, often attended by a large area of low ceiling and low visibility. They are also attended by rapid changes in pressure, necessitating frequent resettings of the altimeter.

When the air moving against a mountain slope is conditionally or convectively unstable, mountain thunderstorms may be severe and continuous and may extend to great heights, presenting dangerous or impossible flying conditions. A thunderstorm presents not only the hazards of excessive turbulence, but also those of hail, lightning, icing, and low visibility. Hail damage is not serious under ordinary circumstances, but occasionally large hailstones do damage aircraft while in flight. A lightning stroke is very likely to put the electrically operated equipment out of operation but otherwise is not dangerous to airplanes of metal construction; however, it may seriously damage fabric, plastic, and plywood construction. Near a thunderstorm, static may interfere with radio communication.

ICING OF AIRCRAFT

The accumulation of ice on the exposed parts of airplanes in flight through clouds, fog, or precipitation is one of the most serious weather hazards of aviation. If high humidities and steep lapse rates prevail, icing conditions are possible at heights where temperatures are below freezing. Icing ordinarily occurs only in the presence of supercooled water droplets. These freeze rapidly when they strike a solid object. Supercooled drops are found even at temperatures of $-20°F$, but are most frequently encountered at temperatures between $15°F$ and $32°F$. Temperatures of $26°F$ to $32°F$ are particularly dangerous, for the air can contain more moisture at these temperatures than at lower temperatures. Any clouds with temperatures between 0°F and 32°F should be avoided as probable sources of icing. Icing may occur when a cold airplane enters an area of falling rain that has a temperature somewhat above freezing; the drops freeze upon striking the cold surfaces of the airplane.

Two principal types of ice deposit occur, namely, *rime* and *clear ice* (or *glaze*). When very small supercooled drops strike the airplane, they do not spread, but freeze as small pellets, forming a rough, granular surface, milky in appearance. This is called rime (Fig. 12.2) It is usually not deposited rapidly enough, nor in sufficient weight, to be a serious danger. It adheres loosely and is frequently dislodged by vibration.

Larger drops break upon contact with the aircraft and spread backward to form a surface of clear ice, which adheres strongly to solid surfaces and therefore is much more dangerous than rime. There is special danger when flying through rain or dense clouds with the air temperature not far below 32°F. In such circumstances, the ice may build up rapidly, even as much as two or three inches in as many minutes. This icing rapidly adds weight, reduces the lift, and increases the vibration and the stalling speed. The rate of deposit depends upon the size and the number of the drops encountered, and therefore, on the speed of the plane and the type, density, and temperature of the cloud. Polar Pacific air masses show a higher frequency of icing than do other air masses in the United States.

In stratiform clouds, the air is usually stable, the drops are small, and icing takes the form of rime. In most cases, it is possible to avoid such clouds by flying over them. In cumuliform clouds, the warm, unstable, rising air causes the drops to grow to large size and carries them into temperatures below freezing. In such clouds, icing is often rapid and dangerous. Fortunately, these clouds are often scattered and the aviator can go around them. At times, when an airplane passes from cold air into a cloud that is not so cold but is below freezing, there is a rapid formation of frost over the entire outside portion of the plane. This occurs most frequently in clouds with ascending currents. It is not so dangerous as the usual types of icing, but it reduces cruising speed and increases stalling speed.

The first impulse of an aviator, after severe icing has reduced air speed or caused loss of altitude, is to climb above the icing condition. This may

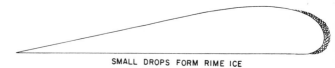

SMALL DROPS FORM RIME ICE

FIG. 12.2

Rime and Glaze on Wing of Aircraft.

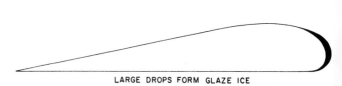

LARGE DROPS FORM GLAZE ICE

be impossible or impractical and creates an additional hazard when the angle of attack is changed very much. The ice then builds up in irregular fashion, thus destroying the air foil, an effect which further increases the drag, reduces the lift, and adds total weight to the plane. Ice may also cause trouble by accumulating on the propeller, windshield, or air-speed indicator. Ice, snow, or frost is especially dangerous on a plane at take-off, and should be removed, especially from the wings, before the plane attempts to leave the ground.

Icing is frequent in the frontal zones of both warm and cold fronts. It is frequently rapid and severe in the cold wedge underlying the warm air in advance of a surface warm front, when rain is falling from the warm air (Fig. 12.3). The drops become supercooled in the cold air or freeze upon contact with the cold aircraft. Snow falling through supercooled drops is especially dangerous, for the snow adheres and adds to the accumulated weight. It also roughens the surface and increases drag. Rime or clear ice, or both, may form also in the cloud area above the inversion in a warm front. The safest plan for the aviator is to fly over the clouds of a warm front when the temperatures indicate that icing is probable.

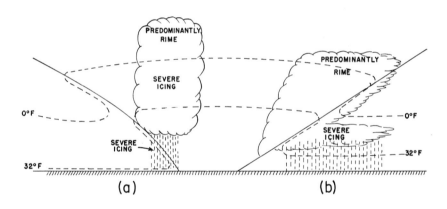

Icing in Frontal Conditions. (a) Cold front; (b) Warm front.   FIG. 12.3

At a cold front, convection is active and icing will probably be rapid to severe along the squall line. Flying through a cold front should be avoided if possible; but, if it is necessary, the course should be perpendicular to the line of the front. Severe icing may occur in flying through the clouds formed in the rising air on the windward side of mountains, even though mountain thunderstorms have not developed. Conditions are especially hazardous if Cumulus clouds are forming.

Small planes are also subject to carburetor icing, which may be more dangerous than any other type because it is not visible and can occur in summer as well as in winter. It is believed that carburetor icing is responsible for more engine failures of light planes than any other single cause.

The carburetor mixes the fuel with air and meters the mixture to the engine. To insure proper mixing and vaporization of the fuel, a venturi (constriction) is built into the air intake at the point of the fuel jet (Fig. 12.4). This increases the speed of the air past the fuel jet as it rushes into the partially vacuumized area created by the intake stroke of the pistons.

FIG. 12.4

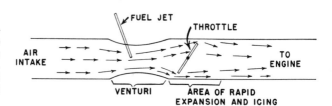

Carburetor Icing. Air pressure is reduced on the engine side of the venturi, causing rapid cooling by expansion. Cooling is further accelerated by vaporization of the liquid fuel.

Rapid expansion of the air, in response to the reduced pressure, cools it adiabatically. Additional cooling results from vaporization of the fuel. The temperature of the air may be reduced 40° to 50°F in this manner, causing moisture to freeze about the throttle. Carburetor icing, under favorable conditions, may accumulate rapidly and cause engine failure with very little warning. It may be avoided by preheating the air before it reaches the venturi.

FOG, VISIBILITY, CEILING

A third major weather hazard in aviation is fog, in its relation to visibility and ceiling. Fog and low Stratus are among the most frequent causes of flying accidents. Flying conditions are considered poor if the horizontal visibility is 1 mile or less, or if the ceiling is 500 feet or less. Conditions are only fair when visibility is between 1 and 3 miles and when ceiling is between 500 and 1,500 feet. Fog often produces these conditions. Radiation ground fogs may be dense near the ground, but are also shallow. In most cases, these fogs have their greatest vertical extent and their lowest visibility about sunrise.

Ground fogs are local in character, often forming as a result of air drainage in lowlands and in river valleys when they do not form over higher ground in the same vicinity. One airport may be closed by ground fog while a near-by airport is entirely clear. Hence, when flying at night or in the early morning, the aviator must be on the lookout for fog at his terminal station, even though there is none at stations en route. The rate of fall of temperature during the night gives a means of estimating when the temperature and dew point will come together and the fog begin. Advection fogs are deeper, more extensive, and more persistent than are ground fogs, and, therefore, are not so easily avoided. They may persist throughout the day. Visibility may be reduced dangerously low, also, by haze, dust, smoke, and blowing snow, and by falling rain or snow.

Low ceilings caused by low Stratus are of frequent occurrence. The aviator loses sight of the ground and must resort to instrument flying. If he is flying low, he runs the risk of striking the ground. The elevation of the base of a Stratus layer, and hourly reports of ceiling height, are of fundamental importance to him. Other forms of low clouds frequently form ceilings dangerously close to the earth.

In emergencies, planes may be able to land safely when the visibility or ceiling is near zero. The pilot must be skilled in instrument flying and have the necessary instruments at his disposal. He may choose the ILS (instrument landing system) approach if his plane is equipped with an automatic pilot capable of accurately bringing the plane in on a radio beam. A more widely used landing method at commercial and military fields is called GCA (ground-controlled approach). Essentially, its success depends on the skill of a GCA controller to watch the plane's progress on a radarscope and direct the aviator by radio to a safe landing approach (Fig. 12.5). A GCA landing requires only that the plane be equipped with radio facilities, and even small private planes have been successfully landed by this method.

Still another technical landing aid used is VOLSCAN; it is reported to be able to pick up planes several miles from the traffic circle and uner-

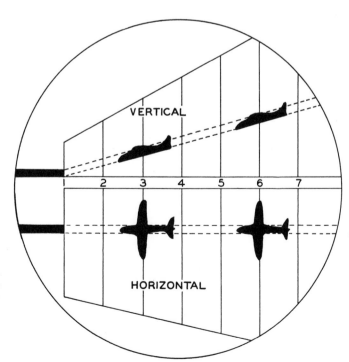

FIG. 12.5

GCA Radarscope. This shows the vertical and horizontal positions of the plane as it approaches the landing field.

ringly direct them to a safe landing approach at the rate of 60 to 120 planes per hour. These navigational and landing aids have rendered fog, smoke, low ceiling, and other obstructions to vision of much less consequence to aviation.

TURBULENCE

The wind is never steady; it is always moving in irregular gusts of varying speed and direction, as has been noted in previous chapters. The degree of turbulence varies with the speed of the wind and its inherent irregularities of flow, with the roughness of the surface over which it is moving, and with the stability of the air. Turbulence is extreme in and around thunderstorms and is great enough to be dangerous in active cumuliform clouds and in high winds blowing against large, abrupt obstructions. Turbulence is ordinarily light in stratiform clouds and where steady rain is falling, and it is usually light at heights of 5,000 feet or more above the ground.

The aviator should be completely familiar with the different types of clouds, their manner of formation, and their range of elevation and thickness. They are visible evidence to him of what is happening in the atmosphere and of its degree of turbulence. In military operations, clouds are often used for concealment. In these cases, it is especially necessary to know the clouds and be able to estimate the comparative dangers of flying through the cloud to that of enemy action.

Turbulence on the windward side of mountains in air moving upslope is ordinarily not dangerous unless thunderstorms or Cumulus have developed. Strong winds moving down the leeward sides have irregular eddies and may cause trouble, especially in landing. The downdraft on the lee side also causes a loss of altitude, and the pilot must approach the mountain well above it in order to avoid crashing into it (Fig. 12.6). In strong winds, the eddies around buildings situated on or near an airport may result in accidents on landing or taking off.

Stability reduces turbulence by checking vertical movement. When there is a temperature inversion in the lower air, the marked stability contributes to quiet, nonturbulent conditions, but it also contributes to

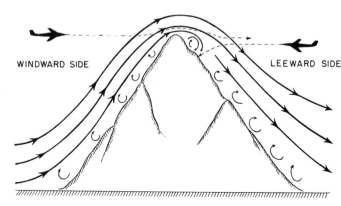

FIG. 12.6

Eddy Turbulence in Mountains. A plane flying upwind in mountainous country requires more altitude for safe flight than when flying in the opposite direction.

WINDWARD SIDE   LEEWARD SIDE the development of fog at the ground and a ceiling of Stratus at the inversion level. Local, daytime instability over a ground surface that is being heated by the absorption of the sun's rays often adds to the turbulence caused by the speed of the wind. This occurs even though the instability is not sufficient to produce Cumulus.

Differences in the heating of the earth's surface over different areas result in such turbulent movements and produce what is known as *bumpiness*. Bumps occur near changes in the character of the surface, as along the borders of forests, and where cultivated and grass-covered areas meet. Even such narrow strips as roads and creeks are often marked by bumps, with ascending currents over roads and descending currents over creeks. Bumpiness due to such irregularities of surface heating is ordinarily greatest within the first 2,500 feet (765 m) above the ground. Although unpleasant, it is usually harmless to airplanes in flight. A somewhat different type of bumpiness is encountered in the waves occurring at the surfaces of different air layers, and these layers may be at any elevation.

A knowledge of the characteristics of warm and cold fronts and of the different air masses of which they are composed is of much importance to the aviator. Accidents sometimes occur at or near cold fronts because of the violent action and rapid changes attending such fronts. Warm fronts are usually more stable and less turbulent, but they present hazards of fog, low visibility, and icing. Visibility is generally better in polar than in tropical air masses because of the greater stability and lower moisture content of the polar masses. Most precipitation falls from tropical maritime air masses.

PRESSURE-PATTERN FLYING

An example of the combination of meteorological knowledge with instrumental improvement and flying skill is found in the development of what is called *pressure-pattern flying*. This procedure was developed to enable aircraft to maintain regular, round-trip flight schedules across the stormy North Atlantic Ocean during the winter months. Hitherto, this route, although the shortest, had been avoided in winter, especially for westbound flights against the prevailing westerlies. Owing to the storminess of the North Atlantic in winter and to the absence of surface stations over wide expanses, serious weather hazards not previously reported were often encountered in flight during World War II. The plan evolved to overcome these difficulties depends upon the use of the radio altimeter, itself a wartime product, in combination with the usual, pressure-actuated altimeter.

The aviator may fly a constant altitude by the use of his radar altimeter and make a record at intervals of the altitude indicated by the pressure altimeter. Likewise, he may fly at constant pressure by the use of the pressure altimeter and note the difference in elevation indicated by the two instruments. In either case, the indicated differences in height may be converted to corresponding pressure values. By plotting these observations at frequent intervals, the aviator gets a map of the pressure distribution at the level of his flight. With this up-to-date pressure pattern before him, he is able to compute the pressure gradient and to determine his position relative to the dominant pressure center. He is able to avoid hazards and take advantage of favorable weather conditions.

PROBLEMS

1.

Assume that you are an official observer for an airfield. Make an observation for an airways sequence report at your locality.

2.

Construct a visibility scale for your home by following these instructions. At the center of a sheet of cardboard, construct a circle 1/2 inch in diameter. Draw nine more concentric circles about the first, each having a radius 1/2 inch greater than the preceding one. Mark the points of the compass about the outer circle. Using a scale of 1/2 inch equals 1 mile, draw in symbols for several of the most distinct objects at appropriate distance and direction from your home.

3.

How can there be carburetor icing when the dew point is above 32°F?

4.

Is the phenomenon of carburetor icing related to the adiabatic processes studied earlier? Explain.

5.

Visit a commercial airfield and ask to see aircraft deicing equipment.

6.

Visit the airfield weather station. Try to read some hourly sequence reports.

7.

Request the guide at the weather station to explain how the altimeter setting is determined. How is it used by the aviator?

8.

Why is pressure-pattern flying not as common over the United States as it is over the oceans?

9.

What kind of continental flights could most easily use pressure-pattern techniques?

10.

If it cannot be circumnavigated in flight, what cloud type does the aviator dread most? Why?

13

the upper
atmosphere

It has long been recognized that the existence of an atmosphere high above the sphere of weather has an important bearing on the habitability of the earth. The concept of the upper atmosphere as a protective umbrella against excessive ultraviolet radiation from the sun is common to most grade-school children. It also serves as a protective shield in another way, for it is in the regions of the upper atmosphere that most meteors disintegrate and vaporize due to frictional heat. Increased interest in space exploration during the last two decades has revealed additional knowledge and opened up many new questions about the significance of the upper atmosphere. Few meteorologists today would deny that there are direct relationships between upper atmospheric phenomena and the weather we experience on the earth.

UPPER ATMOSPHERE DEFINED

The *upper atmosphere*, as used in this book, includes all of the gases of the earth's atmosphere which lie beyond the stratosphere. Boundary levels are not clearly defined, but it is obvious that the lower boundary lies just outside of the reach of typical meteorological sounding instruments. The upper boundary will probably always be determined on some arbitrary basis because the earth's atmosphere seems to fade gradually into a "solar atmosphere" or "solar corona." Even the deepest voids of interstellar space seem to contain many gaseous particles per cubic centimeter which constitute a solar atmosphere, through which the earth and its atmosphere creates a wake like a vessel passing through the water. Observed drag on artificial satellites as well as other evidences confirm this conclusion.

The upper boundary of the stratosphere, or *stratopause,* has been defined as the upper limit of the isothermal layer at about 25 km, but a more logical boundary seems to be at the temperature maximum occurring near 50 km (Fig. 13.3 on page 264). In either case, the upper atmosphere extends from the stratopause to the boundary between the earth's atmosphere and the solar corona. It stands to reason that this boundary will be marked by the altitude at which density ceases to decrease with height. It will also mark the zone across which there is some limited exchange of gaseous particles between the earth's atmosphere and outer space, and it will probably be associated with a change in the temperature gradient. This boundary seems to be located between 500 and 1,000 km above the earth's surface.

THE SCIENCE OF AERONOMY

Interest in studying the characteristics of the upper atmosphere has given rise to a new science known as *aeronomy.* Aeronomy is concerned with the physical and chemical properties of the upper atmosphere and with the processes occurring within it. The term is new, but various aspects of the science have been developing since late in the nineteenth century. The discovery in the 1920's and 1930's that radio waves were reflected by layers in the upper atmosphere has contributed to a steady expansion of the science of aeronomy. The growth has been accelerated during the past twenty years due to advancing technology and to the availability of observations from high-altitude balloons, rockets, and satellites.

A scientific manpower survey in 1961 indicated that there were only about 750 people in the aeronomy labor force of the United States. Most of them had received their training in some other branch of science, but for one reason or another had become interested in studying the upper atmosphere. A few universities have established graduate curricula to train aeronomists, for it is estimated that the United States will need an annual increase of 1,500 aeronomists within the next ten years.

Because of the relative inaccessibility of the upper atmosphere, observational measurements become quite a problem. Late in the 1800's visual observations of the **Probing the Upper Atmosphere** auroras and meteor trails were begun on something of a scientific basis. Radio waves became significant probing tools during the second quarter of this century. Ground-based transmitters and radio receivers were used in a fashion more commonly associated with the techniques of radar. Later it became possible to send sensing devices with radio transmitters aloft, borne up by balloons, planes, rockets, and finally satellites. The ingenuity of the engineering sciences in designing the necessary hardware for these tasks has been phenomenal, as has been the ability of the meteorologists and aeronomists in identifying the kinds of data to be collected for study. Sometimes the data are measured directly, sometimes indirectly, and sometimes they are obtained by interpolation or interpretation. Always there has been the cost factor to be considered, for the task of raising even the simplest instrument from the earth's surface into the reaches of the upper atmosphere is an expensive operation. This partially accounts for the great efforts to pick up any intelligible signals from outer space through the use of optical, auditory, and other sensing instruments on the ground (Fig. 13.1). Spurred on by the successes of the International Geophysical Year and by refinements and improvements in the science of rocketry, sounding rockets have been singled out as probably the most practical and economical mode of gathering most of the specialized data about the upper atmosphere.

Radiowave Receiving Apparatus at Stanford University. This equipment is part of a radioscience laboratory and is used to intercept radio waves from the sun. *Courtesy, Radioscience Laboratory, Stanford University.*   **FIG. 13.1**

THE METEOROLOGICAL ROCKET NETWORK

The use of rockets in the United States for meteorological observations had its beginnings in the middle 1940's. The first efforts were side experiments during tests of the captured German V-2 systems. In the years that followed, special meteorological rockets were designed, tested, and refined. By the late 1950's it became feasible to plan a regular synoptic observational program for the lower regions of the upper atmosphere through the operation of a Meteorological Rocket Network (MRN). This effort is jointly sponsored by the various branches of the armed forces, the U.S. Weather Bureau, and the National Aeronautics and Space Administration.

Since 1959, a dozen or more launching sites in the United States and Canada have been used to launch meteorological rockets into the upper atmosphere. The launches were first scheduled on specific days in the various seasons of the year. Then the schedule intensified to one launch day each month and so on. Within the first four years of the program, over 2,500 rockets were launched.

Two rockets have been extensively tested and are presently being used in the meteorological rocket network. Both reach altitudes within the lower limits of the upper atmosphere. The "Loki" carries 1 pound of S-band chaff as its payload. After ejection at some predetermined altitude, the chaff cloud is tracked by radar. The "Arcas" carries a radiosonde as its payload. When ejected it descends on a metallized 15-foot parachute for radar tracking. Within the next few years, meteorological rockets will be developed to penetrate the upper atmosphere to greater heights, thus closing the gap that exists between rocket observations and those made by meteorological satellites.

METEOROLOGICAL ROCKETS AND THE IQSY

The International Geophysical Year (IGY), from July 1957 to December 1958, marked a period of intense solar activity. By international agreement, a world-wide concentrated and coordinated effort was made to observe the solar and terrestrial atmospheres. As early as 1960 it became apparent that the IGY observations had been highly successful and that it would be desirable to launch a similar coordinated effort during a period of minimum solar activity. The International Year(s) of the Quiet Sun (IQSY) was therefore scheduled to be observed from January 1964 through December 1965 to permit a comparison of phenomena and parameters between the two extremes of solar activity (Fig. 13.2). Since the upper atmosphere is a principal target for investigation during IQSY, it is natural that meteorological rockets will play a prime role in the program.

In addition to the dozen or more observation bases in the United States and Canada, IQSY rocketsonde ascents are being conducted by Argentina,

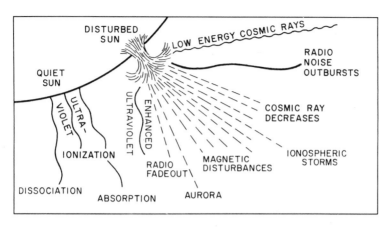

Effects of Solar Activity. **FIG. 13.2**

Australia, England, France, India, Italy, Japan, Pakistan, South Africa, and the Soviet Union. This world network is attempting to make synoptic observations at least once each week, and more often when special conditions warrant the extra effort and expense.

One phenomenon to receive special attention during IQSY is the occurrence of rather sudden but unexplained stratospheric warmings. Rocket ascents will be intensified during such periods in an effort to account for the source and cause of this phenomenon. The World Meteorological Organization has assumed the role of coordination for the STRATWARM system.

The composition of the atmosphere remains remarkably constant to great heights, water vapor being the only significant variable. Ozone (O_3) seems to be present at all levels but gradually increases upward to a maximum at an elevation of about 30 km. Even at this level there is only about one part ozone per million parts of oxygen (O_2), but the ozone is quite effective in shielding the lower levels from deadly ultraviolet rays and in absorbing heat energy from the sun.

Characteristics of the Upper Atmosphere

COMPOSITION

The percentage of oxygen (O_2) remains constant in the atmosphere up to approximately 100 km where a sudden change takes place in its molecular structure. Diatomic oxygen (O_2) is separated into its monatomic form (O_1). This change is brought about by the intense sunlight through a process known as *photodissociation*. These oxygen atoms may recombine in triplets to form ozone (O_3) or in pairs to form oxygen (O_2). Nitrogen (N_2) does not become dissociated as easily as oxygen; so, monatomic

262

nitrogen is not prevalent until much greater heights. In the presence of monatomic gases, heavier gas molecules tend to settle towards the earth due to a process known as *diffusive separation*. This probably accounts for an observed increase in the percentage of oxygen at great heights. Traces of gases in the upper atmosphere include carbon dioxide, carbon monoxide, methane, water vapor, hydroxyl, helium, and hydrogen. A surprising minor constituent in the upper atmosphere is sodium. It plays an important part in certain optical phenomena even though its maximum concentration is very small.

PRESSURE AND DENSITY

Through approximately the first 100 km of the atmosphere the composition remains essentially constant; so, the interrelations of pressure, density, and temperature hold true according to the gas laws. Beyond 100 km the rate of decrease in pressure with increasing altitude is not as rapid, but it continues to decrease at least to 800 km.

TABLE 13.1   Average Density and Pressure Values
with Increasing Height*

ALTITUDE (km)	DENSITY (g cm^{-3})	PRESSURE (mm Hg)
0	1.23×10^{-3}	7.63×10^{2}
10	4.19×10^{-4}	2.01×10^{2}
20	8.89×10^{-5}	4.16×10^{1}
30	1.84×10^{-5}	9.05×10^{0}
40	4.07×10^{-6}	2.17×10^{0}
50	1.02×10^{-6}	5.93×10^{-1}
60	3.04×10^{-7}	1.69×10^{-1}
70	8.84×10^{-8}	4.13×10^{-2}
80	1.94×10^{-8}	7.70×10^{-3}
90	3.12×10^{-9}	1.22×10^{-3}
100	4.78×10^{-10}	2.19×10^{-4}
120	2.44×10^{-11}	1.83×10^{-5}
140	3.07×10^{-12}	5.42×10^{-6}
160	1.11×10^{-12}	2.86×10^{-6}
180	6.59×10^{-13}	1.69×10^{-6}
200	3.61×10^{-13}	1.02×10^{-6}
300	3.34×10^{-14}	1.19×10^{-7}
400	5.09×10^{-15}	2.28×10^{-8}
500	1.17×10^{-15}	6.15×10^{-9}
600	3.45×10^{-16}	2.02×10^{-9}
700	1.19×10^{-16}	7.50×10^{-10}
800	4.60×10^{-17}	3.04×10^{-10}

* *COSPAR International Reference Atmosphere, 1961* (Amsterdam: North-Holland Publishing Company, 1961).

TEMPERATURE

The temperature characteristics of the troposphere are well-known, and the region of the stratosphere has been sounded often enough and in sufficient details to give reasonable assurances of conditions up to about 100 km. Even in the stratosphere, as has been previously noted, there occurs sudden, and as yet, unexplained warmings of the environment. Beyond 100 km, temperature observations have been far less frequent and those that have been made are less reliable. The meaning of temperature in the upper atmosphere becomes vague due to the very low atmospheric densities at these levels. Even though very high temperatures are observed, very little heat is imparted to objects, such as sensing instruments on space vehicles because of the infrequent collisions of gas molecules. The temperature does serve as a measure of the speed of the gas molecules

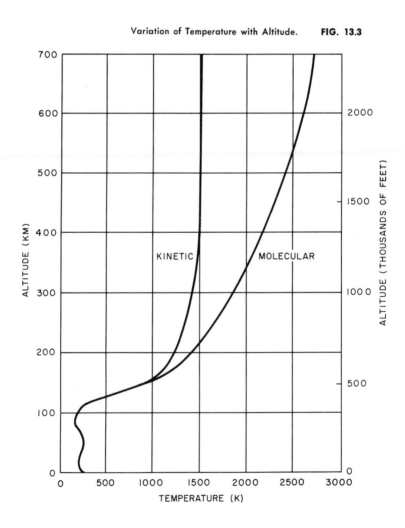

Variation of Temperature with Altitude.   **FIG. 13.3**

and helps to estimate the rate at which different gases escape from the atmosphere into interplanetary space.

Fig. 13.3 shows a revised temperature chart to 700 km which may be adopted as the revised U.S. Standard Atmosphere. It has been recommended by the U.S. Committee on Extension of the Standard Atmosphere (COESA). The two lines above 120 km probably, but not necessarily, represent the extremes in temperature possibilities. To be sure, there is a great variation in the chemical composition of the upper atmosphere because of dissociation and recombination of the atoms. The molecular temperature line assumes mean molecular weight where turbulent mixing is complete. The kinetic temperature line assumes extreme dissociation of the gas molecules.

WINDS

Sufficient data to accurately chart the winds of the upper atmosphere have not yet been collected. It is reliably known that very strong winds occur, especially during the winter months. A velocity of 300 knots has been measured at 58 km over Fort Churchill. Winter winds are westerly, while the lighter summer winds have a prevailing easterly direction.[1] This seasonal reversal in wind direction extends down into the stratosphere. It constitutes an important item for further investigation by the meteorological rocket program. It also remains to be seen if the movements of the gases in regions with very low densities have much significance on the weather. For example, an ordinary satellite may encounter only a fraction of an ounce of air during an entire orbit about the earth. It is difficult to imagine that air movements in these regions can be of real significance to meteorological problems.

CLOUDS

Upper atmospheric clouds have been observed at two greatly different levels for many years. *Mother-of-pearl* clouds, sometimes called *nacreous* clouds, have frequently been observed at altitudes between 20 and 30 km, especially by Norwegian meteorologists. These clouds are believed to be composed of ice crystals. *Notilucent,* or *night-glowing,* clouds are sometimes visible at an altitude of about 85 km. They are very thin and indistinguishable except against the night sky while the sun's rays are still illuminating the cloud material. Their composition is not known, but it is believed that they are composed of dust rather than of water vapor. Both cloud formations have been observed moving rapidly across the sky,

---

[1] The student is cautioned against confusion about wind directions as cited in the literature on the upper atmosphere. Throughout this book wind direction is considered to be that direction from which it blows. Aeronomists generally consider the wind direction to be that toward which the wind is moving.

indicating high wind velocities. Observations of vapor trails from meteors and rockets also confirm high wind velocities with radical shears and considerable turbulence.

STRATIFICATION

The first evidence of stratification in the atmosphere came with the discovery of the stratosphere about 1900. Prior to that time, a common belief held that the temperature continued to decrease with height until it reached absolute zero at some level out in space. Later it was determined that the stratosphere, like the troposphere, has an upper limit. The *stratosphere* is used here to mean that region immediately above the tropopause and extending up to about 50 km where the temperature remains constant or increases slightly with height.

The *mesosphere* (middle sphere) is a region above the stratosphere extending up to about 85 km where the temperature decreases rapidly to a minimum of about 180°K at the mesopause. Photochemical action is important in the mesosphere and plays an important part in determining its characteristics. Airglow emissions are common at this level and aeronomists are interested in studying the diurnal fluctuations arising from atomic and molecular processes due to dissociation and recombination. In spite of this, the mean molecular mass of the prime constituents of the atmosphere remain constant from the earth to the mesopause. For this reason, the troposphere, stratosphere, and mesosphere are sometimes referred to collectively as the *homosphere* (Fig. 13.4). Using the same reasoning, the atmosphere above the homosphere could be called the *heterosphere* because there is a change in the composition and the structure of the gases.

Temperature seems to be the most important characteristic of the heterosphere, however; so, the region is more commonly called the *thermosphere*. As more details are learned about these upper reaches of the atmosphere, it is probable that more spheres will be identified.

It should be noted that the troposphere, stratosphere, mesosphere, and thermosphere are all based on thermal characteristics of the atmosphere at the various levels, while names such as *ozonosphere, ionosphere,* and *chemosphere* are descriptive of regions where certain processes occur.

Ultraviolet light with wave lengths in the vicinity of 1800Å is absorbed by oxygen in the region from the top of the stratosphere up to about 50 km which gives rise to the ozonosphere.[2] Countering this action is radiation at 2550Å which tends to decompose the ozone and maintain a chemical balance in the region. Above the ozonosphere, radiation at 1216Å dissociates oxygen molecules into atomic oxygen, giving rise to the D-Re-

---

[2] Angstrom (Å) is a linear unit commonly used to measure very short wave lengths. An angstrom equals 10^{-8}cm, or one cm equals 10^8Å.

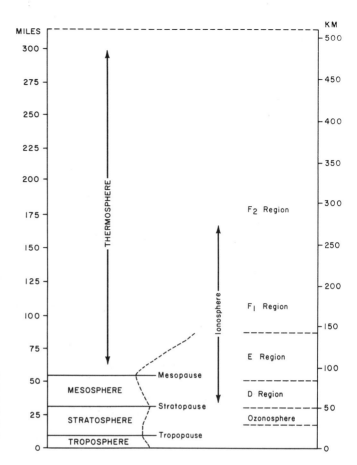

FIG. 13.4

Atmospheric Stratification. The boundaries of the different spheres of the atmosphere are not rigidly defined. The dashed line indicates the principal characteristics of the average temperature on which the various spheres are based.

gion which extends up to about 85 km. The E-Region is centered about 100 km and owes its characteristics to the absorption of X rays which ionize molecules of hydrogen and nitrogen. Less distinct is the F-Region which absorbs radiation between 100Å and 800Å, producing positive oxygen ions. Two subregions, F_1 and F_2, develop during the day, but the distinction tends to disappear at night. The D, E, and F regions have been studied in considerable detail because of their effects on radio communications.

Other High-altitude Phenomena

Many of the characteristics of the upper atmosphere can be explained only in terms of energy gained through absorption at certain wave lengths of the electromagnetic spectrum. The sun emits a spectrum of energy in the form of waves which travel at the speed of light in all directions. The earth and its atmosphere intercepts only about 5×10^{-10} of the sun's total radiations. Essentially all of the waves at both ends of the spectrum are effectively absorbed by selective levels of the upper atmosphere. Only in the ranges of visible light, infrared radiation, and microwaves do appreciable amounts of solar energy reach the surface of the earth (Fig. 3.1 on page 62).

The normal patterns of absorption and transmission of solar energy are seriously disrupted at the times of unusual solar flares on the surface of the sun. These solar storms disturb the earth's magnetic field and especially the characteristics of the ionosphere. Radio signals which are normally reflected by regions of the upper atmosphere may be either absorbed or allowed to escape into space.

RADIATION BELTS

As a part of the International Geophysical Year investigations, instrumented satellites identified two intense radiation belts high above the earth. They are called the *Van Allen radiation belts* after Dr. J. A. Van Allen, of the State University of Iowa, leader of the team of American scientists who discovered them. These belts of radiation particles, composed primarily of electrons and protons, are located high above what is normally considered the earth's atmosphere. The particles are the product of violent actions deep in the atmosphere or in the sun and have their own peculiar motions under the influence of the geomagnetic field (Fig. 13.5). They seem to be alien to the normal atmosphere, since most of the constituents of the atmosphere are totally insensitive to magnetism, but it is possible that unique relationships may soon be discovered between the fluctuating intensities of these belts and the earth's weather cycles.

Van Allen Radiation Belts. The two belts girdle the earth at its geomag-   **FIG. 13.5**
netic equator in doughnut fashion. The inner belt has its maximum intensity between 2,000 and 3,000 miles above the earth. Maximum intensity of the outer belt is at
about 10,000 miles. In both belts, the radiation intensity has been measured to exceed 10,000
counts per second.

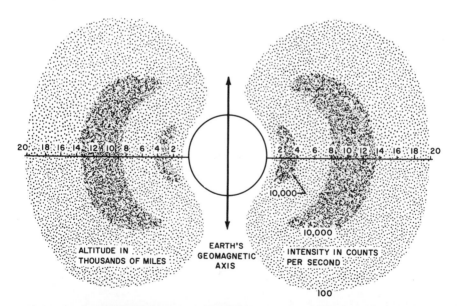

AURORAS AND AIRGLOW

The *aurora borealis,* or *northern lights,* has sometimes been described as the most beautiful natural phenomenon in all creation. In pixie fashion, it drapes the northern skies with dancing colors of red, green, blue, and yellow at altitudes of 75 to several hundred km. Sometimes drapelike in great luxurious folds, sometimes in ribbons or streamers, and sometimes in bands, the aurora provides a thrilling spectacle for all who are fortunate enough to see it (Fig. 13.6). Although the aurora has been seen from essentially all latitudes in the United States, it is primarily a high-latitude and high-altitude phenomenon. The northern parts of the United States and Canada provide good vantage points from which to view the aurora. In the Southern Hemisphere, the comparable phenomenon is called the *aurora australis.*

Auroras are caused by highly excited particles attracted into the fields of maximum flux near the earth's magnetic poles. They are undoubtedly related to the Van Allen radiation belts, and are definitely related to explosions in the sun, for it is during periods of a disturbed sun that the auroras are most spectacular.

On a moonless night, airglow accounts for several times as much radiant energy reaching the earth in visible and ultraviolet wave lengths as all of the stars combined. The astronauts have reported beautiful hues of reds, greens, and yellows along the top of the nighttime atmosphere. It has been determined that highly excited particles of oxygen, hydrogen, and sodium account for most of the airglow as well as the auroral displays. Unlike the aurora, airglow does not seem to be controlled by the earth's magnetic field. Its occurrence is fairly evenly distributed over all latitudes, but by no means uniformly at any given time. Airglow patches move around and change shape in a manner that indicates they are influenced or even transported by air movements. The diffused nature of airglow as it appears from the surface of the earth make it more difficult to study than the aurora, but investigations generally have indicated that the phenomenon is concentrated in the lower reaches of the thermosphere.

METEORS

"Shooting stars" have been of interest to man ever since he developed the capacity to "wonder why." It is ironical that something so obvious remained unexplained so long, and even now the source and cause of meteors is not fully understood. Thomas Jefferson is said to have remarked when told that shooting stars were actually chunks of matter from outer space, "I would rather believe that professors lie than that rocks fall from heaven."

Most meteors are composed of rocklike material and are less than the size of a pea. They enter the earth's atmosphere at speeds up to 10^5 miles

Auroral Displays at Fairbanks, Alaska. The top group of pictures, taken at   **FIG. 13.6**
one-minute intervals, is characteristic of the very active aurora which occurred regularly during the International Geophysical Year. *Photographs of the Aurora by V. P.
Hessler, Geophysical Institute of the University of Alaska.*

(Cont.) **FIG. 13.6**

per hour. Frictional heat soon causes them to burn up, usually at altitudes above 65 km. Only a few meteors are large enough to reach the earth before complete vaporization. One such instance caused Sunset Crater in Arizona and another the Chubb Crater in Canada. Of more significance is the countless number of micrometeors which strike the earth's atmosphere daily. These are too small to be seen as they vaporize, but it is estimated that their debris adds more than 1,000 tons of mass to the earth each day.

There have been some indications of direct correlations between periods of high meteor "falls" and periods of increased precipitation. The time lag in the precipitation is about one month, which would lead to the supposition that it takes the meteoric dust about one month to settle from the level of vaporization to the troposphere. This also presumes that meteoric dust is effective as condensation nuclei and has a widespread effect similar to cloud seeding. All this will require additional investigation before it can be considered more than a theory or hypothesis.

The total contributions of meteors to the chemical, electrical, and thermal characteristics of the upper atmosphere must have a very real influence on the properties of these regions. In addition to serving as a protective umbrella against deadly radiation and a frightful hail of meteors, the upper atmosphere probably holds many more interesting secrets yet to be discovered.

PROBLEMS

1.

How can a space traveler hope to survive for any significant period of time when the temperature in space may be more than 1000°C?

2.

Can you advance a theory to explain the significant temperature lapse rate in the mesosphere?

3.

What is a solar flare? Locate and read two references on this subject.

4.

What can scientists hope to learn by making a world-wide study during a period of "quiet sun"? How does this relate to IGY?

5.

Prepare a report on the development of balloons as weather-observation instruments.

6.

Why does the amount of ozone in the ozonosphere tend to remain essentially constant?

7.

Describe what is meant by "airglow."

8.

Why should a meteorologist be concerned with the auroras or other electrical or magnetic phenomena of the upper atmosphere?

9.

Describe two important reasons why the atmosphere can be considered a protective shield for life on earth. What problems does this same characteristic present to the space traveler?

10.

If a cm^3 of air at sea level contains 10^{19} molecules, how many molecules would be in a cm^3 of air at 100 km? 800 km?

14

climate

The sciences of meteorology and climatology inevitably overlap. No sharp line can be drawn between them. To discuss the weather adequately, one must consider the frequent, usual, or average weather conditions in different parts of the world, and these are what comprise climate. To understand climate, one must know something of the reasons for the various kinds of weather experienced, for climate is the total effect of all the daily weather. In the study of meteorology it is desirable, therefore, to consider also some of the main features of the climates of the earth and their relation to, and influence upon, one another and upon man and his manner of life.

Climatic Elements

The elements of weather and climate are so numerous and combine in such endless variety that the complete description of a climate is extremely difficult. Accurate description involves the extensive use of climatic tables and extensive statistical analysis to reveal the characteristics of the data. To be complete, the tables should include all the elements that affect man and his activities. To acquire from such tables a correct idea of what a given climate is like requires not only a careful comparison of the data with similar data for climates with which one is familiar, but also the exercise of some imagination.

CLIMATIC DATA

Temperature and rainfall are the two most important climatic elements, but the simple tabulation of their average annual values is not sufficient. Two places with the same mean temperature and rainfall may have very different climates because of differences in the distribution of these two elements within the year. For example, San Francisco and St. Louis each has a mean annual temperature of 56°, but San Francisco's January average is 49.9°, and St. Louis's is 31.1°; whereas in July the averages are 58.5° and 78.8°, respectively. Some of the more important data used in the description and classification of climates are:

Mean monthly and annual temperatures, and mean annual ranges of temperature.
Mean daily maximum and minimum temperatures, and mean daily ranges.
Highest and lowest temperatures of record.
Average number of days with maxima above 90°F; above 100°F. Average number of days with minima of 32°F or lower; of 0°F or lower.
Mean monthly and annual relative humidity.
Mean monthly and annual precipitation.
Greatest and least monthly and yearly amounts of precipitation.
Greatest precipitation in twenty-four hours.
Excessive amounts of rainfall for short periods.
Average snowfall by months.
Average number of days with rain, snow, hail, fog, thunder.
Mean cloudiness in tenths of sky covered.
Mean monthly frequency and duration of low ceilings.
Mean percentage of sunshine by months.
Mean wind velocity by months.
Prevailing wind direction by months.
Mean frequency of winds from the different directions.
Mean frequency of gales.
Mean frequencies of the different types of air masses.
Average and extreme dates of first and last killing frosts.

ANALYSIS OF CLIMATIC DATA

A broad, generalized statement of the character of a climate in terms of mean, totals, and extremes is readily obtained by examination of the data recorded under the headings listed in the preceding paragraph. This has long been the standard way of describing climates. It has served well to picture the main features of a particular climate and to distinguish the major types of climate. Military operations, both at the surface and in the air, however, require more specific and detailed climatic information.

The need for such information calls for a new type of statistical treatment that would make possible an accurate calculation of weather risks. Not only the frequencies of individual elements, but also the combined frequencies and interrelations of two or more elements, or of the same element at two or more points, are required. Such problems as the following are illustrative: frequency and duration of fog in the English Channel for each wind direction each month; frequency and duration of low ceilings at a given airport with reference to the time of day or the direction and force of the wind, or with reference to simultaneous conditions at other airports.

The solution of such problems by examining the records of individual stations and making the necessary tabulations and calculations by ordinary statistical methods is impracticable because of the time and labor required. This fact, together with the urgent need for such information, led to the introduction of electrical sorting and tabulating machines using punched cards. These machines take over the entire job of sorting, recording, and adding the numerical data. They quickly furnish a new type of climatological statistics, not previously available. After the data have once been entered by punching holes in standardized cards in accordance with a standardized system, the arrangement and computation for any desired element or combination of elements can be done at the rate of 10,000 cards per hour. The cards become a permanent depository for future studies of many kinds.

The *punched-card method* had previously been used to a limited extent for special climatological studies both in the United States and in Europe, but its wide application to all sorts of climatic problems is now beginning and marks a fundamental development in climatological methods. Punched cards will make much valuable specific information quickly available to a large number of human activities. To have definite information on the probability of favorable or unfavorable climatic conditions at a given time of year and with reference to specific crops or farm activities will be of obvious advantage to the farmer. A knowledge of the frequency of certain weather conditions and combinations of weather conditions is also of direct value in transportation by land, sea, or air, in the design and construction of residences, warehouses, and other buildings, in the construction of airports, in the management of forests, in flood control and irrigation practice, and in many other fields. All these activities could then be planned with more confidence on the basis of calculated weather risks.

Punched-card analysis has been used also to ascertain the relations between the types of weather occurring at the same time in different parts of a large area, such as a state. If a certain pressure-distribution pattern shown on weather charts is attended by rain in western Oregon, for example, what are likely to be the weather conditions in eastern Oregon at the same time? What is the probability of clear weather, of overcast skies, or of rain?

To answer such questions, a long series of daily climatological records covering the entire area under consideration may be analyzed to determine the percentage frequencies of weather conditions occurring simultaneously in different parts of the area. The results obtained constitute a *synoptic climatology* of the region. The method was developed and used primarily in the planning of large-scale military operations but has valuable applications in other fields. It aids the forecaster by contributing to an understanding of weather processes, and it furnishes important additional detail in the description of a climate.

AIR-MASS CLIMATOLOGY

Another new and developing treatment of climatic data is known as *air-mass climatology*. By this method, climates are examined and described with reference to the prevalence of the various types of air masses and the influence of each in giving a place its particular climate. This requires, first, a record at each observing station of the air mass or masses present during each twenty-four hours, and of the time of passage of fronts. From an air-mass calendar obtained in this way, the relative frequencies and durations of the various air masses may be computed by months and seasons. For example, a knowledge of the relative frequency of polar and tropical air masses and of continental and maritime air masses gives new and important information concerning the climate of a region. Not much has yet been done in the field of air-mass climatology because of the lack of the fundamental data. Daily records of air masses were not begun at United States Weather Bureau stations until July, 1945.

SOLAR AND PHYSICAL CLIMATES

If the earth were a uniform land surface without an atmosphere, the temperature of the surface at any given place would be governed directly by the amount of insolation received there. The annual amount of insolation is greatest at the equator and least at the poles, and, under the conditions assumed, we should have a regular decrease of temperature from equator to poles. The actual air temperatures over the earth, as it is, follow this plan of distribution in main outline but not in detail. Insofar as the climate of a place depends directly on the amount of solar radiation received, it is called *solar climate*.

The division of the earth into the five classic zones bounded by the Tropics of Capricorn and Cancer and by the polar circles is of ancient origin and is purely on a solar-climate basis. These are zones of possible sunshine rather than of actual climate. Within the Tropics, the sun is vertically overhead at noon twice each year. Within the polar zones, the sun is below the horizon for at least twenty-four consecutive hours in

winter and above for at least twenty-four hours in summer. In the intermediate zones, the sun is never in the zenith and never below the horizon
for twenty-four hours. The latitudinal zones, notwithstanding their old
names of torrid, temperate, and frigid, merely mark differences in the
elevation of the sun.

The actual or physical climate does not follow the parallels of latitude.
It is modified by geographic conditions, chiefly (a) by the irregular distribution of land and water, (b) by winds and ocean currents, and (c) by
differences in elevation. These modifying influences act in various ways
to produce climatic differences: land and water absorb and radiate heat
differently; cloudiness and humidity are influenced by distance from large
bodies of water; movements of air and water convey large amounts of
heat across latitudinal lines. Nevertheless, the distribution of insolation is
the primary factor determining temperature. Solar climate is the ground-
work upon which modifications are imposed by other factors.

Except in polar regions, the normal distribution of tem-   **Distribution**
perature over the earth is now fairly well determined.   **of Temperature**
Most inhabited land areas have temperature records of
moderate length. Although records over the oceans are less extensive,
nearly all vessels at sea make regular observations, and, because ocean
temperatures are less variable than land temperatures, these serve quite
well to determine the general temperature distribution. The distribution
of temperature is indicated on a map by lines drawn through points of
equal temperature, *isothermal lines.*

For the daily weather maps and for maps of small areas, the actual
temperatures are usually represented, but on maps of extensive areas,
where there are great differences of level, mean temperatures are first
reduced to sea level by using a lapse rate about equal to the average
lapse rate in the free air. This procedure is necessary if the lines are to
show the effects of latitude and of continental land masses on the distribution of temperature. If the actual temperatures obtained at different
altitudes were used, these more general influences would be obscured;
besides, it is not possible to indicate on a small-scale map all the temperature differences found in mountainous regions. Where the isotherms
shown on the maps presented in this chapter pass over elevated regions,
they do not represent the actual temperatures to be found there but have
been thus corrected for altitude.

NORMAL YEARLY TEMPERATURES

The first and most obvious fact noted on examining a world chart of
mean annual temperatures is the decrease of temperature from equatorial

regions toward polar regions (Fig. 14.1). This decrease is evidently due to the different amounts of insolation received; solar climate is dominant in determining the general course of the isotherms. They do not follow the parallels of latitude closely, however, but bend irregularly northward and southward. In equatorial and lower middle latitudes, they bend poleward over the continents, indicating that the continents in these latitudes have an average temperature warmer than that of the oceans, or than the average of the latitude around the globe. In Siberia and northern Canada, the isotherms bend southward, showing that large continental areas in high latitudes are colder than the adjacent oceans.

The isotherms turn far northward in the North Atlantic, disclosing the influence of the warm water that moves from our Florida coast northward and then northeastward across the Atlantic. A similar though less marked northward trend occurs in the Pacific from Japan to Alaska, along the course of the Kuroshio and its extension, the North Pacific Current (West Wind Drift). In the Southern Hemisphere, cold ocean currents flow northeastward toward the west coasts of South America and Africa, bending the isotherms equatorward.

There are thus two major influences producing the irregularities of the annual isotherms: (a) the differing responses of land and water to the influence of insolation and (b) the transportation of warm and cold water by ocean currents. Note how these influences result in a crowding of the isotherms in Alaska and southeastward to New England, and in eastern Asia. The warmest area, as expressed by the annual means, is in central Africa, where the temperature averages more than 85°. The isotherm of 80° extends around the world except for small areas in the eastern Atlantic and eastern Pacific Oceans, and includes large portions of Central and South America, Africa, Arabia, India, and Indo-China, all of the East Indies and the Philippine Islands, and a part of northern Australia. The coldest regions of the world cannot be shown so definitely because records are very incomplete for polar regions, especially for Antarctica. There is a short record from central Greenland which gives a mean annual temperature of −5°F, and a record of one year at Framheim on the coast of the Ross Sea in Antarctica gave an annual mean of −14.4°F.

JANUARY AND JULY NORMAL TEMPERATURES

An examination of the January and July temperature charts (Figs. 14.2 and 14.3) discloses the migration of the isotherms with the seasons. The January isotherm of 90°F includes only small areas in South Africa and in Australia. In July the average temperature is 90° or over in a part of southwestern United States and large areas in North Africa and southwestern Asia. A small area in the Colorado Valley has a July mean of 95°, and a portion of the Sahara Desert, a mean of 100°. In contrast to these high

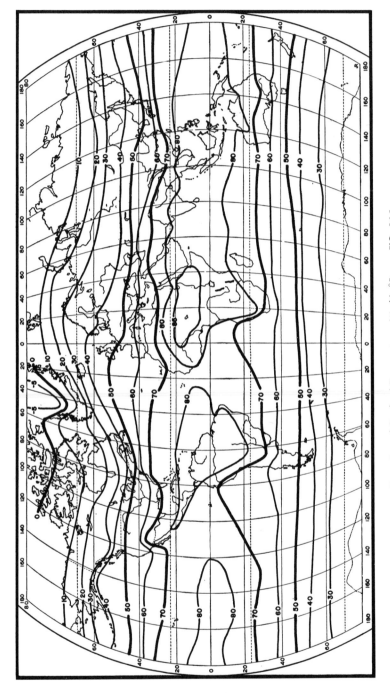

Mean Annual Sea-level Temperatures, World, °F.   **FIG. 14.1**

280

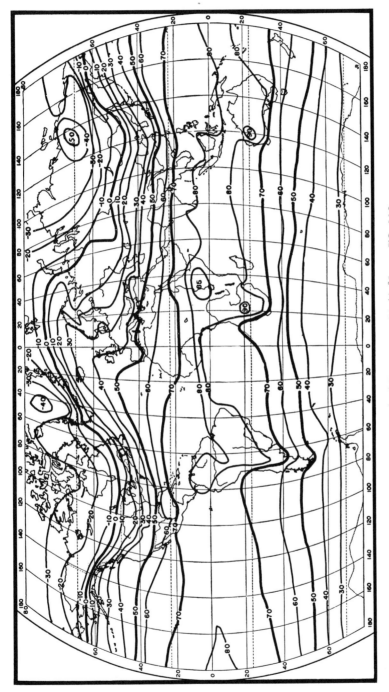

Mean January Sea-level Temperatures, World, °F.   FIG. 14.2

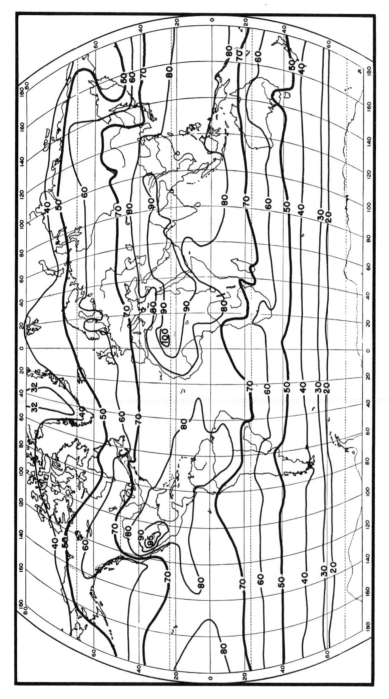

Mean July Sea-level Temperatures, World, °F.　　**FIG. 14.3**

temperatures, the temperature of interior Greenland remains below freezing throughout the year. In January the lowest mean temperatures are in Siberia, —50°F, and in Greenland, —40°F. The lowest mean shown on the map for July is 20°F along the border of the Antarctic continent, but for August, 1958, a mean of —96.8°F was obtained at Vostok.

Note also the migration of the isotherm of 70° in North America; in January it crosses Mexico, and in July it has moved northward to Canada. The change of temperature is less over the oceans than over the lands, and, hence, less in general in the Southern Hemisphere than in the Northern. The migration as a rule is less than that of the sun's rays, which is 47° of latitude. As a result of continental and oceanic influences modifying the effects of insolation, the January temperature off the coast of Norway is 40° higher, while in the interior of North America and Asia it is 30° lower, than the latitudinal average. In July these *anomalies,* or departures from the average temperature of the latitude, are generally less than 10°F, except in the interior of the United States, Asia, and North Africa, where they are from 10° to 20°.

ANNUAL AND DAILY RANGES OF TEMPERATURES

Mean annual ranges of temperature are an expression of the average difference between the mean temperature of the warmest and of the coldest month. They are shown in Fig. 14.4. It will be seen that mean annual ranges are much greater over continental interiors than over large ocean areas in the same latitude, except in equatorial regions. They naturally increase with increase of latitude because of the greater difference between winter and summer insolation as the distance from the equator becomes greater. In the tropical oceans and across equatorial Africa and South America, the annual range is less than 5°F. It increases to 30°F near the tropics in Africa, South America, and Australia, to 80° in the interior of Canada, and to 120° in a small area in Siberia. This progressive change shows clearly the effects of distance from the equator and distance from unfrozen oceans.

In the chart of January mean daily ranges of temperature in the United States (Fig. 14.5), the influences of humidity and of elevation are clearly evident. In portions of the elevated, arid Southwest, the average difference between day and night temperatures in January is 33°F, while in the vicinity of Puget Sound, the marine influence results in a daily range of only 9°F. Note the influence of the Great Lakes in reducing the range. Two physical principles are involved in this influence: first, the water is slow to change its temperature; second, the increased humidity of the air screens out some insolation by day and absorbs earth radiation by night. Note that the extent of the marine influence on the Pacific Coast is greater than on the Atlantic.

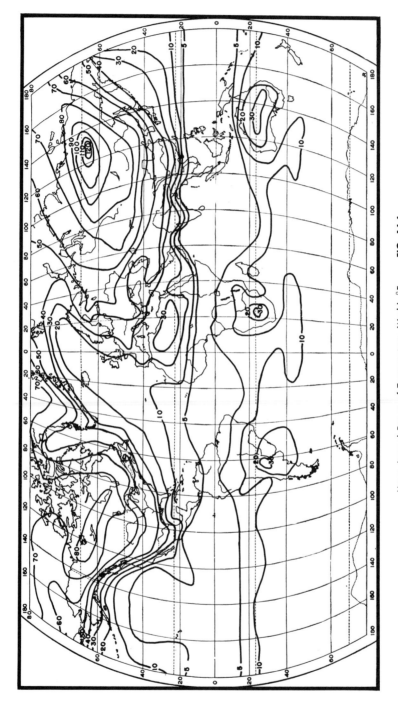

Mean Annual Range of Temperature, World, °F.   **FIG. 14.4**

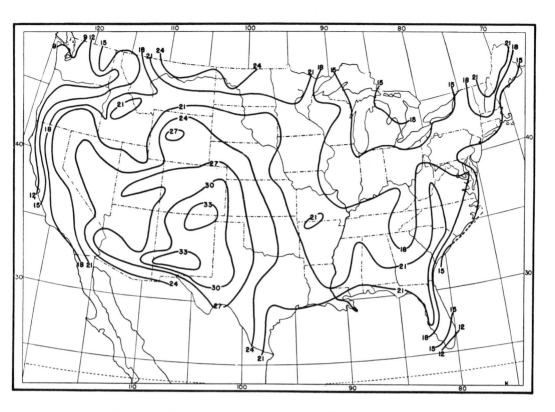

January Mean Daily Range of Temperature in the United States. After **FIG. 14.5** Atlas of American Agriculture.

SOME EXTREMES OF TEMPERATURE

The following are some records of extreme temperatures, obtained under standard conditions of exposure and expressed in the Fahrenheit scale:

Lowest temperature, −126.9°F (−88.3°C), Vostok, Antarctica, August 24, 1960.

Lowest monthly mean temperature, −96.8°F (−71.6°C), Vostok, Antarctica, August, 1958.

Lowest temperature in the continental United States, −70°F (−56.6°C), Rogers Pass, Montana, January 20, 1954.

Lowest mean temperature for one month in the continental United States, −11.4°F (−24.1°C), Bismarck, N.D., February, 1936.

Lowest temperature in Canada, −81°F (−62.7°C), Snag, Yukon Territory, February 3, 1947.

Lowest temperature in Alaska, −76°F (−60°C), Tanana, in 1886. (A minimum thermometer, left for nineteen years near the top of Mt. McKinley, not in an instrument shelter, when recovered indicated a minimum of approximately −100°F).

Lowest mean for one month in Yukon territory, Canada, −51.3°F (−46.2°C) Dawson, December, 1917.

285

Highest temperature of record, 136°F (57.7°C), Azizia, Tripoli, September 13, 1922.

Highest temperature in the United States, 134°F (56.6°C), Greenland Ranch, California, July 10, 1913.

Highest mean temperature for one day in the United States, 108.6°F (41.5°C), Death Valley, California.

Highest average annual temperature in the world, 88°F (31.1°C), Lugh, Italian Somaliland (thirteen-year record.)

Precipitation occurs at irregular intervals and is greatly variable in amount, so that many years of record are required to obtain smooth daily, or even monthly, normals. In fact, it may be questioned whether the word **General Distribution of Precipitation** *normal* in this connection has much significance. Records on land are sufficiently numerous and of sufficient length, however, to justify the use of mean values as tentative normals, with the understanding that several hundred years of record might alter them materially. There is little exact knowledge of the average amounts of rainfall over the oceans. On a chart representing the distribution of rainfall, lines of equal rainfall are called *isohyets*. Isohyets are drawn to indicate the actual precipitation; there is no reduction to sea level as in the case of isobars and some isotherms.

NORMAL ANNUAL PRECIPITATION

From a map of the average annual rainfall of the world we may deduce the following general statements (which the reader should verify by reference to Fig. 14.6):

1. Precipitation is greatest in equatorial regions and decreases irregularly toward the poles. The decreasing amount of moisture in the air as the temperature declines from equatorial to polar regions naturally results in a smaller total precipitation. Also, the general tendency of air to expand and rise in warm areas and to settle in cold areas leads to greater precipitation in the former as compared with the latter regions.

2. Rainfall decreases toward the interior of large continental masses, because the chief source of supply of the moisture of the air is the oceans. Much of the moisture is often precipitated on the near-by land areas, and little is left for the distant interiors. Note the large dry areas in the central portions of Asia and North America. (Other factors are involved besides the inland position of these areas.) Over large land areas there is also an important secondary source of atmospheric humidity in the evaporation from lakes, rivers, soil, and vegetation.

3. Rainfall shows a relation to the general wind systems of the world (discussed in more detail in the next section) and to the direction of the wind, especially whether onshore or offshore.

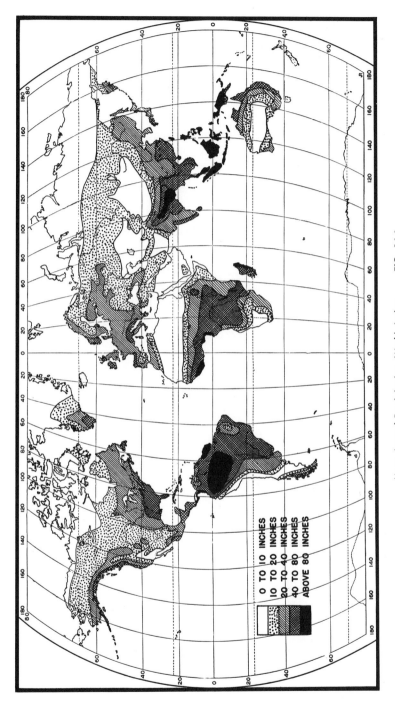

0 TO 10 INCHES
10 TO 20 INCHES
20 TO 40 INCHES
40 TO 80 INCHES
ABOVE 80 INCHES

Mean Annual Precipitation, World, Inches.   FIG. 14.6

4. Ocean currents influence the distribution of rainfall. Warm currents increase precipitation on the neighboring coasts, for there is much water vapor over warm water, and this vapor is cooled when it moves inland, as on the eastern coasts of North and South America. Cold currents diminish precipitation, for the air moving over them is cool and stable and of moderate humidity, as on the western coasts of South America and South Africa.

5. Mountain systems influence precipitation by giving rise to ascending and descending air currents. Most mountain systems have a wet and a dry side, the wet side being toward the ocean or toward the prevailing winds. Outside of the tropics, the wettest parts of the world are mountain slopes facing prevailing winds from the oceans.

SEASONAL VARIATION OF PRECIPITATION

The various types of seasonal distribution of rainfall have great economic significance. There are large areas in equatorial regions where the rainfall is heavy throughout the year, and other areas within the tropics with alternate wet and dry seasons. In the middle latitudes, the west coasts of continents have a winter maximum of rainfall and dry summers. The precipitation is cyclonic in origin and is often increased by orographic factors. In the interiors there is a marked summer maximum, largely of thunderstorm type. On eastern coasts there is a fairly even distribution

Types of Rainfall Distribution by Months.   **FIG. 14.7**

through the year, partly cyclonic and partly convectional, but usually with a summer maximum.

The relation of rainfall to the growing season is of particular importance. For example, in a large portion of the Mississippi and Missouri Valleys, where the total precipitation is light to moderate, the heaviest rainfall occurs in the first half of the growing season, May, June, and July, when it is of the greatest value in the production of crops. A few types of monthly distribution of rainfall are shown in Fig. 14.7.

ANNUAL NUMBER OF RAINY DAYS

The relation of the total rainfall to the number of days with rain is a climatic factor of some importance, indicative of the type of rainfall and of the general impression of dampness or dryness given by the climate. In some places the rain falls in moderate or heavy showers of short duration, and the skies are clear for long intervals. These conditions are characteristic of the interiors of continents and of such regions as our Gulf and South Atlantic Coasts (Fig. 14.8).

In other places there are many days of light rain or drizzle, giving a large number of rainy days but only light or moderate rainfall. In this

Average Annual Number of Days with .01 Inch or More of Precipitation   **FIG. 14.8**
in the United States. Numerous local variations are not indicated.

country the coasts of Oregon and Washington have climates of this character, and in Europe the British Isles, the Netherlands, Belgium, and western France have similar conditions. In both continents, these are marine climates in the prevailing westerlies. The region around the Great Lakes has a similar climate in this respect. Seattle has 151 rainy days and a normal annual rainfall of 34.03 inches, giving an average of 0.23 inch per day of rain; Oklahoma City has nearly as much rain, 31.15 inches, but it falls on 82 days and the rate of 0.38 inch for each day of rain. Marquette, Michigan, has only 32.47 inches per year, but there are 165 days on which a measurable amount falls, each day on the average receiving only 0.20 inch; at Pensacola, Florida, a much heavier rainfall, 57.85 inches, occurs on fewer days, 114, and the amount per day is 0.51 inch, or 2 1/2 times the amount at Marquette.

AREAS OF HEAVY AND LIGHT RAIN

The average annual precipitation is above 100 inches in small areas in Central America, Panama, western Colombia, and southern Chile, as well as in the East Indies, the Himalayas, and along the north coast of the Gulf of Guinea. These are all warm regions, but profitable use cannot be made of the land, because the rainfall is too heavy, and the growth of native vegetation is too luxuriant. Average amounts between 80 and 100 inches occur at places on the west coast of North America from Alaska to Oregon, in tropical South America, many tropical islands, and large areas of the tropical oceans.

At the other extreme, there are areas of less than 10 inches in southwestern United States, the Sahara and Arabian deserts, much of interior Asia from the Caspian Sea to China, the trade-wind belts of the eastern Atlantic, and in north polar regions north of latitude 70°. In the Southern Hemisphere there are regions of less than 10 inches in South America, in southwest Africa, and in much of interior Australia.

Amounts of rain between 20 and 100 inches are favorable for agricultural use of the land. Areas receiving between 10 and 20 inches of rain a year are semiarid. They are suitable for grazing and dry farming, but not

TABLE 14.1   Distribution of Precipitation

ANNUAL RAINFALL IN INCHES	PERCENTAGE OF LAND AREA	CLIMATIC CLASSIFICATION
Less than 10	25	Arid
10–20	30	Semiarid
20–40	20	Subhumid
40–60	11	Humid
60–80	9	Humid
More than 80	5	Very wet

for intensive agriculture except under irrigation. Where the rainfall is below 10 inches, desert conditions exist, and water for irrigation must be brought from wetter regions. Production depends upon the yearly distribution of the rain, and upon other factors, notably temperature. The amounts, 10 to 20 inches, just given, are used as approximate dividing values. Table 14.1 shows approximate percentages of land areas of the earth with rainfall between given values.

SOME EXTREMES OF RAINFALL

Mt. Waialeale, Kauai, Hawaii (altitude 5,075 feet) holds the record of being the wettest place on earth, having received an average annual rainfall of 471.68 inches over a period of thirty-seven years (1912–1949). Not far behind is Cherrapunji, India (altitude, 4,309 feet), with an average annual record of 450 inches (seventy-four-year period). Prevailing winds, together with orographic lifting, account for the unusual rainfall at both stations. While Mt. Waialeale receives copious rains during all months, Cherrapunji receives nearly all of its precipitation during the summer monsoon. During 1860–1861, within a single twelve-month period, Cherrapunji received 1,041.78 inches. The Wynoochee, Washington station receives an average annual rainfall of 150.73 inches.

Precipitation extremes during a single month include Manoyuram, India, 264 inches, Helen Mine, California, 71 inches.

Some of the greatest rainfalls ever recorded in short periods of time are shown in Table 14.2.

TABLE 14.2   Heavy Rainfalls in Short Periods of Time

STATION	AMOUNT IN.	TIME REQUIRED (HRS.)	TIME REQUIRED (MIN.)	DATE OF OCCURRENCE
Unionville, Md.	1.23	00	1	July 4, 1956
Porto Bello, Panama	2.47	00	3	Nov. 29, 1911
Taylor, Texas	2.00	00	10	April 29, 1905
Galveston, Texas	3.95	00	14	June 4, 1871
Guinea, Va.	9.25	00	40	Aug. 24, 1906
Holt, Mo.	12.00	00	42	July 22, 1947
Rockport, W.Va.	19.00	2	10	July 18, 1889
D'Hanis, Texas	21.50	3	00	May 31, 1935
Smethport, Pa.	30.70	6	00	July 18, 1942
Thrall, Texas	34.60	18	00	Sept. 9, 1921
Baguio, Luzon, P.I.	45.99	24	00	July 14–15, 1911

In Romania there is a record of a fall of 8.07 inches in 20 minutes, and in the Sierra Nevada in east-central California, Tamarack (altitude, 8,000 feet) has an average seasonal snowfall of 451 inches. The greatest fall recorded there in a single season is 884 inches, the greatest monthly fall is

314 inches, and the greatest depth of snow on the ground at any time is 454 inches.

At the other extreme, the average annual rainfall in inches is 1.33 at Helwan, Egypt; 1.66 at Greenland Ranch, California; 1.84 at Aden, Arabia; 4.16 at Arequipa, Peru; and 0.02 inch at Arica, Chile (forty-three-year record). There are considerable areas in southeastern California, western and southern Nevada, and extreme western Arizona where the rainfall is less than 5 inches a year.

A broad general description of the climates of the earth **Zonation of Climates** may be made, following a more or less latitudinal division into zones. Each zone includes many climatic variations, but some general characteristics applying to large areas may be mentioned. Although there are many contributing elements to the over-all climate of any area, such as solar radiation, temperature, rainfall, humidity, wind velocity, and evaporation, temperature and rainfall are the most important for general consideration.

TROPICAL ZONE

A simple climate is characteristic of the zone within the tropics. Its central portion is the equatorial low-pressure belt. This *equatorial zone* has a large annual rainfall and frequent and heavy thunderstorms in all months of the year. It is the doldrum region of variable winds and calms, a region of dense tropical forests of rapid growth. Bordering this wet belt on the north and on the south, there are regions which receive rain during the summer of that hemisphere, as the doldrums migrate toward the regions, but little or no rain during a short period of the opposite season, when the doldrums are farthest away. The vegetation of this climatic regime constitutes the true *jungle*, with many trees and a dense undergrowth of tangled vines and other tropical plants. In the Western Hemisphere, these jungles extend intermittently northward into southern Mexico and southward into central Brazil. Toward the poleward sides of these belts, where the rainfall becomes light, there are open grasslands, or *savannas*, bordering the forests. The savannas include the Sudan of Africa, the Llanos of Venezuela, the Campos of Brazil, and the Downs of Australia. In the equatorial and savanna zones, seasonal temperature changes are slight. There are practically no seasons, except where there is a wet and a dry season. Temperatures average high throughout the year, and the climate is oppressive and enervating, especially when the humidity is high, but maximum temperatures are usually not so high as in continental interiors in so-called temperate zones. In large areas of the tropics temperatures never reach 100°. High humidity, dense vegetative cover, and days that are shorter than summer days in higher latitudes are factors in keeping the maximum temperatures moderate.

In the central portions of the trade-wind belts, on the poleward sides of the savannas, the winds blow with great regularity at a moderate speed, storms are very rare, and temperatures are uniformly mild. There are no frosts; the climate is tropical. Although the trade winds move for long distances over the oceans, they move from colder to warmer regions and are therefore rather dry except when there is orographic uplift. On the windward sides of highlands athwart the constant trades, the rainfall is heavy and frequent at all seasons. In other situations, the skies are bright, sunshine is abundant, and rainfall is light. Though not stimulating, this *trade wind climate* is comfortable and healthful in contrast with the mugginess of equatorial climates.

SUBTROPICAL ZONES

In the poleward portions of the trade winds and the equatorward portions of the subtropical high-pressure belts, there are transition zones in each hemisphere with subtropical types of climate, not entirely free of frost. On the west coasts of the continents in these latitudes is the *Mediterranean climate*. These areas have moderate temperatures throughout the year, with moderate rainfall in winter under the influence of the westerlies, and with dry, sunny summers under the influence of the subtropical belts of high pressure. The Mediterranean climate is of greatest extent in the countries bordering on the sea from which it is named, but there are small areas of this type of climate in California, and in South Africa, southern Australia, and central Chile.

The east coasts of continents in these transition areas have a *humid subtropical climate*, more nearly continental in character than is the Mediterranean type, with greater annual temperature ranges, and with no dry season. In parts of southeastern Asia and the Netherlands Indies, a humid, *monsoon climate* prevails, having a short moderately dry season but a heavy annual rainfall from onshore winds.

In the main, the subtropical zones are deficient in rainfall, with large arid and semiarid areas. We have noted that the trade winds are naturally dry. The high-pressure belts are dry because of subsiding air, but they are subject to more variable winds and to occasional invasion by storms from the prevailing westerlies. The natural dryness of these belts becomes evident when we note that the belts include most of the great desert areas in each of the five continents.

INTERMEDIATE ZONES

The middle zones of each hemisphere are regions of the prevailing westerlies, much interrupted and confused by local conditions and by traveling disturbances resulting from the meeting of polar and tropical air masses. Wide temperature ranges and marked changeableness of weather are striking characteristics. There is much variability of rainfall, which is generally heavier on the coasts and lighter in the interiors of the continents. In Russia and Siberia, in middle latitudes, there are large, unwooded, grassy, semiarid plains called *steppes*. These and similar regions in Hungary and the Great Plains of the United States have what is called a *steppe climate*. Such a climate occurs only in large continental interiors. There are, however, large inland areas within the intermediate zones that have adequate rainfall, as do, also, the coastal regions.

POLAR ZONES

About 8 per cent of the earth's surface is included in the polar zones, in which only a minimum of plant and animal life exists. There is almost continuous sunlight for a short time in summer, with some warm days, but the season is so short that the ground remains permanently frozen except in a thin surface layer. Precipitation is light.

ZONES OF TEMPERATURE

The earth may be divided into climatic zones by using isotherms instead of parallels of latitude. On this basis Supan has made the following divisions:

1. *Hot belt:* the area inclosed by the mean annual isotherm of 68°F. This belt is irregular, mostly in the Northern Hemisphere, and somewhat larger than the torrid zone. The poleward boundaries represent approximately the limit of the trade winds and of the growth of palms.

2. *Cold caps:* the area around the poles inclosed by the isotherm of 50°F for the warmest month. This isotherm represents the limit of the growth of cereals and of forest trees. In cold regions it is the temperature of the summer rather than of the year that determines habitability and vegetative growth. Hence the temperature of the warmest month is used instead of the average annual temperature.

3. *Temperate belts:* the area between the hot belts and the cold caps. The northern temperate belt extends north of the Arctic circle in Alaska and in Eurasia, but the cold cap extends south of the circle in the Bering Sea and on the Labrador coast. In the Southern Hemisphere, the temperate belt reaches no farther south than latitude 55°.

For a more detailed study of climate, each of these belts may be divided into numerous subdivisions. Many such subdivisions have been made, both on the basis of temperature and amount and distribution of rainfall, and on the basis of plant growth.

The differences of climate so far discussed have been closely related to distance from the equator, but there are climatic variations wholly independent of latitude. The elevation of an area and its position relative to continents, oceans, and mountain systems give the area certain climatic characteristics in whatever part of the world it may be. Other factors, indirectly related to latitude but producing independent effects on climate, are the influence of prevailing winds and of ocean currents and the prevalence of cyclonic storms.

Climate as Related to Physical Geography

CONTINENTAL CLIMATES

In the interiors of continents the climate is usually rather dry and clear, that is, rainfall is light to moderate, relative humidity is low, and sunshine is abundant. Within the tropics, temperature contrasts are small over large land areas as well as over the oceans. In middle latitudes, continental climates are marked by severe winters and hot summers; in polar regions, the winters are long and severe and the summers short and cool. Steppe climates are dry continental, while a desert is an extreme type of dry continental climate.

MARINE CLIMATES

The climate of the oceans and of lands that are largely influenced by ocean conditions, islands, for instance, is characterized by small daily and yearly ranges of temperature, with nights and winters relatively warm and days and summers cool. That is to say, these climates are equable and moderate in their changes. Because water warms slowly, the springs are late and cool; because water cools slowly, the autumns are late and warm. In the interior of the United States, July is the hottest month, on the average; in San Francisco, where the climate is largely marine, September is the warmest month. Except in the trade-wind belts, marine climates usually have greater humidity and cloudiness than continental climates.

COASTAL OR LITTORAL CLIMATES

The climate along the coasts of continents is intermediate between the marine and the continental types. The prevailing winds and mountain barriers largely determine the distance inland to which oceanic influences penetrate. In the zones of the prevailing westerly winds, west coasts of continents have belts of distinctly coastal climate; but, on the east coasts, continental climates extend practically to the shore. In trade-wind belts, east coasts are under marine influence and west coasts, under continental influence. Oceanic and continental influences on temperature are exemplified by Table 14.3.

TABLE 14.3   Summer and Winter Mean Temperatures
Across Northern North America

STATION	LATITUDE NORTH		LONGITUDE WEST		MEAN TEMPERATURE °F JAN.	JULY
Prince Rupert	54°	10′	130°	6′	35.0	56.0
Edmonton	53°	33′	113°	30′	5.5	61.1
Prince Albert	53°	10′	105°	38′	−4.7	62.7
Winnipeg	49°	53′	97°	7′	−3.9	66.4
Ft. Hope	51°	33′	87°	49′	−7.9	62.2
Moose Factory	51°	16′	80°	56′	−4.8	61.5
Southwest Point	49°	23′	63°	43′	12.2	56.7
St. Johns	47°	34′	52°	42′	23.6	59.3

The relative importance of continental and oceanic influences on the climate of a given region is sometimes expressed numerically by an *index of continentality* based upon the annual range of temperature as modified by a latitudinal factor. Probably a better measure of the relative influence of continents and oceans is the ratio of the frequencies of continental and maritime air masses. Unfortunately, over the greater part of the earth, there are not sufficient records to permit the calculation of this ratio.

MOUNTAIN AND PLATEAU CLIMATES

On mountains and plateaus, the average temperature decreases with elevation at a rate approximating that of the average lapse rate in the free air, but with many local variations. The rainfall increases up to 6,000 or 7,000 feet and then decreases because of reduced absolute humidity. As the air becomes thinner and freer of dust and moisture, it absorbs less radiation, and insolation is, therefore, more intense by day and radiation cooling more rapid by night. However, where there is considerable slope, the daily temperature ranges are kept relatively small by the thorough mixing of the air.

On large, level plateaus, on the other hand, where there is no aid to the mixing of the air, both daily and annual ranges are larger than in lowlands similarly situated. In mountain climates, one is readily warmed in the sunshine by absorption of the intense insolation, while the air itself, which absorbs little radiation, remains cool. At elevations of 12,000 to 15,000 feet, the air becomes so rarefied as to cause mountain sickness in many persons because of insufficient oxygen. Mountain ranges interfere with the free movement of the lower air and often act as climatic divides or barriers, resulting in quite different climates on opposite sides. For example, the west portions of Oregon and Washington have a wet and largely marine climate, while east of the Cascade Range the rainfall is light and the climate has continental characteristics. The Alps are a barrier separating the climate of central Europe from that of the Mediterranean coast.

MAJOR CLIMATIC FACTORS

Some important influences governing the climate of a region and some localities in which each is a prominent factor may be listed as follows:

Latitude: Greenland, Amazon Valley, Antarctica.
Position relative to water: Seattle, San Diego, Boston.
Continentality: Oklahoma City, Minneapolis, Verkhoyansk.
Position relative to mountain barriers: Nevada, Riviera, Ganges Valley.
Altitude: Denver, Bogotá, Addis Ababa, Tibet.
Prevalence of cyclonic storms: New England, Great Lakes region, Germany.
Prevailing winds: Hawaii, India, Azores, Puerto Rico.
Ocean currents: Norway, Labrador, northern Chile.

Irregular distribution and intensity of the climatic fac- **Climatic** tors from place to place often renders a latitudinal or **Classification** topographic zonation of climate unreliable and some- times very misleading. Several classification systems have been devised to overcome this handicap and at the same time present the various climatic types in simplified but usable form. Each system has its merits, but none is perfect. The classification to be reviewed here was first devised by Wladimir Köppen in 1918. It has been revised and refined several times. This modified version by Trewartha is popular in the United States (Fig. 14.9). It is based on an ingenious system of letter combinations to create an exact formula for each climatic region.[1]

MAJOR CLIMATIC DIVISIONS

Five major climatic regions are recognized as follows:

1. A climates, or tropical rainy climates, with no month of the year having a mean temperature below 64.4°F (18°C).

2. B climates, or dry climates, include those arid and semiarid regions of the world where rainfall deficiency is the prime limiting factor in land usability. Evaporation exceeds precipitation, and plow-agriculture is not considered feasible without irrigation. The B climates are further divided into arid or desert regions (BW) and semiarid or steppe regions (BS).

3. C climates, or humid mesothermal climates, lie poleward from the A climates where the rainfall is sufficient for the area not to be classed as B. C climates have a mild winter, the poleward boundary being the 32°F (0°C) isotherm for the coldest month.

[1] Glen T. Trewartha, *An Introduction to Climate* (New York: McGraw-Hill Book Company, 1954). For another recognized classification system, see C. Warren Thornthwaite, "An Approach Toward a Rational Classification of Climate," *Geographical Review*, XXXVIII (January 1948), 55-94.

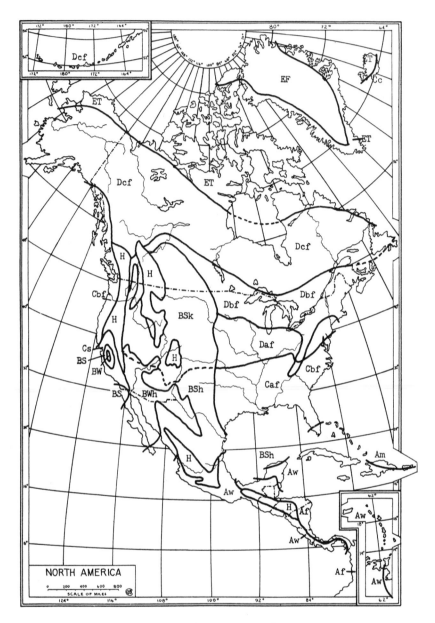

Climates of North America. *By permission from* G. T. Trewartha, An Intro-   **FIG. 14.9**
duction to Climate, 3rd ed. (New York: McGraw-Hill Book Company, 1954).

4. D climates, or humid microthermal climates, lie poleward from the C climates and include those regions with long, cold winters but adequate summers for agricultural and forestry development. The poleward boundary for the D climates is the 50°F (10°C) isotherm for the warmest month.

5. E climates, or polar climates, include those areas having no mean monthly temperature above 50°F (10°C). They are subdivided into *tundra* (ET), with a short growing season, and *ice cap* (EF), where no month of the year has a mean temperature above 32°F.

In addition to these five climatic divisions, an H climate, or undifferentiated highlands climate, is used to designate those mountainous areas with topography and exposure so variable within short distances as to render the standard classifications impractical.

CLIMATIC SUBDIVISIONS

The A, C, and D climatic divisions are further refined according to their rainfall and temperature characteristics. Lower-case letters are used to denote temperature variations (not used with A climates) as follows:

a—warm summers (warmest month above 71.6°F, or 22°C).
b—cool summers (warmest month below 71.6°F, or 22°C).
c—short, cool summers (less than four months above 50°F, or 10°C).
d—long, cold winters (coldest month below —36.4°F, or —38°C).

More specific rainfall distribution data are shown by:

f—no dry season.
s—dry summers (rare in the tropics).
w—dry winters, or during the low-sun period.
m—dry winters with monsoon rain in summers.

Thus by knowing the values of the letters representing a climatic region, as shown in Fig. 14.9, it is possible to visualize the climate of that region. Geographical position within a climatic region is also important, however, and should be considered when the climate of a specific place is of concern. For example, the Caf climatic region may border the Af to the south, the BS to the west, and the Daf to the north. Stations just inside the Caf boundaries on these three sides may be radically different from each other. This is not a fault, but a virtue, of the system, for the gradual but omnipresent variability of climate necessitates a simple classification.

A cycle is the interval of time in which a certain succession of events which repeat themselves again and again in the same order is completed. A cyclical, or periodic, event is one that recurs at regular, equal intervals. There are two very evident weather cycles of such importance that we base our reckon-

Cyclical Changes of Weather and Climate

ing of time upon them, namely, the daily and the annual cycles. It may be noted, however, that, as weather periods, neither of these is absolutely regular in its recurrence. The diurnal period in the weather is governed by the times of sunrise and sunset and is, accordingly, variable in length, except at the equator, and altogether ceases to exist as a twenty-four-hour cycle in polar regions. The annual period in the weather is also of variable length, for the seasons are sometimes "late" and sometimes "early."

WEATHER CYCLES

A brief examination of a climatic table of rainfall shows that a few dry years often occur in succession, followed by a series of wet years, and again by another group of dry years. Such short-period fluctuations are constantly occurring, not in precipitation records alone, but also in connection with other weather elements. It is these variations, and not the daily and yearly periods, that are commonly called *weather cycles*. There can be no doubt of the existence of the fluctuations, but none is truly periodic in its recurrence.

Much attention has been given to the statistical analysis of weather data in the hope of finding periodicities that would be useful as indicators of future conditions, and a great many so-called cycles have been found in this way. There is a list of more than 100 of these, varying in length from 8 months to 260 years, but they all show irregularities: successive recurrences are of different length and intensity; the cycles are interrupted by departures in the opposite direction; after persisting for several periods, a cycle may suddenly fail, sometimes to begin again later in a different phase. There are so many of these "cycles," and they are so irregular, that the result can hardly be distinguished from chance. Most of them are of doubtful reality. They have not proved of practical value in forecasting next year's weather.

Weather cycles, in the sense of fluctuations of an irregular nature, are characteristic of climate throughout the world and often have important social and economic consequences. For example, in the plains of western Kansas, western Oklahoma, and eastern Colorado, there have been series of wet years with accompanying good crops and good prices for land, and series of dry years, causing crop failures and land abandonment. Cycles of this kind are illustrated in Fig. 14.10, which shows, first, the actual rainfall record for the state of Iowa for the years 1873 to 1955, and second, a method of charting the data of rainfall to give a clear picture of cyclical changes.

In the upper curve, the annual total of rainfall is indicated year by year by the distance of a point above the zero line of the figure, and these points are connected by a broken line. Amounts above and below normal occur irregularly, and cycles are not evident in this curve. In some cases, a

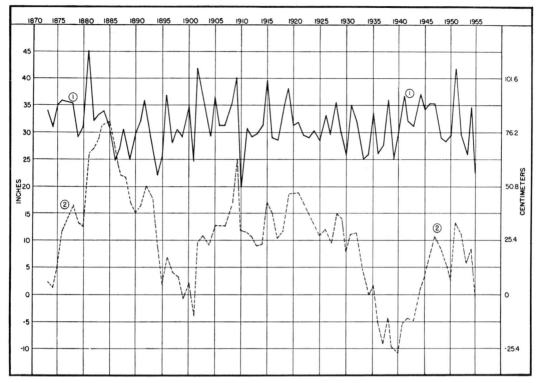

Iowa Precipitation, 1873–1955. (1)—Actual precipitation by years (normal equals 31.60 inches). (2)—Accumulated sums of departures from normal.

FIG. 14.10

few wet or dry years occur in succession; at other times, there are frequent alternations between wet and dry years. The wettest year of the record, 1881, is preceded by two dry years, and the driest year, 1910, is preceded by two moderately wet years.

In the lower curve, the method of *accumulated sums of departures* is used. The departure of the rainfall of each year from the average of the entire series is first obtained, and then, beginning with the first year, the year-by-year accumulated algebraic sums of these departures are calculated and entered. In a series of wet years, there is an accumulating excess of precipitation, and the line moves upward; in dry years, it moves downward. The line slopes up when the year is wet, and down when it is dry, without reference to its position relative to the zero line.

This curve makes certain cyclical tendencies evident. It shows that there was an increasing accumulation of rainfall above normal for eleven years from 1874 to 1885, then a declining rainfall with some interruptions for sixteen years to 1901. There followed a rapid rise for eight years with one slight setback. After 1909 the curve is irregular, with brief periods of excess and deficiency but with an unmistakable downward trend until 1940. The curve again swings upward through another irregular, but distinctive, cyclic trend. Note that the three cycles shown are not of equal

301

length or magnitude. Such imperfectly cyclical variations as are shown by this figure are typical of weather records in general and are to be regarded as the natural, normal behavior of the climate. Any long-time planning should take account of these variations. Unfortunately, planning is hampered by the irregular nature of the variations.

SECULAR TRENDS

In addition to the short-period variations commonly meant by the term *weather cycles,* there are tendencies that persist over longer periods and are known as *secular trends*. In studying the annual growth rings of sequoias, A. E. Douglass found evidence of oscillations in periods of a few centuries in addition to those of a few years. Periods of a similar order of length have been found in the study of glaciers and of lake levels in Europe and Asia. There is some evidence that Persia and Turkestan, Arizona and New Mexico, are drier than they were at the beginning of the Christian era, and that Yucatan and southern Mexico are wetter. If these conclusions are correct, it seems probable that the changes indicated are trends or cycles of a still greater length. However, in most parts of the world, there is no evidence of important trends persisting through centuries.

When we extend our time scale and think in terms of geological eras, we find that climate has changed greatly, but also cyclically, alternating between glacial and interglacial periods. At one time, glaciers covered large areas of northern United States; at another time, some of these areas were

Geologic Evidences of Climatic Changes. *After C. E. P. Brooks.*   **FIG. 14.11**

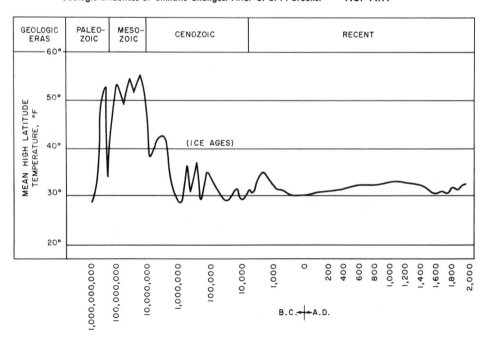

covered by dense tropical forests and inhabited by huge tropical beasts (Fig. 14.11). Plant seeds and spores preserved in peat bogs are now interpreted as giving evidence of several long climatic trends since the glaciers disappeared, periods of perhaps a thousand dry years and then a thousand wet years. The fact that great climatic changes have occurred in geologic time is undisputed, but the causes of the changes are still a subject of speculation. It is certain that alterations in the elevation of the land and in the distribution of land and water have resulted in great changes in climate, but whether or not there were other causes of the geological climatic fluctuations is not known. It seems probable that such slow changes in climate are still in progress, as slow changes in the elevation and distribution of land undoubtedly are.

We conclude that there are numerous oscillations in the atmosphere, some short and some long, and that therefore it is not possible to obtain an absolutely stable "normal" value of the weather elements. The oscillations resemble cycles but are not truly periodic; they resemble the movements of a pendulum, except that the weather does not keep time in its vibrations as a pendulum does. No physical explanation of the origin and continuance of these oscillations is known. They may be the result of variable outside influences, particularly insolation, or they may be due to natural periods of vibration in the atmosphere itself. They are so numerous, so variable and inconstant, that thus far it has not been found safe to trust their extension into the future.

Theories of Climatic Changes

The terrestrial conditions governing the climate of a given portion of the earth have previously been discussed. In connection with the consideration of climatic variability, it is important to examine the larger factors that determine the climate of the earth as a whole, and whether or not they are subject to slow or sudden changes. The four major factors controlling the climate of the world are: (a) the output of solar energy, (b) the earth's distance from the sun and its position relative to the sun, (c) the extent, composition, and dust content of the atmosphere, and (d) the elevation of land and the distribution of land and water.

SOLAR RADIATION

As previously noted, the output of solar energy has small, irregular variations from day to day and in an eleven-year period. There is some evidence, not wholly conclusive, that these variations influence weather changes and short climatic fluctuations. Other changes in solar energy may have occurred and may still be in progress. They may have modified the climate of past ages, but no evidence of such changes in solar output exists. In particular, there is no reason to suppose that *sudden* changes of climatic significance have occurred.

RELATIVE POSITION OF EARTH AND SUN

Aside from the regular seasonal variations in the position of the earth's axis relative to the sun and in the earth's distance from the sun, these undergo slow and slight changes in periods of from 21,000 to 400,000 years. One theory of the cause of glacial and interglacial epochs, *Crolls' theory*, is based upon these recurring slight changes in the earth's orbit. The theory is open to serious objection as an explanation of the known glacial history, and, in any case, such changes as have occurred within the past few thousand years have had no appreciable effect on climate.

ATMOSPHERIC CONTENT

The extent and gaseous composition of the air, by affecting the amount of absorption of incoming or outgoing radiation, affect the climate of the world. Another theory of the cause of the ice ages is based on supposed variable amounts of carbon dioxide in the air in different eras, and the fact that this gas is a good absorber of earth radiation. This theory is not generally accepted, and it appears certain that the proportion of the gases of the air has remained practically constant since the beginning of history, although it probably changed appreciably in geological epochs.

During past geologic ages, there were probably periods of great volcanic activity during which immense quantities of dust were thrown into the air. This volcanic dust, by intercepting much solar radiation, may have been an important factor in the production of climatic changes and, according to Humphreys, was probably one of the chief causes of glaciation. There is observational evidence that large volcanic eruptions in historical times, such as those of Krakatoa in 1883 and Katmai in 1912, were followed by cooler weather for a year or two. These slight temporary results have been observed, but the variation in the amount of volcanic activity in the past few thousand years has not been sufficient to effect a persistent change in climate.

DISTRIBUTION AND ELEVATION OF LAND

Finally, great changes in the elevation of large land areas, in the extent of the land surface, and in the distribution of land and water have undoubtedly caused great alterations in the climates of the world in the past million years. There are evidences of the alternate uplift and subsidence of large land masses, resulting in great variations in the elevation of the land and also in the ratio of the total land surface of the globe to the water surface. We know that elevation has important effects on climate, and we know that changes in the extent and position of land areas would greatly modify climate, not only because of the different responses of land and water to insolation, but also indirectly by producing changes in ocean currents and atmospheric circulation. It seems clear then that these terrestrial changes have been important factors in past climatic pulsations, but the changes are slow in terms of man's history, and such slight changes as have occurred in historical times have had no observable effect.

STABILITY OF HISTORIC CLIMATE

We may disregard geological epochs, because they are too long to be included in the ordinary, everyday meaning of climate, and we may disregard weather cycles as too short, and may consider climate to mean the summation of weather conditions within the recorded life of man. In this sense, climate is about as stable as anything we know on earth, about as permanent as the hills. While there is some evidence in Asia and in our Southwest of changes in the past 1,000 or 2,000 years, in most parts of the world the evidence is to the contrary. Olives are still grown in Palestine and silkworms in China, under apparently the same climatic conditions as prevailed several thousand years ago. In spite of weather cycles and secular trends, the climates of the world appear not to have changed progressively in one direction within the period of history.

There are no sudden, violent changes of climate. That is the conclusion to be drawn from our knowledge of the past, and it is also the conclusion when we consider the causes of climate, that is, the climatic controls discussed in the preceding paragraphs. While all of these factors are more or less variable in the slow course of time and may have been influential in producing geological changes of climate, we have no reason to suppose that any of them ever has or ever will change suddenly or appreciably within a few hundred or a few thousand years. We may therefore expect the climates of the world to remain relatively stable in terms of human history.

Further, it is evident that the activities of man cannot influence these major controls of climate. We cannot yet analyze all the forces affecting weather and climate nor explain their periodic fluctuations, but both reason and experience indicate that climate is much more stable than human institutions or relations. The climatic factors, affecting profoundly the economic, social, and physical life of man, remain comparatively permanent in a changing world. Nations rise and fall, causing changes in trade routes, the rise of new commercial cities, and the decline of old ones. Scientific discoveries and their applications lead to new industries and new habits with resulting changes in economic life and the distribution of the population. Climate, however, remains a practically constant element of man's environment.

PROBLEMS

1.
On three outline maps of the world, draw the isotherms for the year, for January, and for July.

2.
On each of these maps, draw the "heat equator" through the middle of the hottest belt.

3.
Why do higher maximum temperatures occur in North Dakota than in Alabama?

4.
Indicate the normal annual precipitation on a map of the world by different colors or shades for intervals of 10 inches.

5.
Why do continental interiors have their maximum precipitation in summer?

6.
Obtain a local *Annual Meteorological Summary* as published at many weather bureau stations, and list the various items of climatic information published therein.

7.
Plot records of temperature and rainfall, using accumulated sums of departures and also twenty-year moving sums, and report on the character of the variations indicated.

8.
Draw a 5-inch square to represent North America, and schematically subdivide it to show the climatic classification according to Fig. 14.9.

9.
Is the climate of your state changing?

10.
Why do scientists spend a lot of time classifying things? Does the classification of climates help you to recognize other places in the world with similar climate to ours?

15

world weather
relationships
and climatic
influences

A study of the general and secondary circulations makes it evident that the atmosphere is fluid and mobile and acts as a whole. Anything that happens in one part of it affects it all. Local weather and climate are small portions of world weather and climate. The characteristics of weather and climate, and the way in which they vary in time and place, have many important relationships to the life and labors of man. In fact, they are fundamental factors conditioning our life on this planet. In this chapter attention is called, briefly, to some features of the weather in its worldwide relationships and to some phases of man's response to his climatic environment.

The weather vane has long been a symbol of fickleness. **Variability** Change and variety are characteristic of the weather **of the Weather** outside of the tropics, in contrast to the monotony that often prevails in trade-wind and equatorial climates.

COMBINATIONS OF WEATHER ELEMENTS

The weather elements, such as temperature, precipitation, wind direction and speed, humidity, sunshine, and cloudiness, are all continuously variable within rather wide limits, and to a certain degree independent of one another. Hence, the number of possible combinations among them is very great. When 1,440 minutes of changing atmospheric conditions are combined to make a day of twenty-four hours, the number of possible permutations of the weather elements becomes almost infinite, and we see why no two days, as no two human faces, are exactly alike.

It is evident at once, however, that we do not experience our weather entirely by a random sampling of the possible combinations of the weather elements. There is, for example, the seasonal control of temperature; in the United States we do not have zero temperatures in July nor 100° in January. It is also clear that the different meteorological elements do not vary with complete independence. There is an evident correlation between wind direction and temperature, between wind direction and rainfall, and between sunshine, cloudiness, and rainfall. The number of combinations is considerably restricted by these relationships and further limited by the fact that the weather of a given day is not completely independent of the preceding day's weather, as will be noted in the next section. In spite of these limitations, each day is unlike every other, and sometimes the changes from one day to the next are extreme. At Goodland, Kansas, on January 26–27, 1951, the temperature dropped from 79°F to 3°F in eighteen hours. This is an extreme case, having occurred during one of the most severe cold waves in the history of the Weather Bureau. Wide variations in temperature from day to day are frequent in the winter months, however, throughout most of the United States. Rapid and large falls are more frequent than similar rises.

MONTHLY AND ANNUAL VARIABILITY

When these erratic days are combined into weeks and months, and the months into seasons and years, we get an immense number of possible groupings and an infinite variability of detail. Months whose average conditions are the same may in fact be very different, when compared, from day to day. The average temperature of the month of February, 1933, at Des Moines, Iowa, was nearly normal, but half the month was extremely cold, and the other half was unusually warm. There were no normal days, but the month was normal. Rainfall may be equally erratic. The distribution of the various amounts of precipitation in January at Cleveland, Ohio, for sixty-four years, is illustrated in Fig. 15.1, which is called a *frequency polygon*. It will be noted that the figure is one-sided; there are more small values than large ones. The average, or *mean*, value is 2.54 inches, but the most frequent value, or *mode*, is from 1.40 to 1.59 inches, and 2.23 is the *median*, or *middle* value, when the amounts are arranged in the order of their magnitude. A longer record might alter this distribution considerably.

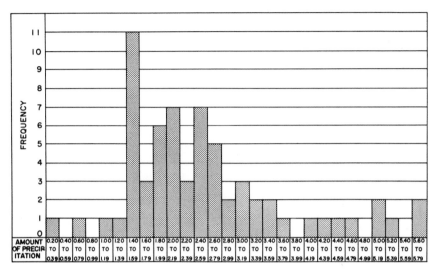

Frequency Polygon of January Precipitation at Cleveland, Ohio, During a   **FIG. 15.1**
Sixty-four-year Period. Mean, 2.54 inches; median, 2.23 inches; mode,
1.40 to 1.59 inches.

Rainfall usually has an unsymmetrical distribution, often more so than is shown in this case, especially in drier regions. In parts of the semiarid West, a rainfall of 12 inches in a year is considered sufficient for the growing of dry-land grains, but in that region an annual average of 12 inches is usually made up of a few years of much more than the average and many years with amounts somewhat less than average. The farmer using the land under these conditions should realize that the land will receive less than 12 inches of precipitation more than half of the time.

In general, temperature data are arranged according to chance and, when plotted, form a symmetrical curve in which the mean, median, and mode coincide. This is illustrated in the polygon and curve showing the variations in the length of the growing season at Indianapolis, Indiana (Fig. 15.2). Frequency curves may be drawn by inspection as in this figure; but if a more accurate representation of the data is required, the algebraic equation of the curve may be calculated. Mathematical considerations also enable us to determine, within a margin of error dependent upon the length and character of the record, how often the rainfall will fall below or exceed any given amount, or to determine the probability of a killing frost after a given date in spring or before a given date in autumn.

By such mathematical means it becomes possible from the examination of a limited number of observations to obtain a reasonable estimate of events as they will occur in the future on the average, a more accurate estimate than can be obtained by simply counting the number of times the given events have occurred in the past. Of course, it is not possible in this

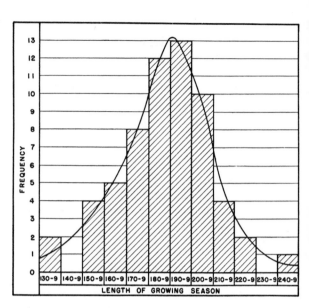

FIG. 15.2

Frequency Polygon for Length of Growing Season at Indianapolis, Indiana, for a Sixty-year Period and Curve Showing the Probable Distribution of Frequencies in a Very Long Record. The curve is approximately symmetrical about the mean value. Mean, 188 days; median, 189 days; mode, 190–199 days.

way, nor in any other way now known, to accurately predict when the favorable or unfavorable seasons will occur. They may appear to happen fortuitously, but in the long run they will occur the number of times indicated by the curve, and it is the performance of the weather and the yield of the land in the long run that determine values, although to the individual owner the events of a few specific years may be of first importance.

In contrast with the character of changeableness which we associate with atmospheric phenomena, we sometimes find the weather in a less fickle mood. There are **Persistence of the Weather** times when similar weather conditions continue day after day for considerable periods. The persistence of the weather is illustrated by what are called *weather spells* and *weather types*.

WEATHER SPELLS

Such phenomena as the occurrence of rain on several successive days and the persistence of hot weather for a week or two are familiar, and are familiarly called *rainy spells* and *hot spells*. When one kind of weather is established, it sometimes has a tendency to continue for several days; if it rained yesterday, the chances of rain today are better than if it was fair yesterday. Today's weather is not independent of yesterday's. As mentioned in the previous section, there are times of rapid variability of the weather, but, on the average, similar weather tends to persist for several days. Reasons for this persistence may be found in the influence of the semipermanent areas of high and low pressure of the general circulation, and in the slow movement or stagnation of cyclones and anticyclones, resulting in the continued inflow of warm air or outflow of cold air.

WEATHER TYPES

Further examination of the records discloses persistence of another kind. We find periods in which the abnormal conditions are not absolutely continuous, day after day, but in which the same kind of weather recurs frequently. It is evident that months of unusual departures, having very heavy rain, for example, or averaging markedly cold or hot, indicate the continuance of abnormal conditions for at least the greater part of a month. Do such departures continue for more than a month? Fig. 15.3 shows the deviation of the mean monthly temperatures from the average at St. Paul, Minnesota.

It will be seen that there are frequent alternations above and below normal, but these do not appear to be systematic; no law of variation is evident. Note that January, 1944 was a very warm month between two cold ones; from February, 1933 to December, 1935 there were fairly regular monthly variations between positive and negative departures, and February, 1936 was a very cold month separating two normal months. Yet, more often than not, we find two or more months in succession on the same side of the normal. Each of the first six months of 1952 was warmer than normal, and the six months from March, 1940 to August, 1940 were all colder than normal. Note especially the long "warm spells" in 1930 and 1931, when there were nine consecutive months with positive departures, and again in 1941 and 1942, when thirteen consecutive months averaged 4.5°F above the normal. In 1948 and 1949, there was a period of seven warm months, and there are a number of other periods in this record with from five to six consecutive months having departures of the same sign.

These records illustrate the tendency for similar temperature departures, that is, similar types of weather, to continue for several months, but, as has been seen, there are many exceptions. Rainfall curves show variations of the same kind. There are dry seasons with the rainfall deficient for several months in succession, and, at other times, wet periods of a few months' duration.

These are examples of the fact, with which students of weather in temperate latitudes are familiar, that similar weather conditions often persist for periods varying from a week or two to several months, and then change abruptly to weather of quite a different character. As has been noted in Chapter 11, upper-air pressure-contour charts give some indication, for short periods in advance, of the tendency toward persistence or toward change. The persistence of a given type of weather probably means that the general pressure distribution remains approximately the same, and that depressions or anticyclones of like characteristics follow one another in succession along about the same paths.

In a warm winter in the United States, for example, many lows move across the northern border, and few cold air masses push southward from

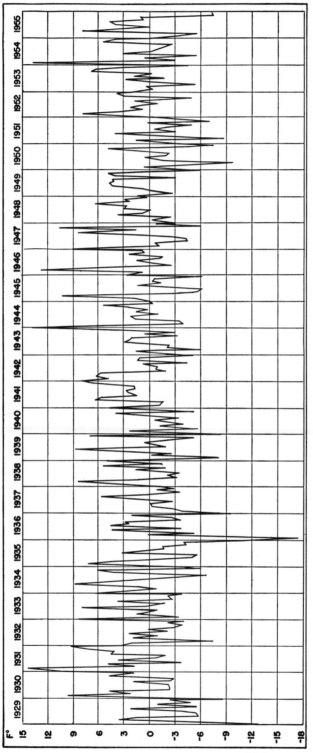

Departures of Mean Monthly Temperatures from Normal, St. Paul, Minnesota, January 1929, to December 1955.

FIG. 15.3

Canada. In a wet season in the Mississippi Valley, many depressions originate in the Southwest and travel northeast, bringing much moist air from the Gulf of Mexico. The change to another type of weather occurs when the highs and lows take a different course. The reason for their taking a different course is to be found in some alteration in the general circulation. In the Northern Hemisphere, such changes in the general circulation are usually shown by modifications in the position and intensity of those seasonal centers of action, the Aleutian and Iceland lows, the Bermuda and Pacific highs, and the continental highs of winter over Canada and Siberia. Modifications in the west-to-east circulation are expressed in terms of the circulation index and appear in the circulation pattern as shown on upper-air charts.

Weather Correlations

Such changes in the general circulation as have been mentioned in the preceding section affect the whole atmosphere and consequently result in weather changes throughout the world, but not necessarily changes of the same kind. An alteration in the paths of traveling disturbances may bring unusually wet weather to one region and dry weather to another, or cold air to some areas and warm to others. Furthermore, the response to pressure changes is not immediate; there is a time lag between cause and effect. A rise of pressure in one part of the world may show itself several months later in changed weather conditions in a distant part of the globe, not necessarily in the same hemisphere.

CORRELATION COEFFICIENTS

A correlation coefficient is a numerical quantity that expresses the degree of linear relationship or correspondence between two sets of data. It is computed by a mathematical process which takes account of and compares the individual deviations from average of the two sets of data. For example, when the average pressure during the summer months at Honolulu is compared for a series of years with the average temperature during the following winter months in the Missouri and upper Mississippi Valleys, a certain degree of correlation is found to exist. It indicates a tendency for high summer pressures at Honolulu to be followed by cold winters in the Missouri and upper Mississippi Valleys, and low pressures by warm winters, but the relationship is not close enough to be of forecasting value.

There is a similar relationship between the pressure in South America and subsequent rainfall in India and temperature in Japan. If the pressure is unusually high in Argentina and Chile during March and April, there is likely to be a heavy monsoon rainfall in India in the following July and August, and a warmer-than-normal August in Japan. There is a negative correlation between summer rainfall in Cuba and the next winter's rainfall in southern England; there is also a relationship between the spring temperatures in Siberia and the summer temperatures in California.

Many other correlation coefficients have been obtained, showing the existence of similar correspondences between widely separated areas. There is a well-know negative correlation between the pressure over Iceland and that over the Azores. When the Iceland low is unusually deep, the Azores high is also strongly developed; likewise, when the low is shallow, the high is weak. A similar oscillation occurs in the North Pacific Ocean between the Aleutian low and the Pacific high. In the Southern Hemisphere, there is a negative correlation of pressure between the South Pacific and Indian Oceans. It is evident that these relationships between distant weather conditions are expressions of the unity of the air. The general distribution of pressure and the general circulation of the air undergo changes that are reflected in world-wide modifications of weather.

The Oceans and the Weather

The study of ocean temperatures and ocean movements in relation to atmospheric changes gives evidence of their interdependence and of the world-wide relationships of weather phenomena. For many years, records of water temperatures at the surface and records of weather conditions have been obtained by ships as they travel their regular routes. A more intensive program was conducted during World War II, and much data were compiled concerning currents, water temperatures at various levels, and surf conditions, and their relationships to wind and weather. Thus our knowledge of the behavior of the air and our ability to foresee its changes have been enlarged, but lack of data from the oceans still limits our knowledge of the complex relationships between the oceans and the weather. A fully adequate scheme of observations would require a great number of continuous records from fixed positions in all the oceans.

RELATIONSHIPS BETWEEN OCEAN TEMPERATURE AND WEATHER

Because water changes its temperature very slowly, the ocean waters are great conservers of heat, and by their movements they are great transporters of heat and equalizers of temperature. The heat carried by ocean currents from the tropical waters of America to the North Atlantic saves the people of northern Europe many thousands of tons of coal each winter, for some of that heat is transported to the land by the winds which are warmed in their passage over the warm water.

Changes in ocean temperature not only effect changes in the temperature of the land to leeward, but they produce other, less direct, effects. Temperature variations over large areas result in a redistribution of atmospheric pressure with varied and far-reaching influences on weather conditions. For instance, the presence of unusually warm water off the southeastern coast of the United States during the winter months probably results in colder-than-normal weather in the eastern states, instead of warmer, as might at first be assumed. A large body of warm water tends to reduce the pressure in its vicinity, and in this case would intensify the pressure gradient between the ocean and the winter high-pressure area over the northern continental interior. Hence, the eastern states would receive more than the usual amount of cold air from interior Canada. In the following paragraphs some specific illustrations of the interrelationships of air and water conditions are given.

EFFECTS OF NORTHEAST TRADES

The changes in the temperature of the ocean water at any place are not due greatly to the heat of the sun there nor to the temperature of the air over the water. They are due chiefly to the effect of the winds in moving the water. For example, strong, steady, northeast trade winds in the North Atlantic cause the warm surface water to drift toward the West Indies and the Caribbean Sea, resulting in an accumulation of warm water in those regions. The place of the water thus removed is taken either by colder water formerly beneath the surface or by colder water drifting in from more northerly regions. Thus, the effect of unusually strong trades is to make the water colder in the mid-Atlantic trade-wind area and warmer in the Caribbean and the Gulf of Mexico.

A portion of this warm water moves through the Straits of Florida and thence along our East Coast and across the Atlantic toward the British Isles and Scandinavia. The amount of water thus transported is probably more than a thousand times the average discharge of the Mississippi River. Since it takes 3,000 times as much heat to warm a given volume of sea water by 1° as to warm an equal volume of air by an equal amount, the effect of such a volume of water on air temperatures is great. It is believed that enough warm water is carried by the North Atlantic Current into the Norwegian Sea each year to raise the temperature of the air over the whole of Europe up to 2 1/2 miles above the surface of the earth by 10 degrees for each degree that the water cools.

POLAR ICE AND THE WEATHER

The surface area of floating ice in the polar seas not only undergoes a seasonal change but frequently shows large variations from one year to another. An increase in the amount of ice is attended by a decrease in the temperature of the air over the ice and over adjacent regions and a related increase in pressure over these regions. In the North Atlantic, when the ice increases, the general tendency is toward a filling up of the Iceland low and a flattening of the Azores high. These conditions result in altering the paths of traveling depressions across the Atlantic. In particular, changes in the amount of ice in the Greenland Sea region are thought to be an appreciable factor in variations in the weather of the British Isles and Norway.

THE PERUVIAN CURRENT AND PERUVIAN RAINFALL

A striking example of the effect of ocean changes upon the weather of near-by land areas occurred on the Peruvian coast of South America from January to April, 1925. Ordinarily the cold Peru current from the south prevails along those shores, somewhat mitigating the heat of the adjacent lands but causing them to be almost rainless, because the cool air is warmed as it moves inland and its relative humidity thereby reduced. During the early months of 1925, this current seems to have disappeared and to have been replaced by a warm northerly current from which warm, moist air moved inland.

The reason for this departure of the ocean from its well-established habit is not known, but it was doubtless meteorological in its nature, caused by some variation from normal temperature and pressure somewhere in the world. The climatic consequences were remarkable. In desert regions where rain was almost unknown, great floods spread destruction and dismay. Counterbalancing these losses came a quick and abundant growth of grass, giving the half-starved animals such a feast as they had not known for years. During April, conditions returned to normal. Such experiences occur at irregular intervals of several years.

The fact is, then, that ocean circulation and ocean temperature are closely connected with air circulation and air temperature. Changes in either cause changes in the other, sometimes in distant parts of the world and after the lapse of considerable time. The various influences interact inextricably, but it seems clear that a more complete knowledge of ocean currents and ocean temperatures and their variations from season to season and year to year, together with a broader knowledge of atmospheric changes over the oceans, would be of value in interpreting what often appears to be the capricious behavior of the atmosphere.

The sun not only governs the movement of the world in its orbit, but also, by its never-ending stream of radiant energy, it rules the earth's life and activity. The
The Sun and the Weather

sun's general control of the earth's weather and climate is evident, but how detailed its regulation of the weather is, remains a question. As previously noted, there are slight variations in the flow of energy from the sun; the solar constant appears to vary slightly from day to day, and in longer periods somewhat more, up to about 3 per cent. Are these solar changes reflected in weather changes on the earth?

SUNSPOTS AND WEATHER

The number of sunspots increases and diminishes in a cycle averaging about eleven years, from one maximum or minimum to the next, attended by changes in the solar output of radiant energy. Evidences of this period appear in some weather records and in the thickness of tree rings and of clay layers deposited by glaciers. Records indicate that atmospheric pressure is relatively low in the tropics and high in high latitudes during periods of great sunspot activity, and the reverse during periods of very little sunspot activity. Sunspot periods are of varying length and intensity, and the weather responses are changeable in amount, difficult to follow, and often obscured by other fluctuations.

SOLAR RADIATION AND THE TURBULENT ATMOSPHERE

A change in the intensity of solar radiation may cause a shifting of the pressure belts, with consequent complex effects on the paths of cyclones and anticyclones and upon the distribution of temperature and precipitation. It is reasonable to assume that the daily fluctuations and the slow cyclical variations in the output of radiation by the sun affect the weather throughout the world by affecting the temperature of the earth and the air, but just how and to what extent they may influence or control the observed weather changes are questions not yet satisfactorily answered. Our erratic day-to-day weather appears to result from innumerable differences in the physical condition of the air. Even with a constant amount of heat from the sun, the physical condition of the lower air would be subject to countless local changes because of such factors as the variations in the surface covering of the earth and differences in elevation, absorption, radiation, evaporation, cloudiness, and dust. The influences affecting the air appear to be so numerous, so immeasurable, and so unpredictable as to create a condition of extreme atmospheric turbulence defying exact analysis and never twice the same in detail.

Seasonal Forecasting

The object of the preceding discussions of weather correlations and solar and oceanic influences has been not to give definite results of immediate application but to emphasize the complexity of world weather relationships. The facts now known about these relationships give us some indication of how the air behaves, but our knowledge is not sufficiently definite or complete to enable us to explain fully the physics of the air in its larger movements. Attempts have been made to apply the existing knowledge of the world-wide relationships of weather to the problem of long-range forecasting—meaning the forecasting of the general character of the weather for a month or more in advance. An attempt is made not to forecast the daily weather, but rather to say whether the precipitation and the average temperature of the period under consideration will be above or below normal, and how much above or below. Seasonal forecasting is the attempt to foresee the general character of a future season, for example, to determine whether the coming winter will be warmer or colder than normal. Such attempts are usually made for seasons not more than six to nine months in the future.

NATURE OF ATMOSPHERIC RESPONSES

It sometimes appears that those atmospheric responses to changing conditions that show themselves in different parts of the world are to be explained as latitudinal shiftings of the pressure belts as a whole or in large areas, such as it has been supposed may be accounted for by changes in insolation. When it is said that the pressure belts shift, it refers to the north or south movement of the doldrums, the subtropical highs, and the polar-circle lows. A movement of these belts occurs annually with the change of seasons; but, if the amount of movement varies from year to year, then, obviously, there will be differences from year to year in the position and development of the trade winds and the prevailing westerlies, and in the paths of cyclones and anticyclones. An abnormal position of these belts results in weather abnormalities of various kinds in many parts of the world.

Sometimes it appears that there is a wavelike swaying of the atmosphere, a resilient movement as in a jelly, as, for example, the oscillation of pressure between the South Pacific and the Indian Oceans. In cases such as this, the indication is that the air has a natural period of vibration, a swinging backward and forward, which continues indefinitely, or at least for a long period when once started. At other times it seems that, when an abnormal condition has been imparted to a large mass of air, the abnormality tends to persist, and the mass maintains a separate existence and movement of its own. This often appears to be the case when successive monthly or quarterly mean pressure departures are charted on maps. The areas of positive and negative departures continue from month to month or from season to season, though changing their position. Probably the atmosphere responds to external influences in each of these three ways: by a shifting of pressure belts, by a wavelike motion, and by retaining properties once acquired. It has not as yet been possible in studying seasonal weather changes to separate the effects of the three.

THE HOPE OF SEASONAL FORECASTS

The methods of correlation have brought to light many interesting and suggestive relationships, and in a few cases have evolved usable formulas, but in general the findings of this method have failed to make forecasts of real value to the necessary degree of exactness. By their nature, correlation coefficients represent only average correspondence between two or more quantities, and can give no indication of when exceptions will occur. Probably their use in conjunction with maps of monthly pressure departures would add to their value, but little has been done on this line, and there is no world-wide arrangement for the prompt collection of monthly means. An arrangement of this nature must be made before correlations and departure maps can be used to their fullest possible value in long-range forecasting.

Active work is continuing on the relation of changes in the solar output of energy to future weather, and some work is being done in the collection and study of ocean temperatures and their correlation with subsequent weather. Other lines of approach to the problem of long-range forecasting are the effort to find recurring cycles in the weather and the effort to identify and classify weather types in the upper air. A consideration of the partial results obtained by the methods described leads us on with the hope that the problem of foreseeing the general weather character of a coming season or year may be solved. The solution does not appear impossible, but it is not yet accomplished. Such general forecasts would not help at all in foreseeing the character of a particular day. We should still have daily changes in the weather and the necessity of daily forecasts based upon a close following of the movements of air masses. But a knowledge that the coming summer would be wetter or drier than average, or the coming winter warmer or colder, would make possible a kind of planned economy not practicable without this knowledge and would make or save millions of dollars for the nation. The search for an answer will doubtless continue.

Everyone is familiar with the influence of the weather **Weather and Health** on physical and mental attitudes. Many persons are depressed and discouraged on dark days, or nervous and irritable on windy days, and others feel the changes in atmospheric conditions in twinges of rheumatism, neuralgia, or old wounds. Temperature, relative humidity, wind, and sunshine are the four weather elements that most directly affect man's physical condition. The branch of the science of biology that deals with the many and complex relationships of weather and climate to life and health is called *bioclimatology*, or *biometeorology*.

TEMPERATURE AND HEALTH

A number of investigations have indicated that the most favorable temperature for persons engaged in active work either indoors or outdoors is about 64°, although it differs somewhat for different individuals. More work will be done with less fatigue at about this average temperature than when it is either warmer or colder. However, frequent moderate changes in temperature are stimulating, especially changes to cooler weather. Autumn, with moderate temperatures changing to cooler, is more favorable than spring with its increasing warmth. Long cold spells and long hot spells are alike depressing. The duration of the extreme temperature is significant. One hot day in summer can be endured, but with each successive day of extreme heat, the output of work decreases, the vitality is lowered, and the death rate increases among those whose bodies are unable to adjust themselves quickly to the changed conditions. The same is true of continued cold weather. Vital statistics indicate that the death rate is lowest when the mean daily temperature is between 60°F and 75°F. Some diseases are directly limited by temperature conditions. Malaria, yellow fever, and some other insect-borne diseases do not occur in cold weather.

HUMIDITY, AIR MOVEMENT, AND HEALTH

Air of moderate humidity is both more comfortable and more healthful than very dry or very moist air. Relative humidity is connected with temperature in its effects on the bodily functions. High humidity with high air temperature increases conduction of heat to the body and at the same time retards evaporation. Hence the body does not cool readily, and the heat is oppressive. High humidity in cold weather increases the conduction of heat from the body at a time when we need to conserve it and intensifies the feeling of cold. High humidity makes us feel warmer in hot weather and colder in cold weather.

With the occurrence of the high temperatures of summer in continental climates, especially in connection with tropical maritime air, humidity is often so great as to become an unfavorable health factor. Under these conditions there is little cooling of the skin, and the mechanism of the body is subjected to a strain to keep its temperature normal. The death rate, especially among infants, is high when a high humidity coincides with a high temperature. On the other hand, humidities may also be too low in hot weather, causing the skin and mucous membranes to parch and crack, especially if the hot weather is attended by moderate or high winds.

The "hot winds" of the Great Plains are uncomfortably dry at times, and *simooms*, the hot, dry winds of the African and Asian deserts, are sometimes fatal even to persons in vigorous health. When these winds blow, there is rapid perspiration and evaporation from the skin. The rate of perspiring has a definite physiological limit, however, and these winds with temperatures well above that of the human body may convey more heat to the body than can be dissipated by evaporation. There is a net gain of heat above the natural blood heat, with resulting fever and death by heatstroke. Similarly, the "hot winds" of the Great Plains cause a wilting and "burning" of the corn fields by overtaxing the moisture-carrying capacity of the plants.

Humidity is especially related to the respiratory diseases, such as pneumonia, influenza, and bronchitis. These are more prevalent in winter, owing probably not so much to low temperatures as to the low humidities existing in our homes, offices, and even hospitals in cold weather, and to the spreading of infections, facilitated by indoor living. Taking in outside air at zero and warming it to 70° without supplying a large amount of water makes it drier than the winds of Sahara and puts an undue strain upon the skin and the mucous membranes of the air passages.

The bad effects of air in heated and crowded rooms are caused not by carbon dioxide or other impurities, except disease germs, but by heat, low humidity, and lack of air movement. For comfort and health, homes and hospitals should have gently moving air. Just as cold and hot weather are unfavorable for vigorous health, so also are extreme humidity conditions in either direction. The same is true of winds. Both high winds and quiet air intensify certain bad effects of other unfavorable conditions. Gently moving air is most favorable. The temperature felt by the body, the effective temperature, is determined by the three conditions, air temperature, relative humidity, and air movement. These three elements determine the "cooling power of the air."

COOLING POWER

Considerable attention has been given to obtaining a measure of the cooling power of the air, particularly with reference to the cooling of the human skin under differing atmospheric conditions. The best-known instrument designed for this purpose is the *kata-thermometer* invented by Dr. Leonard Hill. This instrument, a thermometer of special design, is heated to 100°F, then exposed to the air, and the time it takes to cool to 95°F is observed. From such observations with the kata-thermometer, and other instruments of similar principle, formulas have been developed for expressing the rate of heat loss in terms of the wind speed and the difference in temperature between the air and the body. Formulas have also been derived for computing the cooling power directly from the ordinary meteorological observations of temperature, humidity, and winds, without the use of special instruments.

For general comparative purposes over large areas, it is believed that the values computed from ordinary weather observations are preferable to the observed values obtained by special instruments. In neither case can the results be considered accurate expressions of the actual cooling power experienced by the individual in a specific case; there are too many variable factors, such as the differing conditions of the air and of the human body, and differing clothing worn.

The results obtained do, however, give valuable comparative data concerning the relative cooling powers of different climates in different parts of the world, that is, concerning the effects of varying climates on the comfort of the individual. With the accumulation of such data, it will be possible to make a cooling-power map of the world, with the earth divided into zones of relative climatic comfort or discomfort. These zones could be indicated by a numerical index obtained by formula. More simply, though less accurately, the various regions might be designated *very hot, hot, warm, pleasant, cool, cold, very cold*. Such maps would be a valuable supplement to the usual climatic maps.

ACCLIMATIZATION

When a person moves from the climate to which he is accustomed to a climate having a different cooling power, there is normally a gradual adjustment of the body to the new climatic conditions. This process of adaptation to a new climate is called *acclimatization*. The change occurs primarily in the capillary blood vessels of the skin. In a climate of great cooling power, these capillaries are constricted to conserve heat. In a hot climate they are dilated in order to expose more blood to the lesser cooling power of the air. The dilated vessels have a greater capacity than the constricted ones and require more blood to fill them. Hence there is an increase in the total volume of blood in the process of acclimatization to a warmer climate and a similar decrease in adjusting to a colder climate. The strain resulting from this physiological adjustment ordinarily results only in some discomfort or lowered energy, but in persons not in vigorous health, it sometimes causes heart attacks or other ailments. Such persons, when changing from one climate to another of quite different type, should make the change gradually, by intermediate stages. In continental climates of cold winters and hot summers, a similar but lesser climatic adjustment occurs in spring and autumn.

SUNSHINE AND HEALTH

One other element, sunshine, is generally recognized as of great importance for health. The healing, disinfecting action of sunlight has long been known empirically, and modern medical science has fully confirmed its value, emphasizing especially the action of the ultraviolet portion of the sun's spectrum. Exposure of tubercle bacilli to the direct rays of the sun renders them innocuous within an hour, while they will live in diffuse light for six to twenty-four hours and in dark places for two to eighteen months. All health resorts have a high percentage of sunshine. A certain moderate intensity of sunshine is essential to human life, as it is to most animal and plant life.

IDEAL WEATHER

There are few diseases directly caused by weather or climate, but the condition of the atmosphere in which man lives often influences profoundly his vitality and his susceptibility to infection. Certain states of the weather are bracing and others relaxing. Some air conditions are an aid to health and activity; some are a hindrance. Hot, humid, tropical climates appear to be the most unfavorable, and white men cannot live for long periods in such climates without a general lowering of energy and of ability to resist disease.

The same conditions are not ideal for all persons in all states of health. Sometimes a bracing atmosphere is needed, and sometimes a relaxing atmosphere, but in general, "ideal" weather may be defined as follows: First, a daily mean temperature of about 65°, with moderate changes from day to night and with variation from day to day sufficient to avoid monotony. Second, a relative humidity continuously moderate, say, from 50 to 60 per cent. Third, moderate to brisk air movement. Fourth, abundant sunshine, but not monotonously cloudless and arid weather. In short, our bodies, though capable of withstanding considerable extremes, are best adapted to average or intermediate conditions. Nowhere will a climate be found where conditions are continuously ideal, but some climates are much more nearly so than others.

AIR CONDITIONING

Modern mechanical progress has made possible the maintenance, both winter and summer, of proper temperature, humidity, and air movement within buildings. Air may be conditioned to nearly ideal requirements in these respects in homes, hospitals, shops, offices, factories, railroads cars, steamships, and even automobiles. Air conditioning also involves the cleaning of the air, that is, the removal of dust and organic particles. The removal of these particles has a special value in the prevention of some respiratory diseases.

In maintaining the proper temperature within buildings in winter, it is generally assumed that furnaces will be started when the mean daily temperature falls below 65°F. Note the practical agreement with the most favorable temperature previously mentioned. The difference between 65° and the average temperature of a given day that is cooler than 65° is the number of *degree days of heating* required. For example, if the average temperature of a winter day is 40°, the number of degree days for that day is twenty-five. The sum of these degree days for a month or a season bears a relationship to the amount of fuel consumed, although other weather factors, such as wind, also influence the fuel consumption. When there is summer cooling of air within doors, a temperature of 70°F is sometimes taken as the base, and the number of *degree days of cooling* is the accumulated excess of the mean daily temperature above 70°.

We are what suns and winds and waters make us;
The mountains are our sponsors, and the rills
Fashion and win their nurseling with their smiles.
                              —*Landor.*

**Climate
and
Culture**

As all the people living in a given part of the world are subjected to its favorable or unfavorable climatic conditions for many generations, it is natural that the effects of these influences will be cumulative and show themselves in the energy, physical and social condition, and civilization of the people.

CLIMATIC HYPOTHESIS OF CIVILIZATION

The many ways in which man's climatic environment affects his daily life and activities are manifest, but that the climatic factor of environment largely determines a people's place in the scale of civilization and culture is not so obvious nor so generally recognized. There are those who maintain that the highest civilization is possible only under the most favorable climate, and that a map of civilization today is essentially a climatic map. This is called the *climatic hypothesis of civilization.* This hypothesis does not deny that other factors, such as heredity and religious philosophy, for example, are necessary in the making of a high standard of national life, but asserts that climate is also one of the essential factors.

INFLUENCE OF EXTREME CLIMATES

It is evident that man is limited by extremely adverse weather, and there are many illustrations of the effect of the climate upon man's clothing, food, dwellings, customs, and occupations. The following summary of these effects has been suggested by Professor R. DeC. Ward's discussion of climate in its relation to man. At one extreme of climate, food is almost wholly of fruits, such as bananas, coconuts, and breadfruit; at the other extreme, the Eskimos must depend upon fish and the flesh and fat of animals. In equatorial regions, soil production is abundant and spontaneous; in arctic regions, agriculture is impossible. In large areas of northeast Russia, climatic conditions preclude the possibility of agriculture; food is scarce; fishing, hunting, and reindeer breeding are the chief occupations; and diseases of the eye are common, owing to dazzling snow outdoors and smoke indoors.

In the tropics, shelter and clothing are largely unnecessary, and the simple requirements are easily met; in polar regions, close, unventilated dwellings and heavy clothing of skins and furs must be provided by hard labor and much danger. In Greenland, for example, a large percentage of the deaths is in snowstorms or by freezing or drowning, and deaths are most frequent during the sealing season. The climate of the tropics encourages indolence by its physically enervating influence and permits it by making energetic activity unnecessary. The climate of the polar regions enforces a laborious and dangerous activity in obtaining the bare necessities of existence. In the tropics, life is too easy, and there is no stimulus to activity; in arctic climates, life is too hard, and there is no possibility of accumulation and leisure. In both extremes, climate evidently limits progress.

CLIMATE AND THE BEGINNINGS OF CIVILIZATION

Relative to the influence of climate under less extreme conditions, some suggestion is afforded by the origin and migration of the early centers of culture. Man in his primitive condition probably began to make progress toward civilization and refinement in the less enervating portions of tropical or semitropical regions, where it was possible for him, even with his limited mastery of nature, to obtain leisure for contemplation. The history of civilization since that time discloses a gradual movement into colder regions, as man increased his knowledge of how to make a living on this earth and how to protect himself from adverse weather conditions. Some of the earliest well-developed types of culture were in the valleys of the Nile and of the Tigris and Euphrates Rivers, under arid, semitropical conditions, where agricultural production and the accumulation of food ,were comparatively easy, except that agriculture required irrigation and, hence, coordinated effort and organized society. From these valleys, the center of civilization moved to Greece and then to Italy and, later, northward through Europe into increasingly stimulating climates, from Spain and Portugal to Holland, Great Britain, and Scandinavia.

TEMPERATURE AND CIVILIZATION

The present center of world progress and of western civilization is in the middle latitudes, where there is considerable daily variation in weather and a still greater annual variation. That such climates are the most conducive to human activity and human energy is the conclusion reached by Ellsworth Huntington in his studies of the influence of temperature, humidity, and other weather elements upon individuals and small groups. The climates best meeting the requirements are in a belt of the Northern Hemisphere which includes most of Europe, the British Isles, the greater part of the United States, a narrow strip of southern Canada, and Japan. The same belt includes all the most highly developed nations of today. A map of present-day civilization is, then, practically a map of what has by independent investigation been found to be the most energetic climate. Temperature is probably the most important of the weather factors influencing human energy, and all of these highly developed nations are within a zone where the average annual temperature is between 40°F and 70°F. This has been called *the temperature of civilization.*

These facts do not justify us in assuming that a high type of civilization cannot develop elsewhere, but they seem to indicate that present-day progress, characterized by energy and movement, is largely conditioned upon the stimulating, invigorating climate of the middle temperate regions of the globe. We can agree with Huntington that, "Among the physical stimuli which may control human efficiency, none is more potent than climate."

The subject of agricultural meteorology includes all **Agricultural** those relationships, direct and indirect, between cli- **Meteorology** mate and weather and the life and growth of cultivated plants. It deals with the effects of varying temperatures and varying amounts of sunshine and soil moisture, with the climatic requirements of the important field crops, and with the relationships of the sequence of weather to the progress and yield of crops. Many details of these effects and relationships are not yet unknown, for agricultural meteorology is a new and imperfect science, despite the great age of agriculture as an occupation.

CLIMATE AND CROPS

The close relationship between the climate of a region and the kind of plant life it supports is obvious. Nature decides in the first instance what use can be made of the land, and man adapts himself to her limitations and variations. Precipitation, temperature, sunshine, and length of growing season are the chief factors governing the distribution of plants. In the United States a large area having long, hot, and wet summers produces cotton; another region with a shorter growing season and less water is largely devoted to corn and winter wheat, while spring wheat matures in a still shorter and drier season far northward into Canada. A large region with climate well adapted to hay and pasture extends from Minnesota to the Appalachian Mountains and the middle Atlantic states. More specialized climatic conditions limit the commercial production of sugar cane, sugar beets, potatoes, and fruits to smaller areas in various parts of the country.

Favorable temperature and precipitation are the chief assets of any country. If temperatures are too high or too low, seeds will not germinate, the plant will be retarded in its growth or even killed, blossoms and fruit will be damaged. Different species of plants have different temperature requirements, but for all plants there is some limiting temperature below which they will not grow. Some hardy plants will grow when the temperature is near or slightly below freezing; on the other hand, such tropical plants as date palms require a temperature of about 64°F to start growth. The growth of citrus fruits is limited by temperature to small areas in the United States. Often small local differences of temperature determine the selection of land for oranges in southern California. Outside of the tropics, most agricultural crops begin to grow at about 43°F (6°C), but growth is most vigorous and healthy when the temperature of the soil is between 65° and 70°F. Perennial plants retire into a *rest period* when the temperature is below 43°.

Precipitation is essential to supply the moisture by which food is taken from the soil in solution and carried throughout the plant by the sap. It is also necessary to prevent the drying and wilting of the leaves, from which large quantities of water are transpired to the air in the growth processes. The significance of precipitation as an asset is illustrated by the difference between eastern Kansas and western Kansas in the value of land and the density of population.

WEATHER AND CROPS

Climate largely determines what shall be the staple crops of a region; the weather of the individual seasons largely determines the yields of those crops. It is often not so much the total rainfall and the average temperature that fixes the yield as the distribution of moisture and favorable or unfavorable temperature through the season. There are certain short *critical periods* in the growth of many crops during which their success or failure is largely determined. With some crops and in some climates, temperature is the controlling factor; with others, it is rainfall or sunshine.

For example, corn can recover from earlier droughts, but if it suffers for moisture while tasseling, the yield will be small. J. Warren Smith found that the first ten days of August are the most critical in the production of corn in Ohio. This is the time when a good shower is truly a "million-dollar rain." Winter wheat needs cool and moist weather while growing rapidly; but, warm and dry weather is needed while the heads are forming and filling. Potatoes require cool weather with plenty of moisture, especially during the ten days following blossoming. The rainfall of May largely influences the production of hay in a large part of the United States. A relatively cool and wet August is of importance in the production of cotton in our southern states.

The relationships just mentioned and many similar ones have been discovered largely by the methods of correlation. Records of crop yields are compared year by year with records of temperature, rainfall, and other weather elements, and the influences of the weather's variations on the yield are determined. The knowledge of these influences helps in the adjustment of crops to the most favorable climatic conditions. It helps to decide whether a given crop is well adapted to a given region. Sometimes by the use of different varieties or different methods of cultivation or by varying the time of seeding, the time of occurrence of the critical periods can be adjusted to the time when the weather is most likely to be favorable. It is obvious that a knowledge of the water requirements of plants at different stages of their growth is particularly applicable to farming under irrigation.

The factors influencing the yield of a given crop at a given time and place are many and complex and include condition of soil, tillage, and seed, in addition to the weather. The efficiency of a given amount of rain in producing a crop is influenced, among other things, by the amount of evaporation. In the arid Southwest, evaporation is great, partly because of low humidity and the infrequency of clouds, together with high average temperatures, and crops require more water there than they do in cooler, cloudier regions. In addition to the direct effects of atmospheric conditions on yields, there are the indirect effects resulting from the development of plant diseases and insect pests. Grain rusts are encouraged by hot and humid weather at the ripening stage of the grain; the extent of boll weevil damage to the cotton crop is related to sunshine and humidity during the growing season, and also, since low temperatures kill the weevil, to the minimum temperatures of the preceding winter.

DROUGHTS

A *drought* is a continued lack of moisture, so serious that crops fail to develop and mature properly. The dry period is of particular significance when it is of unusual length as compared with normal conditions in the area. A period of two summer months without rain would not be serious in California, because it is the usual thing, but one rainless summer month in central and eastern portions of the country would constitute a severe drought. The severity and effect of long dry periods depend not only on their duration, but also on the attending temperature and wind, on the kind and previous condition of the soil, and on the condition of the crops. For these reasons, no exact definition of a drought in terms of the number of rainless days can be given.

PHENOLOGY

To a great degree, the growth of plants is a response to the atmospheric influences to which the plants have been subjected—a summation of weather influences. Plants are nature's record of the climate and weather. A record of the progress of plants through the growing season is, then, in part, a weather record. A record of the time of leafing, blossoming, and fruiting gives an indication of the progress of the seasons. Averages obtained from these records are a function of the climate of a region, and the yearly variations from the average are an indication of how the weather has varied. These data form the basis of the science of *phenology*, which may be defined as the study of the phenomena of life, especially plant life, as they recur from year to year, and their responses to weather and climate. Although agricultural practices are in the main determined by long experience, the knowledge gained through phenological records aids in the adjustment of farming operations to the most favorable weather conditions. The data are indispensable in the calculation of correlations between weather and crop yields.

PROBLEMS

1.

Draw frequency polygons and frequency curves from monthly or annual temperature and precipitation tables.

2.

Make graphs of successive departures from normal of monthly temperatures and rainfall and note the character of the curves with reference to variability and persistence.

3.

Chart daily records of temperature and rainfall for evidences of short weather "spells."

4.

Examine records over several months for evidences of weather types.

5.

By spending a month in each of twelve cities in the United States, one might pass the year under nearly ideal temperature conditions, assuming that normal temperatures prevailed. What cities might one select?

6.

Discuss what period without important rain constitutes a drought in your state. How is the length of the period related to the time of year, temperature, wind, and previous condition of the soil?

7.

What amount of rainfall is required to break the drought? How frequently do such droughts occur?

8.

What contributions to the science of meteorology was made by Hippocrates? Aristotle? Copernicus? Kepler? Newton? Torricelli? Fahrenheit? da Vinci? Galileo? Halley? Dalton? Charles? Boyle? Gay-Lussac? Ferrell? Coroilis? Bjerknes?

appendix I

bibliography

**General References
and Elementary
Treatises**

Battan, Louis J., *Cloud Physics and Cloud Seeding.* Garden City, N.Y.: Doubleday & Company, Inc., 1962.

———, *Radar Meteorology.* Chicago, Ill.: University of Chicago Press, 1959.

———, *Radar Observes the Weather.* Garden City, N.Y.: Doubleday & Company, Inc., 1962.

———, *The Nature of Violent Storms.* Garden City, N.Y.: Doubleday & Company, Inc., 1961.

Berriman, A. E., *Historical Meteorology.* New York: E. P. Dutton & Co., Inc., 1953.

Best, Alfred Charles, *Physics in Meteorology.* London: Sir Isaac Pitman & Sons, Ltd., 1957.

Blumenstock, David Irving, *The Ocean of Air.* New Brunswick, N.J.: Rutgers University Press, 1959.

British Meteorological Office, *Cloud Types for Observers.* London: Her Majesty's Stationery Office, 1962.

Byers, Horace R., *Thunderstorm Electricity*. Chicago, Ill.: University of Chicago Press, 1953.

Bygott, John, *An Introduction to Mapwork and Practical Geography*, 8th ed. London: University Tutorial Press, 1962.

Clayton, H. H. (ed.), *World Weather Records*, Vols. LXXIX, XC, and CV of Smithsonian Miscellaneous Collections. Washington, D.C.: The Smithsonian Institution, 1927, 1934, 1947.

Decker, Fred W., *The Weather Workbook*. Corvallis, Oreg.: The Weather Workbook Company, 1958.

Donn, William L., *Meteorology with Marine Applications*. New York: McGraw-Hill Book Company, 1946.

Flora, Snowden D., *Tornadoes of the United States*. Norman, Okla.: University of Oklahoma Press, 1953.

George, Joseph J., *Weather Forecasting for Aeronautics*. New York: Academic Press Inc., 1960.

Haynes, B. C., *Techniques of Observing the Weather*. New York: John Wiley & Sons, Inc., 1947.

Henninger, S. K., Jr., *A Handbook of Renaissance Meteorology*. Durham, N.C.: Duke University Press, 1960.

Humphreys, W. J., *Physics of the Air*, 3rd ed. New York: McGraw-Hill Book Company, 1940.

Huschke, Ralph E. (ed.), *Glossary of Meteorology*. Boston, Mass.: American Meteorological Society, 1959.

International Cloud Atlas. Geneva, Switzerland: World Meteorological Organization, 1956. Vol. I contains the text of descriptions and explanations. Vol. II contains 224 plates, each with an explanatory legend.

Kendrew, W. G., *Weather: An Introductory Meteorology*. New York: Oxford University Press, 1943.

Löbsack, Theo, *Earth's Envelope*. New York: Pantheon Books, Inc., 1959.

Lee, H. D. P., *Aristotle's Meteorologica*. Cambridge, Mass.: Harvard University Press, 1952. English translation.

Lehr, Paul E. and H. S. Zim, *Weather: Air Masses, Clouds, Rainfall, Storms, Weather Maps, and Climate*. New York: Simon and Schuster, Inc., 1957.

List, Robert J. (ed.), *Smithsonian Meteorological Tables*, 6th rev. ed. Washington, D.C.: The Smithsonian Institution, 1951.

Lounsbury, John F., *A Workbook for Weather and Climate*. Dubuque, Iowa: William C. Brown Company, Publishers, 1959.

Marvin, C. F., *Psychometric Tables*, Weather Bureau Bulletin No. 235. Washington, D.C.: U.S. Department of Commerce, 1941.

Massey, H. S. W. and R. L. F. Boyd, *The Upper Atmosphere*. London: Hutchinson & Co. [Publishers], Ltd., 1958.

Middleton, W. E. K., *Vision Through the Atmosphere*. Toronto: University of Toronto Press, 1952.

——— and A. F. Spilhaus, *Meteorological Instruments*, 3rd ed. Toronto: University of Toronto Press, 1953.

Miller, A. A. and M. Parry, *Everyday Meteorology*. New York: Philosophical Library, Inc., 1959.

Namowitz, Samuel N., *Earth Science; the World We Live In*. Princeton, N.J.: D. Van Nostrand Co., Inc., 1960.

Neuberger, Hans and George Nicholas, *Manual of Lecture Demonstrations, Laboratory Experiments, and Observational Equipment for Teaching Elementary Meteorology in Schools and Colleges*. University Park: Pennsylvania State University, 1962.

—— and F. B. Stephens, *Weather and Man*. Englewood Cliffs, N.J.: Prentice-Hall, Inc., 1948.

Newell, Homer E., Jr., *Window in the Sky*. New York: McGraw-Hill Book Company, 1959.

——, *High Altitude Rocket Research*. New York: Academic Press, Inc., 1953.

Orr, Clyde, Jr., *Between Earth and Space*. New York: The Macmillan Company, 1959.

Petterssen, Svere, *Introduction to Meteorology*, 2nd ed. New York: McGraw-Hill Book Company, 1959.

Pulk, E. S. and E. A. Murphy, *Workbook for Weather Forecasting*. Englewood Cliffs, N.J.: Prentice-Hall, Inc., 1950.

Sawyer, John Stanley, *The Ways of the Weather*. London: Adam & Charles Black, Ltd., 1957.

Schonland, B. F. J., *Atmospheric Electricity*. New York: John Wiley & Sons, Inc., 1953.

Sullivan, W., *Assault on the Unknown; The International Geophysical Year*. New York: McGraw-Hill Book Company, 1961.

Sutton, O. G., *The Challenge of the Atmosphere*. New York: Harper & Row, Publishers, Inc., 1961.

——, *Understanding Weather*. Baltimore: Penguin Books, Inc., 1960.

Viemeister, Peter E., *The Lightning Book*. Garden City, N.Y.: Doubleday & Company, Inc., 1961.

Wallington, C. E., *Meteorology for Glider Pilots*. London: John Murray, Publishers, Ltd., 1961.

Yates, Raymond Francis, *The Weather for a Hobby*, rev. ed. New York: Dodd, Mead & Co., 1956.

Special References and Advanced Treatises

Australian Academy of Science, *Antarctic Meteorology*. New York: Pergamon Press, Inc., 1960.

Bolin, Bert (ed.), *The Atmosphere and the Sea in Motion*. New York: The Rockefeller Institute Press, 1959.

Garbell, Maurice A., *Tropical and Equatorial Meteorology*. New York: Pitman Publishing Corp., 1947.

Geiger, Rudolph, *The Climate Near the Ground*. Cambridge, Mass.: Harvard University Press, 1957.

Godske, C.L.S. *et. al., Dynamic Meteorology and Weather Forecasting*. Boston, Mass.: American Meteorological Society, 1957.

Goody, R. M., *The Physics of the Stratosphere*. Cambridge, Mass.: Harvard University Press, 1954.

Gordon, Adrian Hugo, *Elements of Dynamic Meteorology*. New York: D. Van Nostrand Co., Inc., 1962.

Haltiner, George J. and Frank L. Martin, *Dynamical and Physical Meteorology*. New York: McGraw-Hill Book Company, 1957.

Hess, Seymour L., *Introduction to Theoretical Meteorology*. New York: Holt, Rinehart & Winston, Inc., 1959.

Johnson, John C., *Physical Meteorology*. New York: John Wiley & Sons, Inc., 1954.

Kibel, I. A. (ed.), *Collection of Articles on Dynamic Meteorology*. Washington, D.C.: American Geophysical Union, 1960. English translation of Soviet Research in Geophysics.

Landsberg, H. E. *et. al., Meteorological Research Reviews*. Boston, Mass.: American Meteorological Society, 1957.

Malone, Thomas F. (ed.), *Compendium of Meteorology*. Boston, Mass.: American Meteorological Society, 1951.

Molga, Marian, *Agricultural Meteorology*. Washington, D.C.: Office of Technical Services, U.S. Department of Commerce, 1962.

Perrie, D. W., *Cloud Physics*. Toronto: University of Toronto Press, 1951.

Petterssen, Svere, *Weather Analysis and Forecastings*, 2 Vols. New York: McGraw-Hill Book Company, 1956.

Ratcliffe, J. A. (ed.), *Physics of the Upper Atmosphere*. New York: Academic Press, 1960.

Reiter, Elmar, *Jet-Stream Meteorology*. Chicago: University of Chicago Press Inc., 1963.

Riehl, Herbert, *Tropical Meteorology*. New York: McGraw-Hill Book Company, 1954.

Sutcliffe, R. C. (ed.), *Polar Atmosphere Symposium* (Parts I and II). New York: Published for NATO by the Pergamon Press, Inc., 1957.

Sutton, O. G., *Micrometeorolgy*. New York: McGraw-Hill Book Company, 1953.

Taylor, George F., *Elementary Meteorology*. Englewood Cliffs, N.J.: Prentice-Hall, Inc., 1954.

Vaeth, J. Gordon, *200 Miles Up: The Conquest of the Upper Air*. New York: The Ronald Press Company, 1951.

Wexler, H. and J. E. Caskey, Jr., *First International Symposium on Rocket and Satellite Meteorology*. New York: John Wiley & Sons, Inc., 1963.

Willett, Hurd C. and Frederick Sanders, *Descriptive Meteorology*, 2nd ed. New York: Academic Press Inc., 1959.

Climatology
and Related Topics

Aronin, Jeffrey Ellis, *Climate and Architecture*. New York: Reinhold Publishing Corp., 1953.

Brooks, C. E. P., *Climate in Everyday Life*. New York: Philosophical Library, Inc., 1951.

————, *Climate Through the Ages*. New York: McGraw-Hill Book Company, 1949.

Burch, G. E. and N. P. DePasquale, *Hot Climates, Man and His Heart*. Springfield, Ill.: Charles C. Thomas, Publisher, 1962.

Conrad, V. and L. W. Pollak, *Methods in Climatology*, 2nd ed. Cambridge, Mass.: Harvard University Press, 1950.

Critchfield, Howard J., *General Climatology*. Englewood Cliffs, N.J.: Prentice-Hall, Inc., 1960.

Geiger, Rudolf, *The Climate Near the Ground*. Cambridge, Mass.: Harvard University Press, 1950. Translated by M. N. Stewart and others.

Hadlow, Leonard, *Climate, Vegetation, and Man*. New York: Philosophical Library, Inc., 1953.

Hare, F. K., *The Restless Atmosphere*. London: Hutchinson's University Library, 1953.

Jacobs, Woodrow C., *Wartime Developments in Applied Climatology*, Meteorological Monographs, Vol. I, No. 1. Boston, Mass.: American Meteorological Society, 1947.

Kendrew, W. G., *Climatology*, 2nd ed. London: Clarendon Press, 1957.

————, *The Climates of the Continents*, 5th ed. London: Clarendon Press, 1961.

Koeppe, Clarence E. and G. C. De Long, *Weather and Climate*. New York: McGraw-Hill Book Company, 1958.

Shapley, Harlow, *Climatic Change*. Cambridge, Mass.: Harvard University Press, 1953.

Trewartha, Glenn T., *An Introduction to Climate*, 3rd ed. New York: McGraw-Hill Book Company, 1954.

————, *The Earth's Problem Climates*. Madison: University of Wisconsin Press, 1961.

United States Department of Agriculture, *Climate and Man*. 1941 Yearbook. Washington, D.C.: Government Printing Office, 1941.

Visher, Stephen F., *Climatic Atlas of the United States*. Cambridge, Mass.: Harvard University Press, 1954.

Periodicals

Average Monthly Weather Resume and Outlook, published semimonthly in Washington by the U.S. Weather Bureau.

Bulletin of the American Meteorological Society, published monthly by the American Meteorological Society, Boston, Mass.

Climatological Data (by states), monthly bulletins and annual summary obtainable from the U.S. Weather Bureau Section Directors.

Daily Weather Map, published in Washington by the U.S. Weather Bureau.

International Geophysics Bulletin is a monthly survey of plans, activities, and findings in geophysics, with emphasis on U.S. contributions to international endeavors—such as the Year of the Quiet Sun, World Magnetic Survey, Antarctic Research Program, and the International Geophysical Year. Published by the National Academy of Sciences, Washington, D.C.

Journal of Applied Meteorology contains articles of an applied nature. Published by the American Meteorological Society, Boston, Mass.

Journal of the Atmospheric Sciences (formerly the *Journal of Meteorology*) contains original and highly scientific papers; published bimonthly by the American Meteorological Society, Boston, Mass.

Meteorological Abstracts and Bibliography contains abstracts and bibliography of meteorological research all over the world; published monthly by the American Meteorological Society, Boston, Mass.

Monthly Weather Review contains technical contributions in synoptic and applied meteorology and a monthly weather summary; published by the U.S. Weather Bureau, Washington, D.C.

Quarterly Journal of the Royal Meteorological Society contains the results of original research; published by the Royal Meteorological Society, London, England.

Weather, monthly magazine published by the Royal Meteorological Society, London, England.

Weatherwise, a bimonthly magazine of nontechnical articles on meteorology, published by the American Meteorological Society, Boston, Mass.

Miscellaneous Publications of the U.S. Weather Bureau*

Circular A. *Instructions for obtaining and tabulating records from recording instruments.*

Circular B. *Instructions for co-operative observers.*

Circular D. *Instructions for the installation and maintenance of wind-measuring and wind-recording apparatus.*

Circular E. *Measurement of precipitation.*

Circular F. *Barometers and the measurement of atmospheric pressure.*

Circular G. *Care and management of electrical sunshine recorders.*

---

* Obtainable from the Superintendent of Documents, Government Printing Office, Washington, D.C.

Circular I. *Instructions for erecting and using weather bureau nephoscope.*

Circular L. *Instructions for the installation and operation of class A evaporation stations.*

Circular M. *Instructions to marine meteorological observers.*

Circular N. *Instructions for airway meteorological service.*

Circular O. *Instructions for making pilot-balloon observations.*

Circular P. *Instructions for making aerological observations.*

Circular Q. *Pyrheliometers and pyrheliometric observations.*

Circular R. *Preparation and use of weather maps at sea.*

Circular S. *Codes for cloud forms and states of the sky.*

Circular T. *Ocean-station instructions for meteorological personnel* (supplementary).

Climatic Charts for the United States. Twelve charts, 10 × 16 inches.

Cloud Forms. Descriptive pamphlet and thirty-two halftone plates.

Frost Charts for the United States. Five charts, 10 × 16 inches.

Weather Code. Includes Synoptic Code, Radiosonde and Rawinsonde Code, Upper-wind Code, U.S. Weather Analysis Code, and sheet containing Station Model and Explanation of Weather Code Figures and Symbols.

appendix II

conversion factors and tables

Abridged from *Smithsonian Meteorological Tables,* Fifth Edition, 1931.

Equivalent Values

1 foot = 0.3048 meter.
1 meter = 39.37 inches = 3.2808 feet.
1 mile = 1.6093 kilometers.
1 kilometer = 3280.8 feet = 0.62137 mile.

1 inch, mercury = 25.4 millimeters = 33.86395 millibars.
1 millimeter, mercury = 0.03937 inch = 1.3332 millibars.
1 millibar = 0.02953 inch = 0.75006 millimeter.

1 mile per hour = 1.467 feet per second
1 mile per hour = 0.447 meter per second
1 mile per hour = 1.610 kilometers per hour
1 mile per hour = 0.868 knot

1 meter per second = 2.237 miles per hour
1 meter per second = 3.600 kilometers per hour
1 meter per second = 1.940 knots

1 knot = 1.152 miles per hour
1 knot = 1.854 kilometers per hour
1 knot = 0.515 meter per second

TEMPERATURE EQUATIONS

$$F = \tfrac{9}{5}\, C + 32 = \tfrac{9}{5}\,(A - 273) + 32.$$
$$C = \tfrac{5}{9}\,(F - 32) = A - 273.$$
$$A = \tfrac{5}{9}\,(F - 32) + 273 = C + 273.$$

TABLE 1   Barometric Inches of Mercury into Millibars

INCHES	.0	.1	.2	.3	.4	.5	.6	.7	.8	.9
	mb	mb	mb	mb	mb	mb	mb	mb	mb	mb
0	000	003	007	010	014	017	020	024	027	030
1	034	037	041	044	047	051	054	058	061	064
2	068	071	074	078	081	085	088	091	095	098
3	102	105	108	112	115	119	122	125	129	132
4	135	139	142	146	149	152	156	159	162	166
5	169	173	176	179	183	186	190	193	196	200
6	203	207	210	213	217	220	223	227	230	234
7	237	240	244	247	251	254	257	260	264	267
8	271	274	278	281	284	288	291	295	298	301
9	305	308	311	315	318	322	325	328	332	335
10	339	342	345	349	352	356	359	362	366	369
11	372	376	379	383	386	389	393	396	400	403
12	406	410	413	416	420	423	427	430	433	437
13	440	444	447	450	454	457	460	464	467	471
14	474	477	481	484	488	491	494	498	501	505
15	508	511	515	518	521	524	528	532	535	538
16	542	545	549	552	555	559	562	565	569	572
17	576	579	582	586	589	593	596	599	603	606
18	610	613	616	620	623	626	630	633	637	640
19	643	647	650	654	657	660	664	667	670	674
20	677	681	684	687	691	694	698	701	704	708
21	711	714	718	721	725	728	731	735	738	742
22	745	748	752	755	759	762	765	769	772	775
23	779	782	786	789	792	796	799	803	806	809
24	813	816	819	823	826	830	833	836	840	843
25	847	850	853	857	860	863	867	870	874	877
26	880	884	887	891	894	897	901	904	908	911
27	914	918	921	924	928	931	935	938	941	945
28	948	952	955	958	962	965	968	972	975	979
29	982	985	989	992	996	999	1002	1006	1009	1012
30	1016	1019	1023	1026	1029	1033	1036	1040	1043	1046
31	1050	1053	1057	1060	1063	1067	1070	1073	1077	1080

TABLE 2   Conversion of Statute Miles to Nautical Miles to Feet to Kilometers

STATUTE MILES	NAUTICAL MILES	FEET	KILOMETERS
1	0.9	5,280	2
2	1.7	10,560	3
3	2.6	15,840	5
4	3.5	21,120	6
5	4.3	26,400	8
6	5.2	31,680	10
7	6.1	36,960	11
8	6.9	42,240	13
9	7.8	47,520	14
10	8.7	52,800	16
11	9.6	58,080	18
12	10.4	63,360	19
13	11.3	68,640	21
14	12.1	73,920	23
15	13.0	79,200	24
16	13.9	84,480	26
17	14.8	89,760	27
18	15.6	95,040	29
19	16.5	100,320	31
20	17.4	105,600	32
21	18.3	110,880	34
22	19.1	116,160	35
23	20.0	121,440	37
24	20.9	126,720	39
25	21.7	132,000	40
26	22.6	137,280	42
27	23.5	142,560	43
28	24.3	147,840	45
29	25.2	153,120	47
30	26.1	158,400	48
31	27.0	163,680	50
32	27.8	168,960	51
33	28.7	174,240	53
34	29.6	179,520	55
35	30.4	184,800	56
36	31.3	190,080	58
37	32.2	195,360	60
38	33.0	200,640	61
39	33.9	205,920	63
40	34.7	211,200	64
41	35.6	216,480	66
42	36.4	221,760	68
43	37.2	227,040	69
44	38.1	232,320	71
45	39.0	237,600	72
46	39.9	242,880	74
47	40.8	248,160	76
48	41.6	253,440	77
49	42.5	258,720	79
50	43.4	264,000	80

TABLE 3   Fahrenheit Scale to Centigrade

°F	0	1	2	3	4	5	6	7	8	9
					CENTIGRADE					
−60	−51.1	−51.7	−52.2	−52.8	−53.3	−53.9	−54.4	−55.0	−55.6	−56.1
−50	−45.6	−46.1	−46.7	−47.2	−47.8	−48.3	−48.9	−49.4	−50.0	−50.6
−40	−40.0	−40.6	−41.1	−41.7	−42.2	−42.8	−43.3	−43.9	−44.4	−45.0
−30	−34.4	−35.0	−35.6	−36.1	−36.7	−37.2	−37.8	−38.3	−38.9	−39.4
−20	−28.9	−29.4	−30.0	−30.6	−31.1	−31.7	−32.2	−32.8	−33.3	−33.9
−10	−23.3	−23.9	−24.4	−25.0	−25.6	−26.1	−26.7	−27.2	−27.8	−28.3
− 0	−17.8	−18.3	−18.9	−19.4	−20.0	−20.6	−21.1	−21.7	−22.2	−22.8
+ 0	−17.8	−17.2	−16.7	−16.1	−15.6	−15.0	−14.4	−13.9	−13.3	−12.8
10	−12.2	−11.7	−11.1	−10.6	−10.0	− 9.4	− 8.9	− 8.3	− 7.8	− 7.2
20	− 6.7	− 6.1	− 5.6	− 5.0	− 4.4	− 3.9	− 3.3	− 2.8	− 2.2	− 1.7
30	− 1.1	− 0.6	0.0	0.6	1.1	1.7	2.2	2.8	3.3	3.9
40	4.4	5.0	5.6	6.1	6.7	7.2	7.8	8.3	8.9	9.4
50	10.0	10.6	11.1	11.7	12.2	12.8	13.3	13.9	14.4	15.0
60	15.6	16.1	16.7	17.2	17.8	18.3	18.9	19.4	20.0	20.6
70	21.1	21.7	22.2	22.8	23.3	23.9	24.4	25.0	25.6	26.1
80	26.7	27.2	27.8	28.3	28.9	29.4	30.0	30.6	31.1	31.7
90	32.2	32.8	33.3	33.9	34.4	35.0	35.6	36.1	36.7	37.2
100	37.8	38.3	38.9	39.4	40.0	40.6	41.1	41.7	42.2	42.8
110	43.3	43.9	44.4	45.0	45.6	46.1	46.7	47.2	47.8	48.3

TABLE 4   Centrigrade Scale to Fahrenheit

°C	0	1	2	3	4	5	6	7	8	9
					FAHRENHEIT					
−50	−58.0	−59.8	−61.6	−63.4	−65.2	−67.0	−68.8	−70.6	−72.4	−74.2
−40	−40.0	−41.8	−43.6	−45.4	−47.2	−49.0	−50.8	−52.6	−54.4	−56.2
−30	−22.0	−23.8	−25.6	−27.4	−29.2	−31.0	−32.8	−34.6	−36.4	−38.2
−20	−4.0	−5.8	−7.6	−9.4	−11.2	−13.0	−14.8	−16.6	−18.4	−20.2
−10	14.0	12.2	10.4	8.6	6.8	5.0	3.2	1.4	−0.4	−2.2
−0	32.0	30.2	28.4	26.6	24.8	23.0	21.2	19.4	17.6	15.8
+0	32.0	33.8	35.6	37.4	39.2	41.0	42.8	44.6	46.4	48.2
10	50.0	51.8	53.6	55.4	57.2	59.0	60.8	62.6	64.4	66.2
20	68.0	69.8	71.6	73.4	75.2	77.0	78.8	80.6	82.4	84.2
30	86.0	87.8	89.6	91.4	93.2	95.0	96.8	98.6	100.4	102.2
40	104.0	105.8	107.6	109.4	111.2	113.0	114.8	116.6	118.4	120.2

appendix III

mean monthly and annual temperatures and precipitation

TABLE 5 Temperature, Degrees Fahrenheit; Precipitation, Inches

STATIONS	JAN.	FEB.	MAR.	APRIL	MAY	JUNE	JULY	AUG.	SEPT.	OCT.	NOV.	DEC.	ANNUAL
United States													
Abilene: T.......	44.2	47.2	56.5	64.4	72.0	79.2	82.8	82.0	75.3	65.4	53.5	46.0	64.0
Rf.....	0.96	1.01	1.29	2.71	3.96	2.99	2.12	2.24	2.70	2.50	1.35	1.34	25.17
Bismarck: T.....	7.8	10.3	24.2	42.1	54.5	63.7	69.8	67.3	58.1	44.9	28.5	14.7	40.5
Rf.....	0.45	0.44	0.89	1.52	2.32	3.35	2.24	1.82	1.23	0.94	0.57	0.57	16.34
Boise: T.......	29.8	34.8	42.7	50.4	57.1	65.3	72.9	71.8	61.9	51.1	41.0	32.1	50.9
Rf.....	1.73	1.44	1.35	1.18	1.43	0.92	0.24	0.19	0.53	1.24	1.28	1.57	13.10
Boston: T.......	27.9	28.8	35.6	46.4	57.1	66.5	71.7	69.9	63.2	53.6	42.0	32.5	49.6
Rf.....	3.61	3.37	3.57	3.34	3.18	2.89	3.49	3.62	3.14	3.15	3.33	3.45	40.14
Burlington: T....	18.8	19.4	29.1	43.3	56.5	65.7	70.3	67.9	60.3	49.2	36.3	24.4	45.1
Rf.....	1.76	1.57	2.04	2.15	2.85	3.38	3.50	3.37	3.48	2.97	2.66	1.88	31.61
Charleston: T...	49.9	52.4	57.4	64.5	72.7	78.9	81.4	81.0	76.6	67.8	58.1	51.7	66.0
Rf.....	3.02	2.98	3.02	2.53	3.00	4.59	6.89	6.53	4.53	3.27	2.14	2.72	45.22
Chicago: T......	25.1	27.4	36.3	47.7	58.5	68.2	73.9	72.8	66.3	55.1	41.2	30.0	50.2
Rf.....	1.90	2.14	2.58	2.78	3.54	3.30	3.33	3.21	3.14	2.53	2.37	2.04	32.86
Columbus: T....	28.6	30.7	39.1	51.2	62.3	70.9	74.9	73.0	66.5	55.2	41.9	32.4	52.2
Rf.....	3.06	2.67	3.50	2.87	3.59	3.31	3.55	3.26	2.57	2.46	2.77	2.73	36.34

TABLE 5 (Cont.)

STATIONS	JAN.	FEB.	MAR.	APRIL	MAY	JUNE	JULY	AUG.	SEPT.	OCT.	NOV.	DEC.	ANNUAL
United States (Cont.)													
Denver: T.	29.8	32.7	39.3	47.1	56.2	66.3	72.2	70.7	62.9	51.2	39.8	32.3	50.0
Rf.	0.40	0.53	1.04	2.06	2.21	1.38	1.68	1.43	0.99	1.05	0.55	0.73	14.05
Des Moines: T. . . .	20.1	23.7	35.9	50.1	61.3	70.6	75.4	73.1	65.6	53.4	38.4	26.0	49.5
Rf. . . .	1.07	1.12	1.78	2.91	4.56	4.76	3.50	3.52	3.67	2.50	1.43	1.22	32.04
Detroit: T.	24.4	25.3	33.4	46.2	58.0	67.4	72.1	70.3	63.5	52.5	39.3	29.3	48.5
Rf.	2.07	2.18	2.40	2.46	3.21	3.56	3.32	2.78	2.90	2.38	2.44	2.35	32.05
Dodge City: T. . . .	29.0	33.2	42.8	53.6	63.5	72.5	78.4	77.7	69.4	56.1	42.6	32.6	54.3
Rf. . .	0.41	0.77	0.89	1.94	2.89	3.30	3.14	2.67	1.90	1.30	0.73	0.57	20.51
Helena: T.	20.2	23.0	32.4	43.5	51.6	59.2	65.7	65.0	56.6	44.9	33.2	24.2	43.3
Rf.	0.87	0.65	0.79	1.12	2.29	2.34	1.14	0.77	1.25	0.89	0.74	0.78	13.63
Honolulu: T. . . .	70.9	70.8	71.4	73.0	74.8	76.6	77.7	78.4	78.2	76.8	74.5	72.4	74.6
Rf.	3.74	4.26	3.76	2.28	1.88	1.10	1.31	1.46	1.53	1.92	4.21	4.15	31.60
Huron: T.	11.3	14.3	28.9	45.1	56.4	66.2	71.8	69.4	61.3	47.7	31.5	18.7	43.6
Rf.	0.56	0.54	0.91	2.24	2.98	3.79	3.16	2.46	1.57	1.28	0.59	0.57	20.65
Jacksonville: T. . . .	55.4	58.0	62.6	68.7	75.0	79.9	82.1	81.7	78.3	71.1	62.2	56.3	69.3
Rf. . .	2.80	2.97	2.91	2.38	4.02	5.33	6.71	5.81	7.35	4.46	1.98	3.02	49.74
Juneau: T.	26.7	30.0	33.5	40.8	48.0	54.2	57.4	55.0	50.2	42.9	34.8	31.0	42.0
Rf.	6.90	5.27	5.11	5.26	5.16	3.73	5.09	7.38	10.68	10.33	8.29	7.37	80.57
Kansas City: T. . . .	28.2	31.2	42.7	54.8	64.8	73.6	78.1	76.6	68.9	57.7	43.7	32.5	54.4
Rf. . .	1.19	1.75	2.53	3.14	4.65	4.99	4.13	4.09	4.56	2.92	1.83	1.33	37.11
Lander: T.	18.3	22.5	32.4	42.4	51.2	60.5	67.4	65.5	55.7	43.5	30.3	20.4	42.5
Rf.	0.56	0.63	1.19	2.06	2.26	1.15	0.69	0.53	0.92	1.36	0.60	0.68	12.63
Little Rock: T. . . .	41.4	44.9	53.0	62.1	70.3	77.4	80.9	79.8	74.1	63.6	52.1	44.2	62.0
Rf. . .	4.73	3.84	4.62	5.19	4.78	3.76	3.50	3.75	3.17	2.71	4.19	4.14	48.38
Los Angeles: T. . . .	54.6	55.5	57.5	59.4	62.2	66.4	70.2	71.1	69.0	65.3	60.9	56.6	62.4
Rf. . .	3.10	3.07	2.78	1.04	0.45	0.08	0.01	0.02	0.17	0.68	1.20	2.63	15.23
Louisville: T. . . .	34.4	37.2	45.5	56.4	66.6	74.7	78.6	77.0	70.5	59.3	46.7	37.6	57.0
Rf. . .	4.00	3.55	4.39	3.88	3.72	3.82	3.70	3.42	2.78	2.65	3.61	3.74	43.26

TABLE 5 (Cont.)

STATIONS	JAN.	FEB.	MAR.	APRIL	MAY	JUNE	JULY	AUG.	SEPT.	OCT.	NOV.	DEC.	ANNUAL
United States (Cont.)													
Miami: T	66.5	67.1	70.2	72.8	76.4	80.0	81.0	81.4	80.1	77.0	71.8	68.0	74.4
Rf.	2.52	1.83	2.17	3.09	6.22	6.86	5.42	6.17	8.34	8.44	2.91	1.69	55.66
Minneapolis: T	12.7	15.9	29.6	46.4	57.7	67.5	72.3	69.9	61.4	48.9	32.4	19.6	44.5
Rf.	0.86	0.95	1.42	2.23	3.67	4.22	3.73	3.12	3.13	2.08	1.27	0.98	27.66
Montgomery: T	48.2	51.6	57.8	65.3	73.4	79.6	81.7	80.8	76.3	66.6	55.8	49.4	56.5
Rf.	5.20	5.45	5.99	4.30	3.84	3.80	4.86	4.23	2.99	2.46	3.23	4.84	51.19
Nashville: T	38.6	41.6	49.2	59.0	68.2	75.6	79.1	77.8	71.8	61.0	49.0	41.0	59.3
Rf.	4.76	4.13	5.11	4.13	3.87	4.00	3.88	3.71	3.42	2.49	3.50	4.20	47.20
New Orleans: T	54.2	57.3	62.8	68.8	75.4	80.6	82.4	82.2	79.2	71.0	61.5	55.6	69.3
Rf.	4.34	4.25	4.72	5.24	4.60	5.88	6.37	5.80	5.03	3.30	3.14	4.79	57.46
New York: T	30.9	31.3	37.7	49.4	60.6	68.8	73.8	73.1	66.8	56.3	44.2	35.0	52.3
Rf.	3.66	3.82	3.64	3.23	3.24	3.33	4.24	4.33	3.39	3.53	2.96	3.62	42.99
Nome: T	1.3	5.8	8.2	17.2	34.3	44.7	50.1	49.5	41.2	28.9	14.3	6.2	25.1
Rf.	0.97	1.06	0.89	0.61	0.88	1.22	2.87	3.00	2.34	1.47	0.98	1.13	17.42
Oklahoma City: T	36.4	39.6	50.0	59.8	67.7	76.0	80.6	79.7	72.8	61.5	48.8	39.3	59.4
Rf.	1.19	1.11	1.98	3.29	4.88	3.67	2.86	2.89	3.05	2.86	1.87	1.50	31.15
Omaha: T	21.9	25.5	37.0	51.2	62.4	71.6	76.7	74.4	66.8	54.3	38.5	26.4	50.6
Rf.	0.70	0.89	1.37	2.51	3.77	4.56	3.54	3.05	3.21	2.17	1.07	0.93	27.77
Phoenix: T	51.2	55.1	60.7	67.0	75.0	84.5	89.8	88.5	82.7	70.6	59.7	52.0	69.7
Rf.	0.80	0.77	0.68	0.40	0.12	0.07	1.07	0.95	0.75	0.47	0.70	1.00	7.78
Pittsburgh: T	30.7	32.3	39.6	51.2	62.4	70.7	74.6	72.9	66.4	55.7	43.2	34.2	52.8
Rf.	3.05	2.62	3.03	2.92	3.21	3.81	4.05	3.23	2.58	2.52	2.29	2.86	36.17
Portland, Me.: T	22.4	23.8	31.8	43.0	53.3	62.5	68.1	66.4	59.6	49.9	38.0	27.6	45.5
Rf.	3.97	4.00	3.86	3.38	3.40	3.28	3.24	3.14	3.10	3.14	3.46	3.97	41.94
Portland, Ore.: T	39.4	42.1	46.9	51.8	56.9	62.4	66.7	66.7	61.7	54.2	46.8	41.2	53.1
Rf.	6.60	5.36	3.91	2.87	2.19	1.52	0.61	0.64	1.98	3.12	6.10	6.72	41.62
Raleigh: T	41.1	43.2	50.2	59.4	68.5	75.7	78.8	77.0	71.1	62.0	51.0	43.0	60.1
Rf.	3.66	3.92	3.87	3.47	3.81	4.39	5.40	5.41	3.61	2.86	2.28	3.58	46.26

TABLE 5 (Cont.)

STATIONS	JAN.	FEB.	MAR.	APRIL	MAY	JUNE	JULY	AUG.	SEPT.	OCT.	NOV.	DEC.	ANNUAL
United States (Cont.)													
Rochester: T	24.6	24.6	31.8	44.9	57.1	66.1	70.7	69.2	62.4	51.5	38.7	29.3	47.6
Rf.	2.89	2.69	2.76	2.35	2.94	3.00	2.96	2.88	2.45	2.65	2.54	2.72	32.83
St. Louis: T	31.1	34.8	44.1	56.1	67.0	75.0	78.8	77.5	70.5	58.8	45.4	34.9	56.2
Rf.	2.34	2.56	3.38	3.81	4.34	3.82	2.98	2.99	3.46	2.72	2.83	2.21	37.44
Salt Lake City: T	29.2	33.8	41.7	49.6	57.4	67.4	75.7	74.5	64.4	52.5	41.1	31.9	51.6
Rf.	1.31	1.51	1.98	2.05	1.92	0.80	0.51	0.85	0.98	1.44	1.35	1.43	16.13
San Diego: T	54.3	55.1	56.7	58.5	60.8	63.9	67.2	68.7	67.1	63.7	59.7	56.0	61.0
Rf.	2.06	2.03	1.72	0.77	0.35	0.05	0.03	0.04	0.08	0.54	0.76	1.87	10.30
San Francisco: T	49.9	52.2	54.2	55.0	56.8	58.5	58.5	59.1	60.9	60.5	56.3	51.3	56.1
Rf.	4.54	3.85	3.14	1.61	0.80	0.18	0.02	0.01	0.45	1.12	2.35	3.95	22.02
Santa Fe: T	28.8	33.1	39.7	46.7	55.7	64.8	69.0	67.4	60.9	50.4	38.9	30.7	48.8
Rf.	0.67	0.75	0.80	1.00	1.26	1.08	2.38	2.28	1.45	1.18	0.68	0.74	14.27
Saulte Ste. Marie: T	13.3	12.0	21.6	37.4	49.0	58.6	63.8	62.1	55.5	44.6	32.0	20.5	39.2
Rf.	1.95	1.94	1.84	2.20	3.03	2.92	2.89	2.62	4.19	3.74	2.67	2.34	32.33
Seattle: T	39.5	41.1	44.9	49.4	54.5	59.0	63.1	63.1	58.1	51.4	45.6	41.7	51.0
Rf.	4.94	3.89	3.05	2.38	1.87	1.33	0.63	0.70	1.77	2.84	5.03	5.60	34.03
Spokane: T	27.5	31.3	39.7	48.4	55.5	62.8	69.0	68.1	59.2	48.3	38.5	30.5	48.2
Rf.	2.16	1.77	1.20	1.13	1.42	1.28	0.69	0.62	0.90	1.17	2.09	2.19	16.62
Washington, D.C.: T	33.4	35.3	42.6	53.3	63.7	72.2	76.8	75.0	68.1	57.4	45.2	36.6	55.0
Rf.	3.55	3.27	3.75	3.27	3.70	4.13	4.71	4.01	3.24	2.84	2.37	3.32	42.16
Winnemucca: T	28.6	33.5	40.0	46.7	53.9	62.8	70.6	69.3	59.2	48.3	38.4	30.0	48.4
Rf.	1.03	0.91	0.96	0.84	0.88	0.72	0.21	0.20	0.41	0.62	0.68	1.08	8.54
San Juan: T	75.0	74.9	75.4	76.6	78.6	79.7	80.1	80.5	80.5	79.8	78.4	76.3	78.0
Rf.	4.15	2.76	3.15	4.36	5.24	5.30	5.94	5.98	5.91	5.86	6.77	5.50	60.92
North and Central America (except U.S.):													
Calgary: T	11.3	14.5	25.1	39.9	48.9	55.9	60.7	58.7	50.5	41.9	26.4	20.5	37.8
Rf.	0.5	0.6	0.7	0.7	2.4	3.2	2.6	2.6	1.2	0.6	0.7	0.5	16.4

TABLE 5 (Cont.)

STATIONS	JAN.	FEB.	MAR.	APRIL	MAY	JUNE	JULY	AUG.	SEPT.	OCT.	NOV.	DEC.	ANNUAL
North and Central America (except U.S.) (Cont.)													
Kamloops: T	22.4	26.5	37.6	49.7	57.5	64.5	69.6	68.1	58.4	47.8	35.8	28.8	47.2
Rf.	0.9	0.8	0.3	0.4	0.9	1.2	1.3	1.0	0.9	0.6	1.0	1.5	11.0
Quebec: T	10.1	11.7	23.0	37.1	51.5	61.2	66.3	63.0	55.4	43.0	29.8	15.4	38.7
Rf.	3.4	3.3	3.3	2.1	3.2	4.1	4.3	4.0	3.8	3.1	3.0	3.1	40.7
St. Johns: T	24.2	23.3	28.5	35.4	42.7	49.7	58.9	59.3	53.7	45.4	37.6	28.9	40.1
Rf.	6.3	5.7	4.7	4.3	3.2	3.9	3.6	3.7	3.5	6.2	6.0	5.4	56.5
Toronto: T	22.9	21.1	30.2	43.1	53.6	64.6	69.1	67.2	60.8	48.3	37.4	27.7	45.5
Rf.	2.8	2.4	2.1	2.4	2.9	2.6	3.0	2.6	2.8	2.6	2.6	2.6	31.4
Winnipeg: T	−3.5	−0.5	15.2	38.7	51.5	62.6	66.2	62.7	54.1	41.6	22.0	7.2	34.8
Rf.	0.8	0.7	1.2	1.5	2.1	3.0	3.2	2.2	2.1	1.4	1.0	0.9	20.2
Colon: T	79.5	79.2	79.7	79.9	79.9	79.9	80.1	79.3	79.5	79.0	79.0	79.5	79.5
Rf.	3.9	1.7	1.7	4.2	12.6	13.5	16.2	14.9	12.5	14.8	21.5	11.9	129.4
Guatemala City: T	61.3	62.8	65.7	66.2	68.0	66.2	65.8	66.0	65.7	64.8	62.8	61.3	64.8
Rf.	0.3	0.2	0.5	1.3	5.6	11.5	8.0	8.0	9.2	6.7	0.9	0.2	52.4
Havana: T	70.3	72.0	73.4	76.3	79.2	81.3	81.9	81.5	80.4	77.9	74.7	71.6	76.6
Rf.	2.7	2.3	1.8	2.8	4.5	7.2	5.0	6.0	6.7	7.4	3.1	2.2	51.7
Mexico City: T	54.0	56.8	60.4	64.2	64.9	63.9	62.4	62.1	61.2	58.6	56.5	53.4	59.9
Rf.	0.2	0.2	0.6	0.6	1.9	3.9	4.1	4.7	4.1	1.8	0.5	0.2	23.1
South America:													
Buenos Aires: T	73.6	73.0	69.6	61.9	55.9	51.1	50.2	52.3	57.1	61.0	67.3	71.4	61.9
Rf.	3.0	2.5	4.6	3.0	2.8	2.7	2.2	2.4	3.0	3.6	2.8	3.9	36.5
Lima: T	71.1	73.4	72.9	70.0	66.0	62.1	60.6	60.6	61.3	61.9	65.8	69.8	66.2
Rf.	0.03	0.0	0.0	0.03	0.03	0.2	0.3	0.5	0.5	0.1	0.03	0.03	1.8
Para: T	77.7	77.0	77.5	77.7	78.4	78.3	78.1	78.3	78.6	79.0	79.6	79.0	78.3
Rf.	10.3	12.6	13.3	13.2	9.3	5.7	4.9	4.3	3.2	2.5	2.3	5.1	86.7
Quito: T	54.5	55.0	54.5	54.5	54.7	55.0	54.9	54.9	55.0	54.7	54.3	54.7	54.7
Rf.	3.2	3.9	4.8	7.0	4.6	1.5	1.1	2.2	2.6	3.9	4.0	3.6	42.3
Rio de Janeiro: T	77.5	78.1	77.2	74.1	70.7	68.2	67.5	68.7	69.4	71.2	73.4	74.8	72.5
Rf.	5.0	4.3	5.3	4.4	3.5	2.0	1.6	1.8	2.6	3.2	4.3	5.4	43.4

TABLE 5 (Cont.)

STATIONS	JAN.	FEB.	MAR.	APRIL	MAY	JUNE	JULY	AUG.	SEPT.	OCT.	NOV.	DEC.	ANNUAL
South America (Cont.)													
Santiago: T	67.3	66.0	61.9	56.1	50.5	46.0	46.0	48.2	52.2	56.1	61.0	65.7	56.4
Rf	0.0	0.1	0.2	0.6	2.3	3.2	3.4	2.4	1.2	0.6	0.2	0.2	14.4
Europe:													
Athens: T	46.4	47.5	52.3	58.8	67.8	75.7	80.6	79.9	73.9	66.0	57.0	50.0	63.0
Rf	2.0	1.5	1.3	0.8	0.7	0.6	0.3	0.4	0.6	1.7	3.0	2.4	15.4
Belgrade: T	29.1	33.8	43.0	52.0	61.5	67.1	71.6	70.5	63.3	55.2	42.6	34.2	52.0
Rf	1.2	1.3	1.6	2.3	2.8	3.2	2.7	1.9	1.7	2.2	1.7	1.7	24.4
Berlin: T	31.3	32.5	37.0	45.9	54.9	62.1	64.6	63.3	57.0	48.2	38.1	32.7	47.3
Rf	1.5	1.3	1.7	1.4	2.0	2.0	3.1	2.2	1.8	1.8	1.6	1.7	22.2
Constantinople: T	40.6	41.0	45.5	52.3	61.0	69.1	73.2	72.5	67.3	61.3	52.5	45.3	56.8
Rf	3.4	2.7	2.4	1.7	1.2	1.3	1.1	1.7	2.0	2.5	4.0	4.8	28.9
Copenhagen: T	32.2	31.8	34.5	41.7	50.7	58.6	61.9	60.6	55.4	47.3	40.1	34.5	45.9
Rf	1.3	1.3	1.5	1.3	1.5	1.8	2.3	2.6	1.8	2.1	1.7	1.8	20.7
Dublin: T	42.1	42.5	43.6	47.0	51.8	57.1	60.1	60.0	56.0	50.2	45.8	42.7	49.9
Rf	2.3	1.9	1.9	1.9	2.0	2.0	2.6	3.0	1.9	2.7	2.7	2.5	27.4
Geneva: T	32.0	35.6	40.8	48.9	55.9	62.8	67.1	64.9	59.2	49.1	40.8	33.6	49.1
Rf	1.6	1.8	2.1	2.6	3.2	3.0	3.1	3.5	3.1	4.4	3.1	2.2	33.7
London: T	38.9	40.1	42.4	47.3	53.4	59.2	62.7	61.6	57.1	49.9	44.0	40.3	49.7
Rf	1.9	1.7	1.8	1.5	1.8	2.0	2.4	2.2	1.8	2.6	2.4	2.4	24.5
Madrid: T	39.7	43.9	47.5	52.3	59.4	68.5	75.7	74.8	66.4	54.9	47.1	40.1	55.9
Rf	1.3	1.1	1.7	1.9	1.7	1.2	0.5	0.4	1.3	1.8	1.9	1.6	16.4
Marseilles: T	43.3	45.3	48.6	58.7	61.0	67.6	72.1	71.1	66.0	58.1	49.8	44.1	56.8
Rf	1.9	1.4	1.6	1.7	1.9	1.0	0.6	0.9	2.5	4.0	3.1	2.0	22.6
Moscow: T	12.2	14.7	23.4	38.3	53.1	61.5	66.0	62.8	52.2	39.7	27.7	17.2	39.0
Rf	1.1	0.9	1.2	1.5	1.9	2.0	2.8	2.9	2.2	1.4	1.6	1.5	21.0
Odessa: T	25.3	27.7	34.9	47.5	59.2	68.0	72.7	70.9	62.1	51.8	41.0	30.6	49.3
Rf	0.9	0.7	1.1	1.1	1.3	2.3	2.1	1.2	1.4	1.1	1.6	1.3	16.1
Paris: T	36.5	39.0	43.2	50.5	56.1	62.4	65.5	64.4	59.0	50.5	42.8	37.2	50.5
Rf	1.5	1.2	1.6	1.7	2.1	2.3	2.2	2.2	2.0	2.3	1.8	1.7	22.6

TABLE 5 (Cont.)

STATIONS	JAN.	FEB.	MAR.	APRIL	MAY	JUNE	JULY	AUG.	SEPT.	OCT.	NOV.	DEC.	ANNUAL
Europe (Cont.)													
Rome: T	44.1	46.6	50.7	56.8	64.0	71.2	76.6	75.7	70.2	61.7	52.3	45.9	59.7
Rf.	3.1	2.5	2.7	2.7	2.3	1.6	0.7	1.1	2.8	4.6	4.6	3.5	32.3
Trondheim: T	26.	26.	31.	39.	46.	54.	57.	56.	49.	41.	34.	28.	41.
Rf.	4.3	3.0	3.4	2.5	2.2	1.9	2.8	3.4	4.4	5.0	3.9	3.4	40.2
Vienna: T	28.9	32.4	39.0	48.9	57.2	63.9	67.3	65.8	59.4	49.6	38.3	30.9	48.6
Rf.	1.5	1.3	1.8	2.0	2.8	2.8	2.8	2.8	1.7	1.9	1.6	1.7	24.5
Asia:													
Baghdad: T	46.8	53.0	60.3	70.2	80.7	89.6	94.0	93.8	86.9	76.3	60.7	50.3	71.9
Rf.	1.1	1.1	1.2	0.8	0.2	0.0	0.0	0.0	0.0	0.1	0.8	1.2	6.6
Bombay: T	74.5	74.8	78.0	82.1	84.6	82.4	79.5	79.4	79.4	80.7	79.3	76.4	79.3
Rf.	0.1	0.0	0.1	0.0	0.7	20.6	27.3	16.0	11.8	2.4	0.4	0.0	79.4
Delhi: T	57.9	62.2	74.1	86.2	91.7	92.2	86.4	84.5	83.9	78.5	67.6	59.6	77.1
Rf.	1.0	0.6	0.5	0.4	0.7	2.9	7.6	7.0	4.7	0.5	0.1	0.4	26.2
Hong Kong: T	59.7	57.7	63.0	70.3	67.8	80.6	81.7	81.1	80.2	76.1	69.1	62.6	71.6
Rf.	1.4	1.1	2.6	5.5	10.2	15.1	11.4	14.0	11.5	4.5	1.6	1.3	80.1
Jakarta: T	77.9	77.1	78.6	79.3	79.7	79.0	78.4	78.8	79.5	79.7	79.2	78.3	78.8
Rf.	13.0	13.6	7.8	4.8	3.7	3.6	2.6	1.3	2.6	4.1	5.0	8.7	70.9
Manila: T	76.5	77.5	79.9	82.6	83.1	81.9	80.6	80.4	80.2	79.7	78.4	77.0	79.9
Rf.	0.8	0.5	0.8	1.2	5.2	10.2	17.4	17.0	13.8	6.7	5.7	2.8	82.0
Peiping: T	23.5	29.3	41.0	56.7	67.8	76.1	78.8	76.5	67.6	54.5	38.5	27.3	53.1
Rf.	0.1	0.2	0.2	0.6	1.4	3.0	9.4	6.3	2.6	0.6	0.3	0.1	24.9
Singapore: T	78.3	79.0	80.2	80.8	81.5	81.1	81.0	80.6	80.4	80.1	79.3	78.6	80.1
Rf.	8.5	6.1	6.5	6.9	7.2	6.7	6.8	8.5	7.1	8.2	10.0	10.4	92.9
Tokyo: T	37.2	38.3	44.1	54.3	61.5	68.9	75.0	77.7	71.6	60.6	50.4	41.4	56.8
Rf.	2.0	2.6	4.3	5.3	5.9	6.3	5.6	4.6	7.5	7.2	4.3	2.3	57.9
Tomsk: T	-3.3	1.4	14.0	29.8	45.1	59.0	65.7	59.5	47.8	32.2	10.8	1.0	30.2
Rf.	1.1	0.8	0.8	0.7	1.5	2.7	3.0	3.3	1.4	2.4	1.4	1.9	19.9

TABLE 5 (Cont.)

STATIONS	JAN.	FEB.	MAR.	APRIL	MAY	JUNE	JULY	AUG.	SEPT.	OCT.	NOV.	DEC.	ANNUAL
Asia (Cont.)													
Verkhoyansk: T	−58.9	−47.4	−24.0	7.3	35.4	54.5	59.7	49.8	36.3	5.2	−34.4	−52.6	2.7
Rf	0.2	0.1	0.0	0.1	0.2	0.5	1.2	0.9	0.2	0.2	0.2	0.2	3.9
Vladivostok: T	4.8	12.4	26.4	39.2	48.7	56.8	66.0	69.4	61.3	48.6	29.8	13.6	39.7
Rf	0.1	0.2	0.3	1.2	1.3	1.5	2.2	3.5	2.4	1.6	0.5	0.2	14.7
Africa:													
Addis Ababa: T	61.9	59.4	64.0	61.2	63.2	59.2	56.7	58.9	58.0	60.0	61.4	60.0	60.2
Rf	0.6	1.9	2.8	3.4	3.0	5.7	11.0	12.1	7.6	0.8	0.6	0.2	49.6
Algiers: T	53.4	55.4	57.6	61.0	65.8	71.4	77.0	77.5	74.8	68.5	62.4	55.6	64.9
Rf	4.2	3.5	3.5	2.3	1.3	0.6	0.1	0.3	1.1	3.1	4.6	5.4	30.0
Freetown: T	80.9	82.0	82.2	82.0	81.5	79.5	77.6	77.4	78.5	80.2	80.5	81.4	80.3
Rf	0.6	0.5	1.1	5.4	14.8	21.3	36.8	39.6	32.5	15.2	5.3	1.3	174.4
Pretoria: T	71.7	70.6	67.8	62.9	56.7	52.6	51.7	56.7	63.4	67.6	69.2	71.1	63.5
Rf	5.5	3.9	3.5	1.1	0.6	0.2	0.1	0.2	1.1	1.8	3.7	4.2	25.9
Australia and New Zealand:													
Auckland: T	66.6	67.3	65.7	61.3	57.0	53.8	52.0	52.0	54.5	57.0	60.4	64.2	59.4
Rf	2.6	3.0	3.1	3.3	4.4	4.8	5.0	4.2	3.6	3.6	3.3	2.9	43.8
Darwin: T	84.0	83.4	84.1	84.2	81.9	78.9	77.2	79.5	82.7	85.5	85.7	85.3	82.7
Rf	15.3	13.0	9.7	4.5	0.7	0.2	0.1	0.1	0.5	2.1	5.2	10.3	61.7
Melbourne: T	67.5	67.2	64.7	59.6	54.1	50.3	48.5	51.0	53.9	57.5	61.3	64.5	58.3
Rf	1.9	1.8	2.2	2.3	2.2	2.1	1.9	1.8	2.4	2.7	2.2	2.3	25.6
Perth: T	73.5	74.1	71.1	66.4	60.4	56.2	55.0	55.9	58.0	60.9	65.4	70.6	64.0
Rf	0.3	0.3	0.7	1.7	4.9	6.6	6.4	5.6	3.3	2.1	0.8	0.6	33.3

index

index

A

Absolute altimeters (*see* Altimeters, absolute)
Absolute scale, 14
Acclimatization, 322
Adiabatic chart, the, 87, *Fig. 4.5*
Adiabatic processes, 79-90, *Figs. 4.1-4.5*
  lapse rates, 88-90, *Fig. 4.6*
  problems, 98-99
  temperature changes, 83-88, *Figs. 4.3-4.5*
  upper-air observations, 80-83, *Figs. 4.1, 4.2*
Advection fogs, 108-109
Advisory Committee on Weather Control, 118
Aeronomy, 259
Aerovanes, 30-32, *Fig. 2.16*
Agriculture:
  climate and, 326-327
  weather and, 327-328
Air:
  anticyclonic, 128

Air (*Cont.*)
  composition of, 5
  convection in the, 76-77
  convergence of, 113
  cyclonic circulation, 128
  density of, 2
  dry, composition of, *Fig. 1.2*
  effect of solar radiation on, 71-72
  importance of, 2-3
  latitudinal interchange of, 147-150
  mixing processes, 147-148
  orographic uplift of, 113
  penetrative convection of, 111-113, *Fig. 5.4*
  temperatures of, 75
    obtaining, 17
  upper:
    analysis, 218-228
    observations, 80-83, *Figs. 4.1, 4.2*
  weight of, 2
  (*See also* Atmosphere; Wind)
Air conditioning, 323-324
Aircraft, icing of, 249-252, *Figs. 12.2-12.4*

Airglow, 269
Air-mass climatology, 277
Air mass thunderstorms (*see* Thunderstorms, air mass)
Air masses, 169-177
  analysis of, 219
  arctic (*A*), 170
  classification of, 170-171
  cold (*k*), 171
  continental (*c*), 171
  defined, 169
  equatorial (*E*), 170
  identifying, 219-220
  maritime (*m*), 171
  modifications of, 171-172
  of North America, 172-177, *Table 9.1*
  polar continental (*cP*), 173
  polar maritime (*mP*), 173-174
  problems, 183-185
  subsidence, 171
  superior (*S*), 171, 177
  tropical continental (*cT*), 175
  tropical maritime (*mT*), 175-177
  warm (*w*), 171
Airways, weather observations by, 245-248
Albedo, the, 70-71
Aleutian low cell, 144
Altimeters:
  absolute, 27
  pressure, 26-27
  radio, 27
  settings of, 27
Altitude:
  of clouds, 44-45
  corrections in barometer readings, 25
  pressure and, 26-27
  wind velocity and, 32
Altocumulus (Ac), 45, 46, 48, *Figs. 2.26-2.29*
Altostratus (As), 45, 46, *Fig. 2.30*
Anemometers, 30
  wind vanes and, 32-33
Anemoscopes, 29
Angle of incidence, 68-69, *Fig. 3.5*
Annual march of temperature (*see* Temperature, annual march of)
Annual range of temperature (*see* Temperature, annual march of)
Anticyclones, 161-162, *Figs. 8.7, 8.8*
  origin of, 163-164, *Fig. 8.9*
  types of, 164-165
Anticyclonic circulation, 128
Antitrades (winds), 146
Arcas rockets, 261
Arctic air masses (*see* Air masses, arctic)
Argon as an ingredient of air, 5
Aristotle, 4

Asiatic monsoon, the, 148-149, *Figs. 7.4, 7.5*
Aspiration psychrometer, 40, *Fig. 2.20*
Assmann, 96
Atmosphere, the, 1-12
  adiabatic processes, 79-90, *Figs. 4.1-4.5*
  climatic changes and, 304
  composition of, 5
  cross section of, 220-221, *Fig. 11.1*
  density of, 2, 9-10
  dust in, 5-7
  effect of solar radiation on, 71-72
  extent of, 2-3
  gases in, 5-6
  gravity and, 9
  humidity in, 36-44
  importance of, 2-3
  instability, 91-96, *Figs. 4.7-4.9*
  layers of, 96-97
  nitrogen in, 5-6
  normal, 23
  oxygen in, 5
  pressure of, 9-10
  problems, 11-12
  properties of, 7
  the seasons and, 318
  solar radiation absorbed by, *Fig. 3.6*
  stability, 90-91, *Fig. 4.6*
  thickness of, 3
  upper, 258-273
    aeronomy, 259
    auroras and airglow, 269, *Fig. 13.6*
    characteristics of, 262-267
    clouds, 265-266
    composition of, 262-263
    defined, 258-259
    meteors, 269-272
    pressure and density, 263, *Table 13.1*
    probing, 259-262, *Fig. 13.1*
    problems in, 272-273
    radiation belts, 268, *Fig. 13.5*
    stratification, 266-267
    temperature, 264-265
    winds, 265
  water vapor in, 5-6, *Fig. 1.2*
  weight of, 2
  (*See also* Air; Winds)
Atmospherics, 202
Atomic power weather stations, 35-36, *Fig. 2.19*
Aurora borealis, 269, *Fig. 13.6*
Autumnal equinox, 63
Aviation:
  altimeters in, 26-27
  fog, visibility, ceiling, 252-254
  icing on aircraft, 249-252, *Figs. 12.2-12.4*
  observations by the airways, 245-248
  pressure-pattern flying, 255-256

Aviation (*Cont.*)
  problems in, 256-257
  reconnaissance, 82
  thunderstorms, 248-249
  turbulence, 254-255, *Fig. 12.6*
Azores anticyclone cell, 143
Azores high cell, 143

B

Baguio, 187
Ball lightning, 202, *Fig. 10.8*
Balloons, pilot, 80-81
Bar, the (unit of pressure), 23
Barographs, 25-26, *Fig. 2.12*
Barometers:
  aneroid, 25-26, *Figs. 2.10, 2.11*
  corrections, 23-25
  invention of, 10
  mercurial, 21-23, *Figs. 2.7, 2.8*
  scales compared, *Fig. 2.9*
  in weather forecasting, 240-241
Beaufort, Francis, 30
Beaufort scale, 30
Bendix-Friez aerovane, the, 30-32, *Fig. 2.16*
Bergeron ice-crystal theory, 110-111
Bjerknes, V., 163
Bioclimatology, 319
Biometeorology, 319
Black frost, 103
Blizzards, 210-211
Bora winds, 131
Bort, Teisserenc de, 96
Bourdon tubes, 17, *Fig. 2.3*
Boyle, Robert, 8
Boyle's Law, 8
Breezes, 128-131, *Figs. 6.6, 6.7*
Brunt, 163
Buys-Ballot, Christoph, 128
Buys-Ballot's Law, 128

C

Calories, 64
Calvus, 47
Canyon breezes, 131
Capillatus, 47
Carbon dioxide as an ingredient of air, 5-6
Castellanus, 46
Ceiling, aviation and, 252-254
Celsius, Anders, 14
Celsius thermometers (*see* Thermometers, Celsius)
Centigrade thermometers (*see* Thermometers, centigrade)
Charles, Jacques, 8
Charles and Gay-Lussac, Law of, 8-9

Charts:
  constant-pressure, 221-224, *Fig. 11.2*
  mean weather, 228
  pressure-contour, 221-224, *Figs. 11.2, 11.4*
  reproducing, 228-229, *Fig. 11.5*
  space mean, 228
  streamline, of the Caribbean area, 165-166, *Fig. 8.11*
  synoptic, 153, *Figs. 8.2-8.4*
    analysis of, 216-218
Chemicals as ingredients of air, 5
Chemosphere, 266
Chinook winds, 209-210
Circulation index, 226-228
Cirrocumulus (Cc), 45-47, *Fig. 2.23*
Cirrostratus (Cs), 45-47, *Figs. 2.24, 2.25*
Cirrus (Ci), 44-46, 48, *Fig. 2.22*
Civilization:
  climate and, 324-325
  hypothesis of, 324
  temperature and, 325-326
Climate, 274-306
  agriculture and, 326-327
  classifications, 297-299, *Fig. 14.9*
  culture and, 324-326
  cyclical changes in, 299-303, *Fig. 14.11*
    theories of, 303-305
  defined, 11
  elements of, 274-278
  historic, 305
  hypothesis of, 324
  physical geography and, 295-297
  precipitation distribution and, 286-292
  problems in, 329-330
  solar, 277
  temperature distribution and, 278-286
  zonation of, 292-294
  (*See also* Weather)
Climatic hypothesis of civilization, 324
Cloudbursts, 111
Clouds:
  air convergence and, 113
  the albedo of, 71
  Altocumulus (Ac), 45, 46, 48, *Figs. 2.26-2.29*
  Altostratus (As), 45, 46, *Fig. 2.30*
  Cirrocumulus (Cc), 45-47, *Fig. 2.23*
  Cirrostratus (Cs), 45-47, *Figs. 2.24, 2.25*
  Cirrus (Ci), 44-46, 48, *Fig. 2.22*
  condensation and, 110-113, *Fig. 5.4*
  Cumulonimbus (Cb), 46, 48, *Figs. 2.36, 2.37*
  Cumulus (Cu), 44-46, 48, 49, 111-112, *Figs. 2.35, 5.4*
  elevation of, 44-45
  fronts and, 179-180
  genera of, 45-46, *Fig. 2.21*

Clouds (*Cont.*)
high, 44
identification and grouping of, 44-45
low, 44
middle, 44
modification of, 120
Nimbostratus (Ns), 45, 46
observations, 44-55
codes for, 47-49
precipitation and, 110-113
principal forms of, 44
records of, 55
reflective power of, 71
scud, 204
seeding, 118, *Fig. 5.8*
species of, 46-47
Stratocumulus (Sc), 45, 46, 48, 49,
Figs. 2.31, 2.32
Stratus (St), 44, 45, 48, *Figs. 2.33, 2.34*
thunderstorms and, 195-196
tornadoes and, 204, *Fig. 10.9*
in the upper atmosphere, 265-266
with vertical development, 45
wind and, 113
Coastal climates, 295-296, *Fig. 14.3*
Cold anticyclones, 164
Cold waves, 181, 211
Condensation, 38-39
above the earth's surface, 106-110
clouds and, 110-113, *Fig. 5.4*
convective level, 113
nuclei of, 106-107
on solid surfaces, 103-106, *Figs. 5.2,
5.3*
winds and, 149-150
Condensation pressure (*see* Pressure, con-
densation)
Conduction, 74-75
Congestus, 47
Constant-pressure chart (*see* Charts, con-
stant pressure)
Continental air masses (*see* Air masses,
continental)
Continental climates, 295
Convection, 76-77, *Fig. 3.7*
penetrative, 111-113, *Fig. 5.4*
theory of, 162-163
Convective condensation level, 113
Coriolis, G. G., 125
Coriolis force, 124-125, *Figs. 6.3, 6.4*
Cosmic rays, 62
Crolls' theory, 304
Crystals, snow, 115, *Fig. 5.5*
Culture, climate and, 324-326
Cumulonimbus (Cb), 46, 48, *Figs. 2.36,
2.37*
Cumulus (Cu), 44-46, 48, 49, 111-112,
Figs. 2.35, 5.4
Cumulus congestus, 46

Currents, wind, 28
Cyclogenesis, 183
Cyclones, 158-160, *Figs. 8.5, 8.6*
clouds and, 188
the eye of, 187, *Fig. 10.1*
origin of, 162-163, *Fig. 8.9*
tropical, 186-195
characteristics, 187-188
effects of, 193-195
Florida Keys (1935), 188-189
lowest observed pressures, 189
origin and path, 190-193
regions and times of occurrence, 189-
190, *Fig. 10.2*
wave, 182-183, *Fig. 9.5*
Cyclonic circulation, 128

D

Dalton, John, 37
Dalton's law of partial pressure, 37
Day, length of, 67-70, *Table 3.1*
Deep anticyclones, 164
Deflection anemometer, 30
Density:
of air, 9-10
in the upper atmosphere, 263, *Table
13.1*
Dew, 103
Dew point, 38-39
Doldrums, the, 136, 140-143
Douglass, A. E., 302
Drizzle, 107
Dropsondes, 82
Droughts, 58, 328
Dry freeze, 103
Duane, J. E., 188
Dust as an ingredient of air, 5-7
Dust falls, 211-213
Dust fogs, 107
Dust storms, 211-213

E

Earth, the:
atmosphere of, 1-12
distance of, from the sun, 67
distribution of pressure over, 26
orbit of, about the sun, *Fig. 3.4*
radiation from, 63
rotation of, 124-126, *Fig. 6.3*
solar radiation absorbed by, *Fig. 3.6*
temperatures of, 75
Easterly waves, 166-167
Eddy motion, 113
Electromagnetic spectrum, 62
Elements, meteorological, 10-11
Energy:
heat as a form of, 13

Energy (*Cont.*)
  radiant (*see* Radiation)
  for winds, 149-150
Equator, the air movement across the, 149
Equatorial air masses (*see* Air masses, equatorial)
Equatorial belt of low pressure, 136
Equatorial troughs, 165
Equinoxes, 68
Equivalent potential temperature, 86-87, *Fig. 4.4*
Evaporation, 36, 100-102
  fogs and, 109
  measurement of, 101-102, *Fig. 5.1*
Exercises (*see* Problems)
Extratropical cyclones, 158, 167

F

Facsimile equipment, 228-229, *Fig. 11.5*
Fahrenheit, Daniel, 14
Fahrenheit thermometers (*see* Thermometers, Fahrenheit)
Fallwinds, 131
Federal Aviation Agency, 247
Fergusson weighing rain gauge, 56-57, *Fig. 2.39*
Fibratus, 46
Flight Advisory Weather Service, 247
Floccus, 46
Florida Keys storm of 1935, 188-189
Foehn winds, 209-210, *Fig. 10.11*
Fogs:
  advection, 108-109
  aviation and, 252-254
  cost and dispersal of, 110
  defined, 107
  evaporation, 109
  high inversion, 108
  modification of, 120
  radiation, 107-108
  upslope, 109-110
Forked lightning, 201
Fractus, 47
Franklin, Benjamin, 201
Frontal fogs, 109
Frontal thunderstorms (*see* Thunderstorms, frontal)
Frontogenesis, 178
Frontolysis, 178
Fronts, 109-110, 177-183
  clouds and, 179-180
  cold:
    aircraft icing and, 251, *Fig. 12.3*
    characteristics of, 179-181, *Figs. 9.1, 9.3, 9.4*
    defined, 178

Fronts (*Cont.*)
  defined, 177
  formation of, 178
  occluded, 182, *Fig. 9.4*
  problems, 183-185
  squall lines and, 181
  stationary, 181-182
  upper, 192
  warm:
    aircraft icing and, 251, *Fig. 12.3*
    characteristics of, 178-179, *Figs. 9.2, 9.4*
    defined, 178
    wave cyclones and, 182-183, *Fig. 9.5*
    in weather analysis, 217-218
Frost, 103-104
  protection against, 104-106, *Figs. 5.2, 5.3*

G

Galileo, 10
Gamma rays, 62
Gases:
  characteristics of, 7-8
  as ingredients of air, 5-6
  laws of the, 8-9
  relation of volume of, to pressure, *Fig. 1.3*
Gauges:
  rain, 55-57
  snow, 57-58
Gay-Lussac, Joseph, 8
GCA Radarscope, 253, *Fig. 12.5*
General circulation (*see* Winds, general circulation)
Generators, cloud-seeding, 118, *Fig. 5.8*
Geography, meteorology and, 4
George, J. J., 234
George method, the, 234
Geostrophic winds, 127
Glaze, 117
Gradient winds, 127, *Fig. 6.4*
Granular snow, 117
Gravity:
  air and, 9
  corrections in barometer readings, 23
  winds and, 131, 149
Greece, early studies of the weather in, 4
Ground fogs, 107-108

H

Hail, 115-117, *Fig. 5.6*
  soft, 117
  theories of, 116-117
Haze, 107

Health:
  acclimatization and, 322
  air conditioning and, 323-324
  humidity, air movement, and, 320-322
  ideal weather for, 323
  sunshine and, 322
  temperature and, 319-320
Heat, defined, 13
Heat rays, 62
Heaters, orchard, 104-105, *Fig. 5.2*
Height (*see* Altitude)
Helium as an ingredient of air, 5
Hertz, Heinrich, 235
Hertzian electric waves, 62
Heterosphere, the, 266
High-inversion fogs, 107-108
High-pressure centers, 160-165
Hill, Dr. Leonard, 321
Hippocrates, 4
Hoarfrost, 103
Holzman, 102
Homosphere, the, 266, *Fig. 13.4*
Horse latitudes, 136
Humidity:
  absolute, 38, 39
  health and, 320-322
  in identifying air masses, 220
  measurement of, 39-41
  observations, 36-44
  records of, 44
  relative, 39, *Table 2.2*
  specific, 38
Humilis, 47
Humphreys, William Jackson, 132, 304
Hurricanes, 82-83, 187, *Figs. 4.2, 10.3,*
    10.4
  Florida Keys (1935), 188-189
  lowest observed pressures of, 189
  reconnaissance, 191, 194-195, *Fig. 10.3*
Hydrogen as an ingredient of air, 5
Hydrologic cycle, the, 100
Hygrometers:
  dew-point, 39
  electric, 41
  hair, 41
Hygroscopic salts, 106
Hypothesis, climatic, 324

I

Ice, polar, and the weather, 315-316
Iceland low cell, 144
Ice storms, 117, *Fig. 5.7*
Icing, aircraft, 249-252, *Figs. 12.2-12.4*
IGY (*see* International Geophysical Year)
Infrared rays, 62
Insolation, 64
  at a fixed location, 66-70

Insolation (*Cont.*)
  winds and, 149
Instability:
  of the atmosphere, 91-96, *Figs. 4.7-4.9*
  conditional, 93-94, *Fig. 4.8*
  convective, 94, *Fig. 4.9*
Instrument shelters, 17, *Fig. 2.4*
Intermediate zones, climate of, 293-294
International Cloud Atlas, 46, 47
International Geophysical Year (IGY), 2,
    136, 139, 260, 261, 268
International Year(s) of the Quiet Sun
    (IQSY), 261-262
Intertropical convergence, 166
Intertropical fronts, 166
Inversion of temperature, 89
Inversion fogs, 108
Ionosphere, 2, 266
IQSY (*see* International Year(s) of the
    Quiet Sun)
Isallobars, 216
Isentropic analysis, 224-226, *Fig. 11.3*
Isobars, 123-124, *Figs. 6.1, 6.2*
  surface winds in relation to, 127-128,
    Fig. 6.5
Isothermal lines, 278
Isothermal region, 97

J

Jefferson, Thomas, 269
Jet stream, the, 147
Jungles, 292

K

Katabatic winds, 131
Kata-thermometers, 321
Katmai (volcano), 304
Killing frost, 103
Kipling, Rudyard, 201
Knots, 30
Koppen, Wladimir, 297
Krakatoa (volcano), 7, 304
Krypton as an ingredient of air, 5-6

L

Land breezes, 129-130, *Fig. 6.7*
Land surfaces:
  the albedo of, 71
  effect of solar radiation on, 72-73
Landor, Walter, 324
Langmuir, 118
Lapse rates, 88-90, *Fig. 4.6*
  turbulence in relation to, 95-96
  variability of, 89-90

Laws:
    Boyle's, 8
    Buys-Ballot's, 128
    of Charles and Gay-Lussac, 8-9
    Dalton's, of partial pressures, 37
Lenticularis, 47
Lifting condensation level, the (LCL), 84
Light, velocity of, 62
Light rays, 62
Lightning, *Figs. 10.7, 10.8*
    nature of, 201-202
    protection against, 203
    in tornadoes, *Fig. 10.9*
Liquids:
    circulation in, *Fig. 3.8*
    convection in, 76
    temperature and, 8
Loki rockets, 261
Low-pressure centers, 155-160, 162-165

M

McDonald, W. F., 189
Maps, 152-155, *Figs. 8.1-8.4, 11.6-11.8*
    reproducing, 228-229, *Fig. 11.5*
Marine climates, 295
Maritime air masses (*see* Air masses, maritime)
Marvin transmitter, 66, *Fig. 3.3*
Mediocris clouds, 47
Mediterranean climate, 293
Mercurial barometers (*see* Barometers, mercurial)
Mesosphere, the, 266
Meteorographs, 28-29
Meteorologica (Aristotle), 4
Meteorological Rocket Network (MRN), 261
Meteorology:
    defined, 3-5
    normal values of, 11
Meteors, 269-272
Metric system, 21-23
Microseisms, 195
Middle Ages, weather interpretations during, 4-5
Millibars, 23
Mistral winds, 131
Mixing ratio, the, 36-37
Molecular theory, the, 8
Molecules, motion of, 13
Monsoons, 131-132
Mother-of-pearl clouds, 265
Motion of molecules, 13
Mountain breezes, 130, 131
Mountain climates, 296

N

Nacreous clouds, 265
Namias, Jerome, 228
National Advisory Committee on Aeronautics, 196
National Aeronautics and Space Administration (NASA), 261
National Center for Atmospheric Research, 118
National Science Foundation, 120
Navy Oceanographic Meteorological Automatic Device, 35
Nebulosus, 47
Neon as an ingredient of air, 5-6
New York Academy of Sciences, 120
Night-glowing clouds, 265
Nimbostratus (Ns), 45, 46
Nimbus Meteorological Satellite, *Fig. 1.1*
Nitrogen as an ingredient of air, 5-6
NOMAD (*see* Navy Oceanographic Meteorological Automatic Device)
North America:
    air masses of, 172-177, *Table 9.1*
    climates of, *Fig. 14.9*
Northeast trade winds and the weather, 315
Norther wind, 210-211
Northern lights, 269, *Fig. 13.6*
Notilucent clouds, 265
Nuclear power weather stations, 35-36
Nuclei of condensation, 106-107

O

Occluded fronts (*see* Fronts, occluded)
Ocean of air (*see* Atmosphere, the)
Oceans, temperature of, and the weather, 314-316
Orographic uplift, 113
Oxygen as an ingredient of air, 5-6
Ozone as an ingredient of air, 5
Ozonosphere, 266

P

Pacific anticyclone cell, 143
Pacific high cell, 143
Pampero winds, 211
Penetrative convection, 111, 113, *Fig. 5.4*
Peruvian current and the weather, 316
Petterssen, S., 234
Phenology, 328-329
Photodissociation, 262
Physics, meteorology and, 4
Pibals, 81
Plateau climates, 296
Polar air masses (*see* Air masses, polar)

Polar caps of high pressure, 139
Polar easterlies (winds), 145
Polar front, the, 145
Polar low pressure, 138
Polar zones, climate of, 294
Postfrontal fogs, 109
Potential temperature, 85-86
Potentionmeter, 65
Precipitation:
  areas of heavy and light, 290-291,
    Table 14.1
  clouds and, 110-113
  days with .01 inch or more of, 289-
    290, *Fig. 14.8*
  defined, 55
  early measurements of, 10
  excessive, 58
  extremes of, 291-292, *Table 14.2*
  forms of, 114-118
  glaze, 117, *Fig. 5.7*
  hail, 115-117, *Fig. 5.6*
  Iowa, *Fig. 14.10*
  normal annual, 286-288, *Fig. 14.6*
  observations of, 55-58
  rain, 114-115
    gauges, 55-57, *Fig. 2.38*
    stimulation, 118, *Fig. 5.8*
  records of, 58
  seasonal variation of, 288-289, *Fig. 14.7*
  sleet, 117
  snow, 115, *Fig. 5.5*
    gauges, 55-57
    grains, 117
Prefrontal fogs, 109
Pressure:
  of air, 9-10
  barometric tendency of, 26
  circulation zones and cells, 139-140
  condensation, 224, *Fig. 11.3*
  Dalton's law of, 37
  distribution of, 26
  diurnal variations of, 27-28
  of the equatorial trough, 165
  gradients of, 122-124, *Figs. 6.1-6.4*
  height and, 26-27
  high:
    belts, 143
    polar caps, 139
    subtropical, 136-138
  interrelationships with temperature and
    wind, 122-134
  problems, 133-134
  January and July average of, 140-145,
    Figs. 7.4, 7.5
  low:
    equatorial belt of, 136
    polar, 138
  lowest observed, in hurricanes, 189
  mixing processes, 147-148

Pressure (*Cont.*)
  observations, 21-27
    beginnings of, 27
    results of, 27-28
  partial, 37
  units of measurement, 21-23
  upper atmosphere, 263, *Table 13.1*
  upper troposphere, 146
  vapor, 37, 101, *Table 2.1*
  in wind speed, 29-30
  yearly averages of, 136-140, *Fig. 7.1*
Pressure altimeters (*see* Altimeters, pres-
    sure)
Pressure-contour chart (*see* Charts, pres-
    sure-contour)
Pressure-pattern flying, 255-256
Pressure tube anemometer, 30
Prevailing westerlies (winds), 144-145
Problems (exercises):
  adiabatic processes, 98-99
  air masses, 183-185
  the atmosphere, 11-12
  climate, 329-330
  condensation, 120-121
  evaporation, 120-121
  fronts, 183-185
  interrelationships of temperature, pres-
    sure, and wind, 133-134
  solar radiation, 77-78
  special storms, 213-214
  upper atmosphere, 272-273
  weather, 329-330
    analysis and forecasting, 243-244
    observation, 59-60
  winds:
    general circulation, 150-151
    secondary circulation, 167-168
Pseudoadiabatic process, 86
Psychrometers, 40, *Fig. 2.20*
Pyrheliometers, 65, *Fig. 3.2*

R

Radar, 235-236, 253, *Figs. 11.9, 12.5*
Radiant energy (*see* Radiation)
Radiation, solar, 61-78
  characteristics of, 62-63
  climatic changes and, 303-304
  conduction, 74-75
  the constant, 64, 66-67
  convection, 76-77, *Fig. 3.7*
  direct effects of, 70-74
  distribution of, *Fig. 3.6*
  incoming, 63-66
  measurements, 64-66
  at Montpelier, France, 69
  problems, 77-78
  transmission, absorption, and reflection,
    63

Radiation, solar (*Cont.*)
  the weather and, 317
Radiation belts, 268, *Fig. 13.5*
Radiation fogs, 107-108
Radio altimeters (*see* Altimeters, radio)
Radiosondes, 81, *Fig. 4.1*
Radon as an ingredient of air, 5
Rain, 114-115
  gauges, 55-57, *Fig. 2.38*
  stimulation, 118, *Fig. 5.8*
Rainfall (*see* Precipitation)
Raobs, 81
Rawinsondes, 81-82
Rays, 62
Reconnaissance, hurricane, 191, 194-195,
  Fig. 10.3
Richardson, L. F., 239-240
Roaring forties (region), 145
Robinson cup anemometer, 30, *Fig. 2.15*
Rockets:
  effects of, *Fig. 13.2*
  and the IQSY, 261-262
  network of, 261
  sounding, 2
  in upper-air research, 82
  weather forecasting and, 2-3
Rotation, winds and, 150

S

Salinity in evaporation, 101
Satellites:
  Tiros V, *Fig. 4.2*
  in upper-air research, 82
  weather, 2-3, 191, *Fig. 10.3*
Saturation adiabatic rate, 84
Saturation pressure (*see* Pressure, con-
  densation)
Savannas, 292
Schaefer, Vincent, 118
Scud clouds, 204
Sea breezes, 128-129, *Fig. 6.6*
Secondary circulation (*see* Winds, sec-
  ondary circulation)
Sferics, 202
Shallow anticyclones, 164
Shaw, Sir Napier, 150
Sheet lightning, 201
Silver iodide crystals in cloud seeding,
  118, *Fig. 5.8*
Simooms, 320
Sirocco winds, 210
Sleet, 117
Sling psychrometer, 40, *Fig. 2.20*
Smith, J. Warren, 327
Smithsonian Meteorological Tables, 26,
  40, 41, *Tables 2.1, 2.2*
Smoke fogs, 107
Snow, 115

Snow (*Cont.*)
  grains, 117
  granular, 117
  measurement of, 57-58
Soft hail, 117
Solar climate, 277
Solar constant, 64-67
Solar radiation (*see* Radiation, solar)
Solids, temperature and, 8
Solstices, 68-69
Space, solar radiation reflected back to,
  Fig. 3.6
Speed (*see* Velocity)
Spissatus, 46
Squall lines, 181
Squalls, 35
Stability of the atmosphere, 90-91, *Fig.
  4.6*
Stars, "shooting," 269
Static, 202
Stationary fronts (*see* Fronts, stationary)
Steam fogs, 109
Stormy westerlies (winds), 144
Stratification in the upper atmosphere,
  266-267
Stratiformis, 46-47
Stratocumulus (Sc), 45, 46, 48, 49, *Figs.
  2.31, 2.32*
Stratosphere, 96-97, 266
Stratus (St), 44, 45, 48, *Figs. 2.33, 2.34*
STRATWARM system, 262
Streak lightning, 201
Streamline charts, 165-166, *Fig. 8.11*
Sublimation, process of, 36, 103
Subsidence, 94-95
Substances, composition of, 13
Subtropical high-pressure belts, 136-138
Subtropical ridges, 165
Subtropical zones, climate of, 293
Summer, air masses in, 173-177
Summer solstice, 67, 68
Sun:
  distance of, from the earth, 67
  earth's orbit about, *Fig. 3.4*
  rays of, 63
  the weather and, 316-317
Sunshine and health, 322
Sunspots and weather, 317
Superior air masses (*see* Air masses, su-
  perior)
Surface winds, 127-128, *Fig. 6.5*
Surfaces, isobaric, 123-124, *Fig. 6.2*
Synoptic charts, 153, *Figs. 8.1-8.4*
Synoptic climatology, 277

T

Taylor, Dr. H. A., 235
Telepsychrometer, 40-41

Temperatures:
  absolute zero, 9
  adiabatic changes in, 83-88, *Figs. 4.3, 4.5*
  air, 75
    obtaining, 17
  air masses and, 171
  annual march of, 20, *Fig. 2.6*
  annual range of, 20, *Fig. 2.6*
  civilization and, 325-326
  corrections in barometer readings, 23
  daily range of, 20
  distribution of, 278-286
  earth, 75
  equivalent potential, 86-87, *Fig. 4.4*
  in evaporation, 101
  extremes of, 285-286
  gases and, 8
  health and, 319-320
  highest, of the day, 18
  in identifying air masses, 219-220
  inversion of, 89
  interrelationships with pressure and wind, 122-134
    problems, 133-134
  January and July normal, 279-283, *Figs. 14.2, 14.3*
  at Key West, Florida, 20
  liquids and, 8
  in the lower stratosphere, 97
  normal yearly, 278-279, *Fig. 14.1*
  normals of, 18
  observations, 13
    uses of, 18-21
  ocean, and the weather, 314-315
  potential, 85-86
  ranges of, 283, *Figs. 14.4, 14.5*
  retardation of, 20
  solids and, 8
  in the upper atmosphere, 264-265, *Fig. 13.3*
  wet-bulb, 40
  wind and, 128-131
  zones of, 294
Theophrastus, 4
Theories:
  Bergeron ice-crystal, 110-111
  of climatic changes, 303-305
  convection, 162-163
  Crolls', 304
  of hailstones, 116-117
  molecular, 8
  polar-front, 163
Thermographs, 16-17, *Figs. 2.3, 2.5*
Thermometers, 14-17
  Celsius, 14
  centigrade, 14
  deformation, 14
  electrical, 4, 14

Thermometers (*Cont.*)
  Fahrenheit, 14
  invention of, 10
  kata-, 321
  liquid-in-glass, 14
  liquid-in-metal, 14
  major groups of, 14
  maximum, 15, *Fig. 2.2*
  minimum, 15-16, *Fig. 2.2*
  in obtaining temperature of air, 17
  scales compared, *Fig. 2.1*
  wet-bulb, *Table 2.1*
Thermosphere, the, 266
Thornthwaite, 102
Thunderstorms, 186, 195-203, *Fig. 10.5*
  air mass, 198-199
  artificial heat and, 197-198
  aviation and, 248-249
  cells of, 196-197
  clouds and, 195-196
  convective instability in, 197-198
  description of, 195
  frontal, 198-199
  geographic distribution of, 199-200, *Fig. 10.6*
  heat, 197
  lightning in, 201-203, *Figs. 10.7, 10.8*
  structure of, 196-197
  types of, 198-199
  violent movements in, 195-196
Tiros III (weather satellite), 191, *Fig. 10.3*
Tornadoes, 186
  characteristics of, 203-204
  destructive forces in, 204-205, *Fig. 10.9*
  forecasting, 205-208
  lightning in, *Fig. 10.9*
  place and time of occurrence, 205
  at sea, 208
Torricelli, Evangelista, 10, 21
Trade winds, 143
Trewartha, Glen T., 297
Triple registers (*see* Meteorographs)
Tropic of Cancer, 67
Tropic of Capricorn, 67, *Fig. 3.4*
Tropical air masses (*see* Air masses, tropical)
Tropical cyclones (*see* Cyclones, tropical)
Tropics, the:
  atmospheric circulation in, 165-168, *Figs. 8.10, 8.11*
  climate in, 292-293
Tropopause, 97
Troposphere, 97
  upper, 146, *Fig. 7.6*
Turbulence, 32
  aviation and, 254-255, *Fig. 12.6*
  lapse rates and, 95-96
Twisters, 203

Typhoons, 82, 187, *Fig. 10.1*

U

Ultraviolet rays, 62
Uncinus, 46
United States of America:
  daily normals of temperature of, 20
  sounding rockets of, 2
  synoptic weather maps of, *Figs. 8.2-8.4*
  thunderstorms in, 199-200, *Fig. 10.6*
United States Air Force, 82, 196, 235
United States Committee on Extension of the Standard Atmosphere (COESA), 265
United States Navy, 82, 195, 196, 235
United States Weather Bureau, 11, 80, 82, 196, 208, 235, 245, 247, 261
Upper atmosphere (*see* Atmosphere, upper)
Upper fronts (*see* Fronts, upper)
Upslope fogs, 109-110

V

Valley breezes, 130
Values, normal (*see* Normal values)
Van Allen, Dr. J. A., 268
Van Allen radiation belts, 268, *Fig. 13.5*
Vanes, wind, 32-33
Vapor:
  pressure, 37, 101, *Table 2.1*
  saturated, 37
  latent heat of, 36
Velocity:
  of electromagnetic waves, 62
  wind, 29-32, 34-35
Vernal equinox, 68
Vertical temperature gradient, 89
Visibility, aviation and, 252-254
Volcanoes, 7, 304
VOLSCAN (landing aid), 253-254

W

Ward, R. DeC., 324
Warm anticyclones, 164
Water:
  condensation of, 103-120
    above the earth's surface, 106-110
    on solid surfaces, 103-106, *Figs. 5.2, 5.3*
  evaporation of, 100-102, *Fig. 5.1*
Water surfaces, effect of solar radiation on, 73-74
Water vapor, 5-6

Waterman, Dr. Alan T., 120
Waterspouts, 208, *Fig. 10.10*
Wave cyclones, 182-183, *Fig. 9.5*
Waves:
  electromagnetic, 61, 62
  frequencies, 62, *Fig. 3.1*
  heat, 63
  lengths, 62, *Fig. 3.1*
  radio, from the sun, *Fig. 13.1*
Weather:
  agriculture and, 327-328
  aircraft reconnaissance, 82-84
  analysis of, 216-228
    constant-pressure charts in, 221-224, *Fig. 11.2*
    isentropic, 224-226, *Fig. 11.3*
    lows and highs in, 216-217
    placing of fronts, 217-218
    problems in, 243-244
    upper-air, 218-228
  aviation and, 245-257
  correlations, 313-314
  cyclical changes in, 299-303, *Fig. 14.10*
  defined, 11
  early Greek studies of, 4
  elements of, 10-11
    combinations, 307-308
  forecasting, 228-243
    by the airways, 247-248, *Fig. 12.1*
    barometers and, 240-241
    charting of data, 230
    daily, 230-235, *Figs. 11.6-11.8*
    extended, 236-238
    facsimile equipment for, 228-229, *Fig. 11.5*
    jet stream in, 147
    long-range, 238-239
    numerical, 239-240
    pressure changes in, 26
    problems in, 243-244
    radar and, 235-236, *Fig. 11.9*
    rockets and, 2-3
    satellites and, 2-3
    seasonal, 317-319
    short-range, 235-236
    single-station, 241-242
    statistical indications, 241
    of tornadoes, 205-208
  health and, 319-324
  ideal, 323
  maps, 152-155, *Figs. 8.1-8.4, 11.6, 11.8*
  Middle Ages, interpretation during, 4-5
  observing, 13-60
    by the airways, 245-247
    altitude in, 32
    barometers in, 21-26, *Figs. 2.7, 2.8, 2.10, 2.11*
    clouds in, 44-55, *Figs. 2.21-2.37*
    dew point in, 38-39

Weather (*Cont.*)
  observing (*Cont.*)
    humidity in, 36-44
    mixing ratio in, 36-37
    obtaining air temperature, 17
    precipitation, 55-58
    pressure variations in, 26-28
    problems, 59-60
    rain gauges in, 55-58, *Figs. 2.38, 2.39*
    records of, 58-59
    snow in, 57-58
    thermometers in, 14-17
    uses of temperature observations, 18-21
    vapor in, 37
    wind in, 28-36, *Figs. 2.13, 2.14, 2.18*
  the oceans and, 314-316
  problems in, 256-257, 329-330
  proverbs, 242-243
  six fundamental elements of, 10
  spells of, 310
  the sun and, 316-317
  types of, 311-313, *Fig. 15.3*
  variability of, 307-310, *Figs. 15.1, 15.2*
  (*See also* Climate)
Weather station, atomic-powered, 35-36, *Fig. 2.19*
Wet adiabatic rate, 84
Whirlwinds, 208-209
Wind machines, 105-106, *Fig. 5.3*
Wind rose, 34, *Fig. 2.18*
Winds:
  across the equator, 149
  anticyclones, 161-162, *Figs. 8.7, 8.8*
  antitrades, 146
  blizzards, 210-211
  bora, 131
  chinook, 209-210
  clouds and, 113
  currents, 28
  cyclones, 158-160, *Figs. 8.5, 8.6*
  direction of, 28-29, *Fig. 2.14*
  dust falls, 211-213
  dust storms, 211-213, *Fig. 10.12*
  effect of altitude on, 32
  in evaporation, 101
  fall-, 131
  foehn, 209-210, *Fig. 10.11*
  general circulation, 135-151
    problems, 150-151
    zones and cells, 139-140, *Fig. 7.3*
  geostrophic, 127
  gradient, 127, *Fig. 6.4*
  gravity, 131
  gustiness of, 32
  health and, 320-322

Winds (*Cont.*)
  instruments, 28-29, *Fig. 2.13*
  interrelationships with temperature and pressure, 122-134
    problems, 133-134
  January and July averages of, 140-145, *Figs. 7.4, 7.5*
  katabatic, 131
  land breezes, 129-130, *Fig. 6.7*
  local temperature and, 128-131
  mistral, 131
  monsoons, 131-132
    Asiatic, 148-149, *Figs. 7.4, 7.5*
  mountain breezes, 130
  northers, 210-211
  observations, 28-33
    remote, 35-36
    results of, 33-35
  polar easterlies, 145
  polar-equatorial, 132
  prevailing westerlies, 144-145
  sea breezes, 128-129, *Fig. 6.6*
  secondary circulation, 152-168
    problems, 167-168
  sirocco, 210
  sources of energy for, 149-150
  stormy westerlies, 144
  surface, 127-128, *Fig. 6.5*
  three forces affecting, 126, *Fig. 6.4*
  trade, 143
    easterly waves and, 166-167
    and the weather, 315
  in the tropics, 165-166
  upper atmosphere, 265
  upper troposphere, 146, *Fig. 7.6*
  valley breezes, 130
  vanes, 38
  velocity of, 29-32
    altitude and, 32
    variations in, 34-35
  (*See also* Air; Atmosphere)
Winter, air masses in, 173-176
Winter solstice, 67
World Meteorological Organization, 47, 262

X

Xenon as an ingredient of air, 5-6
X rays, 62

Z

Zigzag lightning, 201